N THE TRAIL
OF THE
ASSASSINS

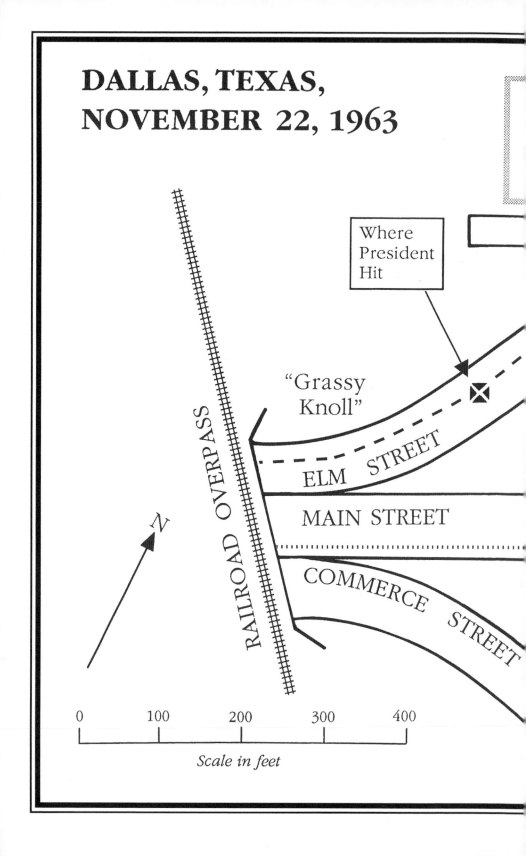

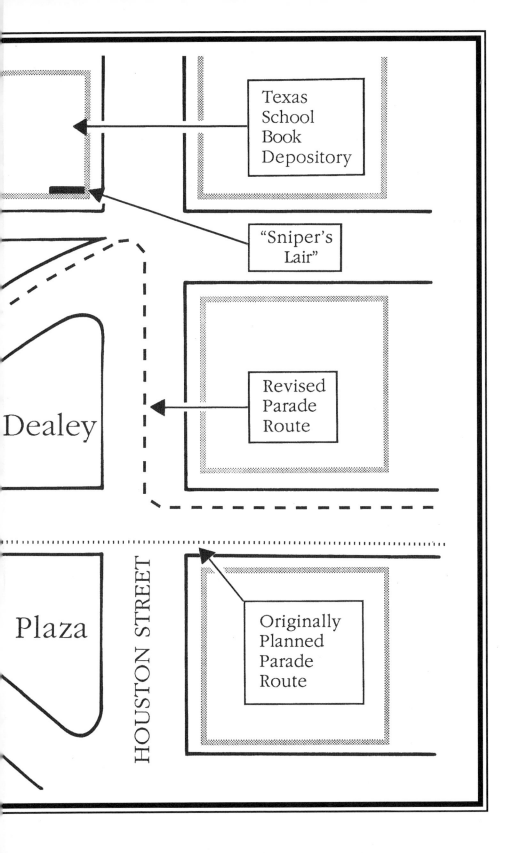

ON THE TRAIL
OF THE
ASSASSINS
ONE MAN'S QUEST TO SOLVE THE MURDER OF PRESIDENT KENNEDY

JIM GARRISON

Skyhorse Publishing

Skyhorse Publishing books may be purchased in bulk at special discounts
for sales promotion, corporate gifts, fund-raising, or educational purposes.
Special editions can also be created to specifications. For details, contact the
Special Sales Department, Skyhorse Publishing, 307 West 36th Street, 11th
Floor, New York, NY 10018 or info@skyhorsepublishing.com.

Skyhorse® and Skyhorse Publishing® are registered trademarks of Skyhorse
Publishing, Inc.®, a Delaware corporation.

Visit our website at www.skyhorsepublishing.com.

10

Library of Congress Cataloging-in-Publication Data is available on file.

ISBN: 978-1-62087-299-4

Printed in China

Dedication

THIS BOOK IS dedicated to the following members of the New Orleans district attorney's staff who served during the 1960s: the late Frank Klein, Andrew "Moo Moo" Sciambra, James Alcock, Louis Ivon, D'Alton Williams, Alvin Oser, and Numa Bertel.

They never stopped fighting to bring out the truth. They only ran out of time.

Acknowledgments

I WANT TO EXPRESS my good fortune in having had Zachary Sklar as my editor, in having benefited from the gifts of his uncommon insight, skills and dedication. I want to express as well my gratitude to my publishers, Ellen Ray and William Schaap, for their unflagging support and confidence, support which in Ellen Ray's case has extended over twenty years. In a time when the hidden machinery of government intelligence intimidates many publishers, the loyalty of Sheridan Square Press was heartening. I also owe a special debt to their researcher, Dan Kryder, for his able and detailed fact-checking. And my sincere thanks to Mary Howell, who first put me and Sheridan Square Press in touch with each other.

I will always be grateful, as well, to Bertrand Russell for his early encouragement of my efforts. And for the constant and crucial advice and support of Carl Oglesby, Mark Lane, Vincent Salandria, Richard E. Sprague, Ralph Schoenmann, Harold Weisberg, Ted Gandolfo, Mort Sahl and Taylor Morris.

I also owe thanks to Louis Wolfson, Cecil M. Shilstone, Willard E.

Robertson, Joseph Rault, Jr., and a small band of New Orleans citizens, the last under the title Truth and Consequences, who helped greatly when it counted.

Others, too numerous to mention, have also had faith in me over the years, and I hope you understand that each of you mattered to me.

Finally, I am deeply grateful to my children—Jim, Virginia, Lyon, Elizabeth, and Darrow—not merely for their sustained efforts, even on school nights, to double-check the manuscript, but especially for their relentless affection during this project.

Contents

Introduction

T H I S   I S   N O T just another of the many books analyzing the dry evidence in the assassination of President Kennedy. It is, instead, a chronicle of the experiences of one man who tried to get to the truth about the murder and prosecute those responsible for it. I write not as a critic but as a participant, a prosecutor and an investigator.

At the time of the assassination on November 22, 1963, I was district attorney of New Orleans. Because the accused assassin, Lee Harvey Oswald, had resided in New Orleans the summer before the assassination, I was immediately drawn into the case. More than three years later, in March 1967, my investigation culminated in the arrest of Clay Shaw, director of the International Trade Mart and fixture of New Orleans high society, on charges of conspiracy to murder John Kennedy.

In the months leading to Shaw's trial in 1969 I publicly suggested that members of the United States government's intelligence community, including Shaw, were responsible for the assassination and had carried it out in order to stop President Kennedy's efforts to break with

Cold War foreign policy. While the jury accepted my argument that there had been a conspiracy, it was not then aware of Shaw's role as a clandestine C.I.A. operative. Unconvinced of his motivation, the jury acquitted him of the charges.

History has a way of changing verdicts.* Twenty-five years ago most Americans readily accepted the government's contention that the assassination was a random act of violence. A lonely young man, his mind steeped in Marxist ideology, apparently frustrated at his inability to do anything well, had crouched at a warehouse window and—in six seconds of world class shooting—destroyed the President of the United States.

When that explanation was announced, shortly after the assassination, the country was in profound shock. We had suddenly lost a very special leader whose personal attributes—freshness, youth, humor, style, intelligence, warmth—had made each of us feel renewed pride in the presidency. The whole country mourned as we watched the now-familiar images of Lyndon Johnson being sworn in as President, the solemn funeral, the grieving first family, Oswald shot by Jack Ruby in the basement of the Dallas police station on national television. Saddened and outraged, Americans wanted an answer. And we got one. The Dallas police closed the case almost immediately, convicting Lee Harvey Oswald without trial. The F.B.I. agreed, virtually closing the case in a matter of weeks. And the Warren Commission, appointed shortly after the assassination, added its official stamp of approval less than ten months later.

But time has undone the official explanation that most Americans at first believed. There were too many contradictions, too many witnesses, too many photographs and motion pictures taken at the scene, too many skeptics. As time passed, previously unheeded witnesses were located, investigative reports of the assassination were found to be false, and other evidence was found to have been altered or destroyed. Even the concealment of assassination evidence for 75 years by the federal government could not prevent independent critics and researchers from uncovering gaping holes in the Warren Commission

* Clarence Darrow lost the Scopes trial, but who remembers that now?

report. By 1967, two-thirds of the public did not accept the conclusion that Lee Oswald was the lone assassin.

In the 1970s the new Freedom of Information Act opened more doors. Material that federal agencies had stored away in their files—believing it would remain secret forever—became available to the public. Since that time able critics have done considerable research. Many books have raised incisive questions about the official story and disclosed new and troubling evidence. Yet much of this information remains unknown to the majority of Americans. For example:

- Five days before the assassination the New Orleans F.B.I. office received a telexed warning that an attempt would be made to assassinate the President in Dallas at the end of the week. The Bureau did not pass on the warning to the Secret Service or other authorities. Shortly after the assassination, the telex message was removed from the file drawer of the New Orleans office of the Bureau.

- The great majority of witnesses at Dealey Plaza in Dallas heard repeated rifle fire coming from the grassy knoll in front of Kennedy. In the chase that followed, the Dallas police apprehended three men and marched them away under shotgun arrest. However, the numerous news photographs of their arrest were never published and no record remains of their mug shots, their fingerprints, or their names.

- On the day of his arrest, Lee Oswald was given a nitrate test, the results of which showed that he had not fired a rifle in the previous 24 hours. This fact was kept secret by both the federal government and the Dallas police for ten months.

- For more than five years, the film of the assassination taken by eyewitness Abraham Zapruder was concealed from the public and kept locked in a vault by *Life* magazine. This moving picture showed Kennedy being slammed violently backwards—clear evidence of his being struck by a rifle shot from the front.

- Approximately an hour before the arrival of Kennedy's motorcade, Jack Ruby, the man who later murdered Lee Oswald, was observed alongside the grassy knoll, unloading a man carrying a rifle in a case. The statement of Julia Ann Mercer, the witness to that event, was altered by the F.B.I. to make it appear that she had been unable to identify Ruby as the man. This fraudulent alteration has never been explained or even denied by the federal government.

- After the President's body was subjected to a military autopsy, his brain disappeared. The brain, which is still missing after 25 years, had been immersed in formalin to harden it and might have shown from what directions the head shots came. Photographs and x-rays of the autopsy, which might also have resolved the issue, were never examined by the Warren Commission.

- The pathologist in charge of Kennedy's autopsy at Bethesda Naval Hospital burned in the fireplace of his home the first draft of the autopsy report.

Such revelations, while not widely disseminated, did eventually force the House Select Committee on Assassinations to conduct another investigation from 1976 to 1979. Its official conclusion, citing acoustical evidence, was that there probably had been a conspiracy to murder President Kennedy—and that more than one man had been shooting at him. However, the investigation was limited and made no further attempt to determine the forces behind the assassination.

This book accepts the responsibility that the House Committee bypassed. Based on my experiences as a district attorney who actively investigated the assassination and on my continuing research since then, I offer in the final chapter an informed historical speculation about what happened—who killed John Kennedy and why. I do not claim, however, to have all the answers about the assassination. No individual could. To uncover the whole truth would require an open-ended, honest federal investigation—the kind that has not taken place to date.

At the outset, I must underscore the fact that the details of the assassination—who pulled a trigger, from what building, what kind of gun, and so forth—are no longer my primary concerns. The assassination was an enormously important event. But even more important, in my view, is what happened after—ratification by the government and the media of an official story that is an absurd fairy tale.

Immediately after the assassination, the federal government and the major media adopted the posture of two giant ostriches, each unyielding to reason, each with its head firmly lodged in the sand. Having ratified the lone assassin theory, they refused to acknowledge any facts that might discredit it and attacked anyone who offered a different explanation.

It was not difficult to figure out what their dilemma was. For the government and the major media to have acknowledged what virtually everyone knew (that Kennedy had been fired at by a number of guns) would have put an end to the sacred pretense that the President's assassination was a chance occurrence. To have acknowledged a conspiracy would have led inevitably to the question of why it had occurred. There then would have followed recognition that there had been powerful opposition in the government to President Kennedy's efforts to end the Cold War. His desire to withdraw from Vietnam, for example, would have been revealed. Correspondingly, the role of those who dragged us into nine years of war in Vietnam also would have become clearer.

When I tried to bring some of these profoundly disturbing connections to light, the United States government and the major media came down hard on me. Both before and after the trial of Clay Shaw, I was denounced by government officials and the mass media for suggesting that members of our own intelligence agencies might have conspired to kill the President. I was vilified in the press as a publicity-seeking politician, a charlatan, and a communist. The federal government brought false charges of corruption against me while I was in the midst of a re-election campaign for district attorney. Although I was found innocent in court, I narrowly lost the election. Thus the government succeeded in its attempt to remove me from office.

In the hostile climate of that time, it was impossible to communicate my view of all that happened. Nearly twenty years later that has changed. We have been through the Vietnam War, Watergate, and the Iran/contra affair. We have learned much about our intelligence agencies and what they have done in our name. Assassination by our C.I.A. is no longer inconceivable; it is established historical fact. The existence of off-the-shelf covert government operations is acknowledged in congressional hearing rooms and on national television. In this more open atmosphere it is time—for history's sake and for the sake of the future—for me to tell the full story of my investigation and allow a new generation to consider it.

As a result of my investigation of the Kennedy assassination and my experiences afterwards, my life and consciousness were changed forever. This book is really about that process of change—of growing disillusionment, anger, and knowledge. My experience as a prominent player in the historical events prevents it from being typical. But our entire country shared, to varying degrees, my change of consciousness. A quarter century later, it is possible to see that the assassination and cover-up by the government and the media were watershed events for this country. They represented the loss of innocence for post-war Americans, the beginning of the current era of discontent and distrust in our government and our most fundamental institutions.

I hope this book will help the younger generation to understand better the political, social, and historical consequences of the assassination and the subsequent cover-up. Today, we still live with those consequences—a continuing and ominous Cold War, a deceptive secret government, a docile press, a pervasive cynicism, and corruption. To bring an end to this era in which the lies of our elected government and the covert operations of our secret government threaten the very survival of our society, we must begin to see the Cold War and our national security in a new light. Our relationship with the Soviet Union and other communist nations must be reconsidered and put into a realistic perspective that looks forward to a new century rather than backward to the 1950s.

In his short three years as President, John Kennedy had already begun to change our attitudes and fundamental assumptions about the Cold War. His adoption of a more enlightened, less polarized view of the earth and its inhabitants, I believe, may have led John Kennedy to his death.

However, it also showed us a way to avoid global catastrophe. In re-examining his tragic assassination 25 years after it occurred, we should not forget his enduring legacy, articulated so eloquently at American University in June 1963: ". . . if we cannot end now our differences, at least we can help make the world safe for diversity. For, in the final analysis, our most basic common link is that we all inhabit this small planet. We all breathe the same air. We all cherish our children's future. And we are all mortal."

ON
THE
TRAIL
OF THE
ASSASSINS

1

The Serenity of Ignorance

I WAS WORKING AT MY DESK in Criminal Court, as district attorney of New Orleans, when the door flew open and my chief assistant rushed in. "The President has been shot!" he yelled. It was just past 12:30 p.m., Friday, November 22, 1963.

Today, a quarter of a century later, I remember my shock, my disbelief. After I grasped what Frank Klein was telling me, I clung to the hope that perhaps Kennedy had merely been wounded and would survive.

Frank and I headed for Tortorich's on Royal Street in the French Quarter. It was a quiet, uncrowded place where they kept a television set in the dining room. On the way, the car radio announced that John Kennedy had been killed. The remainder of that trip was spent in absolute silence.

At the restaurant the midday customers were staring solemnly at the television set mounted high in the corner of the room. I felt a sense of unreality as the unending reportage flooded in from Dallas. There was very little conversation at the tables. A waiter came up, and we ordered something for lunch. When it arrived we toyed with our food, but neither of us ate anything.

The information coming from the television was inconclusive. Although the Secret Service, the F.B.I., and the Dallas police, along with an enormous crowd of onlookers, had all been at the assassination scene in Dallas, for at least two hours the crisp voices of the newscasters provided no real facts about who the rifleman or riflemen had been. However, we were hypnotized by the confusion, the unending snippets of trivia, the magic of the communications spectacle. Concerned with what had happened to the President and with our own hurt, no one left the restaurant that afternoon. The business and professional men who had come for lunch cancelled their appointments. Frank and I made our calls to the office and returned to the television set.

Then, well into the middle of the afternoon, the arrest of the accused assassin suddenly was announced. Approximately 15 Dallas police officers had caught him while he was seated in a movie theatre a considerable distance from the assassination scene. The delayed arrest burst like a bomb on the television screen, and the long silence in the restaurant ended. You could feel the sudden explosion of fury, the outburst of hate against this previously unknown young man. His name was Lee Harvey Oswald.

While Frank Klein and I were transfixed in front of the television set at Tortorich's, a most unusual incident occurred at Guy Banister's office about 12 blocks away, on the other side of Canal Street. At least, it was unusual for Banister, a former special agent in charge of the Chicago office of the F.B.I., a deputy superintendent of police in New Orleans, and a man who had a lifetime reputation as a rigid exponent of law and order.

I knew Banister fairly well. When he was with the police department, we had lunch together now and then, swapping colorful stories about our earlier careers in the F.B.I. A ruddy-faced man with blue eyes which stared right at you, he dressed immaculately and always wore a small rosebud in his lapel.

Although he enjoyed an occasional martini at the International House, Banister had never been known to drink heavily during the day. He was an austere, highly composed individual. However, on the long afternoon of television coverage of the assassination in Dallas, the ex-F.B.I. man made a noble effort to polish off all of the liquor in the Katzenjammer Bar on the 500 block of Camp Street. As the sun was setting over the nearby Mississippi River, he made his way back to his office with Jack Martin, who had been drinking with him. There Banister became embroiled in a heated argument with Martin, a sometime private detective and hanger-on at Banister's office.

The imbroglio erupted after Martin made an injudicious observation. He informed Banister, during the course of their quarrel, that he had not forgotten certain unusual things that had been happening at the office during the summer. At this point Banister whipped out his .357 Magnum pistol and began to massage Martin's head with it.

A .357 Magnum is not an ordinary handgun. It is extraordinarily heavy in order to support its increased muzzle velocity. The brief altercation converted Martin, in a matter of a minute or two, into a bloody, battered mess, and a police patrol car carted him off to Charity Hospital on Tulane Avenue.* Like a tiny seed, the planting of which went unnoticed at the time, that unusual and explosive act by Guy Banister ultimately would lead to the only prosecution ever brought in the case of President Kennedy's murder. Stung by the pain and outrage of his injury, Jack Martin within a day or so would confide to a friend his murky suspicion that David Ferrie, an associate of Guy Banister's and a frequent habitué of his office, had driven to Dallas on the day of the assassination to serve as the "getaway" pilot for the men involved in the assassination.

As Jack Martin sat groggily in the hospital on Friday night, the news scarcity from Dallas abruptly ended. Bulletins were cascading out of the television set. By the following day, the name of Lee Harvey Oswald had been repeated so relentlessly in the media that it had become a household name throughout the world. His resumé was proliferating almost as swiftly, including more and more details about his stay in New Orleans through the summer preceding the assassina-

---

* Banister's violent assault on Martin was memorialized permanently in New Orleans Police Department report number K-12634-63, dated November 22, 1963.

tion. Although I personally had no argument with the official lone assassin scenario so rapidly taking shape in the media, I was not free to ignore Lee Harvey Oswald's unexplained three months in the city. The New Orleans connection meant that, however peripheral the effort might turn out to be, my office had to inquire into Oswald's possible associations in our jurisdiction.

I immediately arranged for a special meeting of a half dozen key members of my staff. On Sunday afternoon, the senior assistant district attorneys and investigators and I gathered in my office. Such weekend meetings had become our custom whenever a crime on the national scene had leads trailing to New Orleans.

In the course of checking out all possible associates of Oswald's in the city, we discovered that the alleged assassin had been seen during the summer with a man named David Ferrie. I got my people on the telephones right away to investigate a possible Oswald-Ferrie relationship.

I had met David Ferrie once. The encounter had been casual but unforgettable. Shortly after my election as district attorney I had been walking across Carondelet Street, near Canal. Half-conscious that the waiting traffic was about to head my way, I began to quicken my step. Just then, a man grabbed me by both arms and stopped me cold.

The face grinning ferociously at me was like a ghoulish Halloween mask. The eyebrows plainly were greasepaint, one noticeably higher than the other. A scruffy, reddish homemade wig hung askew on his head as he fixed me with his eyes. The traffic was bearing down on us as he gripped me, and I hardly could hear him amidst the din of the horns.

I remembered that he was shouting congratulations on my recent election. As I dodged a car, at last escaping his clutch, I recall his yelling that he was a private investigator. Our brief street encounter had taken place sometime in 1962, the preceding year.

This recollection stirred up others. I remembered Ferrie's reputation as an adventurer and pilot. Because I had been a pilot myself during World War II, the legend that he could get a plane in and out of the smallest of fields had stuck in my mind. And so had other vague fragments—his involvement in the abortive 1961 Bay of Pigs invasion of Cuba, his anti-Castro activities, and his frequent speeches to veterans' groups about patriotism and anti-communism. The name of David Ferrie was well known in New Orleans.

Soon one of my assistant D.A.'s, Herman Kohlman, came in with some startling news. He had learned that Ferrie had made a precipitate journey to Texas just 48 hours before—on the very day of the assassination. The source, whom Kohlman verified as thoroughly reliable, was the man to whom Jack Martin had confided after he had been pistol-whipped by Guy Banister. Martin had told this source of his dark suspicions about Ferrie's sudden Texas trip.

A routine review of our files revealed a police report based on a complaint against Ferrie. The complaint, a misdemeanor, had been refused for prosecution, but the report led us to Ferrie's present address on Louisiana Avenue Parkway. I sent Frank Klein and a team of investigators to the place. In Ferrie's unkempt rabbit hutch of an apartment they found an assortment of Army rifles, ammunition clips, military canteens and web equipment, and, on the wall, a large map of Cuba. Adding to the general confusion were two young men awaiting Ferrie's return. They said that Ferrie had headed for Texas in his car early Friday afternoon—approximately an hour after the assassination.

Their account of the timing was confirmed later by other witnesses who had seen Ferrie in New Orleans as late as midday on November 22. This meant that Ferrie probably had not been a "getaway" pilot as Jack Martin believed, but it did not mean that we could regard him as clear of any connection with the assassination.

I left a round-the-clock stakeout at his apartment to await his return. On Monday morning Ferrie appeared and was brought to my office for questioning. He was dressed, as usual, as if he had been shot by cannon through a Salvation Army clothing store. He looked every bit as disconcerting as when I had last seen him on Carondelet Street back in 1962. He denied ever having known Lee Oswald but admitted that he had driven to Houston early Friday afternoon.

Considering his exuberant confidence at our last encounter, he was distinctly ill at ease and nervous. And the more he talked, the less his story held together. For example, when I asked him the reason for his departure from New Orleans only one hour following the assassination, he responded that he had driven to Houston to go ice skating. When I then asked him why he had chosen one of the heaviest thunderstorms in many years as the occasion for his ice skating trip, he had no adequate reply.

Later we would learn that at the skating rink he had never put on ice skates but had spent all of his time at a pay telephone, making and receiving calls. We also learned later that Ferrie continued on from Houston to Galveston, Texas, where he happened to be when Jack Ruby called there the night before he shot and killed Lee Oswald. Needless to say, these details hardly were forthcoming from Ferrie when I questioned him.

From his answers, I did not find anything directly connecting Ferrie with the assassination, but I concluded that further investigation of this odd individual and his curiously timed junket was necessary. I ordered my investigators to take him to the First District Police Station, there to be booked and held in jail for questioning by the F.B.I.

I was confident that an F.B.I. investigation of David Ferrie and any other matters even remotely related to the President's murder would be exhaustive. That faith probably was typical of most Americans in 1963. However, it was particularly strong in my case because of my background. My father had been an attorney as had his father before him. Thus, I had, through osmosis or acculturation, acquired a reverence for the law.

Thomas Jefferson Garrison, my paternal grandfather, had been general counsel of the Northwestern Railway, headquartered in Chicago. One of the members of his staff—a young lawyer named Clarence Darrow—had caused my grandfather much displeasure with his inclination to rebel against some of the more rigid strictures of the law. I have been told that Grandfather Garrison was vastly relieved when Darrow resigned from the railroad's legal staff to represent the Socialist leader Eugene Debs. Darrow, as is well known, went on to become one of America's greatest trial attorneys. Ironically, as much as I admired my grandfather, I developed a high regard for Darrow's unparalleled ability as a trial attorney and his great passion for justice. For this reason (and perhaps because of his relationship with my grandfather) one of my sons is named Darrow.

My maternal grandfather, William Oliver Robinson, was a most patriotic man. He came from a predominantly Irish family and stood seven feet three inches in height. (His two brothers were each seven feet tall.) He had no patience for fools or for anyone who did not believe that the United States of America was the greatest country in the world. Successful in real estate and the coal business, he stood straight as an arrow, wore a magnificent turn-of-the-century moustache, and dressed elegantly, having his clothes tailor-made and sent to him from New York. (There were, of course, no tall men's clothing stores in those days.)

As one of the leading businessmen of Knoxville, Iowa, and undoubtedly as one of its leading characters, he often would represent the town at the railroad station when an important dignitary passed through on the cross-country train. When he did so, he wore a red, white, and blue Uncle Sam costume—including the stovepipe hat—exemplifying the patriotism of the citizens of Knoxville. I have a photograph of him, imposing in this grand regalia, greeting President William Howard Taft, who has just dismounted from the train.

I was born with that Knoxville patriotism in my blood and grew up in New Orleans, but the important formative years of my youth were spent in the military. I entered the Army a year before Pearl Harbor, at the age of 19, and liked it so much that it became a surrogate family to me. After being commissioned a lieutenant in the field artillery in 1942, I volunteered for training as a pilot to fly grasshopper planes for observation of enemy targets. Following tactical flight training at Fort Sill, Oklahoma, I was sent to Europe where I flew in combat over the front lines in France and Germany.

Like the other men in my unit, I had become an artillery pilot primarily for the adventure of it. However, I was also flying to support the United States government's effort to defeat the Nazis and the evil they represented. I was never so conscious of this as when I arrived at Dachau the day after the infantry, supported by my artillery unit, took that Nazi concentration camp and saw the gaunt, starved bodies of the dead inmates piled high alongside the waiting crematorium with its great, heavily sooted brick chimney stacks.

During my five years in the Army in World War II and another 18 years as a field artillery officer in the National Guard, I never encountered deception of any kind. To me, the Army was synonymous with the United States government. I should add that I was still in the National Guard, and still equating the Army with the United States government, when President Kennedy was assassinated and I arrested David Ferrie.

Upon my return to civilian life after World War II, I followed my family tradition and went to law school at Tulane, obtaining both Bachelor of Laws and Master of Civil Laws degrees. Shortly thereafter I joined the F.B.I. As a special agent in Seattle and Tacoma, I was very impressed with the competence and efficiency of the Bureau. However, I was extremely bored as I rang doorbells to inquire about the loyalty and associations of applicants for employment in a defense plant. So I decided to return to the law profession.

My arrival in the position of district attorney of New Orleans was something of an accident. Richard Dowling, the incumbent in the late 1950s and the early 1960s when I was in private practice as a trial lawyer, had been an excellent attorney in civil and domestic litigation. However, the administration of his prosecutor's office left a great deal to be desired. As a former assistant district attorney, a job I had held from 1954 to 1958, I felt a strong concern about that particular office. When Dowling ran for re-election in 1961, I ran against him along with a number of others.

I was given no chance of winning. However, I thought my participation in the election might help one of the others who would produce a better office. For my campaign, I did not go through the streets shaking hands and slapping backs. I did not attempt to have rallies organized for me. I did not have circulars handed out in my behalf. I did not solicit the support of any political organizations. I simply spoke directly to the people on television. And inasmuch as I truly did not have any organizational support except for a handful of friends, I always made it a point to appear on television alone, to emphasize my independence, to turn my lack of political support into an asset.

I ended up in the runoff against Dowling, unexpectedly received the support of the local newspaper, and in the second round campaigned exactly as I had in the first.

To my surprise—and to the astonishment of a good many others—I was elected and took office as district attorney on March 3, 1962. This was the first time in New Orleans history that any public official ever had been elected citywide without any political organization support.

Consequently, I brought to the city a brand new and truly independent D.A.'s office. From the beginning I chose my assistant D.A.'s from among the top graduates of the neighboring law schools and from among the best of the city's young trial attorneys. There was not a single political appointment on my staff. Thus, we were able to operate without obligations to any outside individual or organization.

I was 43 years old and had been district attorney for a year and nine months when John Kennedy was killed. I was an old-fashioned patriot, a product of my family, my military experience, and my years in the legal profession. I could not imagine then that the government ever would deceive the citizens of this country. Accordingly, when the F.B.I. released David Ferrie with surprising swiftness, implying that no evidence had been found connecting him with the assassination, I accepted it.* I assumed that the Bureau had thoroughly examined Ferrie's trip and found it to be of no importance. It irked me a bit that the special agent in charge of the New Orleans office had issued a gratuitous statement saying that the arrest of Ferrie had not been the F.B.I.'s idea but that of the district attorney. It was an unprecedented comment for one law enforcement official to make about another.

I might have expected such an observation from Ferrie's attorney but hardly from another government official. I had assumed that the federal government and I were on the same side. However, I ignored the comment and turned my attention back to the prosecution of burglaries, armed robberies, and other local crimes.

---

* In 1979, when the House Select Committee on Assassinations announced its conclusions, it stated that President Kennedy probably was assassinated "as the result of a conspiracy." It acknowledged that one of the possible indications of a conspiracy was Lee Oswald's apparent association in New Orleans with David Ferrie.

2

The
Awakening

N E A R L Y   T H R E E   Y E A R S   P A S S E D.

These were years of great satisfaction for me. We had rebuilt a bucolic D.A.'s office into a crackerjack operation. The office had gone three years without losing a homicide case—and it would be eight more years before we lost our first one. The pink walls and green pipes of the old office had been replaced with walnut panelling. I regularly attended the National District Attorneys' Association conventions at interesting locations such as Phoenix or Las Vegas or Los Angeles. More often than not, I was able to get away from the office once a week for lunch at Brennan's or Moran's or Antoine's.

By this time our military was deeply engaged in the war in Southeast Asia. Like most Americans, I took it for granted that our government had our troops over there to bring democracy to South Vietnam. Like most Americans, I also took it for granted that our government had fully investigated President Kennedy's assassination and had found it to be indeed the result of a random act by a man acting alone. Certainly, it never crossed my mind that the murder of President

Kennedy and the subsequent arrival of half a million members of the American military in Vietnam might be related.

Of course, I was aware of some of the odd contradictions about the assassination. It was public knowledge that most of the crowd in Dealey Plaza thought they had heard, and even seen, shooting from the grassy knoll in front of the President. Some of them had run up the knoll, behind the wooden fence on top of it, into the railroad yard in the back, and had been stopped by men identifying themselves as Secret Service agents.

Undeniably, there had been some real sloppiness in the security system for the President. Everyone knew that the protective bubble had been removed from his limousine and had seen the photographs of the numerous wide-open windows overlooking Dealey Plaza. But these, I reasoned, were the first things that any investigation would have dug into. The F.B.I. most certainly had done just that and—as if that were not enough—the Warren Commission staff had inquired extensively into the matter for ten months.

The conclusion of these two weighty bodies that all the shooting had been done by one man aiming from behind the President satisfied me that the allegations about activity up front around the grassy knoll, and in the railroad yard behind it, were so much speculation.

That was my view as of late 1966. I was happily married, the father of three children (with two more to come), and I had a great job. I was quite content with the way my life was going and with the world around me. In retrospect, it would be more accurate to say that I was tranquilized by the very world in which I lived.

Then one day that autumn I had a chance conversation with Russell Long, the United States senator from Louisiana. The subject of Kennedy's assassination arose. To this day I recall his words: "Those fellows on the Warren Commission were dead wrong," he said in his blunt fashion. "There's no way in the world that one man could have shot up Jack Kennedy that way."

I was surprised to hear this from one of the most intelligent members of the U.S. Senate, a man I knew personally and deeply respected. This was the first sign I had encountered that doubts persisted about Kennedy's assassination in such high quarters. The force of Senator Long's words aroused my curiosity. I immediately ordered the entire

13

set of the Warren Commission volumes—the hearings, the exhibits, and the Commission's report.

While I waited for the books to arrive, I did some research at the library about how the Warren Commission had come into being. Five days after the assassination, Representative Charles Goodell of New York proposed that a Joint Congressional Committee conduct an investigation. The committee was to consist of seven representatives and seven senators. Two days later, before Congress had taken any action to follow up on Goodell's proposal, President Lyndon Johnson announced that he already had formed an investigative commission and chosen seven members. To avoid any possible criticism that he was taking the investigation out of the hands of Congress, he included two representatives from each chamber.

I looked up biographical information on each of his selections. It was apparent that his investigative group was notably weighted with men whose backgrounds were pro-intelligence or pro-military. Allen Dulles had been director of the C.I.A. for nine years. Representative Gerald Ford was described by *Newsweek* as "the C.I.A.'s best friend in Congress." Senator Richard Russell chaired the Senate Armed Forces Committee and headed its subcommittee on intelligence. John J. McCloy had served as assistant secretary of war and as the United States government's high commissioner in occupied Germany at the end of World War II. At the time of his appointment to the Warren Commission, he was generally regarded as the unofficial top member of the American foreign policy establishment.* At the time, I found nothing questionable about the makeup of the Commission. Nor did I have any reason to doubt the honesty or integrity of these respected leaders.

When the 26 Warren Commission volumes arrived, I immersed myself in the testimony and exhibits for some weeks, mostly at night and on weekends. This was not my idea of a stimulating project, but I did it for the same reason that—back in 1963—I had inquired into David Ferrie's oddly timed trip to Texas. Lee Oswald had spent the summer preceding the assassination in New Orleans. This was my jurisdiction as district attorney.

Considering the lofty credentials of the Commission members and

---

* Rounding out the Commission were Chief Justice Earl Warren, Representative Hale Boggs of Louisiana, and Senator John Sherman Cooper of Kentucky.

the quality and size of the staff available to them, I had expected to find a thorough and professional investigation. I found nothing of the sort. The mass of information was disorganized and confused. The Commission had provided no adequate index to its exhibits (although one was subsequently produced by Sylvia Meagher, a prominent critic of the official version of the assassination). The number of promising leads that were never followed up offended my prosecutorial sensibility. And perhaps worst of all, the conclusions in the report seemed to be based on an appallingly selective reading of the evidence, ignoring credible testimony from literally dozens of witnesses.

The Commission officially concluded, for example, that Kennedy's murder was accomplished by one man shooting from behind the President. This was not merely crucial to the official position; it was sacramental.

Yet I discovered early on in my reading that the statements of many of the witnesses at Dealey Plaza did not support the official explanation of the President's murder. Visualize the scene at Dealey Plaza.* The motorcade, having just made a sweeping left turn from Houston Street, was headed west on Elm Street. At the time the President was hit, the Texas School Book Depository, from which the Warren Commission claimed Oswald did all the shooting, was well behind him, to his right rear. Up in front of him, somewhat to the right, was the grassy knoll with a wooden picket fence—creating a small stockade—on top. There was a grove of small trees clustered along the picket fence. Also on the right front, but slightly closer to the President, was a concrete arcade. All of this was on a terrace high atop the grass-covered slope overlooking Elm Street.

A number of witnesses vividly recalled noticing strange activities taking place in the grassy knoll area in front of the President around the time of the shooting. For instance, an hour before the assassination, Julia Ann Mercer, an employee of Automat Distributors, was driving west past the grassy knoll on Elm Street. Caught in a traffic jam, she found herself stopped alongside a pick-up truck parked part-way up along the curbing. She saw a young man, with a rifle in a case, dismount and clamber up the steep incline onto the knoll. The day

* See the map on the endpapers.

after the assassination, I later found out, she reported this unsettling incident both to the F.B.I.'s local office and the Dallas Sheriff's office. But strangely, Julia Ann Mercer was never questioned by the Commission's staff.

Lee Bowers, the switchman for the railroad yard, had a box-seat view of the grassy knoll from his glassed-in tower, 14 feet above the yard. According to his testimony, a few minutes before the shooting began he observed two men he did not recognize standing behind the picket fence on the knoll watching the approaching parade. Earlier he had seen an unfamiliar man driving a car around in the railroad yard behind the knoll. The man appeared to be speaking into a hand-held microphone.

In an affidavit given to the Sheriff's office, J.C. Price, a Dallas roofing worker, said that following the volley of shots he "saw one man run towards the passenger cars on the railroad siding. . . . He had something in his hand. I couldn't be sure but it may have been a head piece."

Some of the witnesses, contrary to the Warren Commission's conclusions, not only heard shots coming from the picket fence, they saw smoke from rifle fire drifting up through the cluster of trees. Like J.C. Price, an even larger number had the impression that men had run from the knoll after the shooting, heading into the railroad yard behind. Joseph Smith, a police officer who had been a motorcycle escort alongside the President's car, ran up the high grade of the knoll towards the fence.

S.M. Holland, the signal supervisor for the Union Terminal Railroad, described the shooting this way:

> I heard a third report and I counted four shots and . . . in this group of trees . . . there was a shot, a report, I don't know whether it was a shot. I can't say that. And a puff of smoke came out about six or eight feet above the ground right out from under those trees. . . . I have no doubt about seeing that puff of smoke come out from under those trees. . . . I definitely saw the puff of smoke and heard the report from under those trees. . . .

O.V. Campbell, the president of the Book Depository, said the shooting "came from the grassy area down this way," indicating the direction in which the motorcade had been headed once it passed the Book Depository. He said, "I heard shots being fired from a point I thought was near the railroad tracks. . . ."

James Tague, a Dallas car salesman who was cut on the face perhaps by a glancing bullet, said, "My first impression was that up by the, whatever you call the monument or whatever it was . . . that somebody was throwing firecrackers up there . . . and the police were running up to it."

Billy Lovelady, an employee of the Book Depository who was having lunch on its front steps, recollected the shots as having come from "right there around that concrete little deal on that knoll . . . between the underpass and the building right on that knoll."

Abraham Zapruder, who became famous for the home movie he took of the shooting, was standing on a cement slab by the grassy knoll with his back to the picket fence. He described the police officers running past him, headed behind the knoll area. As to where the shooting came from, he added: "I also thought it came from back of me."

Forrest Sorrels, the local Secret Service head, was riding in the front of the parade. He testified that when he heard the shots, "a little bit too loud for a firecracker," he looked over "on this terrace part there, because the sound sounded like it came from the back and up in that direction."

William Newman, a Dallas design engineer, had been watching the parade with his family from the curb at the bottom of the grassy knoll a short distance in front of the picket fence. Newman said:

> We were standing on the edge of the curb looking at the car as it was coming toward us and all of a sudden there was a noise, apparently gunshot. The President jumped up in his seat, and it looked like what I thought was a firecracker had went off and I thought he had realized it. It was just like an explosion and he was standing up. By this time he was directly in front of us and I was looking directly at him when he was hit in the side of the head. . . . Then we fell down on the grass as it seemed that we were in the direct path of fire. . . . I thought the shot had come from the garden directly behind me. . . . I do not recall looking toward the Texas School Book Depository. I looked back in the vicinity of the garden.

L.C. Smith of the Sheriff's office was on Main Street when he heard the shots. He ran "as fast as I could to Elm Street just West of Houston." There he encountered a woman who told him that "the President was shot in the head and the shots came from the fence on the north side of Elm," referring to the picket fence in the grassy knoll area.

Malcolm Summers, the owner of a local mailing service, recalled the moment when the shooting ended:

> Then all of the people started running up the terrace. Everybody was just running around towards the railroad tracks and I knew that they had someone trapped up there. . . .

One lady, Jean Hill, actually chased one of the men. She admitted that she was not sure what she would have done had she caught up with him. She testified that she saw the man go "toward the railroad tracks to the west."

According to Hill's account, the railroad yard—up ahead and to the right of where the President had been hit—plainly was the destination of the men running from the assassination scene. I went back again to the testimony of Lee Bowers, the switchman there, and studied his answers to questions about the aftermath posed by Warren Commission attorney Joseph A. Ball:

> MR. BALL: Afterwards did a good many people come up there on this high ground at the tower?
>
> MR. BOWERS: A large number of people came [from] more than one direction. One group converged from the corner of Elm and Houston, and came down the extension of Elm and came into the high ground, and another line—another large group went across the triangular area between Houston and Elm and then across Elm and then up the incline. Some of them all the way up. *Many of them did, as well as, of course, between 50 and a hundred policemen within a maximum of 5 minutes.*
>
> MR. BALL: In this area around your tower?
>
> MR. BOWERS: That's right. Sealed off the area, and I held off the trains until they could be examined, and *there was some transients taken on at least one train.*

MR. BALL: I believe you have talked this over with me before your deposition was taken, haven't we?

MR. BOWERS: Yes.

MR. BALL: Is there anything that you told me that I haven't asked you about that you think of?

MR. BOWERS: Nothing that I can recall.
[Emphasis supplied.]

The fact that at least one of the trains in the railroad yard had to be stopped by the switchman so that "transients" could be taken off ordinarily would raise the hackles of any good attorney. However, the unperturbed Commission counsel quickly changed the subject, I noted, cutting off further discussion of the accommodating train departure of these unknown men.

I noticed exactly the same legal maneuver when Sergeant D.V. Harkness, the officer in charge of searching the departing trains, testified in response to questions by Warren Commission counsel David Belin:

MR. HARKNESS: I went back to the front, and Inspector Sawyer— helped to get the crowd back first, and then Inspector Sawyer assigned me to some freight cars *that were leaving out of the yard, to go down and search all freight cars that were leaving the yard.*

MR. BELIN: Then what did you do?

MR. HARKNESS: Well, we got a long freight that was in there, and *we pulled some people off of there and took them to the station.*

MR. BELIN: You mean some transients?

MR. HARKNESS: Tramps and hoboes.

MR. BELIN: That were on the freight car?

MR. HARKNESS: Yes, sir.

MR. BELIN: Then what did you do?

MR. HARKNESS: That was all my assignment, because *they shook two long freights down that were leaving,* to my knowledge, in all the area there. We had several officers working in that area.

19

MR. BELIN: *Do you know whether or not anyone found any suspicious people of any kind or nature down there in the railroad yard?*

MR. HARKNESS: *Yes, sir. We made some arrests. I put some people in.*

MR. BELIN: *Were these what you call hoboes or tramps?*

MR. HARKNESS: *Yes, sir.*

MR. BELIN: *Were all those questioned?*

MR. HARKNESS: *Yes, sir; they were taken to the station and questioned.*

MR. BELIN: Any guns of any kind found?

MR. HARKNESS: Not to my knowledge.

MR. BELIN: *I want to go back to this Amos Euins.* Do you remember what he said to you and what you said to him when you first saw him? [Emphasis added.]

This exchange struck me as remarkable. Here counsel Belin has just been told about several strangers using a departing train to leave the area where the President had just been murdered and, rather than ask more than a couple of cursory follow-up questions, he changes the subject. "Amos Euins," another witness, had no connection whatsoever with the activity around the grassy knoll and the interesting occurrence of the timely, departing trains. Belin never asked Sergeant Harkness for further details about the arrested men, particularly who had seen to it that they were "taken to the station and questioned." Neither at the Dallas Sheriff's office nor at the Dallas Police Department was there any record of their arrest or questioning. Nor was there, so far as I could find, any mention of their names anywhere in the 26 Warren Commission volumes.

Also never followed up was equally intriguing evidence indicating that there may have been men impersonating Secret Service agents around the railroad yard area.

Joe M. Smith, the traffic officer at the intersection of Elm and Houston Streets who was told by a woman that the shooting was coming "from the bushes," left the area where he had been stationed and went up on the knoll behind the stockade fence on top. His account, responding to questions from Warren Commission counsel Wesley J. Liebeler:

MR. SMITH: . . . There was some deputy sheriff with me and I believe one Secret Service man when I got there. . . . I felt awfully silly, but after the shot and this woman, I pulled my pistol from my holster and I thought, this is silly, I don't know who I am looking for, and I put it back. Just as I did, he showed me that he was a Secret Service agent.

MR. LIEBELER: Did you accost this man?

MR. SMITH: Well, he saw me coming with my pistol and right away he showed me who he was.

MR. LIEBELER: Do you remember who it was?

MR. SMITH: No, sir, I don't. . . .

However, according to the Warren Commission report, all of the Secret Service agents assigned to the parade had gone along with it en route to the hospital. The Secret Service was on record that not a single one of its agents was at the scene of the assassination, other than those passing through in the motorcade—and all of them were gone in minutes. This meant either that the Secret Service was lying or mistaken or that the man Officer Smith encountered was not really a Secret Service agent.

Sergeant Harkness's testimony revealed that when he first arrived at the rear of the Book Depository (even before his search of the railroad yards) "there were some Secret Service agents there. I didn't get them identified. They told me they were Secret Service agents." From Harkness, therefore, it became apparent that there was not just one, but a number of people purporting to be Secret Service agents in an area where supposedly there were none.

It did not end with Officer Smith and Sergeant Harkness. I found that Jean Hill, who chased a man running from the scene, was halted in the parking lot behind the fence on the knoll. The man, who was wearing a business suit, held out his Secret Service identification for her to see. By the time the interruption was over, her quarry was gone.

Despite these indications that several men may well have been falsely representing themselves as Secret Service agents, or that the Secret Service had no idea where its agents actually were, the Warren Commission and its staff had simply dropped the matter.

As I read, I realized that the Warren Commission and its staff were not alone in their unorthodox handling of the investigation. The Dallas Police Department, which closed its books on the case almost immediately, also conducted a highly irregular inquiry. For example, after his arrest Lee Harvey Oswald was questioned while in the custody of Captain Will Fritz, head of the Dallas Police Homicide Division. As a prosecutor, I knew that recording of such questioning is routine even in minor felony cases. Yet, according to what I read in the Warren Commission hearings, the alleged murderer of the President of the United States had been questioned for a total of 12 hours without any taping or shorthand notes by a stenographer. Nor was any attorney present. The absence of any record of the interrogation of Oswald revealed a disregard for basic constitutional rights that was foreign to me. This could not be mere sloppiness, I realized. A police officer of 30 years' experience like Captain Fritz had to be aware that anything Oswald said under such circumstances would be inadmissible in any subsequent trial.

In my reading, I was also surprised to find how quickly the F.B.I. had wrapped up its investigation, reaching its conclusion that Lee Oswald was the lone assassin within weeks. Judging from the plethora of loose ends I was finding in the Warren Commission's testimony and exhibits, such a rapid conclusion seemed incomprehensible.

The more I read, the clearer it became that all the official government investigations of the assassination had systematically ignored any evidence that might lead to a conclusion other than that Lee Oswald was the lone assassin. At first I did not know what to make of this, so I just kept reading. Then one Friday night I found myself reviewing the testimony of Lieutenant Colonel Allison G. Folsom, Jr., who was reading aloud from Oswald's training record. He described a grade that Oswald had received in a Russian examination at El Toro Marine Base in California shortly before his highly publicized defection to the Soviet Union.

Russian examination! My ears went up.

In all my years of military service during World War II—and since—I had never taken a test in Russian. Never mind Colonel Folsom's additional testimony that Oswald had done poorly on the exam, getting only two more Russian words right than wrong.* I

---

* I am reminded of the man who said his dog was not very intelligent because he could beat him three games out of five when they played chess.

would not have had any Russian words right. In 1959, when Oswald was taking that exam, I was a staff officer in the National Guard in a battalion made up of hundreds of soldiers. None of them had been required to show how much Russian they knew. Even on that night in 1966 when I read Colonel Folsom's testimony I was still in the military service—by now a major—and I could not recall a single soldier *ever* having been required to demonstrate how much Russian he had learned.

Soldiers ordinarily are not taught Russian any more than they are taught philosophy or art or music—not if they are really members of the combat branch to which they are assigned. The government's witnesses and exhibits had described Oswald as a Marine assigned to anti-aircraft duty. A soldier genuinely involved in anti-aircraft duty would have about as much use for Russian as a cat would have for pajamas.

I read no farther that night. I had to digest this first indication that Lee Oswald—in 1959, at least—had been receiving intelligence training. I knew, as did anyone with military background, that Marine intelligence activity was guided by the Office of Naval Intelligence (O.N.I.). Wondering what possible connection there might have been between the O.N.I. and Lee Harvey Oswald, I went to bed. I did not sleep much that night.

The next morning I headed downtown to the seedy, faded sector of town where 544 Camp Street was located. I had jotted down this address some weeks earlier while reading the exhibits section of the Warren Commission volumes. It had been imprinted with a small hand stamp* on some of the material which Oswald had been handing out on the streets of New Orleans in the summer of 1963. Oswald had been spotted participating in several pamphleting incidents. In one on August 9 he was involved in a scuffle on Canal Street with several anti-Castro Cubans and was arrested. The Warren Commission had concluded from this and other evidence that Oswald was a dedicated and ostentatiously visible, if lonely, communist who had joined the Fair Play for Cuba Committee to support Fidel Castro.

* The stamp, later found among Oswald's possessions after his death, was the type available at any dime store.

Because of several inconsistencies, this facile explanation had never sat quite right with me. To start with, I knew that Oswald had stamped the 544 Camp address only on his public handouts of August 9th. It no longer appeared on the subsequent pamphlets he gave out. So now I wanted to look at the place firsthand.

Catty-corner from Lafayette Square, I found 544 Camp to be located in a small mousy gray structure built from a conspicuously unsuccessful imitation of blocks of granite. This modest edifice was called, I was later to learn, the "Newman Building," after its current owner. The entrance at 544 Camp opened onto stairs leading to the second floor.

There was something familiar about the building, and it took me a moment or two to refresh my memory. Then I went around the corner, past where Mancuso's small restaurant used to be, and walked a few steps down Lafayette Street to the other entrance of the building. There I found myself looking at the door of what I knew had been—back in 1963—the entrance to the upstairs private detective office of Guy Banister. Located at 531 Lafayette Street, the door had borne the designation, "Guy Banister Associates, Inc. Investigators." So both entrances—544 Camp and 531 Lafayette—led to the same place. And curiously, the name of Guy Banister, which had come up three years before, had surfaced again.

Banister had died in 1964—about nine months after the assassination—but now it occurred to me why "544 Camp Street" appeared on Oswald's material for only one day. Somebody—presumably Banister or an associate of his—had stopped Oswald from using the address on later circulars. And small wonder. Guy Banister hardly could have been enthusiastic about the young ex-Marine stamping his address on pro-Castro literature.

Even though no longer in the F.B.I., Banister had shared the sentiments of J. Edgar Hoover. I knew that he was heavily involved in anti-communist endeavors of all kinds. A young attorney I frequently played chess with at the New Orleans Chess Club had told me how Banister had hired him when he was a college student to find radical, or even liberal, organizations on the campus, and to join and penetrate them. I knew further that Banister was a leader of the Anti-Communist League of the Caribbean. I had heard about this far-right group from a partner of his in the organization, an attorney named Maurice

Gatlin, who lived at the Claiborne Towers apartment building at the same time I did.

Knowing now that Guy Banister's office was the headquarters out of which Oswald had operated, I began to understand some of the things I had learned about the "Marxist-oriented" pamphleteer. Whenever Oswald was going to hand out pro-Castro leaflets, for example, he regularly had gone to a local employment office and hired men to help him in his leafleting work. I found this out when I noticed that one of the young men shown in local news photos handing out flyers with Oswald looked very much like the son of one of my fellow artillery officers in the National Guard. I called Charles Steele and learned that indeed it was his son, Charles, Jr. We interviewed young Steele and discovered that Oswald had paid him and the others two dollars an hour to hand out pamphlets with him. Oswald had told them that they had to do this until the news photographers departed, after which they were free to go. This recruitment method was highly improbable for a true Marxist group. Most such groups had members to do their leafleting but almost no money. Oswald's Fair Play for Cuba Committee, by contrast, had no apparent members other than himself but enough money that it could hire unemployed people.

This was the first evidence I encountered that Lee Oswald had not been a "communist" or a "Marxist" of any kind. What appeared to be considerably more probable, now that I had seen the setup at 544 Camp, was that Guy Banister—or someone associated with him—had been using Oswald as an *agent provocateur*. For what purpose, and under whose auspices, remained a mystery.

If Oswald had been working that summer under Banister, I reflected, that would help explain some other oddities I had discovered in my reading. According to the Warren Commission report, when Oswald was arrested on August 9 on Canal Street and brought to the police station, he immediately asked to see an F.B.I. agent. Oswald was separated from the other arrested men and brought into a private room where he talked with Special Agent John Quigley of the local Bureau office. Later Agent Quigley burned the notes he had taken during this interview. This is contrary to standard Bureau procedure. Customarily, such notes are placed in the office file, along with the report of the occasion. Such special treatment for a vociferous communist seemed inexplicable—unless Oswald was actually working with Guy Banister, a former high-ranking F.B.I. official, who could have easily arranged it.*

About a week after Oswald's Canal Street arrest, I recalled, someone arranged for him to participate in a radio debate on station WDSU. The subject was, essentially, capitalism versus communism. Oswald represented the left-wing position and duly portrayed himself on the taped program as a Marxist. After Kennedy's assassination, and less than a week after Oswald in turn was murdered, copies of the tape were sent to members of Congress as proof positive that a communist had killed the President.

Could it have been Banister or one of his associates, I wondered, who had arranged for the debate and taped it? Could it have been Banister who sent it to Congress? If Oswald was working under Banister's direction that summer, it was clear that neither his pamphleting nor his radio debating were intended to convert anyone to the cause of Marxism. Rather, they were designed to accomplish only one thing: to create a highly visible public profile for Lee Harvey Oswald as a communist.

I turned away from Banister's old office and looked across Lafayette Street, where the U.S. Post Office Building loomed. Occupying an entire city block, it was majestic and timeless in contrast to its decayed, weatherbeaten surroundings. The building housed the New Orleans Secret Service operation. And, I now recalled, upstairs was the New Orleans headquarters of the Office of Naval Intelligence†—the organization I had been musing about the night before in relation to Oswald's Marine intelligence training. Was it just coincidence, I asked myself, that Guy Banister, who had begun his career in World War II with the O.N.I., had chosen an office right across the street from his old employers? Just as much a coincidence, I supposed, as the location of his previous private detective office—directly across the street from the New Orleans offices of the C.I.A. and the F.B.I.

---

* After Oswald moved back to Dallas, the Bureau also temporarily transferred Special Agent Quigley to Dallas.

† This I had learned earlier from Guy Johnson, a long-time prosecutor in the district attorney's office and a friend of mine who had been active in Naval Intelligence in World War II and subsequently in the O.N.I. Reserves; Johnson went there frequently.

I walked down Lafayette Street, toward the Mississippi River, to look at two other addresses on the 600 block of Magazine Street that I had noted from my reading about Lee Oswald's movements. One was the Reily Coffee Company, where Oswald had been listed as an employee in 1963, shortly before his famous emergence on the city streets handing out circulars calling for fair play for Fidel Castro. You would have to be practically a stranger to the city not to know that William Reily, the coffee company's president, had actively supported the anti-Castro movement for years.

As I walked around the small coffee company building, I wondered whether Lee Oswald actually had labored there as a "second oiler" as company records had indicated, or whether the firm simply had been his nesting place until it was time for him to fulfill his ill-fated assignment as an *agent provocateur* for Guy Banister.

I strolled next door to the other address I wanted to check out—the Crescent City Garage. According to its operator, Adrian Alba, Lee Oswald had spent a great deal of time there when it appeared to Alba that Oswald should have been working at Reily's.* In his testimony before the Warren Commission, Alba described Oswald's interest in the rifle magazines there.

It was not too surprising that there were plenty of gun magazines for Oswald to thumb through. This garage was not exactly a Young Socialists meeting hall. Very much to the contrary, for years it had been the official parking lot of the local headquarters for the Federal Bureau of Investigation. Now, since the Bureau had recently moved to new offices on Loyola Avenue, the Crescent City Garage was still the parking garage closest to the Office of Naval Intelligence and the Secret Service. Furthermore, the Central Intelligence Agency offices, located in the dark gray building known as the Masonic Temple on the 300 block of St. Charles Avenue, stood but a few blocks away.†

Considering the proximity its members maintain with one another, it is hardly surprising that they refer to themselves as the intelligence

---

* Later, Alba testified to more than Oswald's visits to the garage. He testified in 1978 before the House Select Committee on Assassinations that he had "often seen Oswald in Mancuso's Restaurant on the first floor of 544 Camp Street." The House Committee conceded that David Ferrie and Guy Banister also were frequent customers at Mancuso's.

† In the early 1960s the F.B.I. was also located in the Masonic Temple.

community. However, it seemed to me that a man planning to kill the President would have to be exceedingly nonchalant to have chosen the United States government's intelligence complex as the place to spend his spare time until shortly before his lonesome strike.

In most countries, under such circumstances, a serious investigation would have *begun* with the working hypothesis that the intelligence community in New Orleans had used Lee Oswald as an *agent provocateur.* At the outset his extravagantly high profile as a "supporter" of Fidel Castro would have been understood in that context.

However, it was plain from my reading that in the years since President Kennedy's murder, federal investigators never once had glanced in the most obvious directions. Similarly, the highest officers of the United States government appeared totally unaware of the concept of the *agent provocateur.*

By the time I returned home that day I realized I had some serious problems to resolve. The application of every reasonable model to the available evidence had left me with a troubling conclusion. That was the apparent possibility of a *pre-existing relationship* between the man portrayed as the lone killer of President Kennedy and the intelligence community of the United States government.

3

War
Games

THREE YEARS EARLIER our good fortune in stumbling across David Ferrie had been turned aside by the F.B.I.'s assurance that there was no need to investigate him. Now it seemed to me that the best way to get back where we had started was to locate the original source of the information that Ferrie had driven to Texas on the day of the assassination.

Early Monday morning at the district attorney's office I met with Herman Kohlman, the assistant D.A. who had come up with that lead the Sunday after the assassination. He informed me that the source was Jack Martin, the victim of Guy Banister's pistol-whipping.

Within a few hours we had tracked Martin down, and he was seated across my desk, his anxious gaze fixed on my every move. An on-again, off-again alcoholic, he was a thin man with deeply circled, worried eyes. Although he had been written off as a nonentity by many, I had long regarded him as a quick-witted and highly observant, if slightly disorganized, private detective. I had known him casually as far back as my days as an assistant D.A. and always had gotten along well with him.

"Jack," I said, "why don't you relax a little? You should know by now that you're among friends here."

He nodded nervously. He was seated in the roomy, upholstered chair across from my desk, but he looked most uncomfortable. I offered him some coffee. "You're not under cross-examination, Jack," I said. "I just want a little help. Understand?"

His head nodded jerkily.

"What I need is a little clarification about that day when Guy Banister beat you over the head with his Magnum. Remember that?"

"How could I forget it? He nearly killed me."

"Here's my problem, Jack," I said. "You've told me you and Guy were good friends for more than ten years when that happened."

"At least ten," he said. "Could be more."

"And he never hit you before."

"Never touched me."

"Yet on November 22nd, 1963—the day of the President's murder—he pistol-whipped you with a .357 Magnum."

His eyes were now fixed on mine.

"The police report says the reason Banister beat you was you had an argument over telephone bills." I pulled a copy of the police report from my desk drawer and shoved it across to him. "Here, take a look at it."

He bent his head over and examined it as if he had never seen it before. I was sure that he had seen it many times, probably even had a copy at home.

After a moment he looked up without saying a word. His eyes told me he was deeply concerned about something.

"Now, does a simple argument over phone bills sound like a believable explanation to you?" I asked.

I waited. Then, dreamily, he shook his head slowly. "No," he admitted. "It involved more than that."

"How much more?"

Again I waited. He breathed deeply, sucking in the air.

"It started like it was going to be nothing at all," he began. "We'd both been drinking at Katzenjammer's—maybe more than usual, because of the assassination and all. Banister especially."

Pausing to chug down another cup of coffee, he made a real effort to collect his thoughts.

"Well, when we came back to the office, Banister started bitching about one thing and then another. He was in a mean mood. Then all of a sudden, he accused me of going through his private files. Now I never went through his private stuff ever—absolutely never. And that really ticked me off."

He hesitated for a long moment.

"Go on, Jack," I said gently.

"I guess I blew up," he continued, his face flushed with memories of injustice. "That's when I told him he'd better not talk to me like that. I told him I remembered the people I had seen around the office that summer. And that's when he hit me. Fast as a flash—pulled out that big Magnum and slammed me on the side of the head with it."

"Just because you remembered the people you'd seen at his office the past summer?" I asked.

"Yeah, that's all it took. He went bananas on that one."

"And just who were the people you'd seen in the office that summer?" I prodded softly.

"There was a bunch of them. It was like a circus. There were all those Cubans—coming in and going out, coming in and going out. They all looked alike to me."

Someone once commented that whenever you really want to do something unseen, whenever you go to great pains to make sure that you are unobserved, there always turns out to be someone who was sitting under the oak tree. At the strange place that was Banister's office, Jack Martin, unnoticed in the middle of it all, was the one sitting under the oak tree.

He drew a long breath and then went on. "Then there were all these other characters. There was Dave Ferrie—you know about him by now."

"Was he there very often?" I asked.

"Often? He practically lived there."

Then Martin fell silent. I saw by the look in his eyes that he had come to a full stop.

I was not about to let my weekend visit to 544 Camp Street go down the drain that easily, so I gave him a hand. "And Lee Harvey Oswald?" I added.

Jack swallowed, then nodded. It was almost as if he felt relief in finally having a burden lifted from him. "Yeah, he was there too. Sometimes he'd be meeting with Guy Banister with the door shut. Other times he'd be shooting the bull with Dave Ferrie. But he was there all right."

"What was Guy Banister doing while all this was going on?"

"Hell, he was the one running the circus."

"What about his private detective work?"

"Not much of that came in, but when it did, I handled it. That's why I was there."

"So, Jack," I said. "Just what was going on at Banister's office?"

He held up his hand. "I can't answer that," he said firmly. "I can't go into that stuff at all." Unexpectedly, he stood up. "I think I'd better go," he said.

"Hold on, Jack. What's the problem with our going into what was happening at Banister's office?"

"What's the problem?" he said. *"What's the problem?"* he repeated, as if in disbelief. "The problem is that we're going to bring the god-damned federal government down on our backs. Do I need to spell it out? I could get killed—and so could you."

He turned around. "I'd better go," he mumbled. He wobbled as he headed for the door.

Even after talking to Martin, it was still too early for me to create a formal investigative team to look into the assassination. The office was shorthanded,* and we did not yet have enough data. By avoiding the urge to climb onto a horse and ride off in all directions, I felt, we were more likely to be successful.

Informally, I assigned Louis Ivon the job of wooing Martin and persuading him to overcome his mental block about the action at

---

* In the 1960s the New Orleans district attorney's office had only 22 assistant D.A.'s. Even though the city is smaller today because of migration to adjacent suburbs, the office now has 65 assistant D.A.'s.

Banister's place. Ivon was a lanky, laconic young police investigator whose seemingly casual manner belied his intensity of purpose. I knew that Ivon, easily the brightest of the police assigned to my office, had a good relationship with Martin. On occasion, when Martin was given the cold shoulder by the police force on one of his investigations, Ivon had given the man a helping hand.

I also gave Ivon the assignment of developing all possible information about David Ferrie and of establishing liaisons with the police and sheriff's offices in adjacent Jefferson Parish, where Ferrie had lived for many years.

I had already informally brought in Frank Klein. In recent weeks I had been providing him with more and more of the background information I had come across. I even took him on a drive through the back streets in the vicinity of the post office and the Reily Coffee Company. Although I had found much of the Warren Commission material to be worse than useless, I loaned him the volumes so that he, too, could savor the deception—and uncover useful leads.

What I needed from the outset was someone with whom I could brainstorm—trade thoughts and acquire more understanding. In Klein, who had a first-class analytical mind, I had the perfect person.

Finding Klein, and making him the chief assistant D.A., had been a big step forward in forming the kind of prosecutor's office I had in mind. During my years in the field artillery I had observed a characteristic common to the operation of the very best battalions. Invariably, the commanding officer delegated the details of running the organization to what the military calls his "executive officer." This put him in a better position to see his outfit with a bit of perspective as it actually functioned. At the same time, the relative freedom from the day-to-day details gave more opportunity to evaluate policy, implement innovations, and make major decisions.

Klein had served in the Marines, having been decorated in combat in Korea. He was almost Teutonic in his appreciation of discipline and order in administration. I, on the other hand, was more comfortable with the command of a loose ship. We complemented one another perfectly.

One morning about a week after my initial interview with Jack

Martin, I came into my office and found Frank Klein stacking papers on my side table.

"Why," I asked, "are you desecrating my office?"

"Jack Martin stonewalled you on what was happening at Guy Banister's," he said, "so I thought of a way we might find out for ourselves."

"And just what would that be?"

"I've been spending some time at the public library," he said. "These piles are photocopies of the front pages of the *Times-Picayune* for June, July, and August of 1963."

"And what are we going to do with them?" I asked.

"Well," he said, "we might get some idea of what's bothering Martin—of what Guy Banister was up to that summer."

"Seems to me that any operation Banister was running would have too low a profile to show up on the front pages of the paper."

"Maybe so," Klein said, "but I think I found something interesting." He laid in front of me a photostat of the front page of the *Times-Picayune* dated Thursday, August 1, 1963. The heading on the right side story read:

CACHE OF MATERIAL
FOR BOMBS SEIZED

Probe of St. Tammany
Case Continues

I scanned the first paragraph:

> More than a ton of dynamite, 20 bomb casings three-feet long, napalm (fire-bomb) material and other devices were seized Wednesday by Federal Bureau of Investigation agents in a resort area in St. Tammany Parish, between Mandeville and Lacombe.

The story went on to say that the dynamite, bomb casings, and other materials, according to the special agent in charge of the New Orleans F.B.I. office,

> . . . were seized in connection with an investigation of an effort to "carry out a military operation against a country with which the

United States is at peace." This is in violation of Title 18, Section 960 of the U.S. Code.

For such an adventurous foray the local F.B.I. official, with his broad generalities, appeared to me to be keeping his cards very close to his vest. He had not mentioned the country involved and had not mentioned any arrests. Yet the news story had no particular impact on me.

I looked up at Klein. "This is interesting," I said. "But what's the point?"

"Wait a minute," said Klein. "You haven't seen the whole story yet." He pushed another sheet in front of me. This one was a copy of the front page for Friday morning, August 2, 1963. On the left side of the page, I read:

BOMB CACHE COTTAGE LOANED
TO NEWLY-ARRIVED REFUGEE

Owner's Wife Says Mate
Did Cubans Favor

The wife of the owner of a cottage on the north shore of Lake Pontchartrain where a large quantity of explosives and war materials were seized said Thursday that the house was loaned to a newly-arrived Cuban refugee three weeks ago.

Mrs. William Julius McLaney, 4313 Encampment, said that neither she nor her husband, who operates a race horse feed business, had knowledge that the munitions were stored at the house near Lacombe until agents of the Federal Bureau of Investigation questioned her husband Wednesday before making the seizure.

She said that the place was loaned to a Cuban they knew only as "Jose Juarez" as a favor to friends of theirs in Cuba.

The McLaneys had operated a tourist business in Havana, but came to New Orleans in 1960 "because Castro made things impossible down there."

I looked up at Klein, waiting for his comment.

"Remember when we raided Dave Ferrie's apartment three years ago?" he asked. "Remember the map of Cuba that Ferrie had on his wall?"

I nodded, still listening. "Remember the Army equipment and the rifles laying around? He even had an artillery shell sitting there. It was a 155 millimeter."

"And Jack Martin has connected Ferrie with Banister's office," I answered, thinking out loud, "so you think that this news story about the bombs connects with Banister's operation—the one that Martin's afraid to tell us about?"

Klein shrugged his shoulders. "I'm just suggesting a working theory," he said. "Remember Martin mentioned a lot of Cubans being at Banister's place, too. Look at this reference in the second story to the Cuban named Jose Juarez."

"So?"

"So," Klein responded, "what was Lee Oswald handing out? Were they Fair Play for Russia leaflets? Were they Fair Play for Rumania pamphlets? No. They were Fair Play for Cuba leaflets. Did he ever show any interest in Cuba before 1963 when he started handing out those circulars with Guy Banister's address on them?"

"Okay," I said. "You've given me something to chew on. Let me look at these news stories some more."

However, I did not chew on it at all. So, some ammunition had been found north of Lake Pontchartrain. The local F.B.I. chief had not indicated that anything had *happened.* There had been no announcement of any arrests. I pushed the news story off to the side.

Later I would recall having almost tossed away a major lead. The F.B.I. announcement about the "ammunition raid" north of the lake would come to stand as a small milestone. It would represent the last federal government announcement relating to the intelligence community's activity or President Kennedy's assassination that I would not regard dubiously.

Soon we got a new break. Guy Banister's widow unexpectedly agreed to grant us an interview. She was very cooperative, but clearly never knew much about what Guy Banister had been doing at his office. He never had been very communicative about details of his work. However, she did recall one curious thing. After his death, in 1964, she had been removing his effects from his office when she came across a stack of leaflets that she found very peculiar. They had said either "Hands Off Cuba" or "Fair Play for Cuba"—leftovers from Lee Oswald's performances as an *agent provocateur.*

Asked about what had happened to Banister's office files, she recalled that federal government agents had arrived within an hour or two of his death—long before she reached his office—and carted off the locked filing cabinets. She was told that the men had been from either the F.B.I. or the Secret Service—she could not recall which. However, the state police, she added, did not arrive until after she had.

The state police? Apparently in a routine check, possibly because a brother of Banister's had been connected with it, several state police officers had gone through his office. They departed with the index cards to Banister's files, which the federal agents incomprehensibly had failed to take with them.

I had Lou Ivon on the road to Baton Rouge, the state capital, within the hour. That afternoon he returned with a small handful of file cards. They were all that remained of what the state police had found in Banister's office.*

It apparently had occurred to one of the state police officers that the back of these cards would be handy for informal office messages. And so, for three years, this thrifty move had expedited inter-office communications at the headquarters of the Louisiana State Police.

Nevertheless, the few remaining index cards spoke volumes. No local or private matters were referred to whatsoever. The subjects covered were national and even international in scope. From this index list we were able to determine the general nature of the Banister files seized by the federal government:

American Central Intelligence Agency 20-10
Ammunition and Arms 32-1
Anti-Soviet Underground 25-1
B-70 Manned Bomber Force 15-16
Civil Rights Program of J.F.K. 8-41
Dismantling of Ballistic Missile System 15-16

---

* The state police also gave Ivon a book that had been left in Banister's office, a nostalgic reminder of his days in the O.N.I. Written by Admiral Ellis Zacharias, a famous intelligence expert in World War II, it was entitled *Naval Intelligence.* Inside the cover was the inscription: "For Guy Banister, with warmest regards—Ellis Zacharias."

Thus ended the myth of Guy Banister's "private detective agency."

Meanwhile Jack Martin had resurfaced. He had been out of town, and on his return Ivon brought him to my office. After we'd had some coffee, I shoved the August 1, 1963, news story across the table.

"Jack," I said, "is this part of the business Guy Banister was involved in?"

He glanced at the *Times-Picayune* news story and nodded.

"You already know the answer to that," he said, "or you wouldn't have this newspaper on your desk." He read another paragraph or two while I recovered from my pleasant surprise.

"Yeah. That was part of Banister's deal." He looked up. "Can I read the whole story?" he asked.

I nodded and handed him the follow-up story as well.

Martin slowly read through both news stories. Finally he looked at me, a curious frown on his face.

"What's the matter?" I asked.

He shook his head. "It doesn't say anything about the main raid. And it doesn't say a damn thing about all the Cubans who were arrested."

Arrests? The F.B.I.'s statement had not mentioned anything about arrests. Least of all anything about Cubans plural.

"All right then, Jack," I said, "why don't you straighten it out for us? Tell me about the entire operation at Guy Banister's. The whole thing."

And so Jack Martin started to talk. This was the beginning of many long talks—each with frequent interruptions for coffee, upon which he appeared to subsist.

The talks took place over a period of weeks. There were days when I was tied up with other witnesses, there were days when we could not locate Martin, and there even were days when he had found himself a client.

I had to assure him that I would never connect his name with what he told me. Aware of the importance of finally having obtained access to the *sanctum sanctorum* that secretly had harbored Lee Harvey Oswald, I observed this agreement scrupulously. Now that Martin has passed away, I feel released from that vow of silence. Jack would put nothing in writing, nor would he sign his name to anything. But he did tell whatever he could recall about the business at Guy Banister's—although only to me. There must have been occasions later when my staff thought I was psychic when I was able, time and again, to describe the inside workings of Banister's office.

As it turned out, Martin, the tarnished "alcoholic," had told the complete truth about the training camp and the arrests made by the F.B.I. It was the vaunted Federal Bureau of Investigation that had been lying and concealing the full story from the American people.

The actual F.B.I. raid included not only the ammunition described in the news story but also the nearby *undescribed* training camp at which trainees had been arrested (nine of them Cuban exiles and two of them Americans).* This group, later aptly described by two of the better informed journalists as "the Pontchartrain Eleven," was preparing for future C.I.A.-sponsored attacks on Cuba. The F.B.I. raid had come in response to pressure from President Kennedy, who wanted the Bureau to stop the C.I.A.'s unending violations of the Neutrality Act.

In addition to what Martin told me, we learned the full truth about the raid from a supplementary report that the Bureau had sent to U.S. Customs—apparently a matter of course when suspects are arrested for violating the Neutrality Act. A private detective, whose firm worked closely with Customs in its patrol of the New Orleans docks, obtained a copy of the report naming all of the arrested men and turned it over to

---

* One of the Americans was Rich Lauchli, an adventurer and a founder of the extreme right-wing group known as the Minutemen. The other was Sam Benton, also apparently an adventurer of sorts, who once had worked in the Havana gambling casinos. The nine Cubans were all exile trainees. The true circumstances of the arrests are fully described by Warren Hinckle and William Turner in their excellent work, *The Fish is Red*.

my office.* The apparent intended effect of the F.B.I.'s public pronouncements about the raid was to protect and continue to conceal the curious activities at Banister's office.

The Banister apparatus, as Martin described it, was part of a supply line that ran along the Dallas-New Orleans-Miami corridor. These supplies consisted of arms and explosives for use against Castro's Cuba. The security control was so careful that ammunition was kept far-flung in outlying areas. Dispersal was the rule. On the occasions when such explosives were held in New Orleans only small amounts were kept at Banister's office at any one time.

As we later learned from one of the participants, a former C.I.A. employee named Gordon Novel, it was on just such a mission to acquire combat ammunition that David Ferrie, one of the leaders of the local Cuban Revolutionary Front, and a handful of others from Banister's office drove down one night to the blimp air base at Houma, a town deep in southern Louisiana. They entered one of the Schlumberger Corporation's explosives bunkers and removed the land mines, hand grenades, and rifle grenades stored there.

The Schlumberger Corporation was a huge French-owned company, which serviced oil producers worldwide by using explosives and geological measuring devices to determine the probable geology underground. It had been a supporter of the French counter-revolutionary Secret Army Organization (O.A.S.), which attempted to assassinate President Charles DeGaulle several times in the late 1950s and early 1960s for his role in freeing Algeria in North Africa. The C.I.A., which was also supportive of the French O.A.S. generals, had supplied Schlumberger with anti-personnel ammunition and in this operation at Houma, following the demise of the O.A.S., was simply getting its ammunition back.

The expedition, consisting of a car followed by a large laundry truck, returned to New Orleans with its explosive haul, which was then divided equally between Ferrie's apartment and Banister's inner office until the time arrived for its transport to Miami.

Banister's operation also included the processing and handling of

---

* This was a slight reversal of form. Ordinarily, the federal intelligence community eavesdrops on what state and city officials are doing.

anti-Castro trainees passing through the city. Some wearing green combat outfits with black boots and others wearing civilian clothes, they arrived and departed in a steady stream. However, they always were taken in and out of the city in small numbers so that there never would be a conspicuously large gathering at the office.

Many of the exiles were recruits from the West arriving for guerrilla training at the camp north of Lake Pontchartrain. Others were sent on to Florida for similar training being conducted by the C.I.A. there. Occasionally a handful of graduates of the Florida training program would stop at Banister's—a road stop as well as a headquarters—for lodging and eating arrangements to be made on their way back to their homes in the vicinity of Dallas or points west.

As my informal team* talked it out in our brainstorming sessions, we were most conscious that Banister's hidden war games had been played out *directly across the street* from the offices of the O.N.I. and the Secret Service. Furthermore, across Lafayette Park and a short walk down St. Charles Avenue was the headquarters of the Central Intelligence Agency.

It seemed to all of us that, by the late summer of 1963, the parade in and out of Guy Banister's place would have been hard for these intelligence agencies to ignore. We put ourselves in the position of the federal agents in the vicinity and visualized the scene.

To begin with, there was David Ferrie, the defrocked novitiate priest and defrocked commercial pilot. A raffish adventurer with a crudely cut, homemade thatch of reddish mohair, and large greasepaint eyebrows which never quite matched, Ferrie suffered from alopecia, a rare disease that renders its victims completely hairless. Constantly in and out of the office—except when he was across Lake Pontchartrain supervising the guerrilla training of the Cuban exiles—he frequently was garbed in his green combat outfit and combat boots.

There was Guy Banister himself. The austere and downright regal former chief of the Chicago F.B.I. office would necessarily have known a good number of his intelligence community cousins and frequently would have been greeting them, if not stopping to chat.

* This by now consisted of Frank Klein, Lou Ivon, and a young assistant D.A. named James Alcock.

Then there was the ill-starred Lee Harvey Oswald, a thin young man still ramrod straight from his Marine years, periodically marching out of Banister's with a handful of leaflets sufficiently inflammatory to make the average federal agent's hair stand straight up.

Anti-Castro Cubans, many unshaven and wearing green combat garb and boots, regularly tramped up the stairs to Banister's office. More often than not they were talking to each other in Spanish. On their way to and from the guerrilla training camp north of the lake, some of them no doubt dragged Army duffle bags with them.

And, as if all of this was not enough, the Secret Service and Naval Intelligence agents across the street must have grown bored witnessing the movement of ammunition boxes to and from Banister's office: rifles, hand grenades, land mines, whatever had been collected for the secret war against Cuba. During that long busy summer of 1963, it must have been all that the Secret Service and O.N.I. agents could do to concentrate on their business at hand—whatever that might have been.

My small team and I wondered aloud at how it was known in advance that Banister's operation—in such systematic and open violation of the Neutrality Act—was to be protected by the various elements of the intelligence community. For indeed, the F.B.I.'s grossly incomplete announcement of its raid north of Lake Pontchartrain had amounted to an enormous concealment of Banister's continual and considerably more substantial violations of the Neutrality Act within the very heart of the New Orleans intelligence community. It seemed clear to me that the F.B.I.—in its well-publicized "raid" on the ammunition pile supposedly owned by one "Jose Juarez," who never materialized—was going through the motions of giving President Kennedy what he had ordered while its heart continued to belong to the missions being carried out by Guy Banister.

I obtained a copy of the Secret Service's report of its investigation of 544 Camp Street—the entrance to Banister's office—and made it available to my staff. The synopsis of the report, dated December 9, 1963, indicated that "extensive investigation" had revealed that no one at that address ever recalled seeing Lee Harvey Oswald. It went on to indicate that nothing of any consequence had been found at that address.*

Even a layman, across from whose house Barnum & Bailey was operating a circus, would not have to see too many elephants before he realized that this was not an ordinary neighbor. It was the consensus of my informal team that the circus at 544 Camp Street could not have been as invisible as the Secret Service report sought to make it seem.

We did not yet realize it, but we were encountering the first signs that there was a force in this country that—no matter what the cost—wanted the Cold War, and the hot war in Vietnam, to continue.

---

* The Secret Service synopsis stated: "Extensive investigation conducted thus far has failed to establish that the FAIR PLAY FOR CUBA COMMITTEE had offices at 544 Camp Street, New Orleans. It has likewise been impossible to find anyone who recalls ever seeing Lee Harvey Oswald at this address."

The front entrance of the Secret Service's office was located approximately 50 feet from 544 Camp Street. If, after walking those 50 feet, the two Secret Service agents had gone up the stairs, they would have found themselves on the landing outside the door of Guy Banister's office. If they had not known this beforehand, Banister's name was printed there for them to read.

If they had made any effort to investigate him, they would have found that one of Banister's employees had taken off on a bizarre trip to Texas an hour or so after the President's assassination and that later the same afternoon, in a remarkably uncharacteristic action, Banister had pistol-whipped another of his employees. If they had obtained a search warrant, they would have found a stack of left-over "Fair Play for Cuba" leaflets in the office.

Had they questioned Delphine Roberts, Banister's secretary, she might have told them what she later admitted to others: that Banister had been engaged in closed-door meetings with Lee Oswald and that he had arranged for a third-floor room for Oswald's use.

However, the Secret Service investigators did not take these steps. Rather, as their seven-page report reveals, they located a number of individuals whose marginal connection with 544 Camp Street had ended back in 1961 or 1962. The agents engaged these individuals in discursive conversation on matters bearing no discernible connection with President Kennedy's assassination. That was the sum and substance of the Secret Service's "extensive investigation."

4

The Social
Triumphs of
Lee Harvey Oswald

T H E   M O R E   I   T H O U G H T about it, the more the great
disparity gnawed at me. There had been the Lee Harvey Oswald who,
the government told us, was close to being the most rabid communist
since Lenin. On the other hand, at our very doorstep, there had been a
flesh-and-blood Oswald who used as the headquarters for his pam-
phleteering the office of Guy Banister—formerly of the F.B.I. and
Naval Intelligence and, more recently, the Anti-Communist League of
the Caribbean. As if that were not enough, Oswald had been on a first-
name basis with that swash-buckling anti-communist soldier of fortune, David Ferrie, a man who had trained anti-Castro pilots for the
Bay of Pigs in 1961 and by 1963 was giving guerrilla training to more
Cuban exiles for some new venture against the island.

Which one had been the real Lee Harvey Oswald? It seemed to me
that the best way to find out was to go back and study Oswald's short
but varied career. In its conclusions, the Warren Commission had
seemed particularly taken with the idea that Oswald had a "commit-

ment to Marxism." Just how deep that commitment had been was what I was after.

I began with El Toro Marine Base in California, where Oswald was stationed from November 1958 to September 1959. I figured his fellow soldiers should have had a pretty good look at Oswald in the close quarters of military training.

Of all the Marines, Nelson Delgado had lived closest to Oswald and for the longest period, so I headed straight for his testimony. I found that Delgado, who bunked next door to Oswald for the better part of 11 months, had no recollection whatever of Oswald's Marxist leanings. Under oath, Delgado swore that Oswald "never said any subversive things . . . and he didn't show no [sic] particular aspects of being a sharpshooter at all."

Delgado went farther than that. He volunteered that Oswald had been terrible when it came to shooting a rifle on the range and had difficulty meeting the minimum standard for qualifying. "It was a pretty big joke," Delgado testified, "because he got a lot of 'Maggie's drawers,' you know, a lot of misses, but he didn't give a darn." Oswald, he added, "wasn't as enthusiastic as the rest of us. We all loved—liked, you know, going to the range."

The following colloquy between Delgado and Warren Commission attorney Wesley J. Liebeler reinforced the fact that Oswald was inept with a rifle:

> MR. LIEBELER: You told the F.B.I. that in your opinion Oswald was not a good rifle shot; is that correct?
>
> MR. DELGADO: Yes.
>
> MR. LIEBELER: And that he did not show any unusual interest in his rifle, and in fact appeared less interested in weapons than the average Marine?
>
> MR. DELGADO: Yes. He was mostly a thinker, a reader. He read quite a bit.

At one point, the attorney switched away from Oswald's lack of proficiency as a rifleman, only to end up more deeply in the mire.

MR. LIEBELER: This F.B.I. agent says that you told him that Oswald became so proficient in Spanish that Oswald would discuss his ideas on socialism in Spanish.

MR. DELGADO: He would discuss his ideas but not anything against our government or—nothing Socialist, mind you.

Daniel Powers, who had served with Oswald at the Naval Air Technical Center in Florida *and* Keesler Field in Mississippi and El Toro Marine Base *and* in Japan, was questioned closely about Oswald. His response is summed up in the following dialogue with Warren Commission counsel Albert E. Jenner, Jr.:

MR. JENNER: Did he ever express any sympathy toward the Communist Party?

MR. POWERS: None that I recall.

MR. JENNER: Toward Communist principles?

MR. POWERS: None that I recall.

MR. JENNER: Or Marxist doctrines?

MR. POWERS: None that I recall. No, sir.

I examined the testimony of John E. Donovan, who was a first lieutenant at El Toro when Oswald was there. His testimony about Oswald's leftist leanings was explicit: ". . . I never heard him in any way, shape or form confess that he was a Communist, or that he ever thought about being a Communist." The statements of Oswald's other associates at the Marine base were almost uniform in their agreement that he had no inclination in the direction of communism or anything leftwing.*

Only one man who had been at the Marine base with him testified

* Donald Peter Camarata: "I have no recollection . . . of any remarks on his part concerning Communism, Russia or Cuba." Peter Francis Connor: "I never heard Oswald make any anti-American or pro-Communist statements. He claimed to be named after Robert E. Lee, whom he characterized as the greatest man in history." Allen D. Graf: "Oswald never gave to me any indication of favoring Communism or opposing capitalism." John Rene Heindel: "Although I generally regarded Oswald as an intelligent person, I did not observe him to be particularly interested in politics or international affairs." Mack Osborne: "I do not recall any remarks on his part concerning Communism, Russia or Cuba." Richard Dennis Call: ". . . I do not recall Oswald's making serious remarks with regard to the Soviet Union or Cuba."

that Oswald had exhibited Marxist leanings. This man—Kerry Thornley—had not served with Oswald as long as a number of others and had not even lived on the same part of the base at El Toro. That seemed odd to me. Moreover, Thornley's testimony was heard directly by the Warren Commission, and subsequently was given great attention by the media. I noticed, however, that in the Commission volumes, it was separated from the affidavits of the other Marines. This made me wonder if any members of the Warren Commission had actually read the other Marines' affidavits, which overwhelmingly contradicted Thornley's claims.

I thought about the Russian examination Oswald had taken at El Toro and began to look into his earlier Marine service for hints of possible intelligence work. By now I knew that Oswald possessed the characteristics the military looks for in its intelligence recruits. He was from a military family; one brother also had joined the Marines, another the Air Force. He was very close-mouthed by nature, and was well above average in intelligence.

Oswald's assignment at Japan's Atsugi Air Base in 1957 before he came to El Toro was consistent with the possibility that he had been working in military intelligence. Atsugi, I discovered, was the base for all of the daily super-secret U-2 intelligence flights over China. Oswald's anti-aircraft unit, which required a highly classified security clearance, had the duty of guarding a U-2 hangar. It was surrounded by a high, heavily wired fence. Even the mail truck could not enter without a sergeant on foot in front of it giving the password for the day.

I thought Oswald's possible intelligence role at Atsugi might be confirmed by two Central Intelligence Agency documents mentioned in the Warren Commission report: CD 931, "Oswald's access to information about the U-2," and CD 692, "Reproduction of C.I.A. official dossier on Oswald." Unfortunately, these documents, along with many other C.I.A. files, were classified as secret following the Warren Commission inquiry, and I could not gain access to them.

But now I was curious to know just which subjects the government wanted the public to know the least about. I had one of my assistants get together a list of those files concerning Oswald that the government had classified as "unavailable." Here is the list:

CD* 321	Chronology of Oswald in USSR (Secret)
CD 347	Activity of Oswald in Mexico City (Secret)
CD 384	Activity of Oswald in Mexico City
CD 528	re. Allegation Oswald interviewed by CIA in Mexico City
CD 631	re. CIA dissemination of information on Oswald
CD 674	Info given to the Secret Service but not yet to the Warren Commission (Secret)
CD 692	Reproduction of CIA official dossier on Oswald
CD 698	Reports of travel and activities of Oswald & Marina
CD 871	Photos of Oswald in Russia (Secret)
CD 931	Oswald's access to information about the U-2 (Secret)
CD 1216	Memo from Helms entitled "Lee Harvey Oswald" (Secret)
CD 1222	Statements by George de Mohrenschildt re: assassination (Secret)
CD 1273	Memo from Helms re: apparent inconsistencies in info provided by CIA (Secret)

This provocative listing made it more apparent to me than ever that something was fishy.

Next I decided to focus my research on Oswald's movements immediately after he left the Marines. In the summer of 1959—about five months after he had taken his Russian exam at El Toro—Oswald applied for a premature discharge from the Marine Corps. The reason he cited was that his mother was undergoing physical hardships that required his presence and care. In September 1959, he was given an honorable discharge four weeks early, for "hardship/dependency." After spending three days with his mother in Fort Worth, he left for New Orleans.

Oswald's journey out of New Orleans to the Soviet Union was somewhat confusing. His departure for Europe, I found, was by ship. His steamship ticket had been obtained at the Lykes office of New Orleans's International Trade Mart, directed by Clay Shaw, whose name we would come to know only too well later in the investigation. Although Oswald sailed to England, he flew eastward from there. Precisely what kind of air service he used, however, was mysterious. The Warren Commission stated that Oswald flew straight on to Helsinki on Octo-

---

* CD stands for commission document.

ber 9, the very day he arrived in England. However, Oswald's passport showed that he did not leave England until October 10, the following day.

It was known that Oswald checked into his Helsinki hotel on October 10. But this would have been impossible considering the timetable of the only commercial direct route from London. Under the circumstances, the question arose whether he actually flew to Finland aboard a commercial airliner.

Much later, in 1978, James A. Wilcott, a former C.I.A. finance officer, told the House Select Committee on Assassinations that Lee Oswald had been recruited from the military by the C.I.A. "with the express purpose of a double agent assignment in the U.S.S.R."*

Back in 1966 such clear-cut testimony was not in the public record, but the double-agent scenario had crossed my mind. The C.I.A., of course, had denied from the beginning that Oswald was ever employed by the Agency. However, I knew that was its standard position when asked about an employee executing any kind of intelligence assignment.†

After Oswald arrived in Moscow by train from Finland on October 16, 1959, he engaged in a series of contacts with Soviet officials. The initial response of the Soviets was cautious as they evaluated this young American who had not merely left his country behind, but brought the promise of gifts—the secret sweets of American anti-aircraft technology. The newcomer underwent extensive interrogation, although when, where, and under what circumstances have never been revealed.

After two weeks, Oswald made a dramatic appearance at the American Embassy. He flamboyantly handed over his passport and a letter that concluded that his allegiance was with the Union of Soviet

---

* Wilcott testified under oath that he had handled the funding for the project to which Oswald was assigned. Predictably, a chorus line of other Agency witnesses, whose names Wilcott had mentioned, denied all knowledge of such a project. The committee did not pursue the lead.

† In the course of an executive session of the Warren Commission held on January 27, 1964, former C.I.A. Director Allen Dulles acknowledged that U.S. intelligence service officials would lie before revealing that an individual was secretly employed as an intelligence agent and, further, would not hesitate to lie even under oath. Indeed, in 1977, former C.I.A. Director Richard Helms was convicted of failing to answer accurately, while under oath, questions put to him by a Senate committee.

Socialist Republics. He also announced that he had told Soviet officials he would give them information about the Marine Corps and the highly secret radar operations he had been involved in.

As Oswald's dramatic defection hit the world media, the F.B.I., after making a study of Oswald's Marine Corps files, stated that "no derogatory information was contained in the U.S.M.C. files concerning Oswald, and O.N.I. [Office of Naval Intelligence] advised that no action against him was contemplated in this matter." J. Edgar Hoover later explained the F.B.I.'s failure to investigate the Oswald "defection" any further, stating that the American Embassy in Moscow had given Oswald a "clean bill."

In early January of 1960, Oswald was sent to Minsk—one of six Soviet cities to which defectors customarily were sent—and given a job as a metal worker in a radar factory. In a clear demonstration that the Soviet system looks kindly upon defectors, he was given a number of privileges not available to the average Russian worker, including a comfortable apartment and a relatively high salary.

In February 1961, after 15 months in the Soviet Union, Oswald applied at the American Embassy in Moscow to return to the United States. The following month he met Marina Prusakova, a lovely woman with eyes of cornflower blue and also the niece of a lieutenant colonel in the Soviet Union's domestic intelligence service. In April 1961, less than two months after they had met, they were married.

Surprisingly, neither government objected to Oswald's return to America or to Marina's coming with him. It was as if the unending ice of the Cold War had suddenly thawed. Perhaps it was the arrival of spring.

It is noteworthy, for example, that the State Department approved Oswald's return, although it easily could have refused a defector's request. The department's report stated that Oswald "had not expatriated himself" by his actions upon arriving in the Soviet Union in 1959. It added that there was no indication in F.B.I. reports that Oswald was a communist. It authorized the American Embassy in Moscow to lend him the money, on behalf of State, for his return.

Such a repatriation loan, according to State Department regulations, cannot be made unless the recipient's "loyalty to the United States" has been established "beyond question." Considering that

Oswald had supposedly defected and handed military secrets to the Soviet Union, his loyalty hardly would appear to have been "beyond question." Yet the loan of $436 was granted after a few months' delay.

Similarly, the State Department's Passport Office found no reason why Oswald's passport should not be renewed and authorized the American Embassy to renew it in August 1961.* Ordinarily, when a U.S. citizen goes abroad and commits an act indicating allegiance to another country, particularly the Soviet Union, the Passport Office automatically prepares a "lookout" card in case the party ever attempts to renew his passport. No such "lookout" card ever was prepared for Oswald. Like the American Embassy, the Passport Office gave this defector a clean bill of health.

These United States government actions demonstrating almost paternal solicitude for Lee Oswald's welfare even while he was in the Soviet Union comprised, to my mind, a steady, uninterrupted pattern. And the preferential treatment did not end with the arrival of Lee and Marina and their young daughter in New York in June 1962.

Meeting the Oswalds at the New York pier were no agents of the F.B.I. or any other law enforcement agency. There was only Spas T. Raikin, the secretary-general of the American Friends of the Anti-Bolshevik Nations, Inc., a private anti-communist operation with extensive intelligence connections. Raikin also was employed by the Traveler's Aid Society, under whose aegis, according to the Warren Commission, he had been asked by the State Department to meet the returning Oswalds and give them any help they needed.

The government never prosecuted Oswald for his alleged defection. Immediately upon his return to the U.S., Oswald, along with Marina and their daughter, moved to Fort Worth, Texas. There he worked at the Leslie Welding Company until October 7, 1962, when George de Mohrenschildt and his wife came over from Dallas to spend the evening as guests of Lee and Marina at their modest apartment.

Anyone aware of the comparative lifestyles and personal histories of Lee Oswald of the Leslie Welding Company and Baron George de Mohrenschildt of the Dallas Petroleum Club would have to see that

---

* Subsequently, in June 1963, when Oswald applied for his passport again, he received it within 24 hours. Such prompt service is rare in any event but would have been utterly impossible had Oswald's "defection" been genuine.

scene as discordant, an anomaly. While Oswald was quite able to take care of himself intellectually in almost anyone's company, it was also plain that he and de Mohrenschildt had mutual interests, not yet officially revealed, that caused them to find each other's company interesting.

The following day, October 8, Lee packed up and moved to Dallas, 30 miles away, where de Mohrenschildt lived. Oswald wasted no time in seeking a new job at the Texas Employment Office in Dallas.

Oswald's visit to the employment office may well have been an obligatory gesture in accordance with the Golden Rule of the Intelligence Community that the pre-existing economic circumstances of an individual entering clandestine intelligence work are rigidly maintained in appearance after he becomes an intelligence agent. For example, if a newly recruited, previously poor deep-cover agent were to abandon his long-familiar threadbare wardrobe overnight and begin wearing Brooks Brothers suits and driving, perhaps, a new Chrysler LeBaron convertible, he never again would be that same fellow so long undeserving of a second glance and, consequently, so productive to clandestine operations.

In any event, before October 1962 was over, Oswald had obtained a job that, for a former defector to the Soviet Union, seemed quite unlikely. Jagger-Stovall-Chiles, under a contract with the Pentagon, was engaged in the production of charts and maps for military use. Writer Henry Hurt has observed that "part of the work appeared to be related to the top-secret U-2 missions, some of which were making flights over Cuba." This job required an extremely high security classification. Lee Harvey Oswald not only was given the job within one week of his arrival in Dallas, but also had access to a variety of classified materials.

October 1962 was the famous month when, as former Secretary of State Dean Rusk put it, "our government and the Russians were eyeball to eyeball." Our U-2's were making frequent flights over Cuba, and an Air Force plane was even shot down. If Oswald truly had no connection with our intelligence community, if he truly had leanings toward communism—as our government had assured us—then the nonchalance of the security clearance operation of Jagger-Stovall-Chiles (which even then may have been setting the type for names used on maps used by U-2's looking for Soviet missile sites in Cuba) represented great comic movie material gone to waste.

Socially, despite his "defection" and his ostensibly vocal allegiance to communism, Oswald and his family were welcomed with open arms by the White Russian community of Dallas. It should be noted that most of the White Russians shared a political philosophy somewhat to the right of the late Czar Nicholas. A number of them were blue-blooded Russian nobles or large landholders who had been forced by the Bolshevik government to leave their ancestral estates. They lived for the day when the communists would be driven from Russia and they could return to their homeland. Others were of less patrician background, being simple émigrés who had fled from the communists, but their loathing for communism was just as bitter.

Strangely, though, these were the people who helped Lee and Marina find lodging. They saw to it that there was sufficient milk for the baby and that it was taken to the hospital when its temperature was too high. From time to time, they bought pretty dresses for Marina and made her the object of their attention in every way.

Oswald's most frequent associate in Dallas, I discovered, was George de Mohrenschildt. He had been in the United States longer than most of the White Russians and was hardly an ordinary émigré. His father, Baron Sergius de Mohrenschildt, had been governor of the province of Minsk for the czar. The family had fled from the communists after the 1917 revolution. De Mohrenschildt spoke Russian, French, German, Spanish, and Polish. In World War II he had worked for French intelligence. This polished member of the international polo-playing set possessed a doctorate in international commerce and a master's degree in petroleum engineering and geology.

De Mohrenschildt had become a consulting geologist and was a member of the exclusive Dallas Petroleum Club with extremely affluent contacts in the business world. Among his close friends, one of the more interesting was Jean de Menil, the president of the mammoth international Schlumberger Corporation, which had close ties with the Central Intelligence Agency.*

* The C.I.A. and Schlumberger had a mutual interest in the O.A.S., an organization led by former French generals who had revolted against President Charles DeGaulle in 1961 when Algeria was in the process of winning its independence. The Agency had been a staunch, although secret, supporter of the French anti-Gaullist movement. See Chapter 3.

De Mohrenschildt had traveled to the far corners of the world. He had visited Ghana in the role of a stamp collector, although he was actively in the oil business at the time and did not collect stamps. In Yugoslavia he had spent an entire year representing the International Cooperation Administration, a well-known Central Intelligence Agency front based in Washington. He had been in Guatemala when, coincidentally, much of the C.I.A.'s combat training of the anti-Castro Cubans who invaded at the Bay of Pigs took place. And later he moved to Haiti, where he became involved in a "government-oriented" (to borrow the Warren Commission report's phrase) business venture.

This man, obviously a capitalist and very much an anti-communist, was the closest friend in Dallas of the young man whom the Warren Commission had found to have a "commitment to Marxism."

Oswald's charisma seemed to have won over other unlikely friends in the White Russian community as well. Among the first dinner guests to the Oswald apartment in Dallas was Max Clark, a retired Air Force colonel and, at that time, an attorney. Colonel Clark had served as a security officer for General Dynamics, a major contractor for the Defense Department and the world's largest aircraft manufacturer. His wife, Katya—who was also present at the dinner prepared by Marina Oswald—was a member of the royal family of Russia, born Princess Sherbatov. Surely, for a Marxist like Lee Oswald this was a social conquest of the highest order.

Of the many Dallas anti-communist Russians welcoming the Oswalds, only Anna and Teofil Meller had any serious reservations about the couple. This was because Anna, while visiting the Oswalds' apartment, had seen a copy of Karl Marx's *Das Kapital* on a table. She seems to have been unaware that Teofil, her husband, later called the F.B.I. and reported the fact. He was informed by the Bureau's spokesman that Oswald was "all right."*

The Warren Commission handled this potential problem of the F.B.I.'s protection of Oswald with its usual elán. It simply did not call Meller as a witness or even take his affidavit.

---

* It was not until after the assassination, however, that Meller informed the Dallas police that the F.B.I. had informed him that Oswald was "all right." This fact was obtained by researcher Harold Weisberg, one of the most indefatigable critics of the Warren report.

Oswald's treatment following his return, both by the intelligence community and by dedicated anti-communist individuals, led me to a single, unavoidable conclusion: that in the Soviet Union Oswald had been engaged in a clandestine intelligence mission for the United States government.

And I was rapidly becoming aware that in the period after his return from the Soviet Union, anti-communist exiles and parts of the U.S. intelligence community seemed to have a converging interest in the potential value of Lee Oswald. It was no coincidence that Oswald was surrounded by White Russian émigrés in Dallas and anti-Castro Cuban exiles in New Orleans. I had found that the guerrilla training of the anti-Castro exiles was within the exclusive province of the C.I.A. This had a far-reaching pragmatic effect. The F.B.I., ordinarily the most perspicacious of our investigative agencies, seemed careful not to observe what the Agency was doing—nor to whom.

Although most of the government was aware that the C.I.A. had been operating domestically for a long time, I knew that the Agency kept such operations clandestine. The Agency operatives manipulating the émigrés, for example, did not wear uniforms and badges with the emblem "C.I.A." on them. Under deep cover, they were quite indistinguishable from other lawyers, businessmen, engineers, housewives, private detectives, or whatever. At the time I could not be sure just who was guiding Lee Oswald and the exiles surrounding him, but now, with the benefit of hindsight, it seems pretty evident.

Although George de Mohrenschildt probably had been given no indication of the catastrophe waiting down the road, there is now little doubt that he had been operating under deep cover as an agent of the Central Intelligence Agency.* It is equally apparent that his assign-

* George de Mohrenschildt committed suicide in March 1977, hours after arranging to meet an investigator from the House Select Committee on Assassinations. It is theoretically possible for de Mohrenschildt to have been working for another part of the intelligence community. However, the depth of his cover and its subsequent protection by some members of the Warren Commission and the federal investigators supports the likelihood that he was with the Agency, which is forbidden by law to operate domestically. The Warren Commission never called this cosmopolitan man as a witness. Rather, his deposition was taken for the members of the Commission to read.

ment was to bring Oswald from Fort Worth to Dallas and thereafter to serve as one of his "baby sitters."*

My conclusion that de Mohrenschildt was an unwitting baby sitter for Oswald came not only from publicly available evidence but from my conversations with him and Mrs. de Mohrenschildt. Some years after the assassination, after my investigation was well under way, I established phone contact with de Mohrenschildt. To avoid monitoring, we developed a routine of my calling him at the Petroleum Club in Dallas or his leaving a call for me at the New Orleans Athletic Club. Both de Mohrenschildt and his wife were positive that the shooting of the President, or even of a rabbit for that matter, simply was not in Lee Oswald's make-up. They were vigorous in their insistence that Oswald had been the scapegoat. I was particularly affected by the depth of their unhappiness at what had been done not only to John Kennedy but to Lee Oswald as well.

Spring of 1963 arrived and Lee Oswald—as usual, without fanfare or any other preliminaries—left Dallas in late April for New Orleans. His wife and daughter arrived there shortly afterwards. By May 9, Oswald had obtained a job in New Orleans at the Reily Coffee Company, just on the other side of the post office building from Guy Banister's office.

I already had reviewed many of Oswald's activities in New Orleans that summer. Now I was interested in taking a closer look at how he found his way to employment at the Reily Coffee Company. This was a very confusing question because among the Warren Commission exhibits were dozens of photostats of job applications that Lee Oswald *apparently* filed at one place after another before landing his job at Reily. Oswald's familiar chicken scrawl handwriting was apparent at first glance on every application. Judging by this lengthy series of Commis-

---

* A "baby sitter" is a term used by American intelligence agencies to describe an agent assigned to protect or otherwise see to the general welfare of a particular individual. That individual invariably is important to the completion of a mission. Depending upon the nature of the operation under way, the baby sitter may be a "witting" participant (meaning that he knows how his ward is going to be used) or "unwitting" (meaning that he has been given no foreknowledge of what is in store for the "baby" in his custody).

sion exhibits, he had sought employment at half the businesses in the city of New Orleans.

However, the more I pored over these applications, the more puzzled I was. On every one of them the applicant had listed his height as "5 feet 9 inches." The problem was that Lee Oswald happened to have been five feet eleven inches tall. Why, then, should he repeatedly be writing down his height as five feet nine inches?*

I was due to get together the next day with some of the staff for some overdue brainstorming on a number of items, and I added this one to the agenda. The next morning I had hardly arrived at the office when Lou Ivon came in with a lead—picked up by one of his police investigators on the street—that Oswald had visited the Bolton Ford dealership on North Claiborne Avenue. We followed this up as we did even the thinnest of leads and, although the rumor turned out to be false, we ended up finding something potentially more important.

As we later learned from salesmen Fred Sewall and Oscar Deslatte, two men claiming to represent an organization called Friends of Democratic Cuba arrived at the Bolton dealership on January 20, 1961. This was only three months before the abortive Bay of Pigs attempt to invade Cuba, the great turkey that Kennedy had inherited from the preceding administration. One of the men was a powerfully built Latin with a thick neck and a distinct scar over his left eyebrow.† The other was a thin, young Anglo-Saxon who obviously was in charge.

---

* There is considerable confusion over Oswald's height. I believed he was five feet eleven inches because two documents found in his wallet when he was arrested, his local draft board card, dated September 14, 1959, and his Department of Defense ID, undated, but apparently issued about the same time, both gave his height as five feet eleven inches. Also, his September 10, 1959, passport application gave the same height, as did his discharge form DD214, dated the next day. With one exception, all of the documents which give his height as five feet nine inches date from the time John F. Kennedy was President, which is consistent with the theory that during that time, someone was impersonating him.

The exception is Oswald's Marine Corps enlistment card, dated October 24, 1956, which shows him as five feet nine inches. This was only a few days after his seventeenth birthday, and it is perfectly likely that he grew two inches in the next three years.

† After Lee Harvey Oswald returned to New Orleans and began handing out pro-Castro leaflets, this man with the scar was always present on the edge of the crowd. It is standard operating procedure for an intelligence agent engaged in a provocative activity to have a nearby bodyguard to protect him against a violent reaction from the crowd. It seems probable that this man with the scar was Oswald's bodyguard because of the regularity of his presence— invariably on the outer edge of the scene and invariably wearing sunglasses. The sunglasses

The two men indicated that they wanted to buy ten Ford pickup trucks. They wanted a bid from Bolton Ford on the price. The Latin identified himself as "Joseph Moore" but said the bid had to be in the name of "Oswald." The young Anglo-Saxon confirmed this, explaining that "Oswald" was his name and that he was the one with the money. Instead of asking the buyers to sign, Deslatte himself printed the name "Oswald" on the form.* Of course, as all the world now knows, the real Lee Oswald was in the Soviet Union that day and would be for more than another year.

Following President Kennedy's assassination, Sewall and Deslatte remembered "Oswald's" visit and called the F.B.I. When the F.B.I. agents saw the bid form with Oswald's last name on it, according to the two salesmen, they picked it up carefully with solenoid tongs.

After hearing of the Bolton Ford incident, I became very interested in Friends of Democratic Cuba. I obtained a copy of its articles of incorporation. There, among the organization's incorporators, was the ubiquitous name of *Guy Banister.*

I pondered the implications of this staggering information. In the very month that John Kennedy was inaugurated, an intelligence project being run by Guy Banister was using the name "Oswald" in bidding for pickup trucks for apparent use in the Bay of Pigs invasion. More important, the thin young American who had done the bidding either knew Lee Oswald or knew his name. In either case, Oswald was far off in the Soviet Union at the time. At the very least, this strange incident seemed to make Oswald's actual appearance at Guy Banister's operation in the summer of 1963 something less than sheer happenstance.

I called Frank Klein into my office for a long overdue brainstorming session. I summarized the facts of the Bolton Ford incident, and Klein said, "You don't think Sewall and Deslatte were lying, do you?"

---

were large, but they could not conceal the vertical scar that ran up through this man's left eyebrow. We learned of his consistent attendance from our questioning of persons present at the leaflet handouts, many of whom we had identified from our copies of the news photos.

* It is fair to assume that the trucks were intended for the imminent Bay of Pigs invasion and that this indirect purchasing procedure was used to cover the C.I.A.'s involvement in developing and launching the venture. The man who used Oswald's name told the Ford salesman that he ought to sell them the trucks at cost because of the patriotic nature of Friends of Democratic Cuba.

"No."

"But the story doesn't make sense," he continued. "Oswald was in Russia in January 1961. He couldn't possibly have been at Bolton Ford."

"Someone was playing Oswald's part," I said.

"Playing Oswald's part?" said Klein. "But why?"

"I don't know yet," I replied. "But the important point is we now know that whoever was behind the assassination was inclined to have someone impersonate Lee Oswald."

"You're headed somewhere," said Klein, "but I don't know your direction yet."

I pushed the thick volume of Commission documents forward and showed him the job applications. "Notice anything odd?" I asked.

He leafed through them awhile, then looked up. "That's the wrong height," he said. "In every one of these applications he's got the wrong height down."

"Exactly," I said. "If they'll impersonate you in 1961, they'll impersonate you in 1963."

"But why would someone fill out these applications at all these places and continually put down the wrong height?" Klein asked.

"Because the impersonator was only five feet nine," I said. "Since he was being interviewed in person, he had to put down his real height or close to it. Just because someone could imitate Oswald's handwriting perfectly doesn't mean he could stretch himself to Oswald's real height."

Frank agreed with me on the probability of Oswald's impersonation in the job applications. What it amounted to, of course, was that Oswald had been destined from the outset to go to work at the Reily Coffee Company, close by Guy Banister's office. All these applications by someone impersonating him were intended to obscure that.

"You know," said Klein, "you haven't mentioned the most significant thing of all."

"What's that?"

"The time of the visit to Bolton Ford. Using Lee Oswald's name as early as January 1961. That was the month of Kennedy's inauguration."

I paused, considering the enormity of what Frank was suggesting.

"You're asking me if I think the plan to eliminate John Kennedy had begun as early as January 1961," I said.

Frank nodded.

"I would find that hard to believe," I said. "My answer would have to be no."

Many years after that discussion with Frank, I happened to come across a fascinating book about the U.S. intelligence community called *The Armies of Ignorance*, published in 1977. In it, I stumbled upon a fact that stunned me. According to the book's author, William R. Corson, shortly after Kennedy's election in November 1960 the C.I.A. quietly began to put together a "dossier analysis," including a psychological profile, of the President-elect. Its purpose, among other things, was to predict the likely positions Kennedy would take if particular sets of conditions arose. The existence of this study was not made public.

Nowadays I often think back to Frank's question about the implications of the 1961 impersonation of Oswald. And when I do, I wonder—if I had known then about the C.I.A.'s remarkably early psychological profile of Kennedy—whether my answer would have been the same.

5

Setting Up
the Scapegoat

FROM OUR INVESTIGATION so far, I knew that
Oswald could not have shot President Kennedy alone, that some part of
the intelligence community had been guiding him, and that someone
had been impersonating him. In other words, he had been just what he
said he was when he was arrested—a patsy. Precisely what force had set
him up still remained to be seen. Part of the intelligence community
was involved, but I had no idea how broad the base of the operation
might be.

It had always puzzled me why Oswald had left Dallas in April 1963
to spend the summer in New Orleans, only to return to Dallas again in
October. But given what I had learned, this began to make sense.
Clearly, if Oswald was being set up as a communist scapegoat, his close
association in Dallas with the anti-communist White Russians had to
be severed. Likewise, a summer of ostentatiously handing out pro-
Castro leaflets in New Orleans reinforced the image of a crazed communist assassin. In the intelligence community, there is a term for this
kind of manipulated behavior designed to create a desired image:

sheepdipping. It seemed to me that Oswald had been in New Orleans to be sheepdipped under the guidance of Guy Banister and that he had been sent back to Dallas when the mission was accomplished.

To see if I was on the right track, I studied more closely Oswald's return to Dallas and his last two months before the assassination.

On September 23, 1963, a pregnant Marina Oswald and her daughter left New Orleans. They were driven westward to Dallas, I learned, by Mrs. Ruth Paine. It was generally agreed that Lee Oswald left approximately a day later. There were indications that he departed from New Orleans by bus, but that remained unconfirmed.

For the moment, I concentrated—leafing through the large blue volumes to which I had become so accustomed—on the role of Ruth Paine in taking Marina Oswald and her daughter to Dallas and getting them set up there.

Lee and Marina Oswald had met Ruth Paine in February 1963 at a party in Dallas to which George de Mohrenschildt and his wife had brought them. I found that Ruth Paine was the wife of Michael Paine, an engineering designer who did highly classified work for Bell Helicopter, a major Defense Department contractor.

Ruth Paine was a rangy, intelligent woman with widespread interests, among them the Russian language, which she had learned to speak quite well. Her father had been employed by the Agency for International Development, regarded by many as a source of cover for the C.I.A. Her brother-in-law was employed by the same agency in the Washington, D.C. area.

It was on Ruth Paine's way back from a long vacation, during which she had visited her in-laws in Washington, D.C., that she made the stop in New Orleans to pick up Marina Oswald and her daughter for their return to Dallas. I wondered vaguely whether Mrs. Paine herself had been manipulated in the course of this move.

When Marina and her daughter reached Dallas, Mrs. Paine made them at home at her house in Irving, a Dallas suburb. She and her husband, Michael, had separated temporarily, so there was sufficient space for guests.

On October 4, Lee returned to Dallas. He spoke of having been in Houston, looking for work. Ten days later Ruth Paine obtained an interview for him, and he got the job—at the Texas School Book Depository.

For reasons that remain unclear, Oswald rented a series of small rooms in Dallas while his wife and daughter stayed at the Paines' house in Irving. Although Lee kept a number of his personal possessions with him in Dallas, Mrs. Paine made her garage in Irving available to him for his other possessions.

There was no way of guessing what Lee Oswald had in mind with this odd living arrangement, nor who suggested it. However, it was undeniable that this situation worked to the advantage of whoever was behind the assassination. When the President was killed, the scapegoat appeared that much more removed from family and friends, feeding the image of the lonely crazed gunman.

As a routine matter, I wanted to examine the income tax returns of Ruth and Michael Paine, but I was told that they had been classified as secret. In addition to the Paines' income tax reports, Commission documents 212, relating to Ruth Paine, and 218, relating to Michael Paine, also had been classified as secret on grounds of national security. Classified for the same reason were Commission documents 258, relating to Michael, and 508, relating to Michael Paine's sister, as well as Commission documents 600 through 629, regarding relatives of Michael Paine.

What was so special about this particular family that made the federal government so protective of it? Even the duPonts and the Vanderbilts would not have rated this kind of caring guardianship. I wondered if such paternal concern might be related to the fact that the C.I.A. had come to be—for obvious security reasons—a family-oriented organization.

While his wife and daughter stayed with Ruth Paine, Lee Oswald himself, according to the government, was in Mexico City, allegedly contacting the Soviet and Cuban embassies and making himself quite visible. But I was already having doubts about this explanation. Those doubts were confirmed later, when more information on this incident became available.

A C.I.A. memo dated October 10, 1963, reported that in late September and early October Lee Oswald had repeatedly phoned and appeared at the Soviet Embassy in Mexico City, asking if there had been calls for him and talking with a trade consultant who was supposedly a member of the K.G.B.'s "liquid affairs" (murder) bureau. Copies of the memo were sent to the F.B.I. and the State Department. Follow-up Agency leads placed Oswald in the Cuban Embassy as well, where he ostensibly was trying to obtain a visa to go to the Soviet Union via Cuba.

Early in the official inquiry, the C.I.A. informed the Warren Commission of Oswald's alleged activities in Mexico City before the assassination. Uncharacteristically, the Commission asked for more evidence. Perhaps the Commission members, aware that the Agency had 24-hour photographic surveillance of the Cuban and Soviet embassies in Mexico City, were hoping for a good picture to shore up their sparsely documented account of Oswald's trip to Mexico.

Initially, the Agency ignored the Commission's request. But after more pressure, the C.I.A. finally handed over a murky snapshot of a portly, greying gentleman almost old enough to be Oswald's father. This, the Agency claimed, was Lee Oswald at the Cuban Embassy.

The Agency also produced a statement from Silvia Duran, a Mexican who worked at the Cuban Embassy, alleging that Oswald had appeared there. However, the circumstances under which the statement was obtained were tainted, to say the least. On the day after the assassination, the C.I.A. ordered Mexican authorities to arrest Duran and keep her in isolation. The Agency cable said: "With full regard for Mexican interests, request you ensure that her arrest is kept absolutely secret, that no information from her is published or leaked, that all such info is cabled to us. . . ." Duran was not released until she identified Lee Oswald as the visitor to the Cuban Embassy. After her release, the C.I.A. ordered her jailed again. These circumstances were not known to the Commission. Moreover, in 1978 Duran told author Anthony Summers that the man who came to the embassy was blond and about her own height (five feet three)—hardly Oswald.

The Commission did not question the Cuban Consul, Eusebio Azcue, even though he had three angry confrontations with "Oswald." But the House Select Committee on Assassinations did. When Azcue was shown photographs of Lee Oswald, he stated that the young man who visited the embassy was blond and was not the man in the photographs. Nor, said Azcue, was he the man he saw Jack Ruby shoot on television only two months after his face-to-face confrontations with "Oswald."

The allegation that Oswald had been phoning and showing up at the Soviet Embassy did not hold up too well either. There were no photos, and when the Commission asked to hear tape recordings of Oswald's calls, the Agency claimed in one case that surveillance was suspended and in another that equipment was not working. However, the tapes survived long enough for the F.B.I. agents who were present during the infamous 12-hour post-assassination questioning of Oswald to hear them. These agents, according to an F.B.I. memo dated November 23, 1963, and obtained under the Freedom of Information Act, were "of the opinion that the above-referred-to individual [the one on the Soviet Embassy tapes] was not Lee Harvey Oswald."

This evidence, which came out years after my official investigation was over, suggests to me not that Lee Harvey Oswald had been in Mexico City, as the Warren Commission concluded. Rather, it strongly suggests that Lee Oswald was impersonated in Mexico City, as Edwin Juan López, who ran the House committee's extensive Mexico City investigation, believes. This would be consistent with other impersonations of Oswald in New Orleans and Dallas that were carried out in an effort to set him up as a patsy.

Some of the scenes were so preposterous that only the most gullible could swallow them. One of these tableaux occurred in the Mexican Consulate in New Orleans. It was the early afternoon of a mid-September day in 1963. A young man, accompanied by a woman with a scarf tied around her head, appeared at the consulate. On this occasion, Mrs. Fenella Farrington happened to be there to see about getting her family automobile returned from Mexico. It had been left there on a recent visit with her husband.

The young man asked the clerk at the desk, "What is the weather like in Mexico City?"

"It's very hot," she replied. "Just like it is here today."

He then asked her—now striking the sinister theme repeated throughout these pageants—"*What do you have to do to take firearms or a gun into Mexico?*" This was a question that would catch almost anyone's ear. The lady at the consulate asked why he wanted to take a gun, and Fenella Farrington, standing nearby, volunteered that "the hunting's wonderful."

The man, whom Mrs. Farrington described as "tall and very thin," seemed resentful of her contribution, making no effort to show any sign of appreciation. Mrs. Farrington also recalled that he appeared ill-at-ease and not relaxed as were the other tourists seeking visas.

Four days after the President's murder, Mrs. Farrington was visiting relatives in Washington, D.C. when the F.B.I. hunted her down. The F.B.I. agent who called her from the Washington office gave her the office phone number so that she could call back for confirmation of his identity. This done, he informed her that the Bureau had located her because of the scene in the Mexican Consulate in New Orleans. The scene had been photographed, he informed her, by an invisible camera. It had been set in operation when the young man mentioned firearms and, inasmuch as she was present, the Bureau had traced her from the photograph. The young man, he added, was Lee Harvey Oswald, whose picture had been taken at the same time.

The F.B.I. agent suggested to Mrs. Farrington that she had also seen Lee Oswald in Mexico City, even before the scene at the consulate. She replied firmly that she had not seen Oswald in Mexico City. Nonetheless, the agent insisted—despite her repeated denials—that she had met Oswald in Mexico.

Mrs. Farrington and her cousin, Mrs. Lillian Merilh, who had been with her in the Mexican Consulate, later were questioned again by the same F.B.I. agent and others as well. This time the agents produced photographs of Jack Ruby and now insisted that Ruby had been present in the New Orleans Mexican Consulate earlier that day, when both Mrs. Farrington and her cousin were there. Both Mrs. Farrington and Mrs. Merilh informed the agents that the photographs of Ruby did not depict anyone they saw at the consulate.

I heard of her story from Mort Sahl and Mark Lane, who were working with us at the time. Lane took a statement from her at my request. He showed her 17 photographs, asking if any of them appeared to be the young man at the consulate in New Orleans. She replied that two of the pictures could have been the man. She picked out a picture of Lee Oswald. And she picked out a picture of Kerry

Thornley—Oswald's friend from Marine days back at El Toro, who had later moved to New Orleans.

The Farrington affair raised obvious questions. Why, for example, was the F.B.I. trying to bully a witness into saying she saw Oswald in Mexico City? And why was there no picture of Oswald at the consulate? The hidden camera there obviously was good enough to take an identifiable picture of Fenella Farrington and good enough to have the Bureau on her heels in a short time. The F.B.I. agent told her that it had a photograph of the young man who wanted to take a rifle to Mexico, and that it was Lee Oswald. Yet the government had never released that photo. If the photograph had been of Oswald, would the government have been so shy about revealing it?

But the scene at the Mexican Consulate in New Orleans was only the first of several suspicious incidents in which a highly visible "Lee Oswald" caught an observer's attention with a provocative action.

In late September of 1963, another such incident occurred, this time in Dallas. A "Leon Oswald" appeared at the home of Sylvia Odio—an émigré from Cuba—with two Spanish-speaking guerrilla types. One of the two later phoned her, telling her of how crazy "Leon" was and how he wanted to kill the President.

The following month in Dallas, Mrs. Lovell Penn found three men ostentatiously firing a rifle on her property and chased them away. After they left, she found an empty cartridge case bearing the label of "Mannlicher-Carcano"—the archaic and almost useless rifle which, the Warren Commission would announce, Oswald used in his historic exhibition of marksmanship at Dealey Plaza.

In early November a young man using the name of "Lee Oswald" applied for a job at a parking lot at the Southland Hotel. During the course of his conversation with the manager he asked if there was a good view of "downtown Dallas" from the building.

These scenarios were about as subtle as roaches trying to sneak across a white rug. But the most preposterous incident of the bunch took place one afternoon in early November of 1963.

A young man arrived at the Downtown Lincoln Mercury dealership—which happened to be just across the way from where the assassination soon would occur. He announced his intention of test driving and buying a car. The salesman, Albert Bogard, showed him a red Mercury Comet, and in short order they were cruising along the Stemmons Freeway, the customer at the wheel. After they got on the freeway, he revved up the speed to 60 and 70 miles an hour and began driving like Mario Andretti at the Indianapolis 500. He had the car taking even the tightest turns at high speed. As the salesman afterwards told his boss, "He drove like a madman."

When they got back, the customer seemed unhappy upon learning that he would have to pay at least a $200 or $300 down payment to drive out with the brand new car. Eugene Wilson, another salesman, heard him say, "Maybe I'm going to have to go back to Russia to buy a car." The man then told Bogard that he would be back to get the car in a couple of weeks, that he had some money coming in. He gave his name as "Lee Oswald," and Bogard wrote it on the back of one of his business cards. Several weeks later Bogard heard on the showroom radio that Lee Oswald had been arrested. He pulled out "Oswald's" card, ripped it up, and threw it away. "He won't want to buy a car," he said.

Bogard remembered the speed of the ride on the freeway better than he remembered the appearance of the customer. His response was: "I can tell you the truth, I have already forgotten what he actually looked like. I identified him as in pictures, but just to tell you what he looked like that day, I don't remember."

Frank Pizzo, for whom Bogard worked, was much more positive in his recollection. The Warren Commission counsel, Albert Jenner, after unsuccessfully showing him a number of pictures of Lee Oswald with other men, finally showed him a photograph of Oswald taken on November 22 after his arrest.* Here is the dialogue which followed:

MR. PIZZO: He certainly don't [sic] have the hairline I was describing. . . .

MR. JENNER: This was taken the afternoon of November 22 in the Dallas City Police showup.

(Discussion off the record).

(Discussion between Counsel Jenner and Counsel Davis and the witness, Mr. Pizzo, off the record).

---

* It is interesting to note that after Oswald's arrest the F.B.I., which had been informed immediately after the assassination of the "Lee Oswald" visit to Downtown Lincoln Mercury, did not take any of the witnesses from the automobile dealership over to Oswald's lineup.

MR. JENNER: Back on the record. You recall him as being more in the neighborhood of what—5 feet 8 inches, 5 feet 7 inches, more or less, or more or less?

MR. PIZZO: Between 5 feet 7 inches and 5 foot 8½ inches with sort of a round forehead and that V shape is the thing that I remember the most.

MR. JENNER: A widow's peak?

MR. PIZZO: Yes, but very weak.

MR. JENNER: Very weak.

MR. PIZZO: Very weak—not the bushy type that I see in the picture. Well, if I'm not sure—then—I have to say that he is not the one—if you want the absolute statement.

So much, it would seem, for any likelihood of Lee Oswald himself having been the wild driver at Downtown Lincoln Mercury. Oswald was five feet eleven inches tall.

Eugene Wilson, a senior car salesman at the dealership, disagreed even with Frank Pizzo's recollection of the young man's short stature. Wilson said that the young drag racer had been well under "5 feet 7 to 5 foot 8½ inches tall." Wilson, who was five feet eight, said that the man who called himself Oswald was "only about five feet tall."

While the Commission simply bypassed Frank Pizzo's precise testimony, it initially did not present Eugene Wilson's testimony at all. Consequently Wilson is not listed in the index to the hearings. Later, just as the Commission's report was about to go to press, Wilson was discovered, presumably by accident. The belated F.B.I. interview of Wilson, then a car salesman with another Mercury dealership, clearly bothered the interviewing agents. It not only eliminated the possibility of Oswald being the young visitor but underscored the probability of a pretender using Oswald's name. The F.B.I. report emphasized that Wilson had a problem with his vision because of glaucoma. However, he still was selling automobiles, and it was fair to conclude that he could tell when another man was a good deal shorter than he.

The Commission loftily stated that it had carefully evaluated the Downtown Lincoln Mercury incident "because it suggests the possibility that Oswald might have been a proficient automobile driver and,

69

during November 1963, might have been expecting funds with which to purchase a car." Had the Commission said that it had carefully evaluated the incident because it indicated that Oswald had shrunk considerably in height, this would, at least, have been more relevant.

All these heavy-handed tableaux—from the Mexican Consulate in New Orleans to Downtown Lincoln Mercury in Dallas—confirmed my initial instinct that someone had been impersonating Oswald. And now the reason was obvious: A trail of phony incriminating evidence had been carefully laid down prior to the execution of the President, leading to Oswald as the scapegoat. At the same time, the real Oswald had been manipulated by his intelligence community baby sitters. De Mohrenschildt had convinced him to move to Dallas, and then Oswald had been dispatched to New Orleans for sheepdipping, courtesy of Guy Banister. When Oswald returned to Dallas, other guiding hands made sure that he would be at the right place at the right time. Ruth Paine was the one who helped him get the job at the Texas School Book Depository, and although Oswald was called at the Paine household about a better job at the airport, he was never told about it. Consequently, assassination day found him still working at the depository on Elm, the fateful side street that the presidential motorcade took that morning.

I found myself wondering more and more about the accumulating signs of Oswald's manipulation. He was like a pawn on a chessboard, going where he was told to go, ending up where he was placed. When had the manipulation begun? Were there some early signs? My mind was taken back to El Toro Marine Base in California, even before Oswald's trip to the Soviet Union. I thought about Kerry Thornley— the one Marine whose testimony about Oswald was so different from that of the other Marines.

I read through Thornley's testimony again in Volume 11 of the hearings—all 33 pages of it. Most of the testimony of the other Marines around Oswald had been reduced to half-page affidavits, but Thornley had been kept on the stand longer than most of the witnesses in the entire inquiry.

I had my staff begin inquiring about him and learned, to my surprise, that Thornley—who had been in the Marines with Oswald in

1959—had arrived in New Orleans as far back as 1961. In a routine check of police records we found that he was also in New Orleans in 1962. He had been arrested in August for putting a sign on a telephone pole on Royal Street, in the French Quarter, in violation of a city ordinance. We located the arresting police officers. When questioned, however, they no longer could recall the subject of the sign Thornley had posted.

From his own admission, as well as from the statements of Barbara Reid and a number of others, we learned that Thornley had been in New Orleans in 1963, finally leaving the city only a few days after Kennedy's murder. Reid, a long-time French Quarter resident who had known both Thornley and Oswald, described seeing them together on several occasions. One of them was in early September 1963 at the Bourbon House, a combination bar and restaurant in the French Quarter. Thornley, who usually wore his hair extremely long, had just returned from a trip out of town. This time he was wearing his hair unusually short and closely cropped, as Oswald invariably did. Reid recalled having said to them, "Who are you guys supposed to be? The Gold Dust Twins?"

We were eager to talk to Kerry Thornley, but he was not an easy man to locate. It took us a lot of legwork and more than a year to do it. We had investigators going to every place in the French Quarter until we learned what had been his main hangout—Ryder's Coffee House. Except for occasional visits to the Bourbon House on Royal and Bourbon Streets, Thornley seldom went anywhere else.

Ryder's Coffee House had been small, dimly lit, and most unprepossessing. You wondered how such a small place, serving mostly coffee, had survived. However, rent was low at its Vieux Carré location, and apparently beer and wine sales kept it going. Thornley was very much into conversation, and Ryder's was a place where young people gathered to talk. When Ryder's closed down, its regulars simply moved to nearby places.

We picked our most sociable investigators and had them canvass a small cluster of bars that had sprouted up near the old Ryder's. A large number of the patrons knew Thornley. When our investigators found someone willing to help us, they would bring him in to see me and we would have a casual talk. It was all most unauthoritarian, extremely relaxed—and very productive. While Thornley did not seem to be a person inclined toward deep relationships, he had an unusual facility for developing widespread casual relationships. Moreover, Thornley, who moved around quite a bit, was that rarity of the 20th century—an inveterate letter writer. From his friends we obtained a letter here, a postcard there—no address stayed at very long.

However, mostly they came from three cities: Atlanta, Los Angeles, and Tampa, Florida. When we finally caught up with him, he was living in Tampa. It was early 1968, and our case was very far along. I had a Grand Jury subpoena served on him, and a few weeks later we had Kerry Thornley visiting the Criminal District Court Building in New Orleans.

When he arrived, I talked to him briefly. He was quite amicable, even talkative. He said that he had arrived in New Orleans in February of 1961—the month after the Bolton Ford incident—and had been living in New Orleans from that time until late November 1963, a few days after the assassination. He had no reason for leaving at that odd time; he just decided that the time had come to move. He was surprisingly candid about having met both Guy Banister and David Ferrie while in New Orleans, although he described these meetings as brief. He denied having met Oswald during that period when both were in New Orleans.

I had learned that virtually all of the young men connected with Guy Banister's operation, most of whom appeared to be employees of the intelligence community, carried a box key for the Lafayette Square post office. I never learned exactly why, but probably it was for receiving mailed instructions from their intelligence case officers or to provide an explanation for their periodic presence in the building where the Office of Naval Intelligence was located. Fishing, I asked Thornley why, when he lived in New Orleans, he carried a box key for the Lafayette Square post office. He promptly replied that he had possessed such a key because he lived just across the street at the Fox Hotel and it was convenient for him to receive his mail at the post office.

It was something of an eyebrow raiser to learn that, upon his arrival in the city in February 1961, Thornley had moved right into the heart of the intelligence community. However, my eyebrows went up even farther when I learned that while in New Orleans he had been writing a novel "inspired by" Lee Oswald. (He finished the book in February 1963—just nine months before the assassination.) Not many individuals were writing books inspired by Lee Oswald—at least, not before President Kennedy's murder.

One of the reasons I had developed an interest in Thornley was that I suspected he could have been the man who used the name "Oswald" at the Bolton Ford Company in January 1961. He had to have been one of the few men in the world who was in New Orleans around the time, who knew Lee Oswald, and who knew Oswald was in Russia. In addition, Thornley bore a striking resemblance to Oswald. They were of approximately the same height and slight build, both brown-haired and had similar facial features.

I recalled Thornley's testimony concerning their respective heights. Warren Commission counsel Albert Jenner had asked how tall Lee Oswald was. Here is the colloquy that resulted:

MR. THORNLEY: I would say he was about five-five maybe. I don't know.

MR. JENNER: How tall are you?

MR. THORNLEY: I am five ten.

MR. JENNER: Was he shorter than you?

MR. THORNLEY: Yes.

But Oswald had been the *taller* of the two! Why, then, had Thornley described his friend Lee as six inches shorter than he really was? Was Thornley, perhaps, fearful that someone might believe that he had been the young man who acted out the role of Lee Oswald in the early 1960s . . . at Bolton Ford in New Orleans . . . then in Dallas . . . and then in New Orleans . . . and then in Mexico . . . and then in Dallas again?

During my brief questioning of Thornley I did not mention his statement that Oswald had been much shorter than he, saving that for the Grand Jury. I did have time to ask Thornley about his travel schedule in 1963. He said that in the late spring, about the beginning of May, he had gone by bus to visit his parents in California. I asked him whether or not the bus had stopped at Dallas, and he replied that it had. He acknowledged having visited Dallas briefly on that occasion. It was about that time that the Grand Jury was ready to go into session, so we entered the conference room for several hours of testimony by Thornley.

Afterwards, upon reflection, the timing of Thornley's trip to Dallas struck me, although I had said nothing about it while we talked. The Oswalds had just moved from their Neely Street apartment in Dallas to New Orleans in late April, leaving some rent still paid for. Consequently the Oswald apartment had been left unoccupied for some days. Considering their respective travel schedules, Oswald and Thornley had not been very far away from passing each other on the highway, each one in the opposite direction in his respective bus.

I also was aware that at some unknown time, apparently when Oswald was not there, a young man of Oswald's build, wearing a pistol on his hip, had posed for several photographs in the backyard of the Neely Street apartment. In one picture he held aloft a rifle and a copy of the communist newspaper *The Daily Worker.* In the second picture he held a rifle and a copy of *The Militant,* also a leftwing newspaper.

These incriminating pictures purporting to be Oswald had been found in Ruth Paine's garage in Irving, where presumably she had been keeping them for him. When on February 21, 1964, one of the pictures exploded on the cover of *Life* magazine, some people decided the case against Lee Oswald was indisputable. But for most people with common sense, including me, the combination of the brandished rifle and the communist newspaper raised more questions than it answered.

At first glance the photographs appeared to be of Lee Oswald. However, after study it was apparent that in each picture Oswald's face did not precisely fit the neck and body. Furthermore, the facial portrait of Oswald was exactly the same one in each photograph, whereas the posture and the distance of the body from the camera differed. In addition to that, using the length of Oswald's face as a standard of measurement, one of the bodies in one picture was clearly taller than the corresponding body in the other picture.*

Of course, had the photographs actually been the real Oswald posing prior to the assassination with a rifle in his hand, this would have been in conflict with human nature. It is very rare—if not unheard of—in the annals of assassination for the assassin-to-be to provide so much incriminating evidence against himself in advance. It seemed plain enough to me that this was just another part of the process of setting up the patsy.

Thornley had told me that he returned from his summer in California by way of Mexico City. This happened to be very close to the time that the Warren Commission said Oswald was in Mexico. By November 1963, according to his own account, Thornley was living in a New Orleans apartment he rented from John Spencer.

We located Spencer, who turned out to be a friend of Clay Shaw's. As he described it, sometimes Spencer visited Shaw, the director of the International Trade Mart, and sometimes it was vice versa. Spencer told us, however, that Shaw never came by while Thornley was living at his place.

Several days after the assassination, Spencer told us, he came to his house and found Thornley gone. In Spencer's mailbox was a note from Thornley saying, "I must leave. I am going to the Washington, D.C. area, probably Alexandria, Virginia. I will send you my address so that you can forward my mail." Spencer said it was quite unexpected because Thornley had at least a week left in the month before his rent was due. He went to Thornley's apartment, number "C", and found that paper had been left over the entire floor, torn up into small pieces

---

* The Warren Commission and the House Select Committee on Assassinations each concluded that these were genuine photographs of Oswald, taken before the assassination. However, Robert Groden, the photographic consultant to the House Committee, wrote a dissent, printed in the appendix to the committee's hearings. Groden stated: ". . . *in my opinion, no matter what the panel members concluded, the backyard photographs are beyond question fakes. . . .* For the record, the method used here was, almost without doubt, simply posing a man . . . in the backyard with the rifle, pistol and publications as part of this original picture. The only item added was the head of Lee Oswald from the middle of the chin up. . . ." (Emphasis supplied.) In the absence of a rational explanation for such a suicidal picture-posing session on Oswald's part—and none was offered by either the Warren Commission or the House Committee—Groden's conclusion that the photos were fakes remains more persuasive to me.

like confetti. Before being torn up, the paper had been watered down so that the ink was blurred, making it unreadable.

Spencer said he had some conversations with Thornley about his book *The Idle Warriors* and that Thornley had asked him to read a copy of the manuscript, which had been turned down by several publishers before the assassination. Spencer never did get around to reading it. After the assassination Thornley told Spencer that he was going to be a rich man because of the coincidence of Oswald having been the subject of his book.

I later sent Andrew Sciambra to the Washington area, where he traced Thornley's path. Thornley had wound up at Arlington, a Washington suburb, and had moved into Shirlington House, a first-class apartment building where he worked as doorman. Thornley stayed at Shirlington House for six months, until he testified before the Warren Commission. Oddly enough, his salary was less than the rent of his Shirlington House apartment.

In the mid-1970s when I was in the private practice of law, Thornley sent a lengthy, almost biographical, 50-page affidavit to me describing, among other things, evidence he had encountered in New Orleans of "Nazi activity" in connection with President Kennedy's murder. It was apparent that even though I no longer was D.A. Thornley wanted to assure me that he had not been involved in Kennedy's assassination in any way.

Although it did not accord with reality, as I recalled it, the affidavit had, in retrospect, one interesting feature. Purely gratuitously, it mentioned how Thornley had left Washington following his Warren Commission testimony and ultimately returned to California, where he and John Rosselli happened to become friends. The affidavit was mailed to me before Rosselli's name surfaced during the Senate's 1975 investigation of the C.I.A.'s assassination practices. Rosselli, it turned out, had been one of a number of mobsters with whom the Agency had developed a relationship during its pre-Castro activities in Cuba.*

* Rosselli's gambling proclivities in pre-Castro Cuba—the site of numerous casinos—later made him useful to Howard Hughes, the eccentric billionaire. With Rosselli and his connections to ease the way, Hughes moved into the twinkling world of the Las Vegas casinos, buying up whatever caught his eye. It was while he was working for Hughes, and because of his background and gambling contacts in Cuba, that Rosselli was enlisted by the C.I.A.

After the Cuban revolution, Rosselli's assignment from the Agency was to assassinate Fidel Castro. To this end, during 1962 and 1963 Rosselli was given poisoned pills, explosives, rifles, and handguns. However, nothing seemed to work out on the Cuban end. The last effort in this C.I.A.-Rosselli combine ended in mid-February 1963, apparently because "conditions were not right." But Rosselli was not as close-mouthed about his mission as the Agency would have liked. When he appeared before a Senate committee investigating the assassination proclivities of the C.I.A., Rosselli testified that he was aware all along that his murder project was sponsored by the Agency.

Not long afterwards the remains of Mr. Rosselli—garotted and stabbed and cut in pieces—were found floating in an oil drum in Dumfounding Bay, off the Florida coast. Federal investigators were unable to find any leads to the perpetrators. This did not prevent the Justice Department from indicating that it thought the job was the work of organized crime. The C.I.A. said that it thought so, too. It did not seem to have occurred to federal investigative authorities that the mob would not likely have been the unhappy party as the result of Rosselli admitting to the Senate that he had initiated assassination attempts for the C.I.A.*

Whether the murder of John Rosselli was an old-fashioned gesture on the part of the mob or a clever example of what the Agency terms "damage control," it is clear that in the middle 1960s when Kerry Thornley met Rosselli, he hardly was becoming a friend of the average American citizen.

Even after Kerry Thornley's appearance before the Grand Jury, the strange intersections between his life and Lee Oswald's remained enigmatic. Was Thornley an agent of the intelligence community? Had he impersonated Oswald or coached others to do so? Did he know more than he was saying? I did not know the answers back in the late 1960s. And the whole bizarre saga of Thornley became even more

---

Mobsters like Rosselli proved to be valuable assets to the Agency after Kennedy's elimination because their names diverted attention to the mob as a possible "sponsor" of the murder. For more on the C.I.A.'s use of false sponsors after assassinations, see Chapter 20.

* A second mob figure, Sam Giancana, who also had done some business with the C.I.A. regarding Cuba, was called to appear before the same committee and was killed shortly before his scheduled appearance. He was murdered in his home with equal savagery, also dramatically suggestive of a traditional organized crime execution.

6

Deep Cover

"HEY, MY MAN," Dean Andrews said to me. He was a roly-poly lawyer who spoke in a hippie argot all his own. "We've been friends since law school days. Why do you want to treat me like I've got leprosy?"

"Because you keep conning me, Dean. You admitted to the Warren Commission that on the day after the assassination—while you were a patient at Hotel Dieu hospital—you were called on the phone and asked to fly to Dallas and be Lee Oswald's lawyer. When the Warren Commission asked you the caller's name, you replied that it was 'Clay Bertrand'."

"That's right," he said.

"Now, when I tell you I want to know who Clay Bertrand is, you tell me he's a client of yours but you really don't know what he looks like because you never see him."

"Scout's honor, my man," he said.

"That might have been good enough for the Warren Commission, Dean, but it's not good enough for me," I replied.

The puffy, oval face opposite me assumed a look of wounded pride. At least, what you could see of it did. A large part of his face perpetually was concealed by huge black glasses—the kind that let him see you but did not let you see him. He wore them always. Sunny days, cloudy days. Outside, inside. I think he slept in them.

After some nights of reading Andrews's testimony before the Warren Commission, I had arranged for him to meet me for lunch here at Broussard's Restaurant. This was back in early 1967, when I was still frustrated with our futile search for Kerry Thornley. Based on the Warren Commission testimony, I thought Andrews might lead us to an even more important witness.

Broussard's was one of the older places in the French Quarter. The bottom half of the walls around us was of veined marble, the top half was mirrored. The walls had been that way for close to a hundred years and, except for the regular polishing of the mirrors, nothing ever changed in the place. It was one of the least crowded French restaurants, a good place to meet for a quiet conversation. It was a meeting I still recall vividly.

In my reading I had learned that, at the time of his first F.B.I. interview shortly after the assassination, Andrews had described Clay Bertrand, his New Orleans caller, as a man approximately six feet two in height. He had gone on to say that Bertrand was a man who called him from time to time to help young friends of his who had become involved in minor scrapes with the law. Then—and later in more detail—he explained that in the summer of 1963, when Lee Oswald was living in New Orleans, Bertrand had called him and asked him to help Oswald with some citizenship problems his wife, Marina, was having. Oswald, consequently, had met with Andrews several times at his office.

It had readily become apparent to me, however, that the more Andrews realized that his having received a phone call to defend Lee Oswald was a potential danger to him, the foggier the identity of Clay Bertrand became in his mind. By the time Andrews appeared before the Warren Commission in July 1964, Bertrand's height had shrunk from six feet two all the way down to five feet eight inches.

Apparently in response to subtle pressure from the F.B.I. agents, Andrews told them, "Write what you want, that I am nuts. I don't care." The agents obligingly wrote in their final report that Andrews had come to the conclusion that the phone call from Bertrand had been "a figment of his imagination." This not only allowed the Bureau to conclude its investigation into Andrews but harmonized with its announced conclusion that Lee Oswald had accomplished Kennedy's assassination alone and unaided.

I knew Andrews well and had known him for years. He had been at Tulane Law School at the same time I had been there, although we were not in the same class. His practice was focused toward the municipal courts, and he appeared to obtain much of his business from his regular presence in some of the more off-beat bars in the city.

From reading his statements and subsequent testimony, it was clear to me that Andrews indeed had received a phone call from someone in New Orleans about going to Dallas and defending Oswald. And it had come the day after the assassination.

Andrews suddenly leaned forward, his black glasses looming at me. "Pipe the bimbo in red," he said in a low voice.

"What's that?"

I glanced in the direction he was pointing and saw a lissome young lady radiant in crimson, turning heads as she arrived with her lunch date. "She's pretty," I said, turning back to Andrews. His laid-back manner, which seemed to enable him to shed reality as a duck sheds water, was beginning to irritate me. I had been trying to pin him down for half an hour now, and he was well into his second martini, quite unfazed.

"Could we get to the point? Just who is Clay Bertrand? Where do I find him? I want to talk to him."

Andrews swung his arms open wide in exaggerated frustration. "God almighty," he said. "You're worse than the Feebees.* How can I convince you that I don't know this cat, I don't know what he looks like, and I don't know where he's at. All I know is that sometimes he sends me cases. So, one day, this cat Bertrand's on the phone talkin' to me about going to Dallas and representing Oswald." He put his hand over his heart. "Scout's honor, man. That's all I know about the guy."

---

* The "Feebees" meant F.B.I. agents in Andrews's special language.

Andrews resumed eating his Crabmeat Louie with gusto. Apparently he felt that I had my answer and the matter was settled.

For the first time it occurred to me that seated in front of me was a man who took everything in life with a grain of salt. Or perhaps, I reflected, he had up to now.

As he lifted another forkful of his Crabmeat Louie, I reached out and grabbed the fat hand with the fork in it. The black glasses swung my way. The crabmeat halted in mid-air.

"Dean," I said, "I think we're having a communication problem. Let me see if this will help clarify it for you. Now stop eating that damn crabmeat for a minute and listen to me."

I could not see through the glasses, but I knew I had his attention. "I'm aware of our long friendship," I said. "But I want you to know that I'm going to call you in front of the Grand Jury. If you lie to the Grand Jury as you have been lying to me, I'm going to charge you with perjury. Now am I communicating with you?"

Andrews stopped eating his crabmeat and put down his fork. He was silent for a long moment, apparently saddened at the failure of his jive humor. Then he spoke, and for the first time he seemed to be serious—at least, as far as you could tell before the black glasses blocked your vision.

"Is this off the record, Daddyo?" he asked me. I nodded. "In that case," he said, "let me sum it up for you real quick. It's as simple as this. If I answer that question you keep asking me, if I give you that name you keep trying to get, then it's goodbye, Dean Andrews. It's bon voyage, Deano. I mean like permanent. I mean like a bullet in my head—which makes it hard to do one's legal research, if you get my drift. Does that help you see my problem a little better?"

Out of the corner of my eye I saw blue flames flare up. I glanced over to the nearby table. A couple was having crêpes Suzettes, and the waiter had just lit the brandy. He hovered over the burning dessert with great ceremony.

I leaned forward. "Read my lips," I said. I spoke with careful deliberation. "Either you dance in to the Grand Jury with the real moniker of that cat who called you to represent Lee Oswald, or your fat behind is going to the slammer. Do you dig me?"

Andrews froze. I could not read through the huge pitch-black glasses, but I sensed that he was shaken. Then he stood up so suddenly it startled me. "Do you have any idea what you're getting into, my man?" he asked. "You want to dance with the government? Is that what you want? Then be my guest. But you will get sat on, and I do mean hard." He dropped his pink napkin on top of his Crabmeat Louie. "Thanks for the lunch," he mumbled. "It's been lovely."

He wheeled and walked away from the table. When he had entered the restaurant he had jigged in the front door, snapping his fingers to some imagined tune. Looking at him as he walked away, I realized that I had finally gotten through. He was not jigging any more.

My office's search for "Clay Bertrand" began with a discussion by our small group of the back-pedaling by Andrews—as described in the Warren Commission volumes—away from any clear identification of the man. We came to a general agreement that because Andrews himself was known to be a frequenter of some of the bars deep in the French Quarter, such places could be a fertile field for inquiry. It was plain enough that Andrews knew the man who had called him, and the association well might have derived from one of those places where he hung out.

By that time, Andrew Sciambra had become a member of our investigative group. Sciambra had grown up, and had lived much of his life, in the Sixth Ward, which included a large part of the lower French Quarter where the bars Andrews patronized were located. Over the years Sciambra had come to know one and then another operator or employee of these various bars.

To ease the entrée of our people at locales not always enthusiastic about the arrival of law enforcement personnel, we planned for Sciambra first—and, in some cases, friends and acquaintances of his—to contact the various bar owners in the lower part of the Quarter. That done, we formed teams of one assistant D.A. and one investigator each (in this instance, to cover the large area involved, we borrowed liberally from our entire attorney and investigative staff) to sweep the bars and ask if any proprietors knew of a man who used the name "Clay Bertrand."

On the first night of the hunt I went out with one of the teams to one of the bars deep in the Quarter. This particular place, Lafitte's Blacksmith Shop, had been a popular watering hole for classmates of mine back in Tulane Law School days, and I had the distinct impression that I had seen Dean Andrews there—even though that was some years before.

When we arrived at the Blacksmith Shop, I saw that it had changed very little. It was held to be the locale at which Jean Lafitte, the famous pirate whose headquarters was on Bayou Barataria, just outside New Orleans, actually maintained a blacksmith's shop. The place was built around a huge open fireplace and chimney and was constructed almost entirely of ancient brick.

It appeared old enough, given the benefit of occasional rebuilding over the years, to have been standing there since the War of 1812. There was a definite air of intrigue about the place, emphasized by the low ceiling and the thick, uneven rafters which had been hewn by hand rather than cut by machine. From the gaslight lanterns behind the long wooden bar to the chimney lamps at each table there was not an electric light to be seen.

It took very little imagination, amid this unique atmosphere, to envision the pirate, Jean Lafitte, meeting there with representatives of General Andrew Jackson. Jackson's great victory in the Battle of New Orleans has been attributed by some to these meetings, at which he obtained from Lafitte much-needed flints for his rifles.

Unfortunately for our particular expedition, the old owner of the place, who had always been friendly to me, had died a year or two back. The new owner, while friendly enough on the surface, seemed very nervous. Besides, while he was beaming welcome from ear to ear, I noticed that he had eyes like an anxious barracuda, and they definitely were not responding warmly to me. It was evident immediately that I was going to get nothing from him. He had no idea who "Clay Bertrand" was, he said, adding with emphasis that he had never heard the name.

As we left the bar, Lou Ivon came over. "Look, boss," he said gently. "I know you'd rather have me come straight out with this. Your showing up with us like this, without any warning, just about gave that man a heart attack. Seeing the D.A. suddenly walking in doesn't make too many people happy in this area. I think you better leave this operation to us."

So I did. The rest of the sweep was handled by the members of the group. Most of them were better than I was anyway in establishing quick, casual relationships.

These were long evenings for the staff members engaged in the hunt. It was not the kind of thing where one could pop in a place and then pop right out again. Even with Sciambra's help, relationships nevertheless had to be developed at each place visited. If the owner was not there, then it usually meant having to have a few beers while chatting with the bartender. Our investigators learned to go straight to the bar stool nearest the cash register, which resulted in more chances for casual banter with the person tending bar.

At the end of the first week all the scouting patrol had to show for their late nights was a collection of baggy eyes. A number of the owners and bartenders seemed to know well enough who "Clay Bertrand" was, but they felt a professional obligation to protect him, as a regular client, and none whatever to help us.

Still we pushed on. Then at some point—along about the third week—we had our first break. At Cosimo's, a small, crowded tavern deep in the Quarter on Burgundy Street, the bartender had been friendly and receptive on the first encounter but indecisive about knowing who Bertrand was. On the follow-up visit he was cooperative. An uncle of Sciambra's had called him on the phone.

"Sure," he said, "Bertrand comes here a lot. I guess you might say this is a regular stop of his." Did he know whether Bertrand used another name? "Oh, sure," he said. "Clay Shaw. I think most people know that." He went on to mention having seen him on the TV news, usually with important people. He could not understand, however, what the mystery was. As far as he was concerned, everyone in that part of the Quarter knew Bertrand. Did he know why Shaw used the name "Bertrand"? The bartender shrugged. All he knew was that it had been that way for a long time.

After that, two more bartenders—also from places deep in the Quarter—cooperated in quick succession. Clay Bertrand? Sure, they knew him. Everybody around here knew him. His other name? Clay Shaw. Everybody knew about that.

The general feeling seemed to be that Shaw used his pseudonym as some kind of private game, something for his own satisfaction. No one at these bars had any idea why he chose to be "Bertrand" when visiting their places, but that was good enough for them.

Shaw was not particularly discreet in the use of this alias, but he appeared to use it only in the raffish bars in the lower Quarter where his presence might well have tarnished his public image as a prominent civic leader.

Gradually, my men began encountering one person after another in the French Quarter who confirmed that it was common knowledge that "Clay Bertrand" was the name Clay Shaw went by. However, no one would authorize the use of his name or even sign a statement to be kept confidential. No one wanted to get involved. This was quite curious considering Shaw's reputation throughout the city as a man of decorum and distinction.

Finally we located a young man named William Morris who had met Shaw at the Masquerade Bar on St. Louis Street in the French Quarter. He had been introduced to Shaw by Gene Davis, who worked at the Court of Two Sisters. Davis had introduced Shaw to Morris as "Clay Bertrand." Morris had become a friend of Shaw's, not only visiting Shaw's apartment, but encountering him at one private party and, on occasion, again at the Masquerade Bar. Morris said that his tall friend was always referred to as Bertrand.

Then, in a break from a far different direction, the lady who had been the hostess at the V.I.P. room for Eastern Airlines at New Orleans International Airport called us. She had been on duty when a man— apparently meeting a friend who had arrived by plane—signed the guest register as "Clay Bertrand." From some acquaintance she had heard that the D.A.'s office was looking for a man by that name.

The name had stuck in her mind, she said, because each V.I.P. room visitor was supposed to sign the register before leaving. Only this man—not his friend—had signed before they left. She looked at his signature, which she customarily did, and saw the name "Clay Bertrand."

We followed up with a search through the airline's guest registers. As her memory became more specific, the search narrowed down to the sign-in registers for a period of a few months. And then the signature was found. After the printed phrase "Visiting Guest," there was signed with a flamboyant flourish: "Clay Bertrand." Her description of the signer was a tall, elegant, white-haired man with distinguished bearing—obviously Clay Shaw.

Things began to pick up. One lead led to another—or two or three. This was taking weeks, but the team was making steady progress. And slowly, ever so slowly, we were getting a signed statement here, a signed statement there.

Our patient, plodding footwork had taught us that "Clay Bertrand" was actually Clay Shaw—the distinguished director of the International Trade Mart in New Orleans and a civic leader of note. But at the time we had no inkling that Clay Shaw was much bigger and more powerful than his New Orleans persona indicated. It was not until much later, well after the Shaw trial when it could have been of any use to us, that we discovered Shaw's extensive international role as an employee of the C.I.A. Shaw's secret life as an Agency man in Rome trying to bring Fascism back to Italy was exposed in articles in the Italian press which we obtained from Ralph Schoenmann, secretary to the philosopher Bertrand Russell, who had been one of the earliest supporters of our investigation.

According to these articles, the C.I.A.—which apparently had been conducting its own foreign policy for some time—had begun a project in Italy as far back as the early 1960s. The organization, named the Centro Mondiale Commerciale (the World Trade Center), had initially been formed in Montreal, then moved to Rome in 1961. Among the members of its board of directors, we learned, was one Clay Shaw from New Orleans.

The Centro Mondiale Commerciale's new headquarters, according to the Roman press, was elegant. Its publicity, announcing the new, creative role it was going to play in world trade, was impressive. The Centro opened an additional office in Switzerland, also an impressive move.

However, in 1967, the Italian press took a close look at the board of directors of the Centro Mondiale Commerciale and found that it consisted of a very curious collection of individuals. The board contained at least one genuine prince, Gutierrez di Spadaforo, a member of the House of Savoy, whence came Umberto, the last of Italy's kings. Spadaforo, a man of considerable wealth, with extensive holdings in armaments and petroleum, had once been the undersecretary of agriculture for Il Duce, Benito Mussolini. Through his daughter-in-law, Spadaforo was related to the famous Nazi minister of finance, Hjalmar Schacht, who had been tried for war crimes in Nuremberg.

Another director of the Centro was Carlo D'Amelio, the lawyer for other members of the former Italian royal family. Another was Ferenc Nagy, the exiled former premier of Hungary and the former head of its leading anti-communist political party. Nagy also was described by the Italian newspapers as the president of Permindex (ostensibly a foundation for a permanent exposition and an offshoot of the Centro Mondiale Commerciale). Nagy, the Italian newspapers said, had been a heavy contributor to Fascist movements in Europe. Yet another director was a man named Giuseppi Zigiotti, the president of something with the congenial title of the Fascist National Association for Militia Arms.

One of the major stockholders of the Centro was a Major L.M. Bloomfield, a Montreal resident originally of American nationality and a former agent with the Office of Strategic Services, out of which the United States had formed the C.I.A.*

This then was the general make-up of the Centro Mondiale Commerciale, on whose board of directors Clay Shaw served. Judging from the background of its members and the fairly heavy activities in which they were engaged, the organization could not be confused with the Shriners or the 4-H Club. The Centro was described in 1969 by writer Paris Flammonde in *The Kennedy Conspiracy* as apparently representative of the paramilitary right in Europe, including Italian Fascists, the American C.I.A., and similar interests. He described it as "a shell of superficiality . . . composed of channels through which money flowed back and forth, with no one knowing the sources or the destination of these liquid assets."

The Italian government had no problem distinguishing the organization from the Shriners and the 4-H Club. Before 1962 was out, it had expelled the Centro Mondiale Commerciale—and its half-brother, Permindex—from Italy for subversive intelligence activity.

Perhaps because of its Montreal origin, the Centro aroused the

---

* This was significant not only because of his espionage background but because of a curious non-scheduled air trip taken by Clay Shaw and David Ferrie to Bloomfield's home city of Montreal in early 1961 or 1962; see Chapter 9.

interest of a Canadian newspaper, *Le Devoir.* Referring to Ferenc Nagy, one of the Centro's directors, it wrote in early 1967: "Nagy . . . maintains close ties with the C.I.A. which link him with the Miami Cuban colony." Nagy subsequently emigrated to the United States, making himself at home in Dallas, Texas.

With regard to Major Bloomfield, *Le Devoir* observed that although now ostensibly a Canadian, he had been involved in "espionage" in earlier years for the United States government. It went on to point out that Bloomfield was not only a major shareholder of the Centro but of its affiliated group, Permindex, as well.

Summing up the fate of the two related enterprises, *Le Devoir* stated: "Whatever the case may be, the Centro Commerciale and Permindex got into difficulties with the Italian and Swiss governments. They refused to testify to origins of considerable amounts of money, and they never seem to engage in actual commercial transactions. These companies were expelled from Switzerland and Italy in 1962 and then set up headquarters in Johannesburg."

The ultimate evaluation of Clay Shaw's Centro Mondiale Commerciale by the *Paesa Sera* stated: "Among its possible involvements (supported by the presence in directive posts of men deeply committed to organizations of the extreme right) . . . is that the Center was the creature of the C.I.A. . . . set up as a cover for the transfer of C.I.A. . . . funds in Italy for illegal political-espionage activities. It still remains to clear up the presence on the administrative Board of the Center of Clay Shaw and ex-Major (of the O.S.S.) Bloomfield."

Paesa Sera made an additional observation about the Centro. It was, the newspaper observed, "the point of contact for a number of persons who, in certain respects, have somewhat equivocal ties whose common denominator is anti-communism so strong that it would swallow up all those in the world who have fought for decent relations between East and West, including Kennedy." That just happened, as well, to be a trenchant one-line description of the parent organization, the Central Intelligence Agency.

As for Permindex, which Clay Shaw also served as a director, the Italian press revealed that it had, among other things, secretly financed the opposition of the French Secret Army Organization (O.A.S.) to President DeGaulle's support for independence for Algeria, including its reputed assassination attempts on DeGaulle. This observation, had we known about it in 1967, would have brought us full-circle all the way back to the blimp base at Houma, Louisiana, where David Ferrie and others from Guy Banister's operation repossessed the munitions from the Schlumberger bunker which the C.I.A. earlier had given to the assassination-minded O.A.S. It would certainly have helped our case against Shaw to have been able to link him definitively with the C.I.A. Unfortunately, however, with our limited staff and finances, and many leads to follow, our investigation was not able to uncover any of this crucial background information when we needed it most.

7

The Front Page

W E H A D I D E N T I F I E D the once mysterious "Clay Bertrand." Now, for a change, we had a period of calm. Here in New Orleans the usual crimes were being committed, night and day. Despite the syndrome that comes with the job—the feeling that the faster you convict burglars and armed robbers, the faster new ones appear to take their places—the main work of the district attorney's office, the prosecution machinery, had to be maintained and improved. I let the members of the team go back to their regular office positions for a while, and I resumed mine. At night and on weekends, however, I continued my study of the available evidence. Alone in the office or at home surrounded by my family, I would stay up until the early hours of the morning, obsessively poring through testimony, looking for connections and contradictions, thinking, always thinking.

The gunfire coming from in front of the presidential limousine had satisfied me that Lee Oswald was not the lone killer of John Kennedy. The "admission note" at Parkland Hospital, signed by Dr. Robert McClelland, described the cause of death as a "massive head and brain injury from a gunshot wound of the left temple"—a location customarily accepted as being in the front of one's head. And yet it was unanimously acknowledged that at the time of the shooting Oswald was in the School Book Depository, well to the President's rear.

I began to wonder: Had Oswald actually shot the President at all? I studied the statements of witnesses who claimed to have observed unusual activity in the Book Depository and other buildings clustered behind the President. The more I read, the more my doubts grew.

About 15 minutes before the motorcade arrived, Arnold Rowland, a student, and his wife, Barbara, were standing on Houston Street across from Dealey Plaza. Arnold glanced up at the Book Depository, and at the *easternmost* end of the sixth floor (where the alleged "assassin's lair" was located) he noticed a dark-skinned man whom he described as "an elderly Negro." However, at the *westernmost* end of the sixth floor (the opposite end of the building) he saw a man standing, just back from the window, with a rifle in his hands. The man was holding the rifle, barrel pointing upwards, at the 45-degree angle which the military describes as "port arms."

Barbara Rowland, at that moment, was preoccupied by a man having an epileptic seizure in the plaza directly across from them. By the time Arnold got his wife's attention and she looked up, the man with the rifle had stepped away.* They both concluded that the man with the rifle was a Secret Service agent. Arnold testified that on the following day when he described the presence of the second, dark-skinned man on the sixth floor to F.B.I. agents, "they told me it didn't have any bearing or such on the case right then. In fact, they just the same as told me to forget it now."

Carolyn Walther, employed at the nearby Dal-Tex Building, also was standing on the east side of Houston Street. According to a statement she gave to the F.B.I., Walther watched the ambulance arrive for the seizure victim and happened to glance toward the Depository, where she saw a man with a rifle on one of the upper floors. The rifleman was holding the gun with the barrel pointed downward as he

---

* In her testimony in a Commission deposition, Mrs. Rowland recalled her husband telling her about the man with the rifle at the Depository sixth-floor window. She recalled that it was the *westernmost* window which her husband had pointed out to her. She did not look up at the windows again, nor did she remember anything about the second man on the floor.

looked toward the oncoming motorcade on Houston Street. Mrs. Walther said that the rifle was different from any she had ever seen and had an unusually short barrel. The man holding it was wearing a white shirt and was either blond or had light-colored hair. He was standing in the middle of the most easterly window on the floor, leaning forward. In the same window, just to his left, she could see another man standing erect. He appeared to be wearing a brown suit.

Then the motorcade arrived and drew her attention. It did not occur to her to glance up at the window again, not even after the shooting began. She was not called to testify by the Warren Commission.

Toney Henderson of Dallas was waiting for the parade on the east side of Elm near the corner of Houston. After the ambulance departed with the epileptic, she glanced toward the Depository. She recalled that numerous people on different floors were at the windows, looking out. Then on one of the upper floors she noticed two men. They were standing in back of the window and looking out of it at the motorcade. One, a dark-haired man in a white shirt, was dark-skinned and "possibly a Mexican, but could have been a Negro." Mrs. Henderson was unable to describe the other man, except that he was the taller of the two. She did not know exactly which floor the two men were on. The F.B.I. report of her statement did not identify the windows in which she saw the two men.

These statements from witnesses who saw two men on the Depository's top floor were troubling enough, but one night when I came across the testimony of 16-year-old Amos Euins I was so disturbed I could not sleep. Testifying before the Warren Commission, Euins described having waved at the President as the long convertible made its leftward, 120-degree turn onto Elm. He happened to glance upward at the Book Depository and saw what appeared to be "a pipe" sticking out of a window. Earlier, when interviewed by Sergeant D. V. Harkness of the Dallas police, Euins had described the window as being the easternmost one on the floor "under the ledge"—which is the building's famous sixth floor.

After the shooting began, Euins was able to see the trigger and the stock of the rifle. He also noticed that the man doing the shooting had a distinct bald spot on his head. Euins described the bald area as going back about two and a half inches from the hairline and standing out as if it were white in the relative darkness of his surroundings. Immediately after the assassination he described the man as being black. Later in his Commission testimony Euins indicated that he could not be certain whether the man was white or Negro. However, he was immovable on two points. The first was his insistence that the man definitely had a "bald spot" on his head. The second was his denial that he had told a sheriff's deputy that the man he saw on the sixth floor was white. What he had said, he explained to the members of the Commission, was that the bald spot on the man's head looked like it was white.

Considering that Euins was standing just south of the Depository at approximately half past twelve, the sun would have been almost overhead and the bald spot of a man leaning forward might well have appeared to be white, I thought. In any case, Euins's observation of an apparently dark-skinned man with a "bald spot" on his head seemed to coincide with Arnold Rowland's observation of an "elderly Negro." In each instance, the object of their attention was occupying the *easternmost* window in the Depository—the "assassin's lair" where Oswald was supposed to have been—when the parade arrived.* And both of their statements seemed to be supported by Toney Henderson's conclusion that the man she had seen was either a Mexican or a Negro.

Two other men, each of whom was considerably more observant than the average witness, helped to unify the collective observations of the foregoing witnesses into a comprehensive picture of who was on the sixth floor just before—and during—the shooting of the President. Roger Craig, honored in 1960 for his performance as a Dallas deputy

---

* The greatest view by far of the Depository's sixth floor was from the County Jail on Houston Street. The inmates had clustered at the windows to see the Presidential motorcade. Stanley Kaufman, an attorney who testified before the Warren Commission, described a client of his, Willie Mitchell, as not having seen anyone when he glanced over at "that window." However, Kaufman went on to say that "there were people in jail who saw the actual killing."

The inmates of the jail were not called to testify by the Warren Commission. Nor were they questioned by the F.B.I. or the Secret Service. However, one of the inmates, John Powell, surfaced later. Powell, who was in jail for only several days on misdemeanor charges, did not thrust himself forward to testify. Rather, he simply informed acquaintances of what he had seen on the Depository's sixth floor. Ultimately, one of them contacted the media.

Powell and his fellow inmates were on the sixth floor of the jail, so they were able to look right into the sixth floor of the Depository, several hundred feet away. A few minutes before the assassination, Powell and the other inmates stared from their window into the window just across the way and watched two men with a rifle. At first they thought that the two were security guards—until the shooting began. Powell recalled that one of the two men had a very dark complexion.

sheriff, remembered that a few minutes after the assassination he observed the Dallas police questioning a Latin man on Elm Street. As Craig recalled it, the police, frustrated when the man did not answer their questions because he could not speak English, released him. Some minutes afterwards, Craig saw a Nash Rambler station wagon pull up in front of the Depository and recognized the driver as the Latin man who had just been released by the police. Before he could do anything, a young white man—whom Craig later identified as Lee Oswald—came running down from in front of the Depository, jumped in, and the station wagon tore off.* On this occasion—seeing the Latin man for the second time and in a more inculpatory situation—Craig got a closer look at him. He described the man as being not merely dark-skinned but "a Negro."

Meanwhile, Richard Randolph Carr had observed a white man on the sixth floor of the Depository, only in this instance at the next westward window from the "assassin's lair." Carr, who also saw activity on the knoll, was a steel worker on the upper part of the new court-house building under construction at the corner of Houston and Commerce. When the shots were fired, Carr, a combat veteran, glanced over at the Depository. Minutes later Carr was standing on the

---

* A few months after I had read his testimony, Craig came to see me in New Orleans. An alert and idealistic young man who looked more like a cheerleader than a deputy sheriff, Craig had been driven out of Dallas by the law enforcement establishment. His honest testimony had doomed his law enforcement career and he had decided to leave Dallas after someone took a shot at him, grazing his scalp. I got him a job at the Willard Robertson Volkswagen company, and Craig met freqently with me, reviewing in detail what he had seen at Dealey Plaza and at Dallas police headquarters after the assassination.

Shortly after he learned that a suspect had been arrested, Craig told me, he went straight to Dallas police headquarters to see if he could help the homicide department with the identification. He told Captain Will Fritz, the head of homicide who was running the investigation, about the Nash Rambler incident he had seen. The two of them then went into Fritz's private office, where Oswald was sitting. Fritz pointed at Craig and told Oswald, "This man saw you leave." Oswald replied, "I told you people I did." Fritz told Oswald to take it easy, that he was just trying to find out what happened. Then Fritz said, "What about the car?" Oswald answered, "That station wagon belongs to Mrs. Paine—don't try to tie her into this."

Later Deputy Sheriff Buddy Walthers drove out to the Paine residence in the suburb of Irving and confirmed that Mrs. Ruth Paine did have a Nash Rambler station wagon with a luggage rack on top, as Craig had observed. There is no record that Captain Fritz or any other members of the Dallas homicide unit ever followed up this lead. In fact, Fritz later denied that Craig had been at police headquarters or had told him about the Nash Rambler. However, a news photo that turned up six years after the assassination in the autobiography of Dallas Police Chief Jesse Curry clearly shows Craig at police headquarters, corroborating Craig's story.

ground near the Depository when he recognized the very man he had seen earlier at the Depository window on the upper floor. Carr described this man as being a heavy-set individual with horn-rimmed glasses and a tan sport jacket.

Carr followed the man for a block. The man then climbed into a Nash Rambler station wagon (apparently the same car described by Roger Craig), which seemed to be waiting for him, and the car rapidly drove off. Like Craig, Carr noted, in several statements to law enforcement officers, that the driver was "real dark-complected," either "Spanish or Cuban."

It seemed fair to conclude from all the statements that a composite visualization of the Depository sixth floor just before—and during—the assassination added up to at least three different men: two white, one of whom was apparently youngish and either slightly blond or with light brown hair, and the other heavy-set with horn-rimmed glasses; and one distinctly dark-complexioned, very possibly of Latin origin. Whether they had one rifle or two was unclear. The youngish, thinner white man was seen holding one while he stood back of the *westernmost* window (at the opposite end of "the assassin's lair"), whereas the dark-complexioned man was seen firing directly from the *easternmost* "lair."

After reading the statements of these eyewitnesses, I knew that Lee Oswald could not have shot John Kennedy from the "assassin's lair" as the Warren Commission claimed. Unlike the man who was observed shooting from the lair, Oswald did not have a bald spot, nor was he "dark-skinned" or "Spanish-looking." In my mind at this point, it was still possible that Oswald was somehow involved in the assassination, but it seemed clear that others had participated in the shooting, both from the grassy knoll in front of the President and from the Book Depository behind him.

The appearance and reappearance of "dark-skinned," "Spanish-looking" or "Negro" men in the descriptions of the witnesses intrigued me. Not only was the man in the lair identified this way, but the "epileptic" observed in Dealey Plaza was described as a Latin man wearing Army green combat garb.* That description reminded me of the anti-Castro

---

* The incident involving the "epileptic" who had a seizure shortly before the arrival of the President's motorcade aroused suspicion on several counts. First, it effectively made unavailable the ambulance that was on standby in case of injury to the President, which had to be used

Cuban exiles who were constantly traipsing through Guy Banister's office on their way to guerrilla training on Lake Pontchartrain. It occurred to me that the "dark-complected" man whom some observers saw might well have been Cuban. Moreover, given what I knew about Guy Banister's guerrilla training operation and Lee Oswald's proximity to it, the involvement of anti-Castro Cuban exile guerrillas in the assassination of a President whom they despised for "betraying" them at the Bay of Pigs in 1961 and for ordering their training camps shut down in the summer of 1963 seemed a distinct possibility.

In fact, the Cubans began to seem more likely suspects than Lee Harvey Oswald himself. In addition to the eyewitness descriptions, other evidence pointed away from Oswald. For example, Oswald's fingerprints were never found on the Mannlicher-Carcano rifle he was alleged to have used.*

A great deal of confusion surrounded this second-rate Italian rifle

---

to take the epileptic man to Parkland Hospital. Second, the incident created a distraction and caused Dallas police officer Joe Smith to leave his post at the corner of the Depository, making it possible for men on the grassy knoll to move into position as the parade turned off Main onto Houston. Third, a number of witnesses who wrote to our office found it strange that the woman who was treating the epileptic until the ambulance picked him up—he had bloodied his head slightly in falling—and who had promptly appeared and identified herself as a nurse, was nevertheless dipping her handkerchief in the goldfish pond before wiping his head. Some of these correspondents described the epileptic as a Latin man wearing Army fatigues. Fourth, when our office followed up at Parkland Hospital, we found that once the ambulance arrived there the alleged epileptic walked off, refusing to be treated or to identify himself.

* About midnight on November 22, the F.B.I. took the Mannlicher-Carcano alleged to have been Oswald's up to the F.B.I. laboratory in Washington, D.C. The Bureau technicians found no fingerprints or even partial prints identifiable as Oswald's. The following day the Bureau returned the rifle to the Dallas police. Later the Dallas police excitedly announced that they had found "Oswald's palm print" on the rifle. The scientific accuracy of this delayed discovery by the Dallas Police Department was reflected in an internal F.B.I. memo dated August 28, 1964 (but not released until 1968) in which Warren Commission General Counsel J. Lee Rankin is quoted as stating: "Because of the circumstances which now exist there is a serious question in the minds of the Commission as to whether the palm impression that has been obtained from the Dallas Police Department is a legitimate palm impression removed from the rifle barrel or whether it was obtained from some other source and that for this reason the matter needs to be resolved." However, the Warren Commission made no effort to resolve it. It presented the "palm print" in its report as a significant development in the case against Oswald.

In 1984, Agent Vincent Drain, who handled the rifle for the F.B.I., was questioned about the supposed palm print by researcher Henry Hurt. Drain said he did not believe that there ever was such a print: "All I can figure is that it [Oswald's print] was some kind of cushion because they were getting a lot of heat by Sunday night. You could take the print off Oswald's card and put it on the rifle. Something like that happened."

because there was compelling evidence that it was *not* the weapon found in the assassin's lair shortly after the assassination. Officer Seymour Weitzman, part of the Dallas police search team, later described the discovery of the rifle on the afternoon of November 22. He stated that it had been so well hidden under boxes of books that the officers stumbled over it many times before they found it. Officer Weitzman, who had an engineering degree and also operated a sporting goods store, was recognized as an authority on weapons. Consequently, Dallas Homicide Chief Will Fritz, who was on the scene, asked him the make of the rifle. Weitzman identified it as a 7.65 Mauser, a highly accurate German-made weapon. Deputy Sheriff Roger Craig was also there and later recalled the word "Mauser" inscribed in the metal of the gun. And Deputy Sheriff Eugene Boone executed a sworn affidavit in which he described the rifle as a Mauser. As late as midnight of November 22, Dallas District Attorney Henry Wade told the media that the weapon found was a Mauser.

There is, of course, a significant difference between a first-class Mauser and a cheap mail-order Mannlicher-Carcano. It should have been simple to know which weapon had been found. However, to complicate the issue, three empty cartridges from a Mannlicher-Carcano were found in the same room as the Mauser. They were near the easternmost sixth-floor window, close together and almost parallel to each other. Although this arrangement made them easy to find, it defied what any experienced user of rifles knows: that when a rifle is fired, the cartridge is flung violently away. A neat distribution pattern of cartridges like the one found on the sixth floor of the Depository is virtually impossible. It strongly suggested to me that the cartridges were never fired from the assassin's lair but were planted near the window, presumably having been fired earlier elsewhere, so that bullet fragments found in the President's limousine could be described as having come from the Carcano.

There were other problems with the story that the Mannlicher-Carcano had been the murder weapon. For instance, no ammunition clip was ever found. The clip is the device that feeds the cartridges into the rifle's firing chamber. Without such a clip, the cartridges have to be loaded by hand, making fast shooting such as Oswald was alleged to have done impossible. The Warren Commission skirted this problem by never confronting that fact.

Complicating the matter even further, the Mannlicher-Carcano triumphantly produced as the "assassin's rifle" was found to have a badly misaligned sight. So badly was the sight out of line with the barrel that an adjustment was necessary before government riflemen could complete their test firing. Even so, no rifle expert was ever able to duplicate the feat the government attributed to Lee Oswald.

Despite these problems, when the smoke cleared and all the law enforcement authorities in Dallas had their stories duly in order, the official position was that the rifle found on the sixth floor of the Depository was the Mannlicher-Carcano, which allegedly was linked to Oswald under an alias, and not the Mauser, which disappeared forever shortly after it reached the hands of Captain Fritz.

But even this revision of the official story did not explain the third rifle. A film taken by Dallas Cinema Associates, an independent film company, showed a scene of the Book Depository shortly after the assassination. Police officers on the fire escape were bringing down a rifle from the roof above the sixth floor with the tender care you might give an infant. When the policemen reached the ground, a high-ranking officer held the rifle high for everyone to see. The camera zoomed in for a close-up. Beneath the picture was the legend, "The Assassin's Rifle." When I saw the film, I noted that this rifle had no sight mounted on it. Thus it could not have been either the Carcano or the vanished Mauser, both of which had sights.

I was not surprised to find that this third rifle, like the Mauser, had disappeared. But its existence confirmed my hypothesis that Lee Oswald could not have killed John Kennedy as the American public had been told. Setting aside the evidence of two other weapons on the scene, the incredibly accurate shooting of an incredibly inaccurate rifle within an impossible time frame was merely the beginning of the feat we were asked to believe Oswald had accomplished.

I knew from his fellow Marines' testimony that Oswald was a notoriously poor shot. But this job would have been impossible for even the greatest marksman. From the assassin's lair the first thing an assassin would see, when attempting to shoot someone in a motorcade below on Elm Street, was an extremely large tree, still luxuriant in the deep South as late as November. This made it unlikely that the first round fired would have hit anything more than a limb or a handful of leaves from the tree below.

Moreover, Oswald had been seen in the lunchroom down on the second floor of the Depository less than two minutes after the shooting. He not only had appeared composed and relaxed, but was drinking a Coke which he had bought from the vending machine. For him to have finished his historic shooting feat (causing eight wounds in two men in less than six seconds), then hidden the rifle beneath the piles of boxes which Officer Weitzman described, then run down four flights of stairs, then stopped for a Coke at the vending machine—all in less than two minutes without losing his breath—would have required that Oswald move at nearly the speed of light.

Other physical evidence found at the scene pointed away from Oswald as well: a pop bottle that did not have Oswald's fingerprints on it was consequently tossed into the nearest garbage can by Captain Fritz and his investigators.

But the most obvious and compelling piece of evidence exonerating Oswald was the "nitrate" test he was given on the evening of the assassination. Simply put, this test reveals the deposits of nitrate on an individual's cheek when he or she has fired a rifle. The nitrate test results indicated that Lee Oswald had not fired a rifle on November 22, 1963. However, for reasons best known to the government and its investigators, this fact was kept secret for ten months. It was finally revealed in the Warren Commission report.

After going over the government's own evidence, I realized that my earlier conclusion that Oswald had not been the lone killer of President Kennedy was not entirely correct. Clearly there had been others involved in the shooting, but the truth was that Lee Oswald himself had not shot John Kennedy at all. Nor had he even attempted to shoot John Kennedy.

It seemed inescapable to me as a professional prosecutor that the man damned by the world as the criminal of the century was innocent. Only the truly innocent have to be as thoroughly set up as Lee Oswald obviously had been.

* * *

The temporary respite from the investigation did not last long. Frank Klein could not stay away from it, and neither could I. One morning I was in my office reading and rereading a newspaper. I did not hear Frank enter.

"I have never seen you so preoccupied," said Frank.

"It's not just any paper, son," I said. "This is the front page of the *Dallas Morning News* for November 22, 1963."

"Well, what's got you so hypnotized?"

I gestured to the large diagram on the paper's front page, indicating the route of the presidential parade. "Have I ever shown you this before?" I asked.

He shook his head.

I turned the paper around facing his way so that he could read the diagram of the motorcade. It covered almost five-sixths of the front page.

"Frank," I said, "I want you to follow the parade route with me. Let's pick it up right here as it comes down Main approaching Dealey Plaza. Are you with me?"

"Yes," he said, his finger following the thick line indicating the motorcade. "And here is where it reaches Dealey Plaza. . ." He stopped.

"What's the matter?" I asked.

"This diagram indicates that the President's parade was supposed to continue on Main Street through the center of Dealey Plaza—without even leaving Main." He stared at it in disbelief.

"So what's wrong with that?" I asked.

His finger was moving off of Main, inches downward to Elm until he found the Depository area where the President had been shot. "If that was the presidential parade route up there on Main . . ."

I finished the question for him. "How did he get way down here on Elm?"

Frank looked up at me with a slight frown, then looked back at the diagram. He moved his finger back along Main Street to where it reached Houston. "The motorcade turned right on Houston and went down onto Elm," he said.

"Where the motorcade made that sweeping 120-degree left turn you are looking at, which had to slow the President's car down to about ten miles an hour."

Frank looked up again at the thick line indicating the motorcade route continuing on Main through the center of Dealey Plaza as it headed for the Stemmons Freeway.

"Here on Main Street, continuing through the open meadow," he said, "they couldn't have hit him. Are you telling me that at the last moment they just moved the President of the United States off of his scheduled route to here where the Depository is?" He pushed back his chair and stood up. "Hell, I haven't read a damned word about that anywhere. How can they keep something like that a secret for three years?"

I leaned back in my chair. "Now you see why I didn't hear you knock when you came in."

"Where the hell were the Dallas police when they made that last-minute change in the route?" he asked.

"Where indeed?" I asked. "And the Secret Service. And the F.B.I."

"And the city administration of Dallas," he added. "Don't they have a mayor over there in that damned place?"

"Yes, they do. The mayor when this happened was Earle Cabell."

I buzzed the intercom and my secretary, Sharon Herkes, came in. I asked her to take a cab to the public library and find the latest volume of *Who's Who in the Southwest*. "I'm sure you'll find Earle Cabell in there. See if his article indicates any connections with Washington."

"With Washington?" Frank asked.

"Of course," I replied. "You can't tell me it's possible to hijack the President—with the whole world watching—unless there's some kind of cooperation between the city administration and the federal government."

Frank grabbed the front page of the *Dallas Morning News* and pointed to the diagram. "Hell," he said, "was the Warren Commission blind? Didn't they see this?"

"Oh," I said. "Would you like to see the front page that was introduced to the Warren Commission?"

I pulled open my middle desk drawer and took out a copy of the *Dallas Morning News* front page that had been introduced as a Commission exhibit. I handed it to Frank and lit my pipe. I had hardly taken the first puff on it when he yelled.

"Those bastards! They just removed the entire motorcade route from the front page."

That was true. On five-sixths of the *Dallas Morning News* page where the diagram of the motorcade route was supposed to be was nothing but a large square of solid gray. "And this has been printed as an official exhibit by the Warren Commission?" he asked.

I nodded.

"And just what in the hell are we supposed to call this?" he asked, waving the nearly blank exhibit.

I took a puff or two on my pipe. "This is what you call," I replied, "a coup d'etat."

An hour or so later Sharon walked in the door with a large photostat in her hand. "They didn't have anything about Mayor Cabell in the *Who's Who*," she said. "But there's a lot of stuff here about a General Charles Cabell."

I glanced down at the article. Right away it jumped out at me from the page that this Charles Cabell had been the deputy director of the Central Intelligence Agency. Now I found myself looking at that last name with real fascination. It took one phone call to an attorney friend in Dallas to determine that General Charles Cabell was the brother of Earle Cabell, former mayor of Dallas.

Now the eleventh-hour change in the President's motorcade route was even more intriguing to me, and I immediately headed for the public library. Before sunset I had become the leading expert in New Orleans on General Charles Cabell, who, it turned out, had been fired as the C.I.A.'s number two man by President Kennedy. General Cabell had been in charge of the Agency's disastrous Bay of Pigs invasion. In the final hours, while Castro's small air force was tearing the landing effort apart, Cabell had managed to get through a call to President Kennedy in an attempt to halt the disaster. Just over the horizon, by something less than happenstance, lay aircraft carriers with fighter planes on their decks, engines warming up. General Cabell informed the President that these fighters could reverse the course of disaster in minutes and secure the success of the invasion. All that was needed was the President's authorization.

On the preceding day Kennedy had assured the assembled media that if anyone invaded Cuba (and the air had become rife with invasion rumors) there certainly would be no help from the U.S. armed forces. He flatly turned Cabell down. With that the invasion's chances sank, as did the general's intelligence career. President Kennedy asked for Cabell's resignation and the general was subsequently replaced on February 1, 1962, as the C.I.A.'s deputy director. General Cabell's subsequent hatred of John Kennedy became an open secret in Washington.

In most countries, a powerful individual who had been in open conflict with a national leader who was later assassinated would receive at least a modicum of attention in the course of the posthumous inquiry. A major espionage organization with a highly sophisticated capability for accomplishing murder might receive even more. Certainly a powerful individual who also held a top position in a major espionage apparatus and had been at odds with the departed leader would be high on the list of suspects.

However, General Cabell, who fit that description perfectly, was never even called as a witness before the Warren Commission. One reason may have been that Allen Dulles, the former C.I.A. director (also fired by President Kennedy), was a member of the Commission and handled all leads relating to the Agency. During the nine years that Dulles had been the C.I.A.'s chief, General Charles Cabell had been his deputy.

8

Covert Operations

IN 1963 Clinton was a rural hamlet in deep south Louisiana. It was a relic of the long-ago time when cotton had been king, a farmers' center where the cotton crops were weighed and buyers bid for them.

Clinton was the kind of place whose continued survival had no visible basis. Its importance to the cotton industry had faded; it remained only because it had always been there. But in early 1967 we picked up a lead that made that sleepy town very important indeed.

It seemed that back in late summer or early autumn of 1963, Lee Oswald had been seen in Clinton in the company of two older men. The descriptions of these men closely fit Clay Shaw, whose hometown of Hammond we knew was just east of Clinton, and David Ferrie, who had spent a lot of time at Guy Banister's anti-Castro camp a little farther east on Lake Pontchartrain.

It was a slim lead, little more than a whisper in the air which most law enforcement agencies would have waved away impatiently, but such thin leads were what we had been forced to work with from the beginning.

Clinton was a good ways off the beaten path, and I decided that sending assistant D.A. Andrew Sciambra by himself from the city might not be the right way to approach this rural town. Sciambra needed someone else with a bit of country background. I called Governor John McKeithen, and he ordered Lieutenant Francis Frugé, a state police officer of Cajun descent, accent included, to join Sciambra in Clinton immediately.

We soon had an unexpected strike of good fortune. It developed that Oswald's two older companions had selected the most memorable occasion in decades to show up with Lee Oswald in a country town in the Deep South. For the first time in history, a major voter registration drive supported by the federal government was under way. This effort to register more black voters was strongly supported by the blacks in the town and intransigently opposed by the whites. From sunup to sundown almost every adult in Clinton was milling about the vicinity of the registrar's office, the blacks to make sure that the whites did not prevent the registration of new black voters, the whites to make sure that no "outsiders" had come in to encourage the blacks. It was an occurrence never seen before and not likely ever to be seen again. In fact, the first two witnesses located by Sciambra and Frugé traced their recollection of Oswald's presence with the older men in Clinton to the month of September 1963 because that is when the voter registration drive was under way.

A number of the Clinton citizens interviewed found the scene unforgettable because most of the time Oswald was the only white man standing in a long line of blacks. Just as memorable were the two older men who were with Oswald. All of the witnesses described one of the two as wearing a crazy-looking wig and painted eyebrows. There was no doubt that this was David Ferrie.

Ferrie and the other man, who was driving, stayed mainly in the car, which everyone recalled as a large black limousine. One after the other, the Clinton townsfolk described the driver as a tall, very distinguished man. His hair was described as gray or white. Everyone recalled his fancy manners, mentioning that whenever someone passed by the limousine, he nodded politely and said hello.

The town marshal suspected that the two might have been sent from the federal government to help black people register. He called in the limousine license plates to the state police and had them checked. The car, it turned out, was registered to the International Trade Mart, which Clay Shaw—obviously the tall, distinguished-looking man—happened to manage.

The weather was unexpectedly cool, perhaps an early harbinger of summer's end. However, the temperature of the townspeople was warmer than usual, superheated by the emotion of the situation. Everyone seemed to be on the lookout for strangers.

To the townspeople who kept glancing in their direction, Shaw and Ferrie must have presented an incongruous picture. Ferrie, with his wig and painted eyebrows, must have looked like a large, incredibly strange bird. Next to him, Shaw, chain-smoking cigarettes in his imperial manner, must have appeared even more debonaire than usual, even more out of place in this dusty small town. Yet, interestingly enough, Shaw, whose father was an agent for the U.S. Treasury Department, had been born in Kentwood and had grown up in Hammond, just 30 miles east of Clinton.

Those townsfolk who were not staring at the two men in the limousine must have stared long and hard at Lee Oswald. And several months later when the news flashed out that he had murdered the President, a number of them remembered him. Later, at Clay Shaw's trial in New Orleans, Edwin McGehee, the town barber, would recall on the witness stand the moment he saw Oswald for the first time. He had just turned off the air conditioning and opened the door to his barber shop when a young man walked in. Several months later, when the assassination occurred, he promptly recognized that same young man as Lee Harvey Oswald.

McGehee said that he gave Oswald a haircut, which took about 15 minutes, and Oswald showed him his Marine discharge card. Oswald then mentioned that he was trying to get a job at the hospital in nearby Jackson. When McGehee informed him that it was a mental hospital, Oswald seemed genuinely astonished, but continued to express interest in the job. McGehee suggested that he see Reeves Morgan, the state representative for the parish. He also suggested to Oswald that he might have a better chance of getting the job if he were a registered voter.

Oswald then went to Morgan's house. There was a chill in the air,

Morgan recalled, and he sat with Oswald in front of a new fire in the fireplace. He also told Oswald that he would have a better chance for the job if he registered as a voter in the parish. After the assassination he recognized Oswald from the pictures in the newspapers as the young man who had come to see him about the job.

By the time Sciambra and Lieutenant Frugé finished their work in Clinton, they had talked to more than 300 townspeople. After Sciambra returned to New Orleans, I assembled Frank Klein, Jim Alcock, and Lou Ivon in my office. I also called in D'Alton Williams in an effort to strengthen our loose handful of men working on the Kennedy case. D'Alton, unlike the other attorneys present, was not primarily a trial lawyer. His specialty was administrative supervision. However, he was exceedingly intelligent, he long had expressed interest in the project, and there simply were no more trial assistants I could remove from courtroom duty at that time.

As they gathered around the long table in the conference room, it occurred to me that for the first time since we had stumbled into this affair, we had what might be called "a team." We listened and asked questions while Andrew Sciambra reviewed his weeks in Clinton. Alcock wanted to know what conceivable objective could have been accomplished by getting Lee Oswald a job in the state mental hospital in Jackson—if indeed that had been the objective of Shaw and Ferrie. Sciambra replied that he had wondered the same thing. Remembering Oswald's surprise when the town barber informed him that the place was a mental institution, Sciambra had gone to Jackson to see whether or not Oswald had ever filed a job application there.

"And did he?" I asked.

Sciambra nodded. "Yes. I found the lady in personnel who interviewed him. But when she went to the files to get a copy of his application—which she remembers him filling out—it was gone."

By that time we had become so used to the systematic disappearance of evidence that no comment was necessary. The fact remained that Oswald had applied for a job at the mental institution, and that would have been all that his sponsors needed for another touch of sheepdipping. A few weeks of menial work there would have been enough to complete the picture of Oswald wandering haplessly from one job to another, each more obscure than the last. With a bit of luck and a little orchestration, it might even have been possible—with a switch of cards from "employee" to "patient"—to have the right psychiatrist at Jackson describe the problems he had in treating this strange outpatient named Lee Oswald.

Perhaps the most important result of the Clinton work was that we had succeeded in connecting David Ferrie and Clay Shaw. Knowing that Shaw and Ferrie were friends, or even more, that they were jointly engaged in some clandestine association, gave us a better chance to develop information. To investigate Shaw alone—a highly controlled, discreet man with powerful connections—would have been difficult. Now, however, we had found a handle on Shaw. His name was David Ferrie.

When I showed up at the Pere Marquette Building, Wray Gill came out to his waiting room to meet me. One of the city's best trial lawyers, Wray bowed and extended a welcome in his ornate fashion all the way back to his private office, which looked down on the winding Mississippi River, 18 floors below. I was there because David Ferrie had worked as a part-time investigator for Gill in 1962 and 1963.

In Gill's office I waved the small talk aside. "Wray," I said, "I need a favor from you."

"No problem," he replied.

"My intuition tells me that Dave Ferrie might have charged some long-distance calls on your phone when he was around here."

His white eyebrows rose up. "*Some* long distance calls? God almighty! The man almost bankrupted me."

"Can you give me copies of his calls?" I asked.

He sent his secretary to search the bills for 1962 and 1963.

"This is what we have, Mr. Gill," she said when she returned. "You let him go in January 1964. Remember?"

"How can I ever forget?" he muttered. He put his finger on the bill for that month. "I told Dave adios. I told him I could put up with his eccentricities, but not his long-distance calls."

Gill instructed his secretary to draw a penciled line through every call made by the office, leaving exposed the calls made by Ferrie. "They're easy to pick out," he said. "Those cities there didn't have a damned thing to do with this office. You know better than anyone that about ninety percent of my business is right here in New Orleans."

In the course of striking through the office calls, the secretary discovered that the bills for November 1963—the month of President Kennedy's assassination—were missing. She had no idea who had removed them but pointed out that Ferrie still had access to the office files then.

That night I began going through Ferrie's long-distance bills for 1962 and 1963. The first thing I noticed was their remarkable diversity. The calls were not only to many domestic cities but to such distant locales as Guatemala, Mexico, and Canada. Just whom he was calling could have been discovered in short order by a federal agency such as the F.B.I. with its resources and authority. But it had become apparent that no such agencies were going to be willing to help us out.

We had neither the telephone company connections nor the investigative staff to undertake the kind of broad-based, logical approach I would have chosen. Instead, I painstakingly collected and correlated all of the Warren Commission exhibits listing phone calls made by, to, or otherwise connected with witnesses encountered by the federal investigation.

After many evenings of comparing Ferrie's long-distance calls to those in the Commission exhibits, I made a connection. The local telephone bill indicated that one of Ferrie's calls had been made from New Orleans to Chicago on September 24, 1963. This was, according to the Warren Commission's later conclusion, the day before Lee Oswald left New Orleans. The number Ferrie called in Illinois that day was WH 4-4970. The local phone bill did not identify the recipient. Was Ferrie calling, perhaps, to report to some intermediary that the sheepdipping job had been completed or that "the kid is leaving New Orleans" or something of the sort?

In Commission exhibit number 2350 (page 335 of Volume XXV) I found a call made to exactly the same number: WH 4-4970 in Chicago, Illinois. Under Additional Information in the Commission volume was listed "Person call [sic] at 9:09 a.m. credit card used, Kansas City Missouri to Miss A. Asie Room 1405." That exhibit did not identify the caller. However, now at least I had someone's name to connect with the number Ferrie had called.

Some nights later I located Miss Asie—now spelled *Aase*—in Commission exhibit number 2266. There an F.B.I. report identified her more fully as "JEAN AASE" of Chicago, Illinois. The F.B.I. report, dated December 4, 1963, described how she had accompanied "LAWRENCE V. MEYERS" on a business trip to Dallas, Texas, where they arrived the evening of November 20, 1963—two days before President Kennedy's assassination. They checked into the Ramada Motel, the report continued, where they spent the night. On November 21 they moved to the Cabana Motel.

Aase then stated, according to the F.B.I. report, that on the evening of November 21, Meyers took her to the Carousel Club, where he introduced her to Jack Ruby and "the three of them sat at a table near the doorway and chatted."

Considering that Lee Oswald's New Orleans friend Dave Ferrie had called her Chicago number, I wondered if Miss Aase was later curious when Jack Ruby, her partner in casual conversation, killed Oswald three days later.

As I searched through the Warren Commission volumes, my confusion about Jean Aase increased. There had been no index to the testimony volumes to indicate that Jean Asie or Jean Aase existed. As for the exhibit volumes, there was no index to indicate the existence of *anyone*.

Then, in an F.B.I. interview with Lawrence Meyers, I found that she had become Jean *West*. I looked at the Warren Commission's discussion of Meyers. From his interview, Meyers certainly appeared to have been a fairly typical, successful, middle-class businessman. His daughter worked for the government nuclear reactor at Argonne, Illinois,* and his son was in Army Intelligence. As for Meyers's friendship with Jack Ruby, they had happened to meet a few years back—and Meyers had grown fond of the future murderer of Lee Oswald. The members of the Warren Commission were evidently satisfied with this testimony. Meyers was never asked whether or not he knew David Ferrie. Nor did he have anything to add about the mysterious Miss Aase.

---

* Argonne was established in 1946 for scientific research and the development of peaceful uses for nuclear energy. The Argonne National Laboratory is one of the largest scientific research and development centers in the United States. It is financed primarily by the United States Department of Energy.

Miss Aase, or Miss West, or whatever her name was, never appeared before the Warren Commission or gave a deposition to Commission lawyers. I did find a third F.B.I. mention of the mystery woman, this time described as "JEAN WEST," in the same Commission exhibits volume, but it added no illumination. She was not asked whether she knew David Ferrie or how he could have had access to the very phone number by which Meyers also later reached her. Nor did the report reveal a flicker of curiosity about her pre-assassination chat with Jack Ruby.

The timing of this woman's meeting (along with Lawrence V. Meyers) with Jack Ruby was provocative enough. However, the constant changing of her name, which would confuse anyone who wanted to know about her, confirmed for me that something about her—or her phone number—was suspicious.

As I puzzled over this perplexing problem, it suddenly occurred to me that I had stumbled across the use of a "message center"—a customary intelligence community device to throw off the would-be pursuer of a phone-call listing. And in this instance the message center apparently had resulted in a communication with Jack Ruby.

The use of message centers is standard operating procedure for any large government bureaucracy. The message center is so important to the Army, for example, that every unit—from an infantry division headquarters all the way down to a company headquarters—has one and would have difficulty functioning without one.

In the Army, a unit's message center invariably is located by the nearest road of approach and identified for message couriers by a small sign alongside the road. On the other hand, American domestic intelligence does not like to advertise. So shy is it, in fact, that it claims it does not even exist. Nevertheless, its agents also have a need to communicate, and quite often, especially where the circumstances are delicate, they want to obtain *indirection* as well—as appears to have been the case where Jean West, who was contacted by Ferrie, ended up the day before the assassination talking to Jack Ruby.

The time had come for some brainstorming about clandestine message centers, so I got the team together at the office. I used a blackboard to illustrate the routing I had stumbled across: Ferrie calling to West's Chicago telephone; West and Meyers flying to Dallas on

November 20; West and Meyers meeting with Ruby the day before the assassination.

D'Alton Williams, our newest recruit, pointed to the diagram. "Your message center idea looks like a probability to me," he said. "But I think the picture could be made clearer."

We waited for D'Alton to continue.

"Ruby was from Chicago, wasn't he?" he asked.

"Sure," I replied, "and so were Jean West and Lawrence Meyers. Some of these people must have known each other. That's what makes the message center fit so well."

"But there's one problem," said D'Alton. "What if we're dealing with a C.I.A. message center here? Dave Ferrie obviously didn't have enough status to be deciding what message was going to be sent and where. Remember we're assuming this communication went right on through to Jack Ruby."

"Ruby wasn't that much," interjected Ivon.

"That's not D'Alton's point," Klein said. "He's saying that some-one—like the original instigator of the message—knew what was on the schedule for Ruby."

"Right," said D'Alton. "So why don't we start off asking ourselves who Dave Ferrie's boss was."

He paused, then asked innocently, "Didn't Guy Banister used to be the head of the Chicago office of the F.B.I.?"

"I'll be damned," said Ivon. "Chicago to Chicago all the way through to Chicago."

"Do I get a gold star," asked D'Alton, "for figuring out that Guy Banister probably knew Jack Ruby?"

"No," I replied, "because Ruby left Chicago for the Air Force in the late 1940s and there's nothing to indicate that Banister knew Ruby that early. But you get a silver star."

I walked over to the blackboard, scratched out Ferrie's name, and replaced it with Banister's.

"The *probability*," I went on, "is that, with their Chicago connec-tions, they knew some of the same people there."

"But how do we get to know for sure," asked Alcock, nodding toward the blackboard, "that our message center up there is the real thing?" That was standard Jim Alcock. He was always unhappy with uncertainty.

"I don't know," I said. "For now, all we have is a model of a message center. We'll just have to work with that."

About this time, in early 1967, we had an unexpected lucky break. Dick Billings, an editor from *Life* magazine, arrived at the office. He was a slender man with a quick mind and delightful wit. After talking with me at some length, he informed me confidentially that the top management at *Life* had concluded that President Kennedy's assassination had been a conspiracy and that my investigation was moving in the right direction. Inasmuch as *Life* was conducting its own investigation, Billings suggested that we work together. The magazine would be able to provide me with technical assistance, and we could develop a mutual exchange of information.

The offer came at a good time. I had been wanting to increase my stakeout coverage of David Ferrie's home but did not have the personnel to spare, particularly an expert photographer. We had succeeded in establishing a friendly relationship with the couple who lived directly across the street from Ferrie on Louisiana Avenue Parkway. Like him, they lived on the second floor of a duplex and also had a screened porch in the front. I described this situation to the *Life* editor, and within days a top-flight photographer arrived in town. We promptly installed him at his observation post on the second-floor porch across the street.

Meanwhile, out at New Orleans Lakefront Airport, Lou Ivon had located a former airplane mechanic of Ferrie's named Jimmy Johnson and had persuaded him to go back to work for Ferrie but to keep contact with our office. This airport stakeout on Ferrie produced an early dividend. Ferrie told Johnson that a package would be arriving for him shortly. A white compact sports car would be parked squarely in front of the airport administration building, with the windows up but with the door unlocked. Ferrie asked Johnson to check every ten or fifteen minutes to see whether such a car had arrived. When it did, he said, Johnson was to reach under the front seat where he would find— taped to the bottom of the seat—a brown package, which he was to bring to Ferrie.

The car arrived, and Johnson followed the instructions. When Johnson brought the package into the administration building, Ferrie took it to the bathroom to examine the contents. He came out full of excitement and announced that he was going to buy a brand new car.

This cash apparently coming to Ferrie from a mysterious source only made more intriguing another fact that Jim Alcock had uncovered. By serving a subpoena on Ferrie's bank, Alcock found that Ferrie had deposited more than $7,000 in cash to his account in the weeks immediately preceding Kennedy's assassination.

One other lead about Ferrie yielded some provocative information. Ferrie, once a pilot for Eastern Airlines, had been investigated by a private detective agency. I obtained a copy of its report. The investigators had maintained a stakeout near his residence and found that Ferrie was visited frequently by a man named Dante Marachini.

A simple check of the phone book revealed that Dante Marachini resided at 1309 Dauphine Street. This was extremely interesting to me because right next door was the home of Clay Shaw. I wondered who else might be living next door to Shaw. Reaching for the red book (which lists individuals by address) I found that also living at 1309 Dauphine Street was a man named James Lewallen. I recalled from earlier research that James Lewallen had once shared an apartment with David Ferrie in the vicinity of Kenner, a New Orleans suburb.

Now I found myself looking at two unfamiliar names, Marachini and Lewallen, both of whom had in the past been associated with Ferrie and both of whom now lived next door to Clay Shaw. That was something to think about.

Some time later, I came across the name of Dante Marachini again. I had wanted to talk to individuals at the Reily Coffee Company who had worked with Lee Oswald or at a level immediately above him, so I sent Frank Klein over to the company to get their names and respective positions.

He returned rather quickly. "They're all gone," he said. "Anyone who ever had any connection with Lee Oswald left the Reily Company within a few weeks after Oswald did." He laid a sheet of paper in front of me. "Here are the names and the new jobs."

I glanced down at the list. One name jumped out at me immediately: Dante Marachini. He had begun work at the Reily Coffee

Company on exactly the same day as Oswald. Several weeks after Oswald's departure, Marachini also left the coffee company and began life anew at the Chrysler Aerospace Division at the National Aeronautics and Space Administration (NASA), on the eastern side of New Orleans.

I then noticed that Alfred Claude, who hired Oswald for Reily, had also gone to work for the Chrysler Aerospace Division.

Then I saw that John Branyon, who had worked with Oswald at the coffee company, had left for a job at NASA.

At just about the same time, Emmett Barbee, Oswald's immediate boss at Reily, left the coffee company and also inaugurated a new career with NASA.

After seeing what happened to all of these men associated with Oswald at the coffee company and after seeing Marachini's name again, my curiosity about 1309 Dauphine Street returned. I called Lou Ivon in and asked him to find out if James Lewallen, David Ferrie's former apartment mate who now resided at 1309 Dauphine Street, had been as fortunate as some of the workers at Reily had been. It took Ivon a couple of days, but he came back with a now fairly predictable piece of information: Lewallen had gone to work for Boeing out at NASA. Lou and I kicked this interesting situation around a bit, and then we both became curious about what had happened to Melvin Coffee, who had accompanied David Ferrie to Texas on the eve of the assassination.

Ivon was back the next day. Melvin Coffee had been hired by the Aerospace Operation at Cape Canaveral.

Perhaps it was mere coincidence that all these men associated with David Ferrie, Clay Shaw, and Lee Oswald ended up working for NASA, but I doubted it. I knew by now that when a group of individuals gravitated toward one another for no apparent reason, or a group of individuals inexplicably headed in the same direction as if drawn by a magnetic field, or coincidence piled on coincidence too many times, as often as not the shadowy outlines of a covert intelligence operation were somehow becoming visible.

9

The Bonds
of Friendship

I N C L I N T O N our investigation had established a clear link between Clay Shaw and David Ferrie. But we faced a real communications problem. Would most people believe that the urbane, sophisticated Clay Shaw even knew the disheveled, bizarre David Ferrie, much less that he would consort with him? These two men of such disparate personalities not only worked together but were also the closest of friends. The only way to prove this to skeptics was to find more witnesses who knew the odd pair. This we did over a period of months.

One important witness was Jules Ricco Kimble, a member of far-right groups like the Minutemen and the Ku Klux Klan, whose name also surfaced later in relation to the slaying of Martin Luther King, Jr.* A youngster in his teens in late 1960 or early 1961, Kimble was drinking at the Golden Lantern, one of the bistros located deep in the Vieux Carré, when Dave Ferrie introduced him to Clay Shaw. After that, recalled Kimble, he saw Shaw on various occasions. One day in

---

* Kimble was alleged to have known James Earl Ray in Canada, but this was never demonstrated.

late 1961 or early 1962, he received a phone call from Ferrie, who asked if he would like to take an overnight plane trip with him. Kimble was agreeable; he met Ferrie at the airport and at that time learned that Shaw was coming along. They were going to fly to Canada to pick someone up.

Kimble remembered Shaw as seated in the back of the airplane during the trip and either sleeping or thumbing through a book. He also recalled that Shaw carried a brown briefcase with him.

Ferrie landed the plane in Nashville, Tennessee, Louisville, Kentucky, and Toronto, Canada, to gas up, using a Gulf credit card. The final stop was Montreal. Kimble and Ferrie stayed overnight in a hotel in Dorval right outside of Montreal.* Shaw disappeared after they landed, and they did not see him until the next morning at about eight o'clock, the agreed-upon time for departure to New Orleans.

When Shaw arrived back at the plane, as Kimble recalled, he had a "Mexican or Cuban" with him. He described the man as heavy-set, dark-skinned, balding in the front, and in his early or middle thirties. Shaw and the Latin man sat in the back of the airplane together, and the latter spoke to Shaw only in broken English. Kimble described the plane as a Cessna 172, which he thought belonged to a friend of Ferrie's. When they arrived back at the New Orleans Lakefront Airport, Kimble said, they all climbed into his automobile and he drove them into town. About a month or so later, he got another phone call from Ferrie asking if he wanted to make a similar trip back to Canada, but this time he declined.

There were a couple of interesting aspects to this tale. First, Shaw was known to have a fear of flying. Yet here he was in a small Cessna on a long journey. This might well have indicated a more than routine mission for which Shaw felt personally responsible. Second, Ferrie never filed flight plans, so conveniently for Shaw there was no record of this trip or any other he may have made with Ferrie.

Kimble's statement did not end there. He said that he had seen Shaw on different occasions in barrooms and at the International Trade Mart in New Orleans, which Shaw directed. Kimble had heard other

* It may be recalled that Montreal was the hometown of Major L.M. Bloomfield, like Shaw a member of the twin international intelligence combines, the Centro Mondiale Commerciale (World Trade Center) and Permindex. See Chapter 6.

people introduce Clay Shaw as Clay Bertrand, but he had never been introduced to him as Clay Bertrand.

During the period of his association with Ferrie and Shaw, Kimble related, contacts were developed for him with several C.I.A. agents. Their names, as he recalled, were Steinmeyer, who, he informed members of my staff, had since been transferred to Texas; Natt Brown, who still was in New Orleans at the time of Kimble's statement; and a third agent called Red, whose last name he did not know. Kimble used to meet with them in motel rooms, where he would give them reports, pictures, and recordings, and would receive in exchange his paycheck or cash, for which he would sign a voucher. These agents, he added, would often mail instructions to him at his post office box, number 701-30252, at the main office on Lafayette Street.*

There were other occasions when Shaw and Ferrie were observed in each other's company. For example, Ferrie had introduced a young friend of his, David Logan, to Shaw at Dixie's, a watering hole on Bourbon Street at the corner of St. Peter. Earlier Ferrie had brought Logan to a bar called the Galley House, on the corner of Toulouse and Chartres Street, where they also met Shaw. Once again while with Ferrie, Logan met Shaw at a private party on Governor Nichols Street. As a result of these meetings, the young man came to know Shaw quite well and was invited for dinner at Shaw's elegant carriage house at 1313 Dauphine Street. Logan recalled that dinner was served by a uniformed waiter, with each of them sitting at opposite ends of a nine-foot table. Evidently Shaw's passion for grandeur never left him.

In a quite different situation, Nicholas Tadin, the chief of a local musicians' union, and his wife, Mathilda, went out to New Orleans Airport one weekend afternoon to talk to David Ferrie about giving flying lessons to their son. (Ferrie was then operating a flight school.) After they had parked their car, they saw Ferrie coming out of the hangar talking to Clay Shaw. When Shaw turned away from the Tadins and walked to his car, Ferrie waved at him. Mrs. Tadin asked who Ferrie's visitor was, and her husband, who had seen Shaw on previous occasions, informed her that he was the director of the International Trade Mart.

* This was the post office at which Kerry Thornley and so many of the young men who went in and out of Guy Banister's office had postal box keys.

Another individual we located who had met Clay Shaw through David Ferrie was Raymond Broshears, a long-time friend of Ferrie's who occasionally drifted into town from Long Beach, California. We caught up with Broshears, a talkative fellow, some time after Ferrie's death. It was back in 1965, he told us, at Dixie's bar, sufficiently off the beaten path and deep enough in the Vieux Carré for Shaw to be comfortable, where Broshears first met Shaw. Later that evening, on one of the few occasions when Shaw publicly had dinner at a restaurant with Ferrie, Shaw went home and changed from his sport clothes into less casual attire, meeting the other two at the restaurant. Broshears described him as dressed in a "beautiful" gray suit.

On another occasion, Broshears was with Ferrie at a sidewalk cafe on Bourbon Street when Shaw was driven up in a large black chauffeured car. Broshears recalled that Ferrie went over and had a brief conversation with Shaw before the latter was driven off.

Broshears saw Ferrie and Shaw together another time on the corner of Dauphine Street and another French Quarter cross-street that Broshears could not remember. Ferrie brought him to the corner and indicated that they were waiting for Shaw to come by. Shaw drove up, again in an imposing black car, and handed Ferrie a large brown envelope. Then, glancing in Broshears' direction, Shaw informed Ferrie that the F.B.I. was looking for Broshears. After Shaw drove off, Ferrie opened the envelope, which contained cash, and gave Broshears some of the money inside.

Ferrie would never discuss his connection with President Kennedy's assassination, Broshears said, except when he was intoxicated. When he became sufficiently drunk, however, he went to great pains to emphasize that his role had been marginal. He invariably added that providing a service connected with an assassination did not really constitute participation in the assassination.

Over a period of months Ferrie got to know Broshears better and told him more. According to Broshears, Ferrie had driven to Houston, Texas, on the afternoon of the assassination. His assignment was to wait there until he was joined by two members of the assassination team from Dallas. These two men were scheduled to arrive in a single-engine plane piloted by one of the assassins, a man named Carlos, whom Ferrie knew well. Once out of the Dallas area, a twin-engine plane was regarded as more practical, and that was where Ferrie was to have come in. He had been assigned to pick up the two members of the team after the single-engine plane arrived in Houston, thereupon flying them on to a more distant location.

Ferrie said that he had done everything he was supposed to, including going to the ice-skating rink in Houston and waiting for Carlos, but Carlos failed to show up. Broshears at first thought that Ferrie was making this up.

In time, as Ferrie would get drunk and describe again his waiting for Carlos at the ice-skating rink in Houston, Broshears realized that Ferrie was not making it up. It developed that there had been a last-minute change in the departure plans for these two particular members of the assassination team.

Ferrie never revealed to Broshears who gave him his orders. But he left no doubt that he did not consider Carlos qualified to fly any aircraft with a higher rating than single engine. He described Carlos as a Cuban exile, like the other member of the assassination team who had been assigned to arrive in Houston with him. Ferrie had met them both in New Orleans. They were convinced that President Kennedy had sold them out to the communists.

Or so Broshears stated. I had been leery from the outset of details about the assassination volunteered by individuals. I was more interested in bringing into focus the *forces* involved. However, I could not ignore the detail about the Cubans Ferrie said he had met in New Orleans. Ferrie, I knew, had been the guerrilla instructor for Guy Banister and his mix of Americans and Cubans at the training camp north of Lake Pontchartrain. And so this contribution of Broshears's fit the developing picture. I had three separate statements taken from Broshears. There was little variation in detail from one to the next.

As we gathered these statements from Broshears and the other witnesses, we had no idea that Shaw and Ferrie were aware of our investigation and were continuing to meet and plan together in hopes of heading it off. But in September 1967, a man who had spent a number of evenings being courted for his services by Shaw and Ferrie found his way to my office and gave an extensive statement about the pair's activities to Jim Alcock.

Edward Whalen, from Philadelphia, Pennsylvania, was a professional criminal. He had spent most of his adult life in the penitentiary. A friend he would not name got Ferrie on the phone with Whalen in early 1967 in Columbus, Ohio, where Whalen was at least temporarily "at liberty." Ferrie asked Whalen to join him in New Orleans. Whalen learned that big money was to be made by hitting the Jung Hotel and the small jewelry store at the intersection of Baronne and Gravier streets.

Whalen, having recently stolen a new car in Columbus, drove down to New Orleans. He abandoned his recent acquisition on some side street and met Ferrie at the Absinthe House on Bourbon Street. Ferrie, who was wearing his usual eye-catching second-hand threads, appeared intoxicated to Whalen. Whalen pulled up a chair and joined him at the table.

Ferrie began the meeting with a discussion of his flying ability. Not a sentimental man, Whalen cut Ferrie short and said that he needed money because he was on the run from the police. Ferrie assured him that he could earn a large sum of money and, if need be, he himself would fly Whalen out of the country. In this first conversation, which lasted about half an hour, Ferrie did not tell Whalen the details of his plan.

After this meeting, Whalen spent the night at an apartment provided by Ferrie. Ferrie also provided Whalen with a black Ford, a little the worse for wear, for his use while he was in town. It was agreed that the next night Whalen was to meet Ferrie and someone else at the Absinthe House.

Whalen arrived at the Absinthe House first. Shortly thereafter, Ferrie arrived with another man, who was introduced as Clay Bertrand. Ferrie did most of the talking, while Whalen, sizing him up, remained silent. From time to time Ferrie referred to the other man, who from the description was obviously Clay Shaw, as Clay Bertrand. Shaw became nettled but said nothing directly to Ferrie.

Upon leaving the Absinthe House, the three of them drove to Ferrie's apartment on Louisiana Avenue Parkway, which Whalen accurately described down to the shabby furniture.

There Ferrie finally got around to the point. He and Shaw wanted someone killed. Shaw was going to advance $10,000 to Whalen before the job. After it was completed, Whalen would receive another $15,000, Shaw would provide him with a phony passport, and Ferrie would fly him to Mexico. Shaw said the intended victim was going to be a witness against him for something that had been done in the past and that if this man was not stopped, Shaw would end up in the penitentiary for a long time. The victim's name was not mentioned at this time. Whalen was wary of the deal, but he pretended to string along. Before he left, Shaw gave him $300 spending money. Whalen spent that night at a motel on Tulane Avenue. He did not use his real name on the register but could not remember the one he used.

The next day Ferrie met Whalen at Moran's restaurant. After breakfast Ferrie suggested they take a ride. While they were in the car, Ferrie asked him if he had ever heard of Jim Garrison. Whalen said he had not. Ferrie then told Whalen that Garrison was the district attorney and that this was the man they wanted killed. Now Whalen finally told Ferrie he wanted nothing to do with the deal. Ferrie attempted to talk him into going through with the plan, but Whalen refused. They parted with the agreement to meet the next night at the Absinthe House. Whalen spent that night at a motel on Airline Highway. He did not remember the name of the motel or the name under which he had registered.

Whalen and Ferrie met at the Absinthe House the next night as planned. From there, they went directly to Shaw's apartment on Dauphine Street. Whalen recalled that the apartment was on the first floor and that the interior was extremely lavish.

At first only Shaw, Ferrie, and Whalen were in the apartment, and Shaw and Ferrie were trying to persuade Whalen to go through with the plan. After about a half hour, a short fat man wearing dark glasses wandered in. Shaw introduced him as Dean Andrews. Andrews and Shaw conversed for awhile away from Ferrie and Whalen, and shortly thereafter Andrews left the apartment.

Shaw then turned to Whalen and continued to try to persuade him. Shaw said he had done some checking on Whalen and he knew that Whalen's daughter suffered from polio. Shaw said that if Whalen would go through with the plan, he would get Whalen's daughter the finest medical treatment money could buy and also see to it that she was sent to college. However, Whalen insisted that he would not kill a district attorney, and he and Ferrie left.

Once outside, Ferrie told Whalen he was making a mistake; Clay Bertrand, he said, could do a lot for him. Also, Ferrie spoke of Lee Oswald for the first time. He said that Bertrand had done a lot for Oswald and that it was only because Oswald had fouled up that he was killed. Oswald was an agent of the Central Intelligence Agency, Ferrie claimed, and had received money from him and Shaw at one time. Ferrie also said that they had been given "inside" information from Dean Andrews that Jim Garrison was about to start an investigation into the assassination of President Kennedy. Ferrie boasted that he had set up the assassination of Kennedy and mentioned the names of other important people he claimed to know. Whalen said he did not believe these statements, which he regarded as name-dropping in an attempt to get him to change his mind. Whalen insisted he wanted nothing to do with the plan, and he left.

Except for a tendency to be vague about dates and times, Edward Whalen, in my judgment, had given a very accurate statement to Jim Alcock. Particularly persuasive to me was Whalen's knowledge that Dean Andrews had tipped off Shaw and Ferrie about my impending investigation. At the time of Whalen's meetings with Shaw and Ferrie, the only person outside of my immediate staff whom I had told about the investigation was none other than Dean Andrews at our memorable lunch.

I was surprised to learn that I had become a target for removal. But looking back on our investigation, a little gain here, a little gain there, I found it easy to put myself in the place of Shaw and Ferrie. Their desperation, especially after my conversation with Dean Andrews at Broussard's restaurant, was perfectly understandable. But it did not scare me, and it certainly did not stop me. I have always been constitutionally unable to back away from a confrontation. To me, what was happening in my life was a sort of continuation of World War II, except that it was a different kind of combat—and a different enemy. As far as I was concerned, Shaw and Ferrie and whoever was behind them would have to back up before I did.

Shaw well may have had the C.I.A. connections to request that I be eliminated. But the Agency, I had realized by then, had more subtle and sophisticated ways to deal with any threat from me. My guess was that in contacting Whalen, Shaw and Ferrie had created a rogue operation of their own as a solution to their legal problems.

Our investigation had spent months discovering numerous witnesses who had positively linked Shaw and Ferrie together. We still did not know precisely what they had been up to. But if they had reached the point of hiring a hit man to kill me, it had to be something pretty heavy.

10

The Ides
of February

I SHOULD HAVE KNOWN that things had been going
too well for us. Since that lucky weekend when I stumbled on the fact
that Oswald's rubber-stamped address, 544 Camp Street, happened to
be located in the very heart of the local intelligence community, we had
found crucial evidence and witnesses that the Warren Commission and
the media, whether intentionally or not, had ignored. Stumbling from
one unpredictable discovery to another, we had managed to move
steadily forward.

But now the Ides of February arrived, or so we would describe it
until even darker days, yet to come, wiped out this briefly meaningful
title. Internal problems had developed and were beginning to hold
back the investigation.

From the very outset, the two most dynamic individuals in my office
were Frank Klein, my chief assistant D.A., and Pershing Gervais, my
chief investigator. Klein had a first-rate legal mind, meticulous and
precise. A blue-eyed, blond-haired man who took great pride in his
German blood, he believed strongly in discipline and loyalty. His

emphasis on order, system, and responsibility, and his attention to detail were the primary reasons for my prompt appointment of him to the number two position in the D.A.'s office.

Pershing Gervais was totally different from Klein not only in appearance but in background and values. Like Klein, he was highly intelligent and had a sense of humor as quick as a lightning bolt, but there all similarity ended. Whereas Klein tended to be stolid, Gervais was mercurial. Of French extraction, he was black-haired, dark-eyed, restless. His temper was volatile, at times explosive.

Perhaps the greatest difference between the two men was revealed in their attitudes toward authority. Klein tended to welcome it, to support it, to see it as a kind of mortar which held things together. Gervais, on the other hand, was deeply suspicious of it. He tended to distrust it until he had tested it. And even more deeply, so deeply that I could not see it until it was much too late, he was drawn in an animalistic sense toward rebellion—almost for the sake of rebellion.

I had known Gervais since 1941, when we had gone into the Army together as members of the Washington artillery unit of the National Guard. During World War II we had served together on the big guns (155 mm. Howitzers), and together we had gradually risen to become sergeants. By the time I left our unit to go to officers training school, we had become fast and firm friends.

Many years later, when I was elected district attorney, I put this old friend at the head of my investigative staff for routine investigations—which is to say, violations of the law in rackets where citizens might be bilked.* I knew then that he had been involved in some questionable activities years before when he was an officer in the notoriously crooked New Orleans Police Department. But Gervais's testimony had contributed substantially to ending the era of police corruption in the city, and by the time I appointed him, he had become an undercover source of information for the Metropolitan Crime Commission. I felt that a completely honest, "square" D.A.'s office like ours could use a man like Gervais who had once gone wrong and was "born again." We needed some firsthand knowledge of the hidden underworld of the city, and

* At no time was Gervais ever involved in investigating the murder of President Kennedy. He was never even a member of the special team.

Gervais seemed to know what was happening everywhere from Bourbon Street to the farflung edges of town.

I was sworn in at the beginning of 1962, and I recall nothing during our first years in office to indicate that my top assistant district attorney and my chief investigator did not get along. During that time, Gervais had been a virtual tourguide for us as we began to strike at the strip joints, gambling operations, and other racketeer activities that had become synonymous with New Orleans. We hit the B-drinking joints, which were shaking down tourists and offering prostitutes in the back booths. We closed down the last house of prostitution in New Orleans. For the first time in over a century, we ended the lottery operation which had fed upon the poor people of the city. The combination of Klein's efficiency and Gervais's knowledge helped accomplish all this.

By 1966, even as I did become aware of personal differences between Klein and Gervais, I regarded this as a solvable problem. But once we began the Kennedy investigation, the conflict between them escalated. I knew from talking to Gervais that he was indifferent to the assassination. What I did not know at the time, though, was that ever since late 1966 Gervais had been pressuring Klein to try to get me to stop the Kennedy investigation. Klein, who shared my passion for getting at the truth in the case, resented Gervais's intrusions.

I found out just how deep the division was between the two men one weekend afternoon in mid-February 1967. I was returning to the office tired and dusty after three days of special duty with the National Guard at an Army Division staff exercise. Still in my Army field uniform, I found on top of my desk a short note from Frank Klein. The thrust of it was that he could no longer tolerate serving in the same outfit as Pershing Gervais. He said he was informing me reluctantly that if I did not drop Gervais, he would resign. I had to make a choice.

I am afraid that I was very much conditioned from my years in the Army, and one thing that a commander absolutely never allowed was an ultimatum to be issued to him from a lower-ranking officer. I put down the letter, walked to my filing cabinet, and pulled out the evaluations of the work of my various assistant district attorneys. I found that one of the trial attorneys, Charles Ward, stuck out because of his effective record in court. I phoned him and offered him Klein's position. Although surprised, he accepted. With that, I gathered up the rest of my mail from my desk and drove home.

I dismissed the matter from my mind, satisfied that I had handled it the only way an administrator could, and was unaware of what I had really done until I awoke the next morning. Then, however, I realized that my knee-jerk military response had resulted in my letting go the single most important man to our investigation, our best mind.

Within a few days my sense overcame my pride. I called Frank Klein and suggested that we meet for lunch. He was the same old Frank, a little disappointed in me but understanding my reluctance to make a decision based on personalities. I admitted that I had made a mistake, and asked him to return to the office, but he refused as long as Gervais was there. Why he did not tell me then about Gervais's pressure to end the Kennedy inquiry I will never know. But Frank left no doubt about his own continued dedication to the investigation.

I indicated to him that I would find a *modus operandi* which would permit him to continue to be a part of the Kennedy investigation. What we worked out before we parted was that initially he would keep in touch with me or others in the office through Lou Ivon.* And there the lunch ended, curiously enough, with Frank Klein and I as close friends as ever.

As for Pershing Gervais, he remained on as chief investigator for the time being. An old service buddy blinded by sentimentality, I had no idea until it was much too late what his love of money eventually would drive him to. (See Chapter 19.)

Shortly afterwards, on February 17, 1967, I was jolted again. That was the unforgettable day the *New Orleans States-Item* broke its "big story." Jim Alcock was in the midst of showing me how we could use computers to monitor our case load and cut our operating costs when a grim-faced Lou Ivon burst into my office. He ceremoniously laid a copy of the newspaper in front of us. "Happy Valentine's Day!" he said.

Although I knew such a story was coming because a reporter had

---

* Later, when important decisions needed to be made, we would call Frank, and he would meet the rest of the special team at the board room of the New Orleans Athletic Club, participating every bit as much as if he were still with the office.

contacted me, the headlines and leading paragraphs hit me in the face like ice water.

DA HERE LAUNCHES FULL JFK DEATH PLOT PROBE

**Mysterious Trips
Cost Large Sums**

The Orleans Parish district attorney's office has launched an intensive investigation into the circumstances surrounding the assassination of President John F. Kennedy.

The States-Item has learned that the DA's office is pouring out-of-the-ordinary sums of money into a probe of a possible assassination plot.

Dist. Atty. Jim Garrison refused to confirm or deny the existence of such an investigation or to discuss information received by the States-Item. . . .

Trial assistants and investigators assigned to the DA have spent more than $8,000 on unexplained travel and "investigative expenses" in the period since Nov. 25, 1966.

"Damn it to hell," muttered Alcock. For Jim, who confined any displays of anger to courtroom confrontations, this was close to a deckhand's profanity.

"I wonder if those guys dream," growled Lou Ivon, "of how much they've gotten for that $8,000."

We continued to read in silence. The reporter, Rosemary James, having sensed that our office was up to something, had gone through our vouchers requesting judicial approval for withdrawals from our fines and fees account. This was how we had been financing our investigation. We had operated as secretly as possible, assuming this was the most efficient and responsible way to handle such a potentially explosive situation. However, the voucher requests were public records, so they could not legally be concealed.

Finished with the story, Ivon and Alcock shoved their newspapers aside. They were looking at me for my reaction.

I glanced briefly at each of them, saw the anger in their eyes. They expected my contribution of fury.

I shrugged my shoulders.

"That's *it?*" Ivon exploded.

"They hunted down the news," I said calmly. "That's their business. In any event, getting angry doesn't accomplish a damn thing."

Jim Alcock stared in disbelief. "Excuse me a moment," he said. "I've got to go outside and take another look at the front door. I think I might have wandered into the wrong D.A.'s office."

The next morning, coming down Broad Street toward Tulane Avenue, I could see the media people piling on top of each other, trying to get through the narrow entrance to the second floor of the Criminal District Court Building where our office was. I told my driver to circle around the huge, fortress-like structure and come in the other entrance by the coroner's office. This led us to the unmarked door in the basement where the small elevator went straight up to the private bathroom in my office. In my 12 years as district attorney, the press never was able to figure out how I got into my office when they had all the entrances covered.

The early edition of the paper was on my desk, and I immediately began reading the editorial entitled "Garrison Plot Probe." It reminded readers that the federal government had already thoroughly looked into the matter, and then, about halfway through, I saw these words:

> Mr. Garrison's own silence on the subject has itself raised some interesting questions, particularly since more than $8,000 has been spent on unexplained travel and "investigative expenses" since last Nov. 25.
>
> Has the district attorney uncovered some valuable additional evidence or is he merely saving some interesting new information which will gain for him exposure in a national magazine?
>
> Mr. Garrison, it seems, should have some explanation.

I read these lines several times. For a brief moment I thought about throwing the paper up in the air and walking out of the office for good, without a backward glance. Then I reached for one of the long, gold pens from the office set that had been given to me when I was first elected. As Ivon and Alcock sat around me in silence, I carefully bent the pen into a perfect "U". Then, without a word, I dropped it into the wastebasket.

"Is it my imagination," asked Ivon, "or didn't someone tell us yesterday that getting mad didn't accomplish anything?"

"That was yesterday," I said.

Mad hardly was the word for what I felt. Until that moment I had hoped, in spite of continuing signs to the contrary, that the media would understand what I was about, what I was trying to do. More important, I had assumed that they sensed—and cared—that there was something terribly wrong with the Warren Commission's impossible conclusions. Now I saw how naive I had been.

My secretary's voice came over the intercom on my desk. "Mr. Garrison," she said, "I have to tell the press something. They're really piling up outside in the hall. They say they need a statement from you."

"Tell them they got their statement yesterday. It was on the front page of the *States-Item*."

I filled a briefcase full of reference books. Then I took the bathroom elevator express and headed home for an afternoon of uninterrupted work.

Immediately following the *States-Item* articles came a deluge of publicity. I was inundated with requests for interviews. People on the street stopped me day after day. Letters of support arrived at the office from all over the world. Apparently public skepticism about the Warren Commission's official story was far deeper and more widespread than I had realized. The mere fact that I, as an elected official, shared that skepticism and was willing to act on it had sparked a public response the like of which I had never seen.

An unusually strong letter of support came from John Miller, who described himself as an oil man from Denver. It arrived on elegant pale blue stationery, with the small embossed inscription "oil and gas" beneath the name, and hinted that Miller wanted to offer the office financial help to continue our investigation.

Soon Miller came down from Denver. When he arrived, the receptionist brought him back to my office, where Andrew Sciambra and I were waiting.

Our visitor wore a well-cut gabardine suit which had not come off any department store rack. He was a self-assured, impressive man a few years older than I.

Sharon, my secretary, brought coffee for everyone. He savored his. "Your coffee's almost Turkish down here," he said. "But I think I could get used to it very quickly."

Then he turned his attention to me. "You know," he said, "I've been an admirer of your office for a long time now."

He seemed to have no objection to Sciambra's presence—he had not even acknowledged it—so I indicated to Andrew that he should stay.

I had gathered some newly treated photographs to show to Miller. They revealed the shooting of President Kennedy in precise, heart-rending detail. After the small talk was over, I held one out for him to see.

"These have been enlarged," I said, "but they have been specially treated so they show much of the original detail."

"Splendid," he said. "I'd love to see them."

But by this time he was on the other side of the room, picking up some of my war photographs from the credenza.

"Where were you?" he asked. "Europe or the Pacific?"

"Germany," I replied.

"You were lucky," he said. "I spent three years in the Pacific."

"I doubt if you've ever seen these blow-ups before," I said, reaching for some others to show him as well. "We just got them yesterday from New York."

Now our visitor was at the window. He separated some of the blinds so that he could look down on Tulane Avenue.

"I've never seen an avenue," he said, "with such a profusion of bail-bonding companies. Why is that?"

"I imagine it's because this is the Criminal District Court Building," I replied, becoming a little nettled. I had never had a visitor with such mobility.

"All those little places, all that clutter of signs. They make that entire avenue look like a side street."

He had happened to wander back near my desk. I held up the large photograph showing the moment of the fatal shot and, leaning forward, thrust it into his hand. "You may want to see this one," I said. "In this enlargement the explosion looks like it actually was caused by a frangible bullet."

"I know about that shot," he said. He laid the picture back on my desk. "A terrible tragedy."

He leaned across my desk and slid all of the enlarged photographs over to one side. He stacked them neatly in a pile. Then he sat down and faced me. "You don't have to show me these things," he said with a wave of the hand. "It's perfectly obvious to me that you have conducted a most effective investigation, considering your resources."

He studied me reflectively, his fingertips touching together. "I notice where the local press has been working you over the last few days," he said. "Isn't that going to hurt you?"

"Without any question," I responded.

"How much do you have for carrying on your investigation?"

"If you must know," I said, a little unprepared for his sudden assertiveness, "virtually nothing."

"How many men are working with you on this?"

"Less than you would guess," I said. "Most days two assistant D.A.'s, occasionally three. And a handful of police investigators."

"That's all you've had all this time?" he said in disbelief.

"That's it."

"Then how did you manage to make your way into Guy Banister's operation?" he asked.

I hesitated. There had been nothing about Guy Banister in the *States-Item* story. Nor had I mentioned Guy Banister. This man had just told me a great deal more than he reasonably should have known. I could feel Andrew Sciambra's eyes on me, but I did not look back his way. "Shoe leather," I said as casually as possible. I sat back and waited for Miller's next move. Now I was alert and suddenly very curious about why he really was there.

He stood up once more and was pacing the room, only this time more slowly. He continued to ignore Sciambra as if he were a piece of furniture. This was fine with Andrew, who was watching the man quite openly now. Finally Miller spoke up.

"I'm going to be very frank with you," he said. "You've done a great job, an astounding job considering the limited resources available to you. But the best you can ever hope for is to stir up a lot of confusion. You're not going to do this country any good, and you're not going to do yourself any good."

He came back to his seat and sat down, now looking directly at me. I said nothing.

"You don't belong here," he continued. "You're too big for this job. On this Mickey Mouse street with that cluster of bail-bond shops lined up across the way."

"The job manages to keep me pretty busy," I said.

"Nonsense. You should be in a job where you can make decisions that have impact, that affect the world. Here you're trying to climb up the steep side of Mount Everest."

He leaned forward and spoke with intensity, tapping a manicured right index finger on my desk as he made his point. "I suggest that you accept an appointment to the bench in federal district court and move into a job worthy of your talents." He leaned back in his chair and studied me. Half a smile played around his lips. "Do you have any idea," he asked, "do you have any *conception* of how easily such an appointment can be arranged?"

I remained silent and watched him. "I'm not just saying you can move on to the federal bench," he said, "I'm *guaranteeing it.*"

"And what would I have to do to get this judgeship?"

With cool aplomb he said simply: "Stop your investigation."

For a moment no one said anything. Then Miller broke the silence. "The investigation was a magnificent effort. But it's over and done with. Your own local newspaper is already on your behind, and that's only the beginning, my boy, only the beginning."

"How long do you think it would take for me to be appointed?" I asked.

"Ordinarily, these things take a long time. But in your case, with your record, it easily can be expedited. Trust me."

I leaned back in my chair and put both feet on the corner of my table. I looked him over for a long moment before I spoke.

"Mr. Miller," I said, "you and I have met under a great misunderstanding. I haven't the remotest interest in becoming a federal judge. And nothing is going to keep me from going ahead with my investigation of John Kennedy's murder."

I remained where I was so the man couldn't attempt to shake hands with me. I turned to Sciambra. "Andrew, Mr. Miller and I have finished our conversation. Would you mind escorting him to the side door?"

Miller was startled at the sudden change in the course of events. I could see that his jaw bones were tight.

Sciambra guided him out the door and a minute later was back. "Those bastards," Sciambra sneered. "They think they can buy everybody off. Did you see the guy's Annapolis ring?" he continued. I had not noticed it. Sciambra shook his head. "Well, they offered you the carrot, and you turned it down." He paused for emphasis. "You know what's coming next, don't you?"

11

Checkmate

IT WAS FEBRUARY 2 2, 1 9 6 7, and the special
team, as we had begun to refer to each other, was meeting at my house
out in Lakeview, alongside Bayou St. John on the eastern side of New
Orleans. Jim Alcock, Andrew Sciambra, D'Alton Williams, Lou Ivon,
and I were having coffee at the roundtable in the combination kitchen-
dining room. Every now and then my family's big Boxer, Touchdown,
would race by, pursued by my children, pursued in turn by three
cats—and my wife, Liz, valiantly trying to corner the menagerie and
get them out to the backyard.

Although less than a week had passed since the stunning and
premature revelation of our investigation by the press, already I was
learning a lesson: Time and necessity seem to head for your doorstep of
their own volition, with a profound disregard for your particular
problems. Because of my own foolishness, Frank Klein, our best mind,
was not with us. Nevertheless, it was decision-making time. And the
decision staring at us was whether or not the time had come to call
David Ferrie before the Grand Jury.

The unexpected result of the previous week's newspaper stories had been the sudden, stark deterioration of the long-maintained *savoir faire* of David Ferrie. The day the news hit the front page of the *States-Item* Lou Ivon, who was trusted and admired by Ferrie as well as virtually everyone else who knew him, had received an odd telephone call. The caller was halfway through his question before Lou recognized the voice. It was David Ferrie asking if our office had planted the big smear that hit the papers that morning.

"Dave," Ivon said, "do you think we're out of our minds? This building is crawling with reporters grabbing at you when you try to walk through the hall."

Ferrie had responded that he believed Ivon. It was then that Ivon became aware of his caller's unusual excitement. "You know what this news story does to me, don't you?" said Ferrie. "I'm a dead man. From here on, believe me, I'm a dead man."

"What are you talking about, Dave? There's no reason to be jumping to a conclusion like that."

"You'll find out soon enough," said Ferrie. "You'll see."

The following day, Ivon again had a call from Ferrie. This time Ferrie seemed a bit calmer, but his nervousness was still detectable. Now, to Ivon's astonishment, Ferrie asked directly how the investigation was coming along. As Lou mumbled a reply, Ferrie blurted out: "You think your investigation has been all that secret? You know, when you talk to people, they talk to other people."

"Yeah," Lou replied, "I can't argue with that."

Then Ferrie asked if we were still questioning any Cubans.

Ivon followed his instincts and leveled with the man. "Dave," he said, "you know we are. You know that's where this road leads." And then he added, "I only wish you were on our side as a guide. I can guarantee you that the boss would give his right arm to have your mind working with us."

I do not know whether it was the words Ivon used, or the way he used them, but within 24 hours Ferrie called again—this time asking for help. The media somehow had sniffed out that he was one of the targets of our investigation, and they were surrounding his apartment on Louisiana Avenue Parkway like bees on a candy bar.

Ivon told him to wait by the phone. Within ten minutes he would call back with a solution to Ferrie's problem. Lou immediately called the Fontainbleau Motel and reserved a first-class suite under an assumed name. He then called Ferrie back and told him to go to the Fontainbleau, where a suite would be waiting for him. He brushed aside Ferrie's attempts to thank him. "Don't worry about it," Lou had said. "You call us anytime you need us, and we'll give you a hand."

As recently as several nights before, just before midnight, Ferrie had called Ivon at his home and said that the press was still keeping his home surrounded. Ivon had picked him up at a bar on Tulane Avenue, driven him over to the Fontainbleau and again had obtained a suite for him. He also suggested that Ferrie order whatever room service he wanted and try to relax.

You did not have to be a psychiatrist to see that Ferrie was rapidly deteriorating. His emotional stability seemed so precarious that we could not ignore the situation another day. "We have to make a decision, and we're going to make it this morning," I said to the others around the table. I glanced at Ivon. "You saw Frank Klein. What did he say about calling Ferrie to the Grand Jury right now?"

"He said he would wait. His instincts tell him that Ferrie is going to keep on deteriorating and we'll end up getting a lot more out of him. And he also feels that if we call Dave in now he may freeze up and we could lose the best shot we'll ever have."

I turned to Alcock. "Jim, what's your vote?"

Alcock, predictably conservative, shook his expressionless face solemnly. "Looking at it as a lawyer, I don't think it quite adds up to a basis for calling him to the Grand Jury yet."

I looked at Sciambra. "Andrew?" I said.

"Most of me," he replied, "says call him, call him as soon as possible. I've got about fifty questions to ask him, and I'm dying to hear how he answers them. But, speaking as a lawyer, I feel like it may be just a few weeks too early."

I turned to D'Alton Williams.

D'Alton shook his head. "The last thing I like to do is pass when it's decision-making time," he said. "But I don't have the feel yet about what makes Ferrie tick, so I have to abstain."

"Lou?" I asked.

"You know how I've got to vote," he said, flashing an unexpected grin. "I feel sorry for Dave, and I really kind of like the guy. I saw him the other night and I tell you, something or somebody is putting tremendous pressure on him and—well, I'm not a lawyer like the rest of you all. I think if we sit on our behinds too long while we examine the legalities, we'll find we waited too long. I'm for calling him in right now."

"Okay, chief," said Sciambra, looking at me. "How does the vote add up?"

I paused, then said slowly, "We stay cool, hold our fire, and wait a little longer."

The telephone rang, and Liz went over to answer it. "Lou," she called, "it's for you."

Lou was on the phone speaking in low tones. I saw from the intensity on his face that something had happened. Then he turned to look at us.

"Dave Ferrie's dead," he said quietly. "The coroner's already picked up the body at his place."

It took us all a moment to recover from the shock. "Hold onto that phone, Lou," I said. "Before you hang up, get five or six of your best policemen over to Ferrie's place. We're going over there right now and sweep it from one end to the other. And make this clear. This case is in our jurisdiction. I don't want a single man from any federal agency taking over at Ferrie's. Not without an explicit federal court order."

We piled into the cars outside and arrived at Ferrie's apartment less than ten minutes after our own investigators. There was no danger of federal intruders. Our men had sealed it off so a ten-ton tank could not have gotten within 50 yards of the late David Ferrie's apartment.

The first thing that hit me when I went through the door was the smell of the white mice. There had been hundreds of them in the place, kept in wire cages in the living room and dining room as part of the cancer experiments Ferrie had conducted with an established local doctor. The doctor now was long gone, and so were the white mice. But the cages and that unforgettable, stale, oddly sweet smell continued to hang in the air.

The apartment was filthy. It seemed that nothing in it had been washed for years. There was an eclectic accumulation of furniture, no single piece matching any other. An overwhelming library flowed from the living room into the dining room and kitchen. In the bathroom, along both sides of the mirror, we found globs of purplish glue, the residue from Ferrie's periodic application of his home-made wig. And, at one end of his bedroom closet, otherwise cluttered with shabby jackets, we found ourselves staring at the neat but faded lace and satin of some sort of priestly garments.

Ferrie's body long since had been hauled off by the coroner's people. He had been discovered lying nude on the living room sofa, which he often used as a bed, with a sheet pulled over his head. Two suicide notes were found, one on the table alongside of him, and the second on top of the old upright piano against the wall. The table next to him had a variety of medicine bottles on it, several completely empty, the caps removed. I wondered how the coroner's men could have treated poten-tial evidence with such disregard.

Both suicide notes had been typed, and neither bore Ferrie's signa-ture. The first began: "To leave this life is, for me, a sweet prospect. I find nothing in it that is desirable and on the other hand, everything that is loathsome." From that point on the letter became rambling, almost incoherent, as it wandered into a bitter diatribe about the unfairness of life. It made a passing reference to a "messianic District Attorney." The second note, just as bitter, was addressed to a personal friend by name. It began: "When you read this I will be quite dead and no answer will be possible."

Shortly after our arrival at Ferrie's apartment, Lou Ivon had taken off for the morgue to look at the body. One of the numerous legends about David Ferrie and his adventures as a soldier of fortune pilot involved a take-off he had made from the Escambray mountains in Cuba, after delivering munitions to the anti-Castro rebels operating there. As the legend went, a counter-attack almost had trapped him and he was forced to take off in his plane while fighting one of Castro's soldiers with his free hand. He had, according to this tale, received a bad stab wound in his stomach before he got the plane off the ground. When Lou Ivon returned from the morgue, he was holding a freshly taken photograph. The dead man on the slab, his bald head and aristocratic profile somewhat suggestive of Julius Caesar, bore the scar of a knife wound running up the center of his stomach.

The unexpected death of David Ferrie, along with the two suicide notes, created a frenzy of interest in the media, not merely nationally, but worldwide. Reporters descended upon New Orleans to await the coroner's verdict. Each day the crowd of journalists grew larger, filling the halls outside my office and scrambling for every possible bit of information about our investigation.

I was amazed at this development. Previously, the media had scoffed at the idea that President Kennedy had been killed as a result of a conspiracy and that this had been concealed by the federal government. Now suddenly the newspapers, the television, and the radio people had decided that Ferrie's death—and the possibility it may have resulted from suicide or foul play—may have validated my investigation.

On February 25 the coroner announced—rather belatedly, I thought—that Ferrie had died of "natural causes." Instantly the excitement of the assembled journalists vanished, and within hours they were standing in lines at International Airport for flights out of town. Their departure was as mystifying to me as their arrival had been. For, in spite of the coroner's pronouncement, we still were left with two suicide notes, each of which explicitly spelled out that Ferrie was about to depart from this vale of tears.

Unlike most of the media, my special team immediately addressed itself to learning more about the facts of Ferrie's death. I sent the entire group back to Ferrie's apartment to go through it again, this time with a fine-toothed comb.

Meanwhile, at my desk I studied the medicine bottles which had been left on top of the table alongside Ferrie's bed. I wanted to know the effects of each of these drugs, so I looked them up in a thick volume on pharmacology.

I picked up the large bottle of Proloid®, and a recollection came to me. Some years earlier I had a low thyroid condition for a brief period. In order to raise the thyroid production level and increase my metabolism, the doctor had prescribed Proloid for me. Thumbing through the big book, I found that, sure enough, Proloid was medicine to be used *only* when it was desirable to increase bodily metabolism. But David Ferrie, we had learned from several sources, had no problem with low metabolism. On the contrary, he had suffered from hypertension.

I pushed the big book to the side and reached for the phone

directory. One of the forensic pathologists at Louisiana State University medical school had been at the same boarding house with me when he was studying medicine and I was studying law. I had seen him off and on over the years. In a few minutes I had him on the phone and was summarizing the problem before me.

What would happen, I asked, if a man suffering from hypertension were to take—or be forced to take—an entire bottle of Proloid? His answer came without hesitation. Whoever did that, he said, would die shortly afterwards either of a "heart storm" or a brain aneurism (in effect, an exploding blood vessel). The coroner had stated in general terms that the death of David Ferrie was due to "natural causes," but in the autopsy protocol the specific cause had been spelled out as a ruptured blood vessel in the brain.

I asked my pathologist friend if there was any way a coroner might ascertain whether an overdose of Proloid had caused Ferrie's death. He replied that there would be no perceivable signs in a routine autopsy. However, he added that if an examination were made of the blood or of the spinal fluid, an extremely high level of iodine would be encountered, indicating the likelihood that an overdose of Proloid had been taken. He suggested I call the coroner's office and find out if such samples from Ferrie's autopsy had been kept in the refrigerator.

I phoned immediately but was told that no blood samples or spinal fluid from Ferrie's autopsy had been retained. I was left with an empty bottle and a number of unanswered questions. Had Ferrie taken an overdose of Proloid? If so, had he taken it voluntarily? Was it possible that someone else had written the suicide notes and given him the Proloid? The more I reflected upon it, the less sense it made to me. Why should a man kill himself in a way which left no trace—and then leave two suicide notes? Or was I making more out of this than was there? Perhaps it had just been, as the coroner said, "natural causes."

I tossed the empty Proloid bottle in a desk drawer. Throughout the rest of the investigation I kept it as evidence, hoping it would one day be a useful piece of the puzzle. Finally, at a low point many years later, when I felt that my questions would never be answered, I threw it away. I did not want such a souvenir.

*　　*　　*

The sudden death of David Ferrie had brought to us, right on the heels of the previous week's unwelcome front-page news story, our second straight disaster. I could not rid myself of Ferrie's prophetic remark to Lou Ivon immediately following the news story: "I'm a dead man now." Nor could I rid myself of the nagging possibility that his death might as easily have been caused by murder as by suicide. In either case we had lost our best chance for cracking the case.

With David Ferrie around to lead us, however unconsciously, to Clay Shaw and his offbeat companions, I knew we could have continued to develop an ever stronger case against Shaw. With Ferrie gone, it would be a lot harder.

Besides, I was now concerned about how much longer Clay Shaw— who certainly knew as much as Ferrie, if not more—would be around. Ferrie had shown signs of emotional deterioration, had clearly lost a grip on himself, and within five days was lying in the morgue. Would it be any different with Shaw? As with Ferrie, one had to assume that there were others who could see him more clearly than we could. Could we continue to wait for more breaks?

Already, only hours away from the morning meeting at my house, it was decision-making time again. My instincts told me that we had developed a good enough case against Clay Shaw to obtain a Grand Jury indictment of him for conspiracy to assassinate President Kennedy. My instincts also told me, however, that our office had been penetrated to some degree by now, although I had no idea to what extent. Consequently, I did not tell anyone on the staff that I felt it was nearly time to make our move against Shaw.

We had already questioned Shaw once at the office, back when we established that he was the "Clay Bertrand" who had called Dean Andrews about representing Lee Oswald. At that time he had fielded every question flawlessly. No, he had not known Lee Oswald. No, he had never even seen the young man. Did he know a David Ferrie? No, the name was unfamiliar to him. After he had departed, we realized he had given us absolutely nothing.

Now, out of caution, I decided we should interview him again. In response to a subpoena issued by the court, he appeared in our office and we questioned him at great length. This time, perhaps because of the accumulation of details which we had acquired, it was eloquently plain that he was lying. I made the decision that we should arrest him in the very near future, but I continued to say nothing about that to the staff.

On March 1, 1967, the day I had selected, I told the key members of the special team to meet me at 5:30 p.m. in my office. While we waited for the stragglers from the rest of the office to clear out, I reviewed the case we had developed against Shaw.

When the time was right, I walked down the hall, where a judge was waiting for me, and obtained the warrants for Shaw's arrest and the search of his carriage house. While the others waited in my office, I took Lou Ivon and a selected handful of others from the team into another office down the hall. I instructed them to arrest Shaw and search his place thoroughly in accordance with the warrants. I then returned to the remainder of the group and informed them of what I had done.

When Ivon and his men returned to the office with Shaw, I had him taken to one of the senior assistants' offices. We learned that his attorney was Salvadore Panzeca, contacted him, and requested that he come to our office to confer with his client. Then, satisfied that it was useless to question Shaw further at that point, I had Ivon and several of his men escort him to the Criminal Sheriff's office.

An interesting thing occurred during Shaw's booking. Police Officer Aloysius Habighorst, in filling out the booking form, routinely asked Shaw whether he had any aliases. Shaw replied with two words: "Clay Bertrand." Habighorst noted this on the form, then turned to other duties. He had no way of knowing that this amounted to a virtual confirmation to me that it was indeed Shaw who had called Dean Andrews to represent Lee Oswald in Dallas.

Much later, police investigators in my office picked up a faint lead about this incident. In short order I found myself studying a police booking sheet for the first time, observing the name of Clay Bertrand under the classification of "alias," and interviewing Officer Habighorst. A clean-cut young man with an excellent memory, Habighorst recalled the incident in detail, if somewhat stoically. Down the road this incident and his recollection of it would have a memorable result. (See Chapter 18.)

Probably the most interesting single item seized in the course of Shaw's arrest was his address book. It offered some insight into his proclivity for developing casual friendships at lofty levels of European aristocracy. How many Americans have in their address books such fascinating names and addresses as the Marquesse Giuseppe Rey (Vicenza, Italy) the Baron Rafaelo de Banfield (Villa Tripcovich, Triesta, Italy), Sir Stephen Runciman (66 Whitehall Court, London), Princess Jacqueline Chimay (2 Rue Albert Thomas, Paris), Lady Margaret D'Arcy (109 Earl's Court Road, London), Sir Michael Duff (Bangor, Wales) and Lady Hulse (7 Culross Street, London)?

It is true that such a listing could have represented a preoccupation with the past inasmuch as most of the world is no longer run by nobles. However, it is also true that the C.I.A. has a romantic infatuation with fading regimes and that Clay Shaw, with his polished Court of St. James manners, must have been precisely what the Agency needed for assignments involving foreign royalty—such as that in Italy in 1962. (See Chapter 6.)

Amid the names of the international blueblood set, the address book contained the following listing:

"LEE ODOM, P.O. Box 19106, Dallas, Texas."

This odd item was revealed publicly when Shaw's attorneys sought to have the address book returned to him. Our office opposed this move, and in our written opposition we called attention to an interesting fact: The citation of "P.O. 19106" appeared in Lee Oswald's address book as well as Shaw's.

After several days of silence, Shaw's attorneys produced a man named Lee Odom, who at that time rented post office box number 174 in Irving, a suburb of Dallas. He stated that he was from Dallas and that, while P.O. Box 19106 had never been in his name, it had been used for several months by a barbecue company with which he was once associated.

Shaw's attorneys, who now included Edward Wegmann as well as

Panzeca, picked it up from there and explained that Odom had once met Clay Shaw to discuss the possibility of promoting a bullfight in New Orleans.

There were some problems with the bullfight explanation, which had been floated up as justifying the presence of "P.O. Box 19106" in Shaw's address book. For one thing, anyone who was genuinely involved in the promotion of bullfights would have to know that New Orleans, by its very nature, is a city most unlikely to be enthralled by the prospect of death in the afternoon. Second, as we knew from having compiled a summary of all of Clay Shaw's activities since graduating from high school, he had never engaged in any kind of promotion.

Finally, the bullfight explanation seemed weak when juxtaposed to the fact that virtually the same phrase, "P.O. 19106," was memorialized forever on one of the pages of Oswald's address book. The coincidence became even more suspicious when one considered that Lee Oswald had to have written his notation no later than 1963, the year he was murdered, and that as of 1963 Dallas had not yet acquired a post office box with a number as high as 19106.

To me, the explanation that Clay Shaw had written "P.O. Box 19106" in his address book because he was considering the possibility of treating the citizens of New Orleans to a bullfight and that Lee Oswald had written it in his address book years earlier for no reason at all stretched the limits of common sense by a long ways. Once again the people of this country were being asked to swallow a cannon ball, no matter how well lubricated.

Also found by our investigators at Shaw's luxuriously appointed carriage house in the French Quarter were a few more novel items, including five whips, several lengths of chain, and a black hood and matching black cape. The whips had on them what appeared to be dried blood. In the bedroom, about two and a half feet apart, two large hooks had been screwed into the ceiling. These accouterments hardly were inculpatory in themselves. Different people have different hobbies. Had Shaw lived in an earlier era, however, the list of nobles in his address book might have included the Marquis de Sade.

With but one exception, Shaw's entire address book consisted of addresses and phone numbers. That one exception appeared on one of the otherwise unused pages. There, inscribed in Shaw's handwriting, were the words "Oct" and "Nov"—which would appear to mean October and November. Then, after an indecipherable scribble—there was scrawled simply: "Dallas."

12

Confrontation

W H E N   W E   A R R E S T E D   S H A W, the United States government awakened like an angry lion. Whoever in my office was the government's contact had been caught napping by our unheralded apprehension of the man. There followed roars of outrage from Washington, D.C. and shrill echoes from the news media.

From Ramsey Clark, the attorney general of the United States, there came the pronouncement that the federal government already had exonerated Shaw from any involvement in President Kennedy's assassination. This high-level revelation, and the attorney general's subsequent friendly colloquy with Washington reporters, seemed to leave no doubt that the Federal Bureau of Investigation had investigated Clay Shaw and given him a clean bill of health. One newsman asked Clark directly if Shaw was "checked out and found clear?" "Yes, that's right," replied the attorney general. Needless to say, this tableau did not exactly make me look like District Attorney of the Year.

However, the statement that Shaw, whose name appears nowhere in the 26 volumes of the Warren Commission, had been investigated by the federal government was intriguing. If Shaw had no connection to the assassination, I wondered, why had he been investigated? The implications of Clark's statement apparently raised similar questions in Washington, and Clark soon beat a strategic retreat. "The attorney general," a Justice Department spokesman announced, "has since determined that this was erroneous. Nothing arose indicating a need to investigate Mr. Shaw."

Shortly after Clark's pronouncement, however, an unnamed Justice Department official announced that the department had been well aware that Clay Shaw and Clay Bertrand were one and the same individual and that the F.B.I. had indeed investigated Clay Bertrand. This confirmed the facts as we had found them. Nonetheless, despite the backpedaling by the Justice Department, the attorney general's initial pronouncement was the one that got all the headlines. It had struck a serious blow at the integrity of our investigation.

Meanwhile, in New Orleans things were moving fast. In major cases where we were seeking an indictment, I customarily made the presentation to the Grand Jury. This case, however, was different. From the outset, the news media had personalized the investigation, presenting me as a ruthless politician driven by swollen ambition, eager to ride this case to the governor's office or the U.S. Senate or even, as the *New York Times* speculated, the vice-presidency. These stories upset me not so much because of their absurd portrayals of me but because they trivialized a serious legal case concerning the assassination of the President of the United States. The attitude of the media caused me to lean over backwards to establish some personal detachment from the proceedings. Thus, as we sought an indictment of Shaw, I decided not even to enter the Grand Jury room. I left this to the assistant district attorneys on the special team. They presented the evidence we had uncovered, and the Grand Jury returned a true bill. Clay Shaw was indicted for participating in a conspiracy to murder John F. Kennedy.*

Next, I took a step in the *defendant's* behalf. I made a motion for a preliminary hearing. Customarily in major cases it is the defense attorneys who request a preliminary hearing. The object is to force the

---

* In legal terms, the indictment charged that he "did willfully and unlawfully conspire with David W. Ferrie, herein named but not charged and Lee Harvey Oswald, herein named but not charged, and others, not herein named, to murder John F. Kennedy."

district attorney to demonstrate that there is a sound basis for bringing the defendant to trial. This procedure was developed to prevent a prosecutor from holding a frivolous charge over a defendant's head for a long period before trying the case on the merits.

In this case I made the motion out of fairness to Shaw because of the extraordinary seriousness of the charge. My application requested that a panel of three judges be appointed to hear evidence concerning Shaw and that they then determine whether the charges should be dismissed or Shaw held over for trial. This was the first time in the history of Louisiana that such a motion ever was filed by the prosecutor on behalf of the defendant.

Shaw's four-day preliminary hearing began on the morning of March 14, 1967. The large courtroom was filled to overflowing. Reporters and spectators were crowding in everywhere. Although I would be presenting some of the evidence myself, I had determined that I was not going to let the media personalize this hearing. Thus I had delegated the initial questioning of our first important witness to two of my assistants—Charles Ward, the new chief assistant D.A., and Alvin Oser. I would be coming into the courtroom briefly on occasion. Still later I would be bringing in Jim Alcock. But I wanted everyone to know that this was a team effort, not some individual grandstanding by me.

At a preliminary hearing the prosecutor reveals only enough evidence to show that he has a plausible case. At Shaw's hearing we called only two major witnesses. The first was Perry Russo, a 25-year-old Equitable insurance agent from Baton Rouge, who long had been an acquaintance of David Ferrie's. When he heard about our investigation, Russo wrote us a letter, but we never received it. Later he met a reporter from the *Baton Rouge State-Times* and in an interview the morning of Friday, February 24, he told him about a meeting he had attended at Ferrie's apartment at which the assassination of President Kennedy had been discussed. The story appeared in the *State-Times* that afternoon. By late afternoon, the paper was on the stands in New Orleans, and Andrew Sciambra showed it to me. Although it said Russo intended to travel to New Orleans, I told Sciambra to drive up to Baton Rouge immediately.

About 8:00 p.m. Sciambra arrived at Russo's house; Russo had just returned from WBRZ-TV studios, where he had been interviewed for the evening news (and kept away from reporters from the competing local TV station). Sciambra spent several hours with Russo, and showed him dozens of photographs. Russo recognized several Cubans, and then, when Sciambra produced a picture of Clay Shaw, Russo exclaimed, "I know him. I met him at Ferrie's." Of course, he had known him only as Bertrand, but his identification was positive.

Russo was significant because he was the first eyewitness to have overheard Shaw and Ferrie engaging in a discussion of the prospective murder of John Kennedy. In my judgment, even without Russo we had sufficient evidence to support a charge against Shaw of participating in the conspiracy to murder the President. But that evidence was circumstantial. As an experienced trial attorney, I knew that laymen are particularly responsive to eyewitness testimony, and Russo provided that in full measure. Consequently, upon first learning how strong the conversation between Shaw and Ferrie was, I decided to take the additional precaution of confirming the veracity of Russo's recollection. The lawyers on the special team and I considered using a "lie detector" test, but since such tests are highly imperfect and inadmissible in court we rejected the idea. Instead, we chose to use hypnosis and Sodium Pentothal.® Both treatments were administered to Russo under close medical supervision. And both revealed that Russo was indeed telling the truth.

So when we called Perry Russo to the witness stand at Shaw's preliminary hearing we were confident. After the usual preliminary questions, bringing out his background and allowing him to relax in the courtroom surroundings, assistant D.A.'s Ward and Oser asked Russo about a gathering at David Ferrie's apartment.

Russo responded that when he dropped in at Ferrie's place, "somewhere around the middle of September 1963," an informal gathering—which he described as "some sort of party"—was just breaking up. Some of Ferrie's usual bevy of youngsters were there but soon left. Russo said a former girlfriend of his, Sandra Moffett, was also there for a while. After she departed, there remained, according to Russo, a scattering of anti-Castro Cubans—a group which occasionally came by to visit Ferrie. A few of them stayed on for a little while.

Also there was a tall, distinguished-looking man who had what

Russo described as "white hair." Even as he said this, he involuntarily glanced over at Shaw who was continuing to gaze imperturbably at the paneled courtroom wall in front of him. Ferrie introduced the man to Russo as "Clem Bertrand."

Russo remembered having seen the tall, white-haired man once before, when President Kennedy was in New Orleans for the dedication of the Nashville Street Wharf. Russo had noticed the man because he was the only one not looking at Kennedy. The man had kept studying the crowd, and Russo had concluded that he was a Secret Service agent.

At the gathering at the apartment, Russo recalled, Ferrie introduced him to a young man who was called "Leon Oswald." But Russo could not firmly identify this man as the same man he later saw on television as the suspect in the assassination, Lee Harvey Oswald.

After the others departed, only "Oswald," Bertrand, Ferrie, Russo, and several of the Cubans remained. The talk turned to the possibility of assassinating Fidel Castro. This conversation was speculative and strongly anti-Kennedy. No one present—including Perry Russo—had any use for Castro or President Kennedy. Moreover, the conversation was particularly heated because in August the Kennedy administration had established an embargo to stop the flow of arms to South Africa. Some of those present felt a comparable limitation of arms to countries or even guerrilla forces opposed to Fidel Castro might soon follow.

Despite the enthusiasm of Ferrie, Russo, and the Cubans for the elimination of Castro, Russo's testimony continued, the man called Bertrand, who was also basically in favor of the idea, cautiously demurred. "There would be a real problem," he said, "of actually getting at him."

Ferrie immediately produced a map of Cuba and spread it out on a table. He pointed out one potential beach landing area after another, speaking expertly about accessibility, tides and timetables, and routes to Havana.

In this conversation Russo was as much a protagonist as a listener. A tough-minded young man with a high degree of curiosity, Russo was not one of Ferrie's typical playmates. Ferrie, virtually ostracized by most of the adult world, found in Russo an intellectual companion who stimulated him, and so they became close. Russo estimated that Ferrie had been to his house at least a dozen times and that he had been to the pilot's apartment 30 to 40 times. This appeared to be why the man introduced to Russo as Clem Bertrand accepted his presence when the topic later became the removal of John Kennedy.

Russo, his testimony continued, remained after the Cubans had left, assuming that he would get a ride home from Ferrie. There were just the four of them now—Ferrie, Russo, the man called Bertrand, and "Leon Oswald."

Even if it were impossible to get at Castro, Russo recalled Ferrie as saying, it did not mean they could not get at Kennedy. This sudden shift of the objectives, Russo indicated, was inevitable now that the group had grown smaller. In recent months, Ferrie had become obsessed with the subject of Kennedy. He had begun carrying news clippings with him, stories of such actions by the Kennedy administration as an F.B.I. raid on the Schlumberger blimp base at Houma and the August embargo against the shipment of arms to South Africa. At the slightest provocation he would pull clippings from his pocket and denounce the actions bitterly.

Ferrie, Russo said, was pacing back and forth, saying they could get rid of Kennedy and blame it on Castro. That then could be an excuse to invade Cuba. Ferrie was drinking from his constant cup of coffee as he talked. All they had to do, he added, was get Kennedy out in the open.

Ferrie was excited now. Hyperthyroid, he became excited easily and when he became excited, he became loquacious. When he became loquacious, he became magnetic. All eyes were on him as he continued to describe how easily the job could be done.

Ferrie emphasized that "triangulation of crossfire" was the way to do it. Shooting at Kennedy from three directions, one of the shots would have to get him.* Russo recalled the importance Ferrie put on this.

Russo described Ferrie's electric tension when he talked about the

---

* As it happened, triangulation fire does appear to have been used to kill President Kennedy—at least one shooting point from the knoll in front of him and apparently at least two from the buildings behind him. But this does not necessarily mean that Ferrie knew in advance about such a detail. The elimination of an important individual by the covert action machinery of a government intelligence agency is a "need to know" operation. It is doubtful that Ferrie actually knew that fire by triangulation would be used against Kennedy. See Chapters 2 and 7.

assassination of Kennedy, and the contrast of Bertrand, whom he recalled as sitting back, poised and relaxed, smoking his cigarettes. In spite of Ferrie's excitement and his volubility, Russo went on, Bertrand remained the central presence in the group. Now, Russo said, Bertrand spoke up.

Bertrand said it was important for each of them to be in the public eye when it happened. Ferrie responded that he had already decided that he was going to be at the university at Hammond (Southeastern Louisiana University). Bertrand commented that he probably would be traveling, on his way to the west coast.*

Now, Russo testified, for the first time it struck him that these men were talking about where they were going to be *when* President Kennedy was killed. There no longer was speculation here, as in the discussion of Castro's possible assassination.

He testified that Ferrie once again got back on the subject of triangulation (crossfire)—once he got his teeth into a subject, he did not let it go easily—but by that time Russo was tired and his memory of details was hazy. He remembered that Dave Ferrie gave him a ride home.

Some months later, Russo went on to testify, approximately in March 1964, he happened to drive into David Ferrie's new service station. As he arrived there, he saw Ferrie in conversation with a familiar-looking individual. It was the tall, white-haired man who had been at Ferrie's place, the man who then had been introduced to him as Bertrand. At the conclusion of his testimony, Russo was asked to identify the man. Unhesitatingly, Russo indicated the defendant, Clay Shaw.

On cross-examination Shaw's lawyers spent hours trying to discredit Russo and his testimony. They focused particularly on the hypnosis and Sodium Pentothal treatments, implying that we had somehow drugged Russo and brainwashed him into telling this wild story. Their efforts failed, though. We called Dr. Esmond Fatter, a distinguished

---

* As it turned out, Ferrie did go to the university at Hammond, where he slept at the dormitory. However, this was on the way back from his curious trip to Texas, and by then the assassination already had occurred. Clay Shaw, on the other hand, indeed had gone to the west coast when the assassination took place. He had been scheduled to make a speech in San Francisco, which had been arranged for him by Mario Bermúdez, the head of the international relations department for the city of New Orleans, a close personal friend of Shaw's.

physician and hypnotist, and Dr. Nicholas Chetta, the coroner of the city of New Orleans, to explain the treatments they had administered to Russo. Both were evaluated by the three-judge panel as qualified experts on truth verification by Sodium Pentothal and hypnosis. And both testified strongly and clearly under oath that Perry Russo was telling the truth when he recalled hearing Clay Shaw and David Ferrie discussing the details of assassinating President Kennedy.

More than two decades later, Russo's candor about his testimony is startling. "Some people try to thank me," he says, "for helping Kennedy by testifying about the assassination. I didn't do that to help the man. The truth is I hated him for what he did to the Cubans who wanted to fight Castro.

"Why did I testify for the D.A.'s office against Clay Shaw?" he asks in 1988. "That's easy. They learned that I was at that meeting with David Ferrie and him and, when they questioned me, I just wasn't going to lie about it."

The other key witness we called at the preliminary hearing was Vernon Bundy, a black inmate of the New Orleans Parish prison. In his late twenties, Bundy was a narcotics offender who had been in jail because of a parole violation. He had told a prison guard that he had information concerning Lee Oswald. Prison officials with whom we were on good terms passed this on to us, and we interviewed Bundy extensively until we were satisfied that he was telling the truth. During the interviews it had become apparent that Bundy was at ease with me, so I decided to handle his questioning in court.

That day, because of all the publicity, the atmosphere in front of the building was like a circus. A man with colored balloons shaped like rabbits was making brisk sales. At the courtroom door a flock of news reporters descended on me, but I brushed by without comment.

I was on friendly terms with all the judges, but to emphasize my detachment in this case I did not go into their chambers for the customary pre-hearing chat with them and the opposing attorneys.

As I glanced over the scene, the three judges began taking their seats on the bench. Judges Bernard Bagert, Matthew Braniff, and Malcolm O'Hara were among the most competent on the court. Shaw was at the defendant's seat with his attorneys, Irvin Dymond, Edward Wegmann, and William Wegmann. At the bench there was a brief flurry of movement. Judge Braniff, who had a temper like Vesuvius in eruption, had spotted among the spectators a woman with three children, all with rabbit balloons. Judge Bagert grabbed him just in time and signaled to the bailiff to get the lady and her menagerie out of the court.

When things calmed down, I called Vernon Bundy to the stand and led him through his preliminary questioning. The concern of the defense attorneys became evident when they realized that I was about to have him identify Shaw as meeting with Lee Oswald. And they exploded into genuine outrage when Bundy admitted that he was a heroin addict and had gone out to the seawall at Lake Pontchartrain "to get a fix." They were on their feet shouting objections. One of them, for reasons still obscure to me, was calling for a mistrial.

I saw that this was upsetting Bundy and caught his eye. I grinned at him, and he sat back and relaxed. All the defense objections fell of their own weight, and finally I was able to turn Bundy loose to testify in his own narrative style.

He said he had been on the concrete seawall of Lake Pontchartrain on a July morning in 1963, preparing a heroin injection for himself. He was almost out of view because he was sitting a few steps down towards the water.

"I was looking all 'round 'cause I'm skeptical," Bundy testified. At this moment, he said, a black four-door sedan approached and parked.

"A fellow then gets out of the automobile and walks toward me. I am skeptical. I don't know whether he is police or what."

"The guy passed in back of me. . .and he tells me it's a hot day."

Bundy said the man, whom he described as tall and white-haired, walked about 15 or 20 feet away from him and "after five or seven minutes, a young man approached." He said the two talked for about 15 minutes. "The older fellow gave the young guy what I'm not sure, but it looked like a roll of money. The young guy stuck it in his back pocket."

From photographs he identified the young man as Lee Oswald and the man who exited the automobile as Clay Shaw. The two identifications—requiring that he select their photographs from among others—initially had been made without hesitation for us. Now, once again, he unhesitantly picked out the pictures of Lee Oswald and Clay Shaw, identifying them for the judges as the two men he had seen meeting by the seawall.

After overhearing their conversation and after their departure, he testified, he went over to where they had been standing and picked up several yellow leaflets. (It will be recalled that Oswald had been distributing yellow pro-Castro handouts from his 544 Camp Street address.) Bundy used one of the yellow pieces of paper to wrap up his heroin after he "shot the dope."

When I asked Bundy to point out the man who had met with Oswald, he directed an unwavering finger straight at the defendant. During this long moment, the courtroom, which had resembled a noisy carnival before the proceedings began, now was as quiet as an abandoned cemetery at midnight. The defense attorneys occupied themselves with appearing ineffably bored with such timewasting proceedings, a certain sign they were unhappy. As for the three judges and the spectators, they hung onto every word uttered by young Bundy.

When I felt that I had made my point, I asked Bundy to step down from the witness chair and put his hand over the man whom he had seen meeting on the lakefront with Lee Harvey Oswald. Bundy stepped down, walked across the silent courtroom, and put his hand over the gray-white hair of Clay Shaw.

That moment, everyone in the courtroom seemed frozen in shock. Then, apparently receiving a nod from Judge Bagert, the minute clerk announced, "This court will take a recess." It was as the judges were stepping down from their seats behind the bench that the crowd burst into a sustained uproar. I glanced over at the defense table and saw, for the first time, the slightest signs of frowns on the foreheads of the defense attorneys. On the other hand, seemingly above it all—appearing for all the world to be an elegant Gulliver set upon and strapped into his chair by Lilliputians—Shaw continued to savor his cigarette, his eyes above the crowd as he glanced across the courtroom.

On cross-examination, of course, the defense lawyers came at Vernon Bundy like rabid wolves. Disconcerted at first, he appeared to relax and soon was recounting his story steadily and patiently. I knew all the questions they would be asking a hundred times over. It was a long-held custom of mine in trials seldom to object when a witness is standing up firm against the opposing lawyers. I waited a long time for Shaw's attorneys to wear themselves out against Bundy, but in the end they did.

At the conclusion of the preliminary hearing on March 17, the three-judge panel ruled that the prosecution had presented sufficient evidence and ordered Clay Shaw to be held for jury trial.

13

The Assault

ON SEPTEMBER 4, 1967, Chief Justice Earl Warren announced from Tokyo, Japan, that I had presented "absolutely nothing" publicly to contradict the findings of the Warren Commission report on President Kennedy's assassination. Warren, speaking at the Foreign Correspondents Club of Japan, said that he had not heard "one fact" to refute the Commission findings that Lee Oswald was the lone killer.

This was strange behavior for the Chief Justice of the United States. Clay Shaw's trial had not begun. The first juror had yet to be selected. Yet here the highest judge in our land already was testifying as the first witness in the case. He was not testifying under oath, which gave him a unique freedom from the laws of perjury which witnesses following him would not have. And he plainly was loading the dice in Shaw's favor. No witness was going to be eager, in front of all the world, to make the Chief Justice appear to be a liar, or at least mistaken.

But Warren's wholly inappropriate statement was mild compared to the attacks in the media on our case against Clay Shaw and on me personally. Ever since Shaw's arrest the media assault had been vicious and relentless.

Some long-cherished illusions of mine about the great free press in our country underwent a painful reappraisal during this period. The restraint and respect for justice one might expect from the press to insure a fair trial not only to the individual charged but to the state itself did not exist. Nor did the diversity of opinion that I always thought was fundamental to the American press. As far as I could tell, the reports and editorials in *Newsweek, Time,* the *New York Times,* the *New York Post,* the *Saturday Evening Post* and on and on were indistinguishable. All shared the basic view that I was a power-mad, irresponsible showman who was producing a slimy circus with the objective of getting elected to higher office, oblivious of any consequences.

I offer several examples as representative of the American press treatment of our case against Clay Shaw.

In *Newsweek's* May 15, 1967, issue under the heading "The JFK 'Conspiracy,'"* Hugh Aynesworth wrote:

> Jim Garrison is right. There has been a conspiracy in New Orleans—but it is a plot of Garrison's own making. It is a scheme to concoct a fantastic "solution" to the death of John F. Kennedy, and to make it stick; in this case, the district attorney and his staff have been indirect parties to the death of one man and have humiliated, harassed and financially gutted several others.
>
> Indeed, Garrison's tactics have been even more questionable than his case. I have evidence that one of the strapping D.A.'s investigators offered an unwilling "witness" $3,000 and a job with an airline—if only he would "fill in the facts" of the alleged meeting to plot the death of the President. I also know that when the D.A.'s office learned that this entire bribery attempt had been tape-recorded, two of Garrison's men returned to the "witness" and, he says, threatened him with physical harm.

Aynesworth, who seemed a gentle and fair enough man when he interviewed me for several hours in my home, never did get around to

---

* This headline was admirably low-key compared to the *New York Post's* frenzied "A Morbid Frolic in New Orleans." When a particular headline was especially wild, someone on my staff would post it on the bulletin board so we could all get a good laugh.

revealing whose life our office had shortened. As for the $3,000 bribe, by the time I came across Aynesworth's revelation, the witness our office had supposedly offered it to, Alvin Babeouf, had admitted to us that it never happened. Aynesworth, of course, never explained what he did with the "evidence" allegedly in his possession. And the so-called bribery tape recording had not, in fact, ever existed.

If this article was a typical Aynesworth product, one could hardly help but wonder how a newsman with so rampant an imagination continued to find a market for his stories. Yet, in fairness to Aynesworth, I must say that this "news" story was all too typical of what my office staff found itself reading in newspaper and magazine articles by writers from distant cities who had not the remotest awareness of what my office had been attempting to accomplish.

James Phelan, who had written a highly supportive lead article for the *Saturday Evening Post* about my office's successes in fighting crime in New Orleans ("The Vice Man Cometh"), returned to do an article about the J.F.K. investigation. In a piece entitled "Rush to Judgment in New Orleans," Phelan claimed that Perry Russo never told Assistant D.A. Andrew Sciambra about any conspiracy until he was "drugged." The clear implication was that our office had drugged Russo and then planted the conspiracy story in his brain while he was in a highly suggestible state. The truth, of course, was quite different. In fact, Phelan himself was aware of what Russo had told us about the conspiracy well before it occurred to me that we might be able to verify Russo's testimony with medically supervised hypnosis and Sodium Pentothal. I knew this because I was the one who first told Phelan about Russo's story. Phelan's colorful fiction later fell apart at Clay Shaw's trial when it was made clear that Russo had provided Sciambra with a full description of all significant events prior to any medical treatments. (See Chapter 18.) Moreover, as was obvious to the reporters in Baton Rouge (see Chapter 12), Russo gave interviews to the press in which he discussed a conspiracy—although he did not know at the time that Shaw and Bertrand were one and the same—before he had ever met with Sciambra.

The simple truth is that public officials really do not go unobserved so long by the people who elect them. I have never heard of a district attorney who was able to build a career on drugging witnesses so that they would say whatever he ordered them to say. If a prosecutor was so deranged that he resorted to such measures, the word would get around quickly enough and he would not be a prosecutor much longer. It would be much the same if he sought to enhance his career with the aid of thumbscrews and other torture devices.

It is fair to say that the people of New Orleans closely watched the well-publicized charge that their district attorney intentionally drugged a witness to influence his testimony. They listened to the expert testimony of Doctors Esmond Fatter and Nicholas Chetta. They understood that what was sought under controlled medical supervision was the refreshing of memory, if possible. And in the following election of 1969 I was again re-elected to office, this time in the first primary. No previous district attorney ever had been re-elected in New Orleans.

The attacks did not end with Phelan. Without any warning, Dick Billings, the friendly editor from *Life* magazine, suddenly flew in from New York. He seemed amiable enough, but he appeared to have lost a great deal of weight. He had deep circles under his eyes. His Ivy League clothes hung loosely on his thin frame. He informed me that *Life* would no longer be able to support me and work with me in the investigation. The magazine, he said, had come to the conclusion that I was not the vigorous opponent of organized crime that it had first thought I was.

"What on earth are you talking about?" I asked. He then mentioned a name, asking me if I knew of the man. I shook my head and answered that I had never heard of him. The editor held out his hands. "There you are," he said. "You should have had a dossier on him by now."

I pulled over a phone directory and located the name he had mentioned in the small town of Covington, a listing which indicated that he lived immediately north of the lake. "Is this who you mean?" I asked.

"That's the man," he said. "He's one of the top racketeers down here."

"And you're the starting quarterback for the Green Bay Packers," I

responded. If that fellow had been engaged in any extended criminality in and around New Orleans, I would have known his name well.
As it turned out, I could find no one in the office who ever had heard
his name. Nor did the name ever come up again.

I studied my visitor. It was obvious that he was an unhappy man
executing a bad assignment which he had been ordered to carry out. I
was angry, but not at him. He was considerably more sensitive and
intelligent than most of the media representatives I had encountered.
Soon he would be assigned to stories about the birth of quintuplets in
Bangor, Maine, or a scientific breakthrough in increasing the fertility
of rabbits.

Apparently, the *Life* magazine gambit had been planned for some
time, if not from the very outset. Within a few weeks my name
appeared in the second of two *Life* articles about organized crime. It
gave particular attention to me as a free-wheeling visitor at Las Vegas
casinos from time to time. The writer of the article had some problems
working me into the scenario because, as it happens, I do not gamble
at all. It is not that I am too virtuous. I simply observed a long time
ago that the house always wins.

However, that detail did not inhibit the editors of *Life*. I was
described as having a special Las Vegas connection who was a "lieutenant" of a New Orleans "mobster." I reportedly was "granted a $5,000
credit in the cashier's cage." The implication was that I used this credit
to sign chits during my alleged forays at the gambling tables.

It was true that I filled out a form once when I had to cash a check at
the Sands Hotel. This apparently is where I acquired such credit, if
indeed I had that much. It was also true that I took trips to Las Vegas
about twice a year, but they were entirely for the purpose of getting out
into the dry western climate, which I happen to love, and catching up
with some sunshine. That was all that was needed for me to become
Life's version of The Man Who Broke the Bank at Monte Carlo.

Around the time of the *Life* article about my fictional gaming
proclivities at Las Vegas, *Time* magazine—a sister publication of *Life*'s
and a part of the Luce empire—ran a series of articles on our investigation. It was pictured as an indefensible sham, and I as a demented
buffoon, hungry for headlines.

None of the publications I read seemed to consider the possibility that our investigation might have some legitimate evidentiary basis and that John Kennedy may indeed have been the victim of a conspiracy. The *New York Times Magazine* once—and then very briefly—did confront the issue of a conspiracy. The article appeared under the catchy title "No Conspiracy, But—Two Assassins, Perhaps?" The author, an Englishman named Henry Fairlie, stated, incredibly enough, that neither in Europe nor in America had he found much popular interest in the possibility that the Warren Commission had reached the wrong conclusions. He did acknowledge, however, that "doubt has been aroused" and went on to express his concern that such doubt "may become an obsession in at least some quarters—perhaps eventually in the popular mind, which has so far been resistant."

The thesis of the article eventually emerged in the following sentences:

> The fact that more than one person is engaged in an enterprise does not necessarily make it a conspiracy. This is the leap which alarms me, and it is a leap (I do not wish to imply any conscious motive) which ambitious authors perhaps find a little too easy to take.

If I understood it correctly, the reasoning here in the newspaper of record was that just because more than one individual may have been shooting at President Kennedy at the same time, this did not necessarily mean that a conspiracy had occurred.

After the early harassing fire which we had been receiving from the print media, the big guns of TV news moved in. In the spring of 1967, local sources alerted us that the advance men of a special N.B.C. investigative team had arrived in New Orleans. The ostensible chief investigator was a man named Walter Sheridan. He was quartered at the Royal Orleans, and it soon became clear that he was in New Orleans to stay a spell.

Sheridan was a poised man of apparent substance whom I passed several times in the hotel lobby, each of us giving a casual nod to the other. After a while it occurred to me that he did not quite fit the picture of a man simply on his way up in the business of gathering

165

news. In time I would learn that our visitor had unusually high connections, not merely in New York but in Washington, D.C. as well. He often made reference to his service in the Office of Naval Intelligence, Guy Banister's alma mater.

The N.B.C. news team did not seem interested in interviewing anyone from the office, which was fine with us. We were naive enough to assume that they were investigating the President's murder. The continued absence of any signs of real curiosity from the N.B.C. team about the facts of Kennedy's murder simply indicated to us that another fictional pre-fabricated "lone killer" product was in the making.

However, we were beginning to wonder why Sheridan and the various people working on his project were staying so long in town. We kept seeing the blue and white cars of WDSU—the local N.B.C. TV affiliate—parked for hours at a time in the vicinity of the courthouse where our office was located.

In time we learned that the N.B.C. investigators had found their way to the State Penitentiary at Angola, where they had been questioning Miguel Torres, a professional burglar, and other inmates.

It was just about then that we suddenly realized that N.B.C. was not investigating the assassination at all. It was investigating *us*—me, my office, my staff, and our investigation. One of the sources who told us of N.B.C.'s plans was Marlene Mancuso, who had once been married to Gordon Novel.* She wrote in a memo to us that she had been contacted by a reporter for N.B.C.:

> Richard Townley told me that he had been trying to contact me for a couple of weeks. He said that he worked for N.B.C. and that his intuition told him that I would be involved eventually. . . .
>
> He said Mr. Garrison would get a jail sentence. He said he figured that I was going to be Mr. Garrison's star witness, and that Mr. Garrison was going to use me to discredit Gordon and make him appear as a second Oswald. He kept going back that he

---

* I was at this time attempting to extradite Novel from Ohio to question him about the munitions he, along with David Ferrie and the anti-Castro Cubans, had taken from the Schlumberger bunker at the Houma blimp base. From Novel, N.B.C. had found its way to Marlene Mancuso. See Chapter 14.

wanted a taped interview that would show me in a good light. He said that otherwise I would probably be subpoenaed and there would be a lots [*sic*] of newspapermen around me and a state of confusion and I would look very bad. . . .

Townley kept telling me that it would be more intelligent to be presented nicely than to be shown in a bad light coming out of the courtroom. . . . He said they are going to expose Mr. Garrison as a fraud and that he is working with N.B.C., out of WDSU, on this. . . .

Even bolder was N.B.C.'s approach to Perry Russo. Russo told Andrew Sciambra that before the program he had been contacted repeatedly in an effort to persuade him to change his recollection of having heard Clay Shaw discuss President Kennedy's assassination with David Ferrie.

While the facts were fresh in his mind, Sciambra wrote a memorandum based on what Russo had told him. Here are some representative paragraphs summarizing Perry Russo's statements about what the N.B.C. people were up to:

> Over the past few weeks, I have been in constant contact with Russo discussing N.B.C. personnel and agents who have been coming to his residence to discuss with him the Garrison probe in general and the N.B.C. Television White Paper Report on the probe in particular. In regard to this, Russo has informed me that during the past few weeks Richard Townley of WDSU Television has been to his house twice and James Phelan of the *Saturday Evening Post* has been to his house four times. Some of the highlights of those conversations are as follows. . . .
>
> Townley also told Russo that he would contact him in a few days and let him know what moves Clay Shaw's attorney had in mind, as they were working together. Russo also said that Townley told him that he and N.B.C. had contacted all of the witnesses that they know about and that they would try to find out what else the District Attorney's office had but that it was getting harder to get information out of the District Attorney's office because now the District Attorney's office is insulating the leaks. . . .
>
> Russo said that Walter Sheridan of N.B.C. News told him that the President of N.B.C. contacted Mr. Gherlock who is in charge of management at Equitable's home office in New York and

Gherlock assured the President of N.B.C. that if Russo did cooperate with N.B.C. in trying to end the Garrison probe, that no retaliation would be taken by Equitable [Russo's employer] against Russo by the local office on instructions from the home office.

Russo said that he told Sheridan that he needed a rest as the news people have been bothering him day and night and that he would take a seven to ten day vacation in California after the baseball season was over. Sheridan then asked him if he would like to live in California. He advised him that *if he did side up with N.B.C. and the defense and bust up the Garrison probe that he would have to run from Garrison and move from Louisiana.* Sheridan, Russo continued, said that they could set him up in California, protect his job, get him a lawyer and that *he could guarantee that Garrison could never get him extradited back to Louisiana.* [Emphasis added.]

Sheridan then told him that N.B.C. flew Novel to McLean, Virginia, and gave him a lie detector test and that Garrison will never get Novel back in Louisiana. Russo said that Sheridan told him that what he wants Russo to do is to get on an N.B.C. National television show and say, "I am sorry for what I said because I lied, some of what I said was true but I was doctored by the District Attorney's staff into testifying like I did". . . .

Perry said that James Phelan of The Saturday Evening Post told him that he was working hand in hand with Townley and Sheridan and they were in constant contact with each other and that they were going to destroy Garrison and the probe. . . "

By now I was becoming concerned about the severe intensity of N.B.C.'s assault on the case we had developed, not to mention the corresponding effort to smear my office. We had already been the targets of numerous distortions, exaggerations, and even fabrications in the news media. But these "media" people were going far beyond word games. They were engaged in an organized effort to derail an official investigation of a major city's district attorney's office. They were attempting to persuade witnesses to alter their testimony, even attempting to move major witnesses permanently to another part of the country.

When the White Paper entitled "The Case of Jim Garrison" was broadcast nationwide to an audience of millions in June 1967, it required only a few minutes to see that N.B.C. had classified the case as criminal and had appointed itself as the prosecutor.

The three lead-off witnesses were John Cancler, a convicted burglar and pimp better known to local law enforcement officials as "John the Baptist"; Miguel Torres, a convicted burglar serving time at the State Penitentiary at Angola; and a man named Fred Leemans, whom I had never heard of, who turned out to be the proprietor of a "turkish bath" in downtown New Orleans.

On the program, "John the Baptist" announced that he had been a cellmate of Vernon Bundy's. Bundy, he confided, had told him that his story concerning Clay Shaw and Lee Oswald was untrue. This, of course, was an outright lie, but it was merely the first of many to follow.* Cancler also described a callous attempt of the district attorney's office to get him to place false evidence in Clay Shaw's home. Cancler said he rejected out of hand such a questionable suggestion.

In his interview, Torres claimed that the district attorney's office had tried to get him to testify falsely that Clay Shaw had made indecent advances towards him. Even worse, he said, the D.A.'s office tried to get him to say that he knew Shaw to be Clay Bertrand. To help induce him to tell these lies, he revealed, the D.A.'s men had offered him a supply of heroin and a three-month vacation in Florida. Torres, according to the rest of his story, preferred to return to cutting sugar cane at the Louisiana State Penitentiary rather than accept such an unethical vacation.

Then there appeared Leemans, who informed the network interviewer that the D.A.'s office had offered him $2,500 if he would testify that Clay Shaw had visited Leemans' downtown steam emporium with Lee Harvey Oswald. At first he had agreed to the proposal, he indicated. However, after he thought it over, the idea of participating in such an immoral act had begun to eat away at him and he could not go along with it.

And then the round face of Dean Andrews filled the screen as he announced solemnly that it had not been Clay Shaw who had called him the day after the assassination to be Lee Oswald's lawyer. In fact,

---

* One that my staff particularly enjoyed was the network's solemn description of one of its witnesses, William Gurvich, as "the Chief Investigator of the District Attorney's office." A private detective, Gurvich had volunteered to help the investigation but had disappeared from the office months before. He had never been a regular investigator, let alone the chief investigator, of my office.

he said, he would not know Clay Shaw if he fell across him lying dead on the sidewalk.

After the program was over, in view of John Cancler's demonstrated willingness to discuss the veracity of Vernon Bundy, the Orleans Parish Grand Jury wanted to hear Cancler under oath. Its members asked him to repeat what he had told N.B.C. about Bundy having testified falsely concerning Oswald and Shaw. The Grand Jury also wanted to hear him confirm under oath his N.B.C. allegations of improprieties by my office.

Cancler, now citing the Fifth Amendment, refused to repeat his charges on the ground that to do so might cause him to incriminate himself. At the request of the Grand Jury, he was then brought before one of the Criminal Court judges, who again asked him to repeat the charges he had made in front of the entire country. Once more, he took the Fifth Amendment and refused. The judge found him guilty of contempt of court and sentenced him to six months in jail in addition to the servitude awaiting him on his burglary conviction.

Also in response to the Grand Jury's request, Miguel Torres was brought down from the State Penitentiary at Angola to appear before it. Torres, as well, was asked to repeat under oath the accusations he had made nationwide on N.B.C. Like Cancler, Torres refused to respond under oath on the ground that it might incriminate him. In court he took the Fifth Amendment again and also received an added jail sentence for his contempt.

The Grand Jury gave so little credence to Fred Leemans's outlandish steambath story that it did not even bother to call him. As for Dean Andrews, shortly following the N.B.C. program, he was indicted by the Orleans Parish Grand Jury for committing perjury when he testified before it that Clay Shaw was not the "Clay Bertrand" who called him about being Lee Oswald's lawyer. Subsequently, in August 1967, Andrews was found guilty of perjury by a jury of New Orleans citizens.

Within several days after N.B.C. aired the program, I sent off a furious letter of complaint to the Federal Communications Commission. I requested equal time to reply personally to the network's rapacious attack on my office.

The F.C.C. made N.B.C. provide me with a half hour to reply to the hour-long White Paper. Not exactly equal time, but all I needed. I made my reply live from the network's local affiliate, WDSU-TV, and it was broadcast across the country.

Afterwards, I felt I had communicated my message, but I was not left with a satisfied feeling. I kept asking myself, why had N.B.C. worked so long and hard to tear our case apart? Indeed, to tear our office apart.

I had known for years, without having ascribed any particular significance to it, that N.B.C. was a subsidiary of Radio Corporation of America. Now I wanted to know, just what *was* Radio Corporation of America?

At the public library, I learned that R.C.A. had become an integral part of the American defense structure during World War II with its development of the expanded use of radio by the armed forces. This partnership had grown even stronger as R.C.A. went on to develop a new, extremely effective altimeter for high-altitude bombing missions. From there it had moved on into advancing of radar and other sophisticated machinery for the armed forces. Like the American military, R.C.A. had grown from a relatively simple service into a powerful collossus. Its prime military contract awards had increased more than one billion dollars from 1960 to 1967. It no longer was a mere "radio business." Now it was a part of the warfare machine. And its chairman, retired General David Sarnoff, was well known for his belligerent, pro-Cold War public pronouncements and activities.

Given this background, it made more sense to me why R.C.A. and its subsidiary N.B.C. might want to discredit a local district attorney who kept raising the unpleasant possibility that the President had been assassinated by the cold warrior establishment of the United States intelligence community.

Compared to the brutality wrought on the facts by N.B.C., the Columbia Broadcasting System's documentary was civilized— although much of it was untrue. It was aired on four successive evenings in June and, unlike N.B.C.'s White Paper, focused on the assassination rather than on me and my office.

I had been invited by C.B.S. to participate in its epic presentation. I was reluctant because I knew that, one way or another, I would once again receive the shaft from the media. However, I knew of no one else who had been invited to present the case against the lone assassin scenario, so I went.

To my surprise, the network interviewed me extensively, for at least half an hour, during which I explained how President Kennedy had been removed as the result of a conspiracy and described the probable reason.

When the C.B.S. program was shown across the nation, my half hour had been reduced to approximately 30 seconds. This gave me just about enough time to be a discordant bleep in the network's massive four-hour tribute to the Warren Commission.

14

The Company

FROM THE BEGINNING I was concerned about the insufficient size of my staff and budget for an investigation of the J.F.K. assassination. Early on there might have been a chance of obtaining a special increase in our budget, but that had been blown to smithereens by the editorial in the local press and the national onslaught that followed.

The dilemma was solved in an unexpected way. Practically out of the blue, volunteers who had heard about the investigation came to help us. Some arrived on the scene personally, some wrote, others called. By the spring of 1967 we had acquired an "assistant special team" made up of the volunteers. The extra help turned out to be a great lift to the morale of the special team.

One volunteer we picked up was a young Englishman who had been working at the National Archives in Washington. He sent us copies of his excellent research work, and inasmuch as we had no one in Washington to do archive research—in particular to obtain copies of Commission documents for us—we added him to the staff. Later, we had him move down to New Orleans to maintain our own accumulating investigative files, which we called "the Archives."

Next there drifted in a most impressive volunteer—a broad-shouldered, square-jawed former case officer of the Central Intelligence Agency named William Wood. Recognizing that this was a rare opportunity to understand the workings and the mentality of the Agency, we were eager to grab him. However, before we did, we wanted to make sure that he actually had been with the C.I.A.

His story was that he had been with the Agency seven years but had been dropped after he became an alcoholic. While he bore no ill will against the Company,* he felt strongly about what we were trying to do in our Kennedy investigation and wanted to be of help. He was a newsman from Austin, Texas, and had credentials supporting his considerable experience as a newspaperman and investigator.

Wood saw that we were not completely satisfied about his past Agency connection, so he made a suggestion. He had the impression, he said, that an old friend of his from Agency days was still in charge of the Agency infirmary at Langley, Virginia. He gestured to Lou Ivon, who had been sitting in on our long initial interview. Why not, he suggested, have Ivon call the C.I.A., get the doctor on the phone, and then listen in on the conversation between Wood and the doctor?

When the doctor was on the phone and Wood responded, it became obvious that they knew each other well. Wood told the doctor that his drinking days were over, and while he missed the Agency, he had been doing well in the newspaper business. The doctor wished him good luck. Satisfied that Wood had a, genuine Agency background, we welcomed him to the team.

Because of the curiosity of the news media about our activity, we decided it would be best to keep it quiet that we had a former Agency man aboard. So from that time on we used the name "Boxley" instead of Wood. Bill Boxley became a familiar figure in and out of the office. He always carried a loaded .45 automatic pistol, which he kept in a holster under his armpit. This indicated to me that his original intelligence service had been in the U.S. Army, because all of the other American intelligence services used the .38 caliber revolver. He also

---

* "Company" is the term generally used in the intelligence community to refer to the C.I.A.

always carried with him a large rectangular black briefcase. He was an indefatigable worker, and it was apparent that he was dedicated to our effort.

Additional volunteers helped handle the burgeoning leads coming in. One was an urbane, very bright young man who had grown up in Latin America and spoke Spanish like a native; he was useful in interviews with Cuban exiles. Jim Rose, another former C.I.A. employee, was accepted after a strong recommendation from Boxley, who had known him back in his Agency days. Rose had a number of photographs showing himself instructing anti-Castro guerrilla trainees at the No Name Key training camp in Florida back in the early 1960s. Another volunteer was a private detective whose substantial business offered us access to technical equipment we needed. Another volunteer from the west coast had family money which provided him with plenty of free time and a useful travel capability.

With the enthusiasm and the fertile minds of the volunteers, the outlook appeared excellent for a real increase in our productivity. The only problem, as we would learn later, was that many of the volunteers were with us at the behest of the C.I.A. In fact, during one period there were almost as many men on our special team working for the federal government as were working for the New Orleans D.A.'s office. As time passed, however, one would make a mis-step, and I would winnow that one out.

At the beginning of the investigation I had only a hunch that the federal intelligence community had somehow been involved in the assassination, but I did not know which branch or branches. As time passed and more leads turned up, however, the evidence began pointing more and more to the C.I.A.

For example, one of the key players, Guy Banister, had past ties to the O.N.I. and the F.B.I., but his work in New Orleans with the Cuban guerrillas had to be C.I.A. David Ferrie, of course, had trained guerrillas for the Bay of Pigs invasion, a C.I.A. operation. And Jules Ricco Kimble, who had flown on a strange mission to Montreal with Shaw and Ferrie, admitted to getting assignments from C.I.A. case officers. (See Chapter 9.)

The impersonation of Oswald in January 1961 at Bolton Ford, where trucks were being purchased for the Bay of Pigs invasion, smelled of the C.I.A., as did the involvement of George de Mohrenschildt with Lee Oswald. The last-minute change in the parade route in Dallas was highly suspicious and raised serious questions about the mayor of Dallas, Earle Cabell, and his brother, former Deputy Director of the C.I.A. Charles Cabell, who had been fired over the Bay of Pigs fiasco. The parade route change, along with other leads pointing to the C.I.A., had been covered up neatly by the Warren Commission and its point man for intelligence issues, former C.I.A. Director Allen Dulles. Everything kept coming back to Cuba and the Bay of Pigs and the C.I.A.

But why, I kept asking myself, would the C.I.A., entrusted with protecting national security, want to assassinate its own President? All the evidence kept pointing to that, but it just did not make sense. To try to get some handle on it, I began reading everything I could get my hands on concerning the Cold War, the Kennedy presidency, and the intelligence community. With the whole house dark except for a circle of light around my desk, I would stay up until the early hours of the morning, engrossed in books. Somewhere I hoped to find a clue about what might have motivated the C.I.A.—or parts of it—to want to get rid of Kennedy. As I gained more knowledge over a period of months, a possible reason for the assassination started to emerge.

Beginning with his refusal to make air support available to help rescue the C.I.A.'s disastrous invasion of Cuba at the Bay of Pigs in April 1961, President Kennedy had adopted a highly distrustful stance toward the cold warriors at the C.I.A. More important, he had taken significant steps toward a détente with the Soviet Union. Over the initial protests of the Joint Chiefs of Staff, he had authorized Secretary of State Dean Rusk to sign a nuclear test ban treaty with the Soviet Union in 1963. During the Cuban missile crisis he had rejected his advisers' recommendations to bomb and invade Castro's Cuba. Instead, using a naval blockade, he had reached a private understanding with Soviet Premier Nikita Khrushchev, which included Kennedy's commitment that the United States would abandon any plans to invade Cuba. The F.B.I. raid in the summer of 1963 shutting down the

C.I.A.'s anti-Castro guerrilla training camp north of Lake Pont-chartrain was part of the implementation of that understanding.

All of this defied more than a decade of Cold War foreign policy engineered largely by John Foster Dulles, President Eisenhower's secretary of state, and his brother, C.I.A. Director Allen Dulles. By June of 1963 President Kennedy had directly and eloquently renounced the Cold War in a landmark speech at American University in Washington, D.C., underscoring that the United States and the Soviet Union had to live together peacefully on one small planet.

But none of these policy changes was as significant, in retrospect, as Kennedy's intention to withdraw all American military personnel from Vietnam. Why this decision so horrified the foreign policy establishment could be understood only by going back to the beginnings of U.S. involvement in Vietnam.

The American cold warriors' view since the end of World War II, I learned, was that under no circumstances could the U.S. lose control of Vietnam and its valuable natural resources. As early as 1952 a secret National Security Council memo stated bluntly:

> Communist control of all of Southeast Asia would render the U.S. position in the Pacific offshore island chain precarious and would seriously jeopardize fundamental U.S. security interests in the Far East.

In 1954, after French troops surrendered to Ho Chi Minh's forces at Dien Bien Phu, all the relevant powers, except the United States, signed the Geneva Accords temporarily separating the country along the 17th parallel until unification elections could be held. To rescue the American investment, Secretary of State Dulles, General Nathan Twining, and Admiral Arthur Radford initiated a plan for the American military to invade Vietnam, but President Eisenhower blocked it. Instead, Eisenhower, in effect, approved a permanent division of the country by canceling the scheduled elections and creating a separate government in South Vietnam. Under C.I.A. control, military advisers were used to prop up a puppet dictatorship against Ho Chi Minh's forces from the North and the Viet Cong forces in the South, both seeking unification of the country.

This was the situation John Kennedy inherited as incoming President. At first he went along with C.I.A. pressure and authorized an increase in the number of U.S. military advisers. However, he refused to send combat troops. At the time of his death, observed his adviser Kenneth O'Donnell, he was determined to limit American assistance to Vietnam to technicians, helicopter pilots and Green Beret advisers, saying, "I'll never send draftees over there to fight."

In October 1963, seeing the U.S. bogged down in a no-win situation, Kennedy instructed Defense Secretary Robert McNamara to withdraw immediately 1,000 American military advisers from Vietnam—"an order that was quietly rescinded after his death"—and he planned to withdraw all American forces by the end of 1965.

This decision, on top of the new Cuba policy and the signing of the nuclear test ban treaty, added up to nothing less than a fundamental break with Cold War foreign policy, which had been the lifeblood of the C.I.A. Here, it seemed to me, was a plausible motive for the assassination. Though my thinking at this stage was not very developed, at least I could see that the C.I.A.'s vested interest as well as its ideological commitment were to the continuation of the Cold War. John Kennedy had not only threatened to end that but had also, as recalled by Senator George Smathers, threatened to strip the C.I.A. of its "exorbitant power." Along the way he had made implacable enemies—from top-level C.I.A. cold warriors like Allen Dulles, General Charles Cabell, and Richard Helms (then deputy director in charge of covert operations) down to anti-Castro Cuban exiles who felt betrayed at the Bay of Pigs.

While it was difficult for me to accept that an entire agency as enormous as the C.I.A. could have sanctioned and carried out a plan to assassinate the President, it did not seem unreasonable that rogue elements within the Agency or contract agents who had been working with them on other projects might well have. That encompassed a lot of people, among them Clay Shaw, Guy Banister, David Ferrie, and a plenitude of Cuban guerrillas who had been trained north of Lake Pontchartrain.

Although none of the evidence we had gathered definitively implicated the C.I.A., I realized that sophisticated intelligence agencies rarely left smoking guns lying around. Amazingly, though, leads pointing to the Agency continued to come in. This must have worried somebody at Langley because my staff was infiltrated and gradually, over time, I learned that the Agency was actually attempting to obstruct our investigation. This only added to my suspicions that the C.I.A.—or some part of it—had been deeply involved in the assassination.

The Agency's attempted obstruction of our investigation became increasingly perceptible when we tried to extradite Gordon Novel from Ohio. This legal maneuver grew out of the clandestine visit by some of Guy Banister's associates to the blimp base at Houma, Louisiana. (See Chapter 3.) They had removed munitions from the Schlumberger bunker in the middle of the night and brought them into New Orleans.

Some time after we learned about this jaunt, an informant advised us that Novel had taken a photograph of the truck used in picking up the munitions. Subsequently, Novel had sold the photograph to Walter Sheridan of N.B.C. I discussed this unusual case with the D.A. of Houma, and he insisted that as far as his jurisdiction was concerned, the removal of the munitions from the Schlumberger bunker had been a burglary. In my judgment, the transport of the burglarized material into New Orleans had been a felony, and the disposal of evidence relating to the offense (sale of the photograph to N.B.C.) also was a crime committed in New Orleans.

However, before I could question Novel about this latest adventure involving Guy Banister and his personal war against Cuba, Novel picked up word that I was looking for him (probably from one of the half dozen C.I.A. men I had naively embraced as associates) and hit the road.

We located Novel in Ohio and moved for his extradition in April 1967. We wanted to know why the ammunition had been taken from the Schlumberger bunker, why it had been brought into New Orleans, and why the photograph of the truck had been sold to Walter Sheridan.

In the following weeks, Gordon Novel, through interviews and press conferences in Ohio, began providing the public with more enlightenment about some of the C.I.A.'s activities than we had been able to develop in the previous several months. Among other things, he announced that the Schlumberger bunker business had been a C.I.A. enterprise all the way.

Even the *New Orleans States-Item,* which had shown no great interest in our investigation, headlined an article "Evidence Links C.I.A. to D.A. Probe." The article stated that "the strongest C.I.A. ties lead to Gordon Novel." It went on to say that Novel had informed a number of acquaintances that he had been a C.I.A. operative and would use this fact to clear himself of charges that he had participated in the burglary of the Schlumberger bunker.*

"To polygraph operators and to friends and associates," the paper wrote, "Novel has said the munitions burglary was no burglary at all—but a war materiel pickup made at the direction of his C.I.A. contact." Novel indicated that the Schlumberger bunker at the blimp base was in actuality "a C.I.A. staging point for munitions destined to be used as part of the abortive Bay of Pigs attack on Castro's Cuba."

Novel identified the other men present at the removal of the munitions from the bunker as all working for the C.I.A., among them David Ferrie, Sergio Arcacha Smith (former head of the Cuban Revolutionary Front in New Orleans, who moved to Dallas, Texas, following this incident) and a number of anti-Castro Cubans whom he did not know.

Approximately one month later, new evidence indicated more strongly Novel's apparent linkage to the Central Intelligence Agency. A few weeks after Novel had departed the New Orleans scene, two young ladies moved into his apartment in the French Quarter. While cleaning the apartment, they found a penciled draft of a letter wedged under a plastic cover alongside the kitchen sink. The note came to the attention of Hoke May, a *States-Item* reporter, and May subsequently showed the letter to me. When he asked me for permission to publish it, I told him to go ahead.

The authenticity of the letter was confirmed by Novel's attorney, Steven Plotkin, who stated, "Everything in the letter as far as Novel is concerned is actually the truth." Gilbert Fortier, a leading New Orleans handwriting expert, concluded after comparing the letter

---

* The notion that knowledge of one's activities by the C.I.A. could constitute a defense in a criminal proceeding is not that far-fetched. In 1982, five Irish-Americans were acquitted by a Brooklyn federal court jury of gun-running charges which, they argued, the C.I.A. had known about, and tolerated, for years.

with other samples of Novel's handwriting that it indeed had been written by Novel.

The letter was addressed to Novel's apparent New Orleans C.I.A. contact, a man identified only as "Mr. Weiss." It should be added that this letter was written in January 1967, before our investigation had surfaced. In his letter Novel stated:

> I took the liberty of writing you direct and apprising you of current situation, expecting you to forward this through appropriate channels. Our connection and activity of that period involves individuals presently about to be indicted as conspirators in Garrison's investigation. . . . Garrison has subpoenaed myself and an associate to testify before his grand jury on matters which may be classified TOP SECRET. . . .

Novel's letter went on to say that the Agency should take "appropriate counteraction relative to Garrison's inquisition concerning us." He suggested that this could "best be handled through military channels vis-a-vis D.I.A. [Defense Intelligence Agency] man. Garrison is presently colonel in Louisiana Army National Guard and has ready reserve status."

Here we had Gordon Novel suggesting to the C.I.A. that it have the military assign me to active duty as a way to get me off his back. In the end, I was not called for active duty. Nonetheless, we were unable to extradite Novel from Ohio. Even a personal call by Governor John McKeithen of Louisiana to Governor James Rhodes of Ohio, requesting him to extradite Novel, resulted only in Novel's continued protection as a fugitive. Ohio returned Novel's extradition papers to us, stating that they contained "technicalities which do not comply with the law."

This was the first time our office had ever failed in an extradition case, but unfortunately, as we continued to investigate the J.F.K. assassination, it would not be the last. Most of the extraditions I sought in this case were blocked as if a giant foot had stepped on my office. These included an attempt to extradite from Nebraska Perry Russo's ex-girlfriend Sandra Moffett, who had been at the party at David Ferrie's about which Russo had testified.

We received even less cooperation from the federal government than from the states. We tried, for instance, to subpoena F.B.I. Agent Warren DeBrueys, who we believed could enlighten us on a number of issues. An informant had told us that DeBrueys was so involved with Guy Banister, David Ferrie, and the anti-Castro Cubans that instead of operating out of local Bureau headquarters, he had a special office at the Customs House on Canal Street, close to the scene of anti-Castro activity. DeBrueys was summoned by the Parish Grand Jury, but on instructions of the Justice Department, he pleaded executive privilege and refused to testify.

Later I felt it was time for the Grand Jury to hear from Allen Dulles. I wanted to know many things from him, specifically whether or not Clay Shaw, Lee Oswald, David Ferrie, Gordon Novel, and Guy Banister had been associated with the C.I.A., and why his former deputy, General Cabell, had not been questioned by the Warren Commission.

I sent off a subpoena to our nation's capital. A brisk letter from the United States Attorney in Washington, D.C. came back shortly. It informed me that he "declined" to serve the subpoena on Mr. Dulles.

Meanwhile, relatives of Richard Case Nagell, a federal intelligence agent, had been in touch with me. They said that in mid-1963 he had discovered an operation to assassinate President Kennedy. His attempt to warn the government of this, they explained, had resulted in his being sent to the federal penitentiary for three years. He was in the process of being released and wanted to meet with me in another city. If I could not go see him, the family would visit me.

I agreed, and two members of his family flew from New York down to New Orleans to set up the meeting. Their confirmation of the story—although lacking in the background which only he could provide—was convincing. However, he refused to travel outside of New York City, where he recently had arrived following his release from federal prison. I agreed with his family to discuss the matter further the next day.

At home that night I went through the Warren Commission material. According to the hearings index, the name of Nagell had never come up. It did not seem to be in the Commission exhibits either.

Nevertheless, I was curious about this unusual story and determined to find whatever I could about Nagell. If he had been close enough to the assassination planning to have learned about it in advance, I reasoned, then the federal bureaucracy would have produced a report on Nagell. Even if it had been altered to point in the wrong direction, somewhere there had to be a report.

Then, in the Commission documents, I finally stumbled across it. The F.B.I. report said, in full:

> For the record he would like to say that his association with Oswald (meaning Lee Harvey Oswald) was purely social and that he had met him in Mexico City and in Texas.

Nagell indeed had been on the fringe of things, at least, or he would not have been in the Bureau's report. It was evident, however, that it had been heavily sanitized. It was one of the shortest reports produced in the entire F.B.I. investigation. There was no reference to Nagell's occupation. There was no hint of why the F.B.I. had questioned him. There was no reference to the federal charge against him at the time the report had been written. Yet the charge had been real enough that he only now—three years later—was getting out of prison.

The next morning I met with Nagell's family again at my office, and in a few minutes I was talking to him on the phone. He was explicit in his requirements for a rendezvous. It had to be in New York City. I had to be the one to go there; he would not talk to anyone simply representing me. The meeting had to be in the open air, not in a hotel or other enclosed building.

A very uptight guy, I thought, but I assumed he had his reasons. I described a spot in South Central Park, just across 59th Street from the Plaza Hotel, near the great pond. It was an area of light trees and scattered shrubbery and benches. He was agreeable to our meeting there.

So I flew to New York.* A few minutes before the appointed time, I stepped out of the Plaza Hotel and walked across the crowded street into the park. The area was deserted except for a tall, lean man who was

---

* The air fare, as well as the hotel, now had to be paid by me personally, and this was the way things would be from now on because of the newspapers' watch over our fines and fees fund.

standing there with his hands in his pockets. His blondish hair was thinning. He studied me as I approached him.

We shook hands and sat down on a bench together. It was hard to believe that we were in the heart of New York. There was no one nearby. It was a sunny day, with a light breeze riffling through the small trees. There followed, as I recall it, one of the most provocative and frustrating conversations I have ever had. I cannot say he did not warn me at the outset.

"I am not going to identify the organization I worked for in 1963," he said. "You simply will have to draw your own conclusions about that. Nor will I say exactly what I was working on. I am bound by some laws in this area, and I've already had enough problems from the government without having any new ones."

Nevertheless, I could not withhold the query. "Were you with the Company?" I asked.

He shook his head. "I cannot answer that question."

"Then just what information can you give me?" I asked. I had not come all the way to New York to hear him recite the standard secrecy agreement that all agents in the intelligence community are required to sign.

"I am already on record about my learning that the assassination was scheduled and about my effort to contact the Bureau and warn them about it. As far as I am concerned, I have a right to go into that because I have already done so before. I just thought that you should know firsthand what I have to say. Is this of any interest to you?"

I nodded.

In mid-1963 he had been working for the United States government, so Nagell's story began, in an agency which he would not identify. The people for whom he worked, a vagueness from which he never departed, were curious about a project involving a fellow named Lee Oswald and some other men. Consequently, Nagell was assigned to spend some time establishing the necessary relationships and observing. In late August or early September of 1963, for reasons he would not spell out, it became apparent that an exceedingly large—he emphasized the word "large"—operation, pointing toward the assassination of President Kennedy, was under way. At just about the time of this discovery, for reasons he would not explain, the individual who had given him his assignment was moved to another part of the country, and Nagell suddenly found himself without a direct contact.

It was a strange tale, Nagell being "frozen out" by the very government agency which had assigned him to conduct a penetration of the ongoing activity. I can only say that Nagell impressed me as being utterly honest and sincere in his account.

Knowing what was going to happen, he went on, but having no way of knowing when, he decided that the best solution was to notify J. Edgar Hoover, the director of the F.B.I. He wrote Hoover a letter spelling out all that he had been able to learn about the proposed assassination. He sent the letter registered, return receipt requested. Then, as the days and weeks passed with no answer from the F.B.I. chief, he concluded that his attempt to warn of what was approaching had been in vain. Worse, he sensed from the silence which his letter had met that there was a very real danger of his being drawn into a trap. After all, he had been in the company of Oswald, and others with him, during much of the summer of 1963.

Finally, in what he admitted was an act of desperation, he decided that his one safe course was to insure that he was in a federal institution on the day the assassination occurred. He would rather be charged, he reasoned, with malicious mischief than be drawn into a giant trap involving the assassination of a President. He walked into a federal bank in El Paso, fired several shots in the ceiling, then waited outside sitting on the curb until the guard came running by. He had to call back the guard, who in his haste had rushed past him.

But Nagell was not charged with malicious mischief. The government charged him with armed robbery. Moreover, at his trial he was convicted, and the judge sentenced him to ten years imprisonment.*

Nagell answered a few questions. Had he actually been in physical association with Lee Oswald? Right there with him? Yes, he replied. And with other men connected with Oswald? The answer was yes. Where did this occur? In New Orleans and in Texas.

I asked him whether these other men and Oswald all were working

---

* He had served three years. Two years later, his conviction was reversed on the grounds there was no evidence of intent to rob.

together on the project or whether the others were manipulating Oswald. He thought this question through at some length. Then he said that he did not pretend to have been close enough to know for sure, but his intuition was that the others had manipulated Oswald from the outset.

I asked him the names of the other men. He hesitated, but when the answer came, it was specific: Guy Banister, Clay Shaw, and David Ferrie.

With what organization were these men connected? Now he looked at me with a half smile and shook his head slowly. I pressed. Were they connected with the C.I.A.? "I cannot discuss or name any government organization," he replied. In spite of the troubles he had been through, he would not say a word about the intelligence community at large, with the single exception of the F.B.I.'s having ignored his warning letter about President Kennedy's murder. And that was the sum of Nagell's story. Beyond the precise parameters he had established he would not be budged a centimeter.

During most of my flight home I reflected long and hard on my Central Park meeting with Richard Case Nagell. I had studied him closely for all of the three hours or so we were together, and I was satisfied that weaving a fabricated tale was not in this man's makeup. On the other hand, there seemed to be no getting around the fact that his account was not easy to digest. I concluded that I would probably have to chalk up the Central Park scene to experience.

Many years down the road I found myself reading an account of Nagell's arrest by East German police as he attempted to cross back into West Germany. Richard Case Nagell definitely was not your basic insurance salesman.

Whether Nagell had come to me on his own or had been sent by some intelligence apparatus to set me up in some unknown way I never learned. But another incident that followed made me realize that I could be entrapped and discredited at any time.

Increasingly I had begun making speeches at various universities, hoping that by communicating with students throughout the country I could offset the hysterical assault of the plainly unified mass media.

Equally important, I had fast been using up my savings from the National Guard, and the fees from these talks were becoming helpful in continuing to finance our investigation.

So here I was about to go on the road again. This time I had a speech coming up at New Mexico University, and it was on this trip that our domestic intelligence structure made its first attempt to entrap me. I arrived at the university in Albuquerque in the afternoon and that evening spoke for several hours to the students. I received a heart-warming and encouraging response, as I usually did at universities.

Almost immediately after the talk Bill Boxley, the former C.I.A. man who had become one of my volunteer investigators, appeared in the lobby of my motel. I was surprised to see him because I thought he was back in New Orleans.

Pulling me off to the side, he told me with great concern that word had been received that an attempt was going to be made to kill me. He had been left with no alternative but to fly to New Mexico where he could act as my bodyguard. He expressed relief at having made it there in time.

I had always had a high regard for Boxley's intelligence and ability. For once, however, I was furious. I found an empty table and led him to it. "I notice," I said, "that you always carry a forty-five." He nodded, patting his shoulder holster. "What branch of the Army were you in before you went into the C.I.A.?" I asked.

He paused, uncertain where I was headed. "The infantry. I was a dogface for years. Then the Army Counter-Intelligence Corps. Then into the Agency. What's the problem?"

"When you were in the Army," I asked, "did you have a chance to find out what an order meant?" He nodded. "Do you happen to remember," I continued, "my ordering everyone on my staff not to participate in passing on these horror stories, these endless rumors about how somebody is going to be killed?"

"Yes, but——" he began.

"There is no but," I said. "I don't appreciate your dumping this paranoid garbage on me. And I don't appreciate your inability to follow a simple order. Especially," I added, "when it means that I personally am going to end up paying for your flight out here and back." The last I growled at him almost savagely because Boxley was always out of money, and I continually had to write checks for him.

Over my angry objections, still adamantly protesting that I needed protection, Boxley shared my suite at the motel that night. Placing his large .45 automatic pistol on the table beside him, he slept on the sofa. The next morning he went with me to the airport and saw me off to Los Angeles, where I had some people to meet in connection with our investigation.

When I arrived at the Los Angeles airport, I went straight to the magazine rack to buy something to read. There were no seats at the Los Angeles airport baggage claim area, and I have always been allergic to standing around wasting time. Consequently, as I had remarked to Boxley a month or so earlier when the flight to Los Angeles had been mentioned, at the L.A. airport I always went to the men's room, sat down in a toilet booth, and read a magazine for about ten minutes until my luggage arrived. Then I would pick it up, hail a cab, and be on my way.

This time something unusual happened. After buying a copy of *Life,* I went into the men's room to read it. I opened to an article by General James Gavin recommending that we adopt new techniques of defense in the Vietnam War. At just that moment, I heard the door in the booth right next to me open and close. I had taken the first in a long line of empty booths. When someone almost immediately entered the very next booth, I knew that something was wrong. I closed the magazine on my lap and listened.

Then I heard low whispering voices at the door. I did not wait a second longer. Since all I had intended to do was read, I was already fully dressed and thus was able to open the door of the booth quickly. Two fat uniformed airport policemen were stuck momentarily in the exit door of the men's room as they sought to rush out of it simultaneously, apparently in response to my unexpected emergence. The three of us left together.

Then I saw a ring of at least half a dozen additional airport police in uniforms, gathered in a semi-circle around the entrance to the men's room. Even as it was dawning on me that I had been set up, the sergeant in charge of them addressed me sharply. "Hey, mister!" he said in an accusatory tone. "How long were you in that men's room?" The answer, of course, was two or three minutes at the outside. However, under the circumstances, that hardly was the point.

Even as he addressed me, I noticed that two women assistants working at the counter for one of the rent-a-car services were staring at me and had recognized me. As a by-product of the intensive media assault, I had been receiving almost continual television coverage. This was one occasion when it was useful.

"That's none of your goddamn business," I yelled at him. I turned and, as I walked past the other policemen toward the luggage ramp, I saw the sergeant in charge shake his head. The other policemen, who had been standing in my way, moved apart and let me through.

Climbing into a cab, I knew how lucky I had been to get away. As I had a chance to reflect, I realized that there was more to the snare than had then been visible. I remembered a curious phone call I had received about three weeks earlier from Los Angeles. The call had come to my house in New Orleans, where I had an unlisted telephone number. The caller was a man I had not seen in many years. I had once represented him briefly on a federal case. I recalled him as a grimy, furtive, and disheveled homosexual who sold pornographic photographs for a living. Such a client was hardly to my choosing, but at the time I was in the business of representing criminal as well as civil cases, and so I had accepted his case. But this man failed to pay me, and I notified the court that I was no longer his attorney.

Years later, only three weeks before the bizarre incident at the airport, this character had called me out of the blue. After he identified himself, I asked him how he had obtained my unlisted number. He responded vaguely that he had connections. I then asked him why he was calling me, and he launched into a weird explanation. He was thinking of visiting New Orleans during the next Mardi Gras, he said, and he thought perhaps we could get together. I told him that I had no intention of getting together with him anytime or anywhere and slammed down the phone.

Now, I suddenly realized who had been placed in the booth next to me just prior to my intended arrest at the Los Angeles airport. As an experienced prosecutor, it was not difficult for me to envision what would have happened had I not shot out of the men's room so quickly, emerging along with the two policemen. One way or the other, my seedy former client would have arranged to come out of his stall at about the same time as I emerged from mine. Any of a variety of eminently prosecutable scenes would have been created. The airport police would have responded, and at my subsequent trial for violating some obscenity misdemeanor under California law, I would have found myself as the defendant under cross-examination. At the appropriate moment a prosecutor would have asked me if I still had any relationship with my former client, who would have just finished testifying for the prosecution. I would have responded, of course, that I did not. Then the prosecutor would have produced the man's Los Angeles telephone bill. It would have on it a long distance call to me at my unlisted home number in New Orleans. That would have been the end of the ballgame.

My conviction of the sex misdemeanor charge would have made headlines across the nation, the Louisiana legislature would have been left with no alternative but to remove me from office, and the C.I.A. would have accomplished one more dirty trick in the name of national security.

I analyzed the whole affair repeatedly during my visit in Los Angeles and my flight home. But I could not figure out how the Los Angeles airport police knew exactly what flight I would be on.

The answer came much later when Vincent Salandria, a distinguished Philadelphia attorney who was the most prominent critic of the Warren Commission's explanation of President Kennedy's bullet wounds, came down to see our investigative team in action. On the day Salandria arrived, Bill Boxley was presenting to the special team some evidence he had tracked down in Dallas on a recent trip.

After the meeting broke up, Salandria asked me if he could look at other material—memos, notes—from Boxley. I picked out some samples from the files, and Salandria spent the rest of the day going through the folders. When we got home, he suggested we go into the living room and talk.

"You once mentioned your concern about your office being penetrated," he said almost idly as he turned over the papers on his lap. Salandria had an unusually soft, unruffled voice, suggestive of silk sliding across silk.

"That's right," I said. "Perhaps you get paranoid in this sort of thing. It's just a feeling I've had."

"Jim," he said softly, "I'm afraid your friend, Bill Boxley, works for the federal government."

I had a cold feeling over my entire body.

And then Salandria methodically showed me why that had to be the case. Boxley's memos and summaries—each impressive in its own right—did not add up when evaluated as a whole. It was embarrassingly apparent that Boxley's material had been designed, first, to intrigue me and, second, to lead nowhere at all.

Salandria picked up the phone and called Boxley. "Bill," he said, "Jim and I have been having a conversation. We're over at his place. We wondered if you could come by."

Two hours later I looked at my watch. "He's not coming over," I said.

"I think you'll find that Mr. Boxley has gone," he replied.

I got Lou Ivon on the phone and told him to come over. Then we drove to Boxley's rented room on Canal Boulevard. I had never been in it. The landlady let us in the front door. "No," she said, "I haven't seen the man since he rented the room earlier this year. He just sends me a check every month."

She showed me Boxley's room. A shirt, folded from the cleaners, had been tossed on the bed. "He left that shirt here six months ago," she said. I showed her Boxley's home number in my address book. She shook her head. "There's no phone with that number here."

"Somewhere around here," Salandria purred, "the government has to have a very comfortable safe house. But I doubt if we'll ever see it."

I did not reply. I was thinking about the incident at the L.A. airport. It finally hit me. It was Boxley who had told the airport police which flight I would be on. He had called them from New Mexico after seeing me get on the plane. The story about an attempt to kill me was concocted. His real mission had been not to protect me but to set me up.

I was disgusted with myself. I had been so blind. In contrast, Vincent Salandria had taken a single day away from his law practice in Philadelphia, flown down, and had pegged Boxley virtually in one sharp-eyed glance.

The next day we learned that Boxley had traveled to Beaumont, Texas, following Salandria's phone call. From there, using the name of Wood, he sent telegrams to the editors of the *Times-Picayune* newspaper and each of the local television stations stating that he had resigned as an office investigator upon learning that I was addicted to drugs.

A reporter from one of the TV stations gave a copy of the telegram to Lou Ivon and asked him curiously who this man Wood was, but that's as far as the story got; Boxley's eleventh-hour riposte disappeared like a stone dropped in the center of Lake Pontchartrain, leaving not a ripple.

Still, the man had been sitting in on our innermost meetings for months. With his big briefcase always in his hand, he had been in and out of our file room a hundred times. I had to admit that I had been badly fooled. And worse, every one of our files now had to be considered duplicated by the federal government.

15

Shell Game

NEARLY TWO YEARS ELAPSED between Clay Shaw's arrest on March 1, 1967, and the beginning of his trial. Our office spent much of that time prosecuting routine local crimes, countering legal maneuvers by Shaw's lawyers, and preparing our case against Shaw. The leads we pursued took us in many directions, some of which had little to do with Shaw. For me, the most fascinating research in this latter part of the investigation involved the "cover-up" of the truth about the assassination by law enforcement officials and the media.

The manipulations of evidence by the Warren Commission and the Dallas homicide unit in their investigations of the murder of J.D. Tippit were prime examples. Tippit, of course, was the Dallas police officer who was shot to death approximately half an hour after the assassination. The murder took place across the dry Trinity River from Dallas in the suburb of Oak Park, not too far from where Lee Oswald was boarding at the time. Though the case was never tried, both the Warren Commission and Dallas homicide agreed that the killer, who left the scene with an icy nonchalance, flicking away used shells from his gun, was Lee Oswald.

This was a useful conclusion. Among other things, it provided the government with a motivation for the assassination: Lee Oswald was a troubled and temperamental young man so violent that he was capable of shooting down a police officer in cold blood with no provocation; therefore such a savage madman was also capable of murdering the President for no reason. Or as one member of the Warren Commission's legal staff rhetorically posed the question and the answer: "How do we know that Lee Oswald killed President Kennedy? Because he killed Officer Tippit." Conveniently, the converse also worked: Only a man who had just killed the President and knew he was being hunted down would have any reason to shoot a police officer in a quiet suburb at mid-day.

The only problem with this scenario was that, as so often before, when I examined the evidence, the damning conclusions about Oswald just did not hold up.

First of all, given what was known about Oswald's movements, it was highly improbable that he could have been physically present at the time of Tippit's murder. According to several eyewitnesses at the scene, Tippit was shot anywhere from 1:06 p.m. to 1:10 p.m. Deputy Sheriff Roger Craig, who was at the Book Depository at the time, confirmed this. When he heard the report of Tippit's death on the radio, he looked at his watch; it was 1:06 p.m. And yet Oswald, it was generally acknowledged, had returned to his rooming house at around 1:00 p.m. He left quickly and Earline Roberts, the housekeeper, observed him standing by the northbound Beckley Avenue bus stop at 1:04. The area where Tippit was killed was in the opposite direction— a mile to the south. Using the broadest interpretation of the time element, even if Oswald had changed his mind about the bus and run southward, it was virtually impossible for him to have arrived at the scene before the shooting of the police officer.

The Warren Commission simply ignored these time anomalies and presented various eyewitnesses whose testimony quickly fell apart. Domingo Benavides, who had been the closest of all the witnesses to the shooting (a few yards), would not identify Oswald as having been there.

Warren Reynolds, who had seen a gunman running on Jefferson Street a block from the shooting, did testify that the man he had seen was Oswald. But the circumstances of his testimony were highly suspicious. Reynolds initially had told the F.B.I. that he would "hesitate" to identify Oswald as the running man. Shortly afterwards, Reynolds had been shot in the head in the dark of a car lot basement. After a miraculous recovery in the hospital, Reynolds had second thoughts about what he had seen and decided the running man actually was Oswald.

The inconsequential testimony of these and several other witnesses left Helen Markham as the centerpiece of the government's case against Oswald. As I read Markham's testimony, it occurred to me that few prosecutors had ever found themselves with a witness at once so eager to serve their cause and simultaneously so destructive to it.

While the other witnesses at the scene unanimously agreed that Tippit died instantly, Markham explicitly recalled trying to talk with him for 20 minutes before the ambulance arrived. Despite the Warren Commission's lawyers' excruciating attempt to lead her to an identification of Lee Oswald (a fairly tall and skinny young man with thinning, light brown hair), she informed Mark Lane, a well-known critic of the government's investigation, that Tippit's killer was stocky and had "bushy hair." Thereafter, under oath she denied having done so and only admitted it after hearing a tape recording of the conversation. Then, making matters even more confusing for the government, Markham described the killer she saw as having "black hair."

Before her testimony was completed, Markham had raised doubts in the minds of some observers that she even was at the scene of Tippit's murder. At least two witnesses did not recall seeing her there.

Yet, with all that, Markham was the government's best witness, the only one who identified Lee Oswald as the killer of Officer Tippit. And here is how that identification went before the Warren Commission:

MR. BALL: Now when you went into the room you looked these people over, these four men?

MRS. MARKHAM: Yes, sir.

MR. BALL: Did you recognize anyone in the line-up?

MRS. MARKHAM: No, sir.

MR. BALL: You did not? Did you see anybody—I have asked you that question before—did you recognize anybody from their face?

MRS. MARKHAM: From their face, no.

MR. BALL: Did you identify anybody in these four people?

MRS. MARKHAM: I didn't know nobody.

MR. BALL: I know you didn't know anybody, but did anybody in that line-up look like anybody you had seen before?

MRS. MARKHAM: No. I had never seen none of them before.

MR. BALL: No one of the four?

MRS. MARKHAM: No one of them.

MR. BALL: No one of all four?

MRS. MARKHAM: No, sir.

Ultimately, out of desperation the Commission's attorney had to resort to putting a leading question to his own witness—absolutely inadmissible in any real court—in order to telegraph to the witness what he wanted to hear:

MR. BALL: You recognized him from his appearance?

MRS. MARKHAM: I asked—I looked at him. When I saw this man I wasn't sure, but I had cold chills just run over me.

This brief exchange constituted the totality of the witness testimony identifying Lee Oswald as Tippit's murderer.

There were other significant witnesses, of course. Among these were the ambulance driver and his helper, who could have clarified the time of Tippit's death and which witnesses were present at the scene; Mr. and Mrs. Donald Higgins, who lived directly across from the murder scene and observed some of what occurred; and T. F. Bowley, who used the dead officer's car microphone to inform the police radio dispatcher that Tippit had just been killed. But none of these was ever called by the Warren Commission.

There were also three important eyewitnesses to the murder who changed the whole face of the case for me. I discovered them in the rapidly burgeoning body of work by legitimate critics of the Commission. Mark Lane, the critic who later came to New Orleans to work with our investigation, had tracked down and interviewed one of these witnesses—Acquilla Clemons. Before the first shot, she observed *two* men standing near Officer Tippit's police car. She saw one of the men with a pistol, waving away the other, as he trotted toward Jefferson Street on the far side of the block.

The running man, the one she recalled as having shot the police officer, was in her words "kind of short, kind of heavy." The second man she recalled as tall and thin, wearing a white shirt and khaki slacks— clothing which no other witnesses recalled Oswald wearing that day. Clemons said Dallas police officers told her not to tell anyone what she had seen lest she be killed, a familiar piece of law enforcement advice in Dallas that day.

I also learned about Frank Wright from Lane.* Wright saw the last part of the scene that Clemons had described. It was Wright's wife who called the ambulance that carried Tippit's dead body away.

Mr. Wright, who had been inside the house, came out in time to see Officer Tippit roll over on the ground, probably the last move of his life. Wright observed another man looking down on the fallen officer. Then the man circled around the police car and got into an old, gray car on the other side of it. He drove off rapidly.

It seemed to me quite probable that this was the second man Clemons had observed, the one who was waved off by the short, heavy one who ran away. It began to dawn on me that these witnesses were saying something no one else had said: Officer Tippit was killed by two men, neither of whom was Lee Oswald. The implications, I realized, were staggering. If Oswald was innocent of the Tippit murder, the foundation of the government's case against him collapsed.

Three years before, F.B.I. Director J. Edgar Hoover must have come to the same conclusion I did, because he explicitly ordered the special agent in charge of the Dallas Bureau office not to permit his agents to question Acquilla Clemons or Mr. and Mrs. Wright. I did not know this until many years later when the F.B.I. memo from Hoover to

* Mark Lane's locating and interviewing of key witnesses to Officer Tippit's shooting probably was the earliest and most outstanding work done by all the critics of the official conclusion concerning the assassination.

Gordon Shanklin was revealed in a book by Michael Kurtz. But one thing I did know at the time was that I could not find a shred of testimony from Clemons or the Wrights in the Warren Commission materials.

As I continued my research, I discovered that beyond the eyewitnesses there was other evidence gathered and altered by the Dallas homicide unit showing that Lee Oswald had been framed in the Tippit murder. For instance, I read transcripts of the messages sent over the Dallas police radio shortly after the murder. These were recorded automatically on a log. Just minutes after a citizen first reported the murder on Tippit's radio, Patrolman H.W. Summers in Dallas police unit number 221 (the designation for the squad car) reported that an "eyeball witness to the getaway man" had been located. The suspect was described as having black wavy hair, wearing an Eisenhower jacket of light color, with dark trousers and a white shirt. He was "apparently armed with a .32, dark finish, automatic pistol," which he had in his right hand. Moments later, Sergeant G. Hill reported that "the shell at the scene indicates that the suspect is armed with an automatic .38 rather than a pistol."*

It seemed clear to me from this that the hand gun used to shoot Tippit was an automatic. But the gun allegedly taken from Lee Oswald when Dallas police later arrested him at the Texas Theatre was a revolver. Unless Oswald had stopped and changed guns, which no one had ever suggested, this fact alone put a severe hole in the government's case.

---

* To appreciate the injustice described here, it is necessary to understand the difference between an automatic hand gun and a revolver. An automatic contains the bullets in a clip, which fits inside its handle. Each time the gun is fired, the empty cartridge remaining in the chamber is automatically flipped out by the ejector mechanism as the new cartridge and bullet are pushed up into place by a spring at the bottom of the clip. A revolver, typified in American tradition by the long-barreled hand weapon of the Old West, holds its cartridges and bullets in a circular, revolving chamber and does not automatically eject each cartridge as fired. One of the major differences between the two weapons is that each time the automatic flips out a used cartridge it leaves on it an ineradicable mark of the ejector mechanism. A revolver does not do this; it leaves only the mark of the firing pin.

Another difference is that revolvers are usually all metal and have a relatively small gripping handle, whereas an automatic has a large flat handle, which ordinarily has a dark blue metallic finish.

The bullets found in Officer Tippit's body and the cartridges found at the scene of his murder yielded further evidence of the frameup. The Dallas coroner had conducted an autopsy on Tippit's body and had removed four bullets from it. Three of them, it turned out, were copper-coated and had been manufactured by the Winchester Western company. The fourth, however, was a lead bullet made by the Remington-Peters company.

This was awfully strange, I thought, because bullets were never sold in mixed lots. Gun users bought either a box of all Winchesters or one of all Remingtons, but not some of each. The discovery of two different makes of bullets in Tippit's body indicated to me—and would indicate to most experienced police officers—a likelihood that two different gunmen did the shooting. This was consistent with the eyewitness testimony of Acquilla Clemons and Mr. and Mrs. Wright.

When a homicide occurs, it is standard operating procedure for the police homicide division to send off the bullets and cartridges to the F.B.I. laboratory in Washington, D.C. for study and possible identification of the gun that fired them. In this case, the Dallas homicide unit, understandably shy about advertising the coroner's discovery, sent only *one* bullet to the F.B.I. lab, informing the Bureau that this was the only bullet found in Tippit's body.

To everyone's surprise, the Bureau lab found that the bullet did not match Oswald's revolver. When it discovered this oddity, the Warren Commission was inspired to look for other bullets that might match up better. Although the Commission never received a copy of Tippit's autopsy report, somehow it found out that four bullets—rather than merely one—had been found in Tippit's body. The ordinarily incurious Commission asked the F.B.I. to inquire about the three missing bullets, and they were found—after four months—gathering dust in the files of the Dallas homicide division.

These bullets were sent to the F.B.I. lab. But Special Agent Courtlandt Cunningham, the ballistics expert from the lab, testified before the Commission that the lab was unable to conclude that any of the four bullets found in Tippit's body had been fired by the revolver taken from Lee Oswald.

The cartridges allegedly found at the scene proved even more problematic. While the bullets had initially been under the control of the coroner who found them in Tippit's body, the cartridges—the metal casings which provide propulsion power to the bullets—were Dallas homicide's responsibility from the outset.

On the very day of Officer Tippit's murder, Dallas homicide had made a summary of all the evidence it had in the case—a most important standard police procedure. Although a number of witnesses mentioned that they had seen cartridges strewn around after the shooting and the early recorded radio messages had described the murder weapon as an automatic because of the ejector marks on cartridges found at the scene, this summary did not include cartridges of any kind.

It was not until six days after it had sent the single bullet to the F.B.I. lab in Washington that the Dallas homicide division finally added four cartridges allegedly found at the scene to the Tippit evidence summary. The cartridges were then sent off to Washington, and the Bureau lab promptly reported back that they indeed had been fired by the same revolver that Oswald allegedly purchased through the mail under the alias of A. Hidell.

The Dallas police force may have been relieved to hear this result, but to me the late appearance of the cartridges only focused more attention on the Dallas homicide unit's unconscionable manipulation of evidence. I knew that if the cartridges had actually been fired by Oswald before his arrest, they routinely would have been included in the summary of evidence and sent off to the F.B.I. lab on the evening of the murder. But these cartridges were not sent until well *after* Dallas homicide had learned that the lab could not find positive markings from Oswald's gun on the single bullet. (This evaluation would have come from the Washington lab to the Dallas Bureau office by telex within 24 hours.)

It seemed clear to me what had happened. Having failed to get a positive identification with Oswald's revolver from the bullet, Dallas homicide was not about to send off cartridges with an automatic hand gun's ejector marks on them even if these were the actual cartridges found at the scene. Instead, someone in the homicide division or cooperating with it had fired the confiscated revolver *after* Oswald's arrest, thereby obtaining the needed cartridges bearing its imprint. Then those cartridges were sent to Washington.

However, competence was not the Dallas homicide unit's strong suit, even in fabricating evidence. The F.B.I. lab found that *two* of the cartridge cases had been manufactured by Western and *two* by Remington. Since the lab had already concluded that *three* of the bullets found in Tippit's body were copper-coated Westerns and *one* was a lead Remington, these numbers simply did not add up.

Worse yet, at the Warren Commission hearings it became embarrassingly apparent that the used cartridges that the Dallas homicide team had sent to the F.B.I. lab were not the cartridges actually found at the scene of Tippit's murder. One witness, Domingo Benavides, found two used cartridge shells not far from the shooting and handed them to Officer J.M. Poe. Dallas Police Sergeant Gerald Hill instructed Poe to mark them—*i.e.,* to scratch his initials on them in order to maintain the chain of evidence. This is standard operating procedure for all homicide officers everywhere.

Poe informed the Warren Commission that he believed he had marked them, but he could not swear to it. At the Commission hearing Poe examined four cartridges that were shown to him but was unable to identify his marks on them. Sergeant W.E. Barnes informed the Commission that he had received two cartridges from Officer Poe back at police headquarters and had added his own initials to them. However, he too was unable to positively identify the two shells.

After I had gone through all the evidence, I knew I had some serious thinking to do. My study suggested that two men had murdered Officer J.D. Tippit. This did not surprise me. For the architects of the assassination of the President to have sent one layman armed with a .38 caliber hand gun to eliminate a trained police officer would have been a bad mistake. Any experienced officer wounded once or even twice by a .38, the heaviest caliber used in the Tippit murder, could still, with some luck, end up shooting his assailant through the head. So if the removal of Tippit was important to the plot—perhaps as a way to set up Oswald and show that he was indeed brutally violent—then at least two men were needed to do the job properly.

The overwhelming evidence that Oswald had not committed the Tippit murder confirmed all the prior research I had done indicating that Oswald was a mild-mannered man incapable of such violence. In the Shaw trial to come, I knew that if I could convince a jury that Oswald was incapable of murdering John Kennedy or J.D. Tippit, this would improve our chances for a conviction immensely. It would immediately force the jury to consider the possibility of a conspiracy as a realistic alternative to the Warren Commission scenario.

But the Tippit case was most significant to me because it revealed the extent of a cover-up perpetrated by the Dallas Police Department—or rather by the Dallas homicide unit. I had to remind myself that in a city of Dallas's size, the homicide unit was small, ranging from six to nine police officers. A sophisticated planner of the assassination would have been able to predict who would be investigating after the crime was committed and might well be able to control the key people. But just because this unit, under the iron command of Captain Will Fritz for more than three decades, had concealed and manipulated evidence was no reason to condemn the entire department.

I recalled what I knew about the homicide unit's behavior in the Kennedy case. It had discovered a possible murder weapon, a 7.65 Mauser rifle, in the sixth-floor "lair" of the Texas School Book Depository and promptly lost it. (See Chapter 7.) It had questioned Lee Oswald for 12 hours and failed to record a word of the interrogation. (See Chapter 2.) It had allowed several suspects arrested in the vicinity of Dealey Plaza to be released without as much as getting their names or mug shots. (See Chapters 2 and 16.) It had failed to check out the Nash Rambler station wagon that Deputy Sheriff Roger Craig had spotted taking Oswald away from the Book Depository. Indeed, it had lied about the incident, denying that Craig had ever been at police headquarters. (See Chapter 7.) Worst of all, it had allowed Oswald to be killed in the basement of its own headquarters surrounded by dozens of police officers and then immediately closed its books on the assassination, considering it solved.

Now added to this appalling record was the blatant manipulation of evidence in the Tippit case—the concealing of three bullets, the disappearance of automatic cartridges found at the scene, the tardy "discovery" of revolver cartridges, the failure to pursue any leads to the two men who had been seen by eyewitnesses.

At first it seemed to me that Dallas homicide's objective had been to develop a case against Oswald, the man it had hastily decided was the assassin. No matter what it took, it wanted to pin the Tippit murder on Oswald, thus bolstering the proposition that he was indeed capable of killing the President for no apparent reason.

But as I reviewed the record, a second more horrifying thought occurred to me. Perhaps Dallas homicide had systematically altered evidence not just to nail Oswald in a fit of misguided patriotism. Perhaps it had behaved as it had *intentionally, to protect* the actual killers of both John Kennedy and J.D. Tippit. If that were true, it would mean we were dealing with something beyond incompetence, even beyond cover-up. It would mean that Dallas homicide—or key members of it—had at worst colluded in the assassination before it happened or at best actively ratified it afterwards.

16

Escape of
the Assassins

WHO ACTUALLY PULLED the triggers had never interested me as much as who organized, paid for, and benefited from the assassination of John Kennedy. But the fact that so many suspects in and around Dealey Plaza on November 22, 1963, had been allowed to go free by the Dallas authorities interested me a great deal. If those suspects had been properly detained and questioned, I felt, one of them might well have led authorities to the planners behind the assassination.

From Deputy Sheriff Roger Craig and other witnesses I already knew about the exodus of three suspicious men from the Book Depository shortly after the fatal shots were fired. The vehicle they departed in was a Nash Rambler station wagon, light in color, with a luggage rack on top. During the shooting it was parked on Houston Street, adjacent to the back entrance of the Depository and facing *north*—the wrong direction for traffic on Houston. No one observed a driver sitting in it while it was parked.

After the shooting was over, the three men came running out of the back entrance of the Depository and poured into the station wagon. It headed north on Houston so fast that one door still was flapping open. From Craig I knew that it circled back, pausing right in front of the Depository to pick up another young man. This young man jumped into the station wagon, which quickly sped off.

The astonishing thing about this brief trip was not that law enforcement officials did not interfere but that the station wagon's movements were so bold. They suggested that the driver virtually anticipated no interference. In fact, the average American encounters more trouble driving downtown on an ordinary mid-afternoon than this driver encountered driving rapidly in the wrong direction on a one-way street at the scene of the murder of the President of the United States. Roger Craig's report of this incident to Dallas Homicide Chief Will Fritz, it will be recalled, got nowhere. No one even bothered to check on who owned the station wagon.

Witnesses behind the presidential motorcade heard shooting not only from the Book Depository but also from the Dal-Tex Building near Houston and Elm. At least one man arrested immediately after the shooting had come running out of the Dal-Tex Building and offered no explanation for his presence there. Local authorities hardly could avoid arresting him because of the clamor of the onlookers. He was taken to the Sheriff's office, where he was held for questioning. However, the Sheriff's office made no record of the questions asked this suspect, if any were asked; nor did it have a record of his name. Later two uniformed police officers escorted him out of the building to the jeers of the waiting crowd. They put him in the police car, and he was driven away. Apparently this was his farewell to Dallas, for he simply disappeared forever.

Another man was arrested at the Dal-Tex Building. According to Dallas law enforcement authorities, he gave his name as Jim Braden and was released after being checked out. Astonishingly, this time the federal government offered a considerable amount of information about the suspect. His real name, it was said, was Eugene Hale Brading, and he was an ex-convict with a history of several dozen arrests. In the several months before the assassination he had begun using the name Jim Braden, under which his oil business in Los Angeles was listed. He explained to authorities that he had been in Dallas on business, with the approval of his parole officer. Only a few days earlier, he had

had an appointment with one of the sons of H.L. Hunt, the oil billionaire. Braden had been in the Dal-Tex Building at the time of the assassination, he claimed, because he wanted to make a phone call. When he discovered the pay phone there was out of order, he walked out to find himself arrested.

This story contained several provocative leads to what I now recognized as "false sponsors"* of the assassination. Not only had the man's explanation for being in the Dal-Tex Building been vague, but he had a long arrest record with connections evocative of "organized crime," the number one false sponsor that the media vaguely alluded to; and his trail led to H.L. Hunt, a representative of the "Southwest oil magnates," the number two false sponsor that always seemed to come up. After sustained analysis, however, it was clear that Braden's contribution to the assassination was a large zero. This, I concluded, was probably the reason why his name—and his alone of all the suspects— was made available to the public.

I was aware that the local authorities also had ignored suspects on the grassy knoll in front of the presidential motorcade. Long before, I had learned that Julia Ann Mercer had seen a man carrying a rifle case up the grassy knoll an hour before the assassination. Police officers standing on the nearby overpass observed what was happening and made no move to interfere. (See Chapters 2 and 17.)

Only much later did I learn of yet another suspect who got away immediately after the shooting by literally sliding down the back side of the grassy knoll to his car. Tom Tilson, an off-duty police officer, had heard about the shooting over his car radio and had seen the President's car moving at high speed. As he drove near the overpass, he saw a man "slipping and sliding" down the slope west of the overpass, which was the far side from the Book Depository. This was the only man Officer Tilson could see running away from the shooting, so he watched him. The man came down against the side of a car parked there, threw something in the back seat, then jumped in the front seat and took off at high speed.

---

* "False sponsors" are fictitious suspects routinely created by the intelligence community's disinformation machinery following some covert action to lead the unwary down the wrong path away from government intelligence. See Chapter 20 for a more detailed treatment of the use of false sponsors.

Tilson followed the car in a wild chase. When he got close enough, he called out the license number and the make and model of the car to his daughter riding with him. She wrote the information down, and after the car got away, he called it in to the Dallas homicide squad. But there was no response from homicide. Officer Tilson never heard another word about the suspect he had chased.

At the time I was looking into the matter of the escaped suspects, a computer consultant from New York named Richard E. Sprague contacted me. Sprague had collected and studied extensively many of the approximately 500 still photographs and motion pictures taken at Dealey Plaza on the day of the assassination. He was particularly excited about several news photos that showed three men arrested in the railroad yard, behind the grassy knoll, being marched away by police armed with shotguns.

By studying many photos taken of the grassy knoll area to President Kennedy's right front, Sprague had traced the flight of these three men to the empty boxcar in the railroad yard, in which they were caught after running from the knoll. I recalled these men from the testimony of Sergeant Harkness before the Warren Commission. (See Chapter 2.) The "tramps and hoboes," as Harkness described them, had been taken from a boxcar just as the freight train, by luck or planning, was starting to pull out of the railroad yard. The moving train had been stopped by the switchman, Lee Bowers, with controls in his 14-foot tower, allowing pursuing police to climb aboard the boxcar. According to Harkness, the three suspects "were taken down to the station and questioned." Yet no record of these suspects existed—no names, no mug shots, no fingerprints, no nitrate tests. Somewhere along the line, they too had been set free by Dallas authorities.

The photos of the "tramps" had been taken by news photographers William Allen of the *Dallas Times Herald* and Joe Smith of the *Fort Worth Star** as the suspects were marched by the Book Depository,

---

* Pictures of the same scene were also taken by Jack Bears of the *Dallas Morning News*. But Sprague obtained Bears's photographs later. All the photographs are now in the archives of Western New England College, Springfield, Massachusetts. A representative example appears in the photo section of this book.

presumably on their way to be questioned. Sprague believed that these photos, which amazingly enough had never been published, might help unlock some mysteries about the assassination. If either the "tramps" or the officers escorting them could be identified, new avenues for investigation would be opened.

I said that I wanted copies and asked Sprague to send me some immediately. It so happened that I was about to fly to New York to appear on the Johnny Carson show. This would be a rare opportunity for me to speak directly to the American public about our investigation, and I wanted the photos with me as documentation. So Sprague arranged for them to be delivered to me at the New Orleans Airport.

The chance to appear on the Carson show had arisen unexpectedly through the efforts of Mort Sahl. The articulate satirist, who was spending an extended period of time in New Orleans helping the office in a variety of ways, was well aware of my problems communicating with the public through the news media. Even the simplest press conference involved a process of "translation," so that what came out in the media never seemed to be precisely what I had said. Sahl, being in show business, had access to places I did not, like the Johnny Carson show. One night when he was on the program, the conversation drifted to the subject of the assassination and my investigation. Suddenly Sahl turned toward the audience and asked if they did not think Carson should invite me to be a guest on the show so that I could explain my side of the case. The response was so demonstrably affirmative that it left Carson and the network with no alternative. A few days later I received a telegram of invitation, which I promptly accepted.

On the plane to New York, I opened the package of photographs Sprague had sent. There were about a half dozen of them. I studied the figures in the photos carefully. One of the three men under arrest was medium tall, big-shouldered, with tousled blondish hair and a half smile on his face. The other two were both short, and their faces showed no serious concern. One of the short men wore a crumpled felt hat, but it was on the back of his head, revealing trimmed hair on the sides.

This detail immediately raised questions in my mind. As far as I knew, the hoboes and tramps who used to ride the rails in bygone days wore their hair shaggy and overgrown, an inevitable result of life on the road. But each of these men had a noticeably short and recent haircut. And the 8" x 10" pictures left no doubt that each was clean shaven as well.

The three men had on rough, shabby clothing, but it appeared to be quite clean. And while real hoboes invariably had thin, worn-out soles on their shoes, befitting their precarious economic status, there were no thin soles in these photos.

Several details raised questions about the police officers too. First of all, the arrested men were not handcuffed. This was strange. For offenses much less serious than murdering a President, police officers handcuff their prisoners every day. Certainly if these men were dangerous enough to be marched away under shotgun guard, they were dangerous enough to be handcuffed as well. Yet for some reason, the suspects in the photos were spared the customary discomforts of having been caught fleeing the scene of a murder.

Another odd thing was that the officers in the photos were not carrying their shotguns at port arms as would be customary in most cities. Each was carrying his gun differently, casually, as if he were going bird hunting. And then there was the curious fact that the trousers of one of the officers did not come close to fitting him. The Dallas Police Department, I presumed, had some form of dress code, but this officer's attire could not have been within its guidelines.

Finally, there was something interesting about the police officer marching in the front—the apparent leader of the arresting officers. A tall, lean man, he was wearing a miniature radio receiver earclip—a plastic device less than half an inch by a quarter of an inch in size.* In 1963, I knew, most intelligence agencies possessed these devices, but I knew of no local police force that did.

All of these details together made me wonder not only if the

---

* Another group of pictures taken at Dealey Plaza shortly after the assassination by Jim Murray of Blackstar Photo Service and William Allen of the *Dallas Times Herald* revealed another individual wearing exactly the same kind of radio receiver in a semi-invisible earclip. In this series of photos, Deputy Sheriff Buddy Walthers is shown looking down at a bullet while a neatly dressed blond man is reaching down to pick it up. The unidentified blond man was wearing the plastic radio receiver clipped to his ear lobe. The bullet was never seen again. The Warren Commission did not ask Walthers about the bullet or the blond man with the earclip, and he did not volunteer anything about them. Walthers subsequently was murdered, so it is safe to conclude that this bullet will remain on the long list of missing or destroyed evidence.

shabbily dressed suspects were actually tramps but also if the uniformed men with the shotguns were actually Dallas police officers.* The knowledge that the suspects had been released without any record of their arrest naturally did not reassure me on either of these points.

I was not sure if the Dallas police force had been penetrated, or impersonated, or both. But I did know that a remarkable number of suspects had mysteriously disappeared without a trace left behind and that the photographs Sprague had sent me could help prove that to the American people. As I put the prints of the shotgun arrests in my briefcase, I resolved that anyone watching the Johnny Carson show the following night was going to get to see them.

The next day I went to Carson's N.B.C. offices as scheduled in the early afternoon. The show was to be that night. Someone explained to me that on special occasions the guest was interviewed before the live appearance so that Carson would have some idea of what the area of discussion would be. I readily agreed to this. Thereupon, three or four well-dressed men, obviously all attorneys, entered the room. They questioned me for several hours on just what my responses would be if I

---

* The Warren Commission never dealt with this question at all. It made no reference to the "tramps." However, the House Select Committee on Assassinations did. One might wonder how it went about trying to identify these suspects. Did its staff, perhaps, arrange with Dallas authorities to produce the uniformed officers in the photographs? These custodians of the prisoners might have been able to provide some clue about their identity. After all, the very first thing police officers ask, even in a purse-snatching case, is the name of the suspected offender. Furthermore, the captors might well have helped explain why these three characters were allowed to wander off with less discomfiture than if they had been nabbed for shoplifting.

Unfortunately, there is no record of any attempt by the committee to identify the uniformed men. Nor did it send for command-level members of the police department who, at a glance, might have given the names of the custodians of the vanished prisoners.

Rather the House Committee approached the matter as if they were from some other planet. They set up a team of expert anthropologists and provided them with the photographs of the arrested men. These anthropologists carefully measured the noses and foreheads and other features of the arrested men with calipers. Then the anthropologists measured the nose, forehead, and so on of various persons believed to have harbored a strong dislike for John Kennedy. When the measurements did not match, the chief anthropologist then testified at the hearing that those suspects were not among the arrested men.

In a nation of well over 200 million people, such a process of elimination could take a very long time. What the House Select Committee on Assassinations—or, at least, its investigative staff—had invented was a scientific method of making certain that the men arrested following the assassination would never be identified.

were asked particular questions. I fielded the questions, and my answers were recorded.

Carson himself popped into the room briefly for the obligatory pre-show greeting of a guest. He seemed stiff and ill at ease. To make some small talk, I mentioned that my birthplace had been in western Iowa, a few miles away from his in Nebraska. He glanced at his watch in reply and was gone. I was surprised to discover that someone so jovial, so full of smiles on camera, could be such a cold fish off stage.

That night I arrived early at the network. One hour had been set aside for Carson to interview me. After a brief wait in a small green room, someone brought me out, pulled aside a very large curtain, and there I was, with great bright lights all over the place, standing on the television stage. The audience was applauding so warmly that they made me feel like a million dollars, and I gave them a big smile and waved back at them.

As I sat down next to Carson, I noticed that his desk was covered with typewritten questions and answers. It took but a glance for me to recognize that these were the questions I had been asked earlier in the afternoon, followed by the answers I had given the attorneys. After that there had been typed the suggested responses for him to make to me.

Carson began by reading me a long, rambling question of the "When did you stop beating your wife?" type. It was a gumbo made up of weird and inane crackpot speculations about the assassination—none of which came close to any statement I ever had made.

After a couple of minutes I saw that he had finished and was waiting for me to answer. His small humorless eyes, like a pair of tiny dark marbles, were fixed on me. Apparently he really believed that I had been the source of such intellectual rubbish. Suddenly it was hard for me to keep from laughing, and I know it showed.

"Johnny," I said, "how long do I have to answer that one?"

When he saw that I had completely dismissed the question, he looked down and began reading the next one. Now it was apparent to me that he was going to parrot each question, read my known response, and come up with some new brain teaser the lawyers had put together for him. This was fine with me. As a lawyer, I was used to adversarial proceedings. On the other hand, I knew Carson was accustomed to guests who smilingly agreed with everything he said.

I had actually looked forward to an open exchange of thoughts with Johnny Carson. But I was not about to play any games with him in which I was the ball. So I promptly changed my whole *modus operandi*. As casually as you might move from one chair in a courtroom into a nearby chair, I began changing my answers from what I had told the lawyers that afternoon.

Of course, I did not change the substance. I just altered the form or, in some cases, the emphasis. For example, when the answer was in two parts, I now gave the second part first—the opposite of what I had done that afternoon. After a few questions I saw from the up-and-down movement of Carson's fingers that he had lost his place. He never found it again.

I was not trying to be cute. Nor was I about to try to match wits with a great comic talent like Carson. As an attorney, I simply was doing what I do best. Very gradually, I shifted the emphasis of our colloquy to where I was asking the questions. Naturally he was not prepared to handle a subject as complex as this one. When in frustation he asked me why the government still was concealing evidence, as I had contended, I knew that my moment to show the photographs had arrived.

"Don't ask me, John," I said opening my briefcase. "Ask Lyndon Johnson. You *know* he has to have the answer."

He stared at me blankly, without responding.

"Maybe I'd better show you pictures," I said, reaching into the briefcase.

Before anyone could stop me, I was holding in front of the camera one of the big photographs showing the three men being marched off by the Dallas police with their shotguns. It took Carson a moment to recognize the scene, but when he realized what it was, he lunged at my arm like a cobra, pulling it down violently so that the pictures were out of the camera's view.

"Photographs like this don't show up on television," he said sharply.

I held the picture up again for display in front of the camera. "Sure they do," I replied. "The camera can pick this up."

This time he yanked my arm down even harder. "No, it can't," he snapped.

Nevertheless, I swung the picture up for the third time. This time, however, I saw the red light blink off and realized that the director of the show had cut the camera off. Another camera—probably panning the audience—was now beaming its more comforting picture out across America.

Then, before anyone could change the subject, I said loudly, "Those arrested men you just saw were never seen again. They all got away."

At that moment, I knew I had communicated what I wanted. Of course, I had an angry host on my hands the rest of the show. But that was his problem, not mine.

During my flight back to New Orleans I found myself reflecting on the mind-set of Carson and the N.B.C. attorneys who had debriefed me. They were unnerved by my viewpoint, I realized, not so much because it differed from their own but because I was explicitly advocating the existence of a *conspiracy* in President Kennedy's assassination. I recalled the thinly veiled contempt of the attorneys whenever they touched upon the concept of a conspiracy. I felt as if I were a German citizen back in the mid-1930s who had publicly questioned Adolf Hitler's sanity and was being given the obligatory questioning before being shipped away to a mental institution. I remembered that Carson himself had nearly come unglued during the heat of our argument as I zeroed in on the idea that a conspiracy had occurred.

Why was it, I asked myself, that these people at the very heart of the New York media industry were so allergic to the very concept of conspiracy? What was it that was so inconceivable, that was so utterly unthinkable about the idea of a conspiracy?

Then, perhaps for the first time, I realized what it was that petrified these people, that froze their brains into gridlock. To acknowledge that an organized conspiracy had occurred was to recognize that it had been done for a purpose—to change government policy. Having told the world for so many years how wonderful we all were, here in the greatest country in the world, the media people were not willing to admit that our national leader could be removed in such brutal fashion in order to change government policy. That would put the lie to

American democracy. That just could not be. Therefore, in their minds, the assassination had to be a random event, the work of a deranged loner.

I found myself, once again, thumbing through the photographs of the men under shotgun arrest. The journalists who had taken these photographs certainly had not tried to conceal anything. Plainly, they had arrived at the scene as soon as possible and taken as many pictures as they could. They had rushed back to their editors with the results.

Any one of these photographs was a potential Pulitzer Prize winner a hundred times over. Collectively, they were among the most important photographs ever taken. Why, then, had the editors and the publishers of the newspapers involved not seized the opportunity to be the first into print with these great photographs?

The idea of a gigantic, highly organized media conspiracy I found unacceptable. It was simply too unwieldy. Yet something had caused the photos never to see the light of day.

And something had happened to me in New York City as well. Why had I been debriefed in advance so that Carson could be apprised of my likely answers? Why had Carson pulled my arm away so that the photographs were out of camera range? And why had the director and the control room switched off the cameras so that the photographs could not be seen?

The only reasonable, realistic explanation, I found myself concluding, was control. It was not the kind where a small cabal in Washington or New York called all the shots about what could get into print and on the air. It was control of a looser sort: here a call from a high-ranking federal intelligence official explaining to a newspaper publisher the overwhelming national security consequences that might result from irresponsible publication of pictures before the government had studied them; there a call from a Texas politician, a lifetime friend of Lyndon Johnson's, to a network president explaining the great harm that could befall the republic if such photographs were shown to the public.

It was difficult for me to accept, because if I had been a publisher and received such a call, I would have made sure not only that the photograph was on the front page but that it was as large as possible so no one could miss it. However, I had to admit that I did not think like most publishers, and most publishers did not seem to think like me.

It was tragic, but in the final analysis, the mainstream media had somehow been persuaded to go along with the official story. Whether out of incompetence or intention, they, as much as the Dallas authorities who let so many suspects escape, had also ratified the assassination.

17

The Reluctant
Investigators

SOME OF THE BEST WITNESSES to the assassination found their way to us after it became apparent to them that the federal agents and the Dallas police really were not interested in what they saw. Julia Ann Mercer was just such a witness. In fact, no other witness so completely illuminated for me the extent of the cover-up.

Mercer had been but a few feet away when one of the riflemen was unloaded at the grassy knoll shortly before the arrival of the presidential motorcade. Consequently, she was a witness not only to the preparation of President Kennedy's murder but also to the conspiracy involved.

She gave statements to the F.B.I. and the Dallas Sheriff's office, and then returned to the F.B.I. and provided additional statements, but she was never called by the Warren Commission—not even to provide an affidavit.

Much earlier, I had read Julia Ann Mercer's statements in the

Warren Commission exhibits, but I had never had a chance to talk to her. Then one day in early 1968 her husband called me at the office. He said that he and his wife were in New Orleans on business and had some things to tell me. I agreed to meet them at the Fairmont Hotel, where they were staying.

Arriving at their suite, I found a most impressive couple. A middle-aged man of obvious substance, he had been a Republican member of Congress from Illinois. Equally impressive, she was intelligent and well-dressed, the kind of witness any lawyer would love to have testifying on his side in front of a jury. After he had departed on business, I handed her copies of her statements as they had been printed in the Warren Commission exhibits. She read them carefully and then shook her head.

"These all have been altered," she said. "They have me saying just the opposite of what I really told them."

About an hour before the assassination she had been driving west on Elm Street and had been stopped—just past the grassy knoll—by traffic congestion. To her surprise (because she recalled that the President's parade was coming soon), she saw a young man in the pickup truck to her right dismount, carrying a rifle, not too well concealed in a covering of some sort. She then observed him walk up "the grassy hill which forms part of the overpass." She looked at the driver several times, got a good look at his round face and brown eyes, and he looked right back at her.

Mercer also observed that three police officers were standing near a motorcycle on the overpass bridge above her and just ahead. She recalled that they showed no curiosity about the young man climbing the side of the grassy knoll with the rifle.

After the assassination, when Mercer sought to make this information available to law enforcement authorities, their response was almost frenzied. At the F.B.I. office—where she went the day after the assassination—she was shown a number of mug shots. Among the several she selected as resembling the driver was a photograph of Jack Ruby. On Sunday, when she saw Ruby kill Oswald on television, she positively recognized him as the driver of the pickup truck and promptly notified the local Bureau office. Nevertheless, the F.B.I.

altered her statement so it did not note that she had made a positive identification.

She laughed when she pointed this out to me. "See," she said, "the F.B.I. made it just the opposite of what I really told them." Then she added, "He was only a few feet away from me. How could I not recognize Jack Ruby when I saw him shoot Oswald on television?"

The Dallas Sheriff's office went through the same laborious fraud and added an imaginative touch of its own. Although Mercer had never been brought before any notary, the Sheriff's office filed a sworn affidavit stating that she did not identify the driver, although she might, "if I see him again," and significantly changing other facts.

"See that notarized signature?" she asked me. "That's not my signature either. I sign my name with a big 'A' like this." She produced a pen and wrote her name for me. It was clear that the signature the Dallas Sheriff's office had on its altered statement was not even close to hers.

Julia Ann Mercer then wrote on the side of my copies of the F.B.I. and the Dallas Sheriff fabrications the correct version of what she had seen then. That version had not been acceptable in Dallas, but it was more than welcome to me. Conscious of the sudden deaths of some witnesses who appeared to have seen too much for their own survival, I thought that she should sign her maiden name as she had back in Dallas right after the assassination. At my suggestion she did so.

When I got back to my office, I thought about Julia Ann Mercer. She had been only a few feet away from one of the most crucial incidents of the assassination and had tried in vain to tell the federal and Dallas law enforcement authorities the simple truth. The implications of her experience were profound. First of all, Mercer's observations provided further evidence that there was another rifleman on the knoll ahead of the President.

But to me the responses to her statements were even more chilling. They proved that law enforcement officials recognized early on that a conspiracy existed to kill the President. Both local and federal authorities had altered Mercer's statements precisely to conceal that fact.

I already had concluded that parts of the local Dallas law enforcement establishment were probably implicated in the assassination or its cover-up. But now I saw that the highly respected F.B.I. was implicated as well. After all, the Bureau had to have known on Saturday, November 23, when it showed Jack Ruby's photo to Mercer, that Ruby might have been involved in a conspiracy.* This was the day *before* Ruby shot Oswald.

The Bureau's failure to locate Ruby immediately for questioning, along with its rewrite job on Mercer's statements,† made me uncomfortable. Just how deeply, I wondered, was my former employer involved in this assassination?

The answer to my question began to emerge quite soon. Mark Lane had been working temporarily in New Orleans on his book *A Citizen's*

---

* Jack Ruby had a special relationship with the Dallas office of the F.B.I. In 1959 Ruby met at least nine times with one of the Dallas Bureau's agents. At that time he also purchased a microphone-equipped wrist watch, a bugged tie clip, a telephone bug, and a bugged attaché case. These facts suggested that Jack Ruby was probably a regular informant with the local Bureau office.

But Ruby may well have been working for the C.I.A. also. Individuals on the payroll of one agency are sometimes hired as contract employees for another agency within the intelligence community. During 1959, the same year in which Ruby was meeting with the F.B.I. agent, he took two flights to Cuba. One was for eight days. The other was an overnight turn-around flight. Earlier in the 1950s he had consulted a war supplies dealer about the purchase of 100 jeeps, one of the most valuable items for the rebels in Cuba whom the C.I.A. was supporting at that time. On a later occasion, he was deeply involved in gun running for the Cuban rebels supported by the Agency.

† There was a coda to the Julia Ann Mercer story. In the late 1970s, when I was in private law practice, the House Select Committee on Assassinations convened. Because I had seen too much critical material disappear in the hands of federal investigators, I was not enthusiastic about sending the committee anything.

However, Mercer's observations, as well as the government's alteration of them, were of overriding importance. There was no evidence more conclusive of the frontal shooting of Kennedy, of the conspiracy, and of the subsequent cover-up. Consequently, I sent the committee copies of Mercer's statements to the F.B.I. and the Dallas Sheriff's office as they appeared in the Warren Commission exhibits, with her description of the alterations written on the sides of each.

Because of the exceptionally high casualty rate among important assassination witnesses, I described her only by her maiden name, which she had signed on her statements. In an accompanying letter, I explained the reason to the committee and said that if they intended to call her as a witness and would assure me that there would be a serious effort to protect her, I would be happy to send her married name and present address.

I never received a reply from the House Committee. Some years later I happened to be thumbing through the published hearings of the committee when I stumbled on an interesting passage. It said that I had sent to the committee *alleged* statements made by one Julia Ann Mercer. The House Committee's investigators, the report continued, "had been unable to locate her."

Dissent and helping me with the investigation. One night he gave a talk on the assassination at Tulane University. Afterwards he happened to meet a former F.B.I. employee named William S. Walter. During their conversation Walter mentioned that on November 17, 1963—five days before the assassination—he had been the night clerk on duty at the Bureau's New Orleans office when a warning about a possible presidential assassination attempt came chattering through on the teletype machine. Walter immediately called five agents who handled the relevant local investigatory units, and considered his duty done. When he heard this, Lane promptly pulled Walter off to the side, interviewed him, and made out a statement concerning the substance of their conversation. Sometime later I located Walter and followed up, talking to him at length a number of times.*

In 1976, Walter gave a copy of the text of the F.B.I. telex to the Senate Intelligence Committee chaired by Senator Richard Schweiker of Pennsylvania. After the Freedom of Information Act was passed, Lane also obtained a copy of the warning telex and made it available to me. This is what it said:

---

* Later, after Walter got to know me better, he told me that during our investigation of the assassination, the Bureau recorded all my home telephone conversations. Ordinarily, the Bureau intercepts phone conversations of citizens with no effort whatsoever. But I was a public official, so out of caution it retained a private detective agency from a city in north Louisiana. A sleuth temporarily moved down to New Orleans and, operating out of the Warwick Hotel, handled the monitoring of my phone for the Bureau. Every morning the local Bureau office would receive a tape recording of my conversations of the preceding day and night, which were promptly typed up.

After the Freedom of Information Act was passed, Lane requested copies of all material in the F.B.I. files referring to me. When the package arrived, much of it was blacked out. There was no reference to the phone monitoring inasmuch as the Bureau's elaborate phone interception system and its equally elaborate informer system are automatically excluded by the Bureau's own administrative decision from the F.O.I.A. requirements. But we did find ample evidence that the Bureau had tracked me on every trip I made away from New Orleans during the J.F.K. investigation.

No detail was omitted, from the time of my arrival in a city to the hotel where I stayed. In some instances, after I had more publicity than I wanted, I paid for my airline ticket or registered at a hotel under a pseudonym. On one trip, as the Bureau's summary duly observed, I registered at a hotel as W.O. Robinson, which was my maternal grandfather's name. On two others, I used Claude Culpepper and Clyde Ballou, appellations I had plucked out of thin air. The F.B.I. reports treated this with great seriousness and referred darkly to my use of "aliases."

Of course, I had become so used to the surveillance of everything I did that none of this surprised me. However, in looking back, I now wonder why I ever reached a state where something like that was taken for granted.

URGENT: 1:45 AM EST 11-17-63 HLF 1 PAGE
TO: ALL SACS
FROM: DIRECTOR
THREAT TO ASSASSINATE PRESIDENT KENNEDY IN
DALLAS TEXAS NOVEMBER 22 DASH TWENTY THREE
NINETEEN SIXTY THREE. MISC INFORMATION
CONCERNING. INFORMATION HAS BEEN RECEIVED
BY THE BUREAS [sic] BUREAU HAS DETERMINED
THAT A MILITANT REVOLUTIONARY GROUP MAY
ATTEMPT TO ASSASSINATE PRESIDENT KENNEDY ON
HIS PROPOSED TRIP TO DALLAS TEXAS NOVEMBER
TWENTY TWO DASH TWENTY THREE NINETEEN
SIXTY THREE. ALL RECEIVING OFFICES SHOULD
IMMEDIATELY CONTACT ALL CIS, PCIS LOGICAL RACE
AND HATE GROUP INFORMANTS AND DETERMINE IF
ANY BASIS FOR THREAT. BUREAU SHOULD BE KEPT
ADVISED OF ALL DEVELOPMENTS BY TELETYPE.
OTHER OFFICES HAVE BEEN ADVISED. END AND
ACK PLS.

We learned from Walter that when the assassination occurred, he was eating lunch but immediately ran back to the New Orleans Bureau office. In the file he found the warning telex along with a duplicate which had soon followed it. At the time he copied the exact phraseology of the telex warning and kept it. Shortly afterwards he checked the file again to see if the warning was still there. It had been removed. No sign of it, nor any reference to it, remained.

The telex had been most explicit, naming both a place and dates for the attempt to assassinate the President. It was addressed to all special agents in charge, which meant every one in the country, including Dallas. And yet the F.B.I. did nothing. There is no record that it notified anyone—not even the Secret Service, which as the President's bodyguard should have been informed immediately.

Had the November 17 warning been distributed to all concerned agencies, I realized, the last-minute change in the parade route could have been scrutinized more closely, spotted as a trap, and the parade might have been canceled. Even if the parade had been held, the limousine's movable plastic bubble, which might have saved the President, could have been used. And the iron-clad rules of keeping windows closed and rooftops empty along the motorcade route could have been enforced by the Secret Service. Instead, as the parade approached the Dal-Tex Building and the Book Depository on the substituted route, the proliferation of open windows and the open limousine left no doubt that security for President Kennedy had been abandoned.*

When I learned of the telex warning from William Walter, nearly five years had passed since the assassination. But in that time none of the five agents Walter had called the morning of November 17 ever hinted to the American people or to the Warren Commission that the F.B.I. had received a specific warning about the assassination five days before it occurred. Nor had any of the special agents in charge across the country, to whom the warning had been addressed. Nor had the F.B.I. itself, or its director, J. Edgar Hoover, under whose name the warning had gone out in the first place. If such conspicuous silence did not smell of cover-up, I did not know what did.

The five-day warning telex soon took on added significance when I belatedly learned of some remarkable information made public years before by C.A. Hamblen, the early night manager of Western Union's Dallas office. A week or so following the assassination, I discovered, Hamblen had stated to a number of individuals that approximately ten days before the assassination, Lee Oswald had been in the Western Union office and had sent a telegram to Washington, D.C. It was his impression that Oswald's telegram had been directed to the secretary of the Navy. I already knew that Oswald, although relatively mild-mannered, was assertive enough to have sent other complaints to the secretary of the Navy—a fact which Hamblen could not be expected to have known.†

---

* The Secret Service's performance was less than exemplary in other ways. Even after being informed by Texas officials at Parkland Hospital of the law requiring an autopsy in Texas, the Secret Service hijacked President Kennedy's body and got it aboard Air Force One for a military autopsy in Bethesda, Maryland. And before the day was over, the Secret Service also cleaned out the President's limousine—washing away bullet fragments with buckets of water. Governor John Connally's clothing (bullet holes, bullet traces, and all) was sent to be cleaned and pressed. Preservation of important evidence was clearly not high on the Secret Service's agenda.

† On these earlier occasions, Oswald had written the Navy secretary protesting the "dishonorable discharge" which had replaced his honorable discharge after his pronouncements from the Soviet Union. As a former Marine, Oswald came under the jurisdiction of the secretary of the Navy.

Hamblen also recalled that on several occasions Oswald had come to the Western Union office to collect modest money orders which had been sent to him. According to Hamblen, for identification Oswald showed him a library card and a Navy I.D. card. This was very close to what Oswald routinely carried for identification: a library card and Marine I.D. card.

With Hamblen's recollection an intriguing situation arose: About *ten days before* the assassination Lee Oswald had sent a telegram to the secretary of the Navy. Then, *five days before* the assassination F.B.I. headquarters had sent a detailed telex warning of the impending attempt to kill the President to all Bureau offices. Might the two messages, I wondered, somehow be related?

My earlier research about Oswald's relationship to the F.B.I. seemed relevant to this question. I had learned long before that Oswald's address book contained the name of F.B.I. Agent James Hosty of the Dallas Bureau office. Immediately following Hosty's name, Oswald had written a telephone number. I obtained a Dallas phone directory for the year 1963 and found that this was not the phone number of the local F.B.I. Yet, as I discovered, Hosty's home phone number was not in the directory. It was apparent, then, that Oswald had written down Hosty's unlisted home number or some message center. Hosty himself, I presumed, had given the number to Oswald.

I also knew that when the F.B.I. gave the Warren Commission a list of the contents of Oswald's address book, it omitted Special Agent Hosty's name and unlisted number, as noted down by Oswald. Even the Warren Commission was disturbed when it found out about this oversight. The F.B.I. explained that the omission had been made because the person who transcribed the list was only interested in "lead information."

Then, years after the Warren Commission inquiry, an item appeared in the press describing Oswald's visit to the Dallas F.B.I. office shortly before the assassination. The news story said that Oswald had left a note addressed to Agent Hosty. The woman at the Bureau office who first received the message stated that it contained a threat by Oswald to blow up the F.B.I. office. On the other hand, Hosty explained that it was merely a warning to him to stop questioning Oswald's wife at their home while Oswald was not present. If the note was a threat to blow up the F.B.I. Dallas headquarters, then Oswald should have been placed immediately on the "Dangerous Character" list for special attention prior to the President's arrival in Dallas. Even if the note was a much milder threat than that, Oswald ordinarily should have been given a prompt evaluation interview, if not confined outright to his residence during the President's visit to the city. However, in this case the Dallas F.B.I. took no action whatsoever.

What the note actually said will never be known for sure. Hosty claims that Special Agent in Charge Gordon Shanklin ordered him to destroy it, which he promptly did. Interestingly, Hosty said that he had never mentioned the note to the Warren Commission because "he had been instructed by the F.B.I. not to volunteer information."

This was not unlike the earlier incident in New Orleans when F.B.I. Agent John Quigley destroyed the notes of his interview with Oswald at the police department's First District Precinct Station following Oswald's arrest for his Canal Street imbroglio with the anti-Castro Cubans. (See Chapter 2.) What was it, I found myself wondering, that so consistently compelled the F.B.I.—traditionally compulsive about hanging on to notes and records—to cremate or tear up anything describing an encounter between the seemingly innocuous Lee Harvey Oswald and any special agent of the Bureau?

The image of Oswald bringing a note for Hosty to the Bureau office and leaving it at the front desk is compelling. I recall the way that the confidential informants often communicated with their contact agents during my brief tour with the F.B.I. in Seattle and Tacoma. Most of the informants would leave messages or information concerning an assignment at the front desk in a sealed envelope addressed to their contact agent. The informants were paid moderately, but regularly, for the secret information they provided on a variety of projects. And their identity was carefully protected. Even in Bureau files the informant was always identified by code.

In any event, I began to wonder if, in the weeks before the assassination, Lee Oswald was a confidential informant for the F.B.I., reporting to Special Agent James Hosty.

This possibility had been raised early in 1964 by Waggoner Carr, then attorney general of Texas. A man of high integrity and repute, Carr had told the Warren Commission in a secret session on January

22, 1964, that evidence he had acquired from Allan Sweatt, the chief of the criminal division of the Dallas Sheriff's office, indicated that Lee Oswald had been an undercover informant. More specifically, Oswald had been employed by the F.B.I. as confidential agent number 179 at a salary of $200 a month, beginning more than a year prior to and continuing up to the very day of the murder of President Kennedy.

This shocking news leaked into the media, appearing in articles by Joe Goulden in the *Philadelphia Inquirer* on December 8, 1963; by Lonnie Hudkins in the *Houston Post* of January 1, 1964; and by Harold Feldman in *The Nation* on January 27, 1964. After considerable debate, the Warren Commission agreed that it was necessary to conduct thorough hearings on this matter. Unfortunately, no such hearings were held. Of the three bylined writers just mentioned, not one was called as a witness by the Commission. Nor was the original source, the chief of the Sheriff's criminal division, ever called.

Over the years Waggoner Carr's allegations had been lost in the tidal wave of information, theories, and speculation about the assassination. But now the idea that Oswald had been a confidential informant for the F.B.I., which I had discarded at first as a strained premise, began to make sense to me.* It could explain the presence of Hosty's name and unlisted number in Oswald's address book, Oswald's visit to the Dallas Bureau office, and his threatening note to Hosty.

And the confidential informant possibility threw a most intriguing light on another curious fact: The F.B.I. did not mention Lee Oswald as a suspect in the assassination until two and a half hours after the shooting, shortly after Air Force One had departed for Washington with new President Lyndon Johnson and John Kennedy's body aboard.

---

* Years later I heard a story about Oswald's status as an informant from a Milwaukee resident named Jim Gochnour. Gochnour told me that a former F.B.I. agent named Carver Gaten had been his landlord in Seattle, Washington. Gaten, one of the few black agents in the F.B.I., had told Gochnour that he knew James Hosty in the Bureau's Kansas City office when both were assigned there.

The two agents developed a close relationship, and on several occasions Hosty complained about the unfairness of his transfer shortly after the assassination from Dallas to Kansas City, widely considered at the time the "Siberia" of the F.B.I. Hosty confided to Gaten that Oswald had been paid regularly for information but provided very little. As Oswald's contact agent, Hosty apparently got a lot of heat from his superiors for not prying more from Oswald and was bitter that he had taken the blame for Oswald's shortcomings.

My attempts in recent years to locate Gochnour and Hosty to verify this story have not been successful.

According to Dallas Police Lieutenant Jack Revill, an F.B.I. agent came up to him at Dallas police headquarters at 2:50 P.M. and said that the Bureau had "information that this suspect was capable of committing the assassination." The agent who brought this welcome news and was the first to mention the name of Lee Harvey Oswald was none other than James Hosty.

Was Hosty merely an innocent messenger, or had he and possibly others in the Bureau been involved in a plot to set up Oswald as the patsy? If F.B.I. employees had been part of the conspiracy, then that might explain why the Bureau had mysteriously failed to act on the warning sent over its telex system five days before the assassination and why no one responded to. the letter of warning that Richard Case Nagell claimed to have sent to J. Edgar Hoover. (See Chapter 14.) It also might explain why Oswald, who evidently did not get along with Hosty and may have sensed that he was being set up, had sent a telegram to the secretary of the Navy ten days before the assassination.

I began to formulate a possible scenario. Long in advance, the engineers of the assassination had selected the idealistic and gullible Oswald as a patsy. His close-mouthed intelligence background helped assure not only success in the venture but subsequent support from the government, which would not want to admit that the assassination originated in its own intelligence community.

If Oswald was on the government payroll as a confidential informant in Dallas and New Orleans, he might well have believed that his job was to penetrate subversive organizations, including Fair Play for Cuba and perhaps Guy Banister's apparatus, in order to report back to the F.B.I. about them. Along the way, he was allowed to penetrate a marginal part of the assassination project, again with the idea that he was engaged in an officially sponsored effort to obtain information about it. He may even have filed reports on the plot to kill the President with his contact agent, James Hosty. When Oswald sensed that Hosty was not responsive, he may have gone over his head and telegraphed some kind of warning to the secretary of the Navy, who in turn may have informed the F.B.I.'s Washington headquarters, which then sent out its warning telex.

But it was equally possible that Oswald had been acting as an informant for some other branch of the intelligence community as well, such as the O.N.I. or the C.I.A. represented by Guy Banister, and was withholding relevant information about the conspiracy from Hosty and the F.B.I. Then, when Hosty had innocently begun to harass Oswald and his wife to get more information, Oswald had responded with his threatening note and a telegram to the secretary of the Navy.

It was impossible to know what was in Lee Harvey Oswald's mind. But whatever he thought he was doing, he had clearly acquired more information than the assassination's engineers could tolerate. That is why he had to die so suddenly in Dallas less than 72 hours after John Kennedy.

I knew I could never take any of this into the courtroom. It offered no real link to Clay Shaw, and it was only conjecture. But it did seem to me that there was no better way to draw in and set up a scapegoat like Oswald than to persuade him that he had penetrated the planning for a great public murder and was in a position to give an eleventh-hour warning about it to the proper authorities.

The question that troubled me, and may well have troubled Oswald, was: If the Dallas police, the Sheriff's office, the Secret Service, the F.B.I., and the C.I.A. were all potentially involved in the plot, who were the proper authorities?

18

The Trial
of Clay Shaw

YOU MAY REMEMBER Ernest Hemingway's novel *The Old Man and the Sea.* Santiago, the old fisherman, managed to catch a great fish, a monster fish, so huge that he had to tie it alongside the boat to bring it back in. By the time Santiago reached shore, the fish long since had been picked apart by sharks. Nothing remained but its skeleton.

Looking back, I can see that this is pretty much the way it turned out when we finally got Clay Shaw to trial in Criminal District Court. It had been a long, tedious, and frustrating uphill fight getting even that far. Our office had been infiltrated by the federal government, and Bill Boxley had stolen many of our files. As if that were not enough, a week or two before the trial began Lou Ivon learned that the young Englishman from Oxford who was in charge of our archives had given copies of many of our files to the defense. Almost as important, some of our key witnesses—*e.g.,* David Ferrie, Gordon Novel, Sandra Moffett—had died or been scared off or moved from New Orleans with no chance of my extraditing them.

Before the trial, we had to make decisions about which witnesses not to use. A prosecutor cannot simply put witnesses on the stand because they happen to be available and because their testimony, under direct examination, supports the prosecutor's case. He or she must also consider whether one of these good witnesses will blow the case out the window on cross-examination.

For example, there was Richard Case Nagell. He arrived shortly before the trial, willing to testify against Shaw. I met him at the New Orleans Athletic Club and had a long session with him. He was as intense as he had been when I last talked to him. He was as accurate and precise in his recollection of details. He felt as strongly as ever about J. Edgar Hoover's silence after his early letter of warning about the operation to assassinate President Kennedy.

However, he was also as inflexible as ever about identifying the intelligence agency with which he had been associated—and might still be associated. I understood his concern about the non-disclosure agreement which he apparently had signed with his parent agency. But it was all too clear to me what a field day the defense lawyers would have when they discovered on cross-examination that he would not disclose his affiliation. In short order they would be coming at him just as the sharks had come at Santiago's fish. By the time they finished with Nagell, the jury would have been left with the impression of a crackpot. One such incident, one such discrediting, is all it takes to undo an entire case. I decided that with Nagell we could not take that risk.

Then there was Julia Ann Mercer, possibly the most important witness we encountered during our investigation. An hour before the assassination she had seen Jack Ruby unload one of the riflemen at the grassy knoll in front of where Kennedy later would be shot. What Mercer had seen virtually added up to a *prima facie* case of conspiracy. However, her testimony would be peripheral to our case against Clay Shaw, who was only a small part of the overall conspiracy. Considering the number of witnesses who had been murdered or otherwise disposed of by "accidents," I decided that we could not needlessly endanger her life. For the same reason, I continued not to make available to the press or the federal government her married name and her residence.

As for the witnesses we decided to use, Jim Alcock, whom I had assigned to be the chief prosecutor, and the rest of the special team arranged the order of their appearance and how to handle them. One witness, an accountant from New York named Charles Spiesel, came to us very late in our investigation and presented us with a dilemma. He claimed to have met Ferrie and Shaw on a trip to New Orleans and heard them discussing the possible assassination of the President. Alcock brought me his statement and asked what I thought about using him. By this time I had become quite suspicious because of all the tricks played on us. While I could find nothing specifically wrong with the statement, I told Alcock I found it simply too pat. But Alcock decided he wanted to call Spiesel, and since I did not have time to interview the witness myself, I agreed. It was a decision we would soon come to regret.

On January 29, 1969, the case of *State of Louisiana versus Clay Shaw* finally came to trial. As we walked into the majestic courtroom that morning, I put my hand on one of the massive white oak pews. I felt a great sense of nostalgia. This was the same room in which I had tried my first case as an assistant prosecutor approximately 15 years earlier.

Just as it had been during the preliminary hearing, the courtroom once again was a circus and, if possible, even more crowded. After having made our way through the horde of reporters at the entrance, we had to forge our way through even more tightly packed bodies to reach the prosecution table. The crowd was noisy to the point of unruliness. Suddenly there was a hush. Everyone craned their necks to see Clay Shaw and his attorneys entering the court. Shaw, tall and impeccably dressed, naturally caught the eye. He was a dark man, his complexion almost olive in color. As he towered above his defense counsel, his high cheekbones loomed larger than ever.

The defense group at the opposite side of the room hardly had settled into their chairs when the gavel started pounding. As the crowd quieted, Judge Edward Aloysius Haggerty swept into the courtroom in his black robe and took the bench. A stocky, red-faced man with alert blue eyes under his bushy eyebrows, Haggerty had been born and bred in the heart of the Irish Channel of New Orleans and still lived there. I knew him well from my years in the great building.

The judge began by addressing a matter of enormous interest to the local spectators. Contrary to all custom, this major trial had been unthinkingly scheduled by the clerk for the midst of the Mardi Gras season. Apparently a major concern of Haggerty's was that the jury not have to miss all the fun, particularly the parades. The Rex parade, featuring the king of Mardi Gras, was the most important and often the most beautiful. Rex invariably was a prominent New Orleanian whose name was never revealed until the morning of the parade, when a photograph of him and his queen would appear on the front page of the *Times-Picayune*. The "truck parade" of the Elks Crew, which traditionally followed Rex, was probably the most enjoyable of all the parades. Made up of a hundred trucks or more, each carrying a movable day-long Mardi Gras party, it was always a wild, imaginative, and unpredictable sight to behold.

Judge Haggerty proudly announced that he had made arrangements for the jury to be able to watch not only the Rex parade but the "truck parade" of the Elks Crew as well from the balcony of a residence on St. Charles Avenue. This important local business taken care of, the trial could now get under way.

I left the selection of the jury to Jim Alcock and Assistant D.A. Alvin Oser while I went back to the office and concentrated on persuading reluctant witnesses to leave Dallas and even more distant cities for the trial.

By the time the jury was picked, January had become February and I joined Alcock and Oser in the courtroom. Every now and then, you could hear the sounds of Mardi Gras drifting up from revelers cruising by on Tulane Avenue.

After assuring himself that each side was ready, Judge Haggerty nodded his head in my direction, indicating that I should commence the prosecution's opening statement. I walked over to the jury and, slowly pacing back and forth in front of them, explained what our case was about. I told them what the conspiracy law said and what evidence we would present to prove that Clay Shaw had violated it. Since fancy dramatics in the courtroom had never been my way, my voice was low-key, devoid of histrionics.

When I was through, F. Irvin Dymond, one of the best trial lawyers in New Orleans, made the opening statement for the defense. I had opposed Dymond in court many times. He had a way of leaning forward as he addressed the jurors, standing with his feet widely separated and his shoulders slightly hunched, his hands gesturing to drive home a point. He rarely moved from this firm posture. Dymond's style, though unconscious, was certainly effective, emphasizing to the jurors his great intensity and concern.

Following the opening statements, we called as our first witnesses the citizens of the small town of Clinton, Louisiana, who had seen Lee Oswald there in the company of Clay Shaw and David Ferrie two months before the assassination. (See Chapter 8.) Because Andrew Sciambra had located the Clinton witnesses for us and knew that aspect of the case better than anyone else, I sent him in to handle their questioning. His powerful body, the result of years of boxing at L.S.U., was hardly hidden by his business suit. But he had a soft way of questioning, and he had established an excellent rapport with the witnesses from Clinton—conservative whites and liberal blacks alike.

Reeves Morgan, a former state legislator, testified that after the assassination he notified the F.B.I. of Oswald's presence in Clinton. Morgan said that the special agent thanked him but told him that the F.B.I. already knew about Oswald's visit to the Clinton area. He heard nothing further from the Bureau.

John Manchester, the Clinton town marshal, testified that he "checked out" all strange cars visiting Clinton during the voter registration drive, including the big black car parked near the office entrance of the voting registrar. "I walked over and talked to the man behind the wheel of the car," said Manchester. "He was a big man, gray hair, ruddy complexion. An easy-talking man, he said he was a representative of the International Trade Mart in New Orleans."

Manchester pointed to Clay Shaw as the man he had questioned. Shaw gazed back at him impassively. As Sciambra had learned in Clinton, Manchester contacted the state police and confirmed that the limousine was the property of the International Trade Mart in New Orleans.

Responding to Sciambra's questioning, the Clinton witnesses not only pointed to Shaw as the man who had been sitting at the wheel of the black limousine but identified photographs of David Ferrie as the man who had been sitting next to him. Everyone remembered the anomalous scene of Lee Oswald, who had come to Clinton with them, standing in a long line of black voting applicants. As virtually the only white man waiting, and a stranger to boot, he was unforgettable.

During the testimony, I glanced over at the defendant and his staff of attorneys. Shaw was as imperious as ever, his cigarette tilted upward as he always held it, the smoke spiraling toward the ceiling.* His nobility of manner, every gesture courtly, made me think that this must have been the way Louis XVI had been at his trial. He seemed detached, even slightly bored, by the mundane proceedings around him.

Next to him sat his chief counsel, Irvin Dymond. Like Shaw, he also smoked cigarettes incessantly, his eyes narrowing down to slits each time he inhaled. Also present at the defense table were Edward Wegmann and his brother, William, who handled legal matters involving Shaw's property interests. Edward, the older brother, seldom smiled but was constantly making notes on a yellow legal pad. William, the more animated of the two, frequently conversed with Dymond.

Another apparent member of Shaw's defense team was an attorney named Richard Matthews. He was not a counsel of record and was not at the defense table. But every day he sat in the first row of spectators directly behind Shaw and from time to time would approach the defendant. There would be a long whispered exchange between them while Matthews crouched alongside Shaw's chair. This phenomenon, which I had never seen before in a courtroom, continued throughout the trial.

I knew Matthews from years earlier, before he moved from Louisiana to Japan. Back then, while he was closing up his office, I asked him how he expected to practice law in Japan. His response sounded to me like double-talk, and I wondered at the time what he would really be doing in the Far East. Now I suddenly found myself looking at him for the first time since his departure. It seemed odd that he was abruptly here in the middle of this trial, whether officially or unofficially, acting as one of Shaw's primary advisers.

Seeing Matthews in this context cast a new light on his mysterious move to Japan. I had no evidence, but my instincts told me now that the man had been working for the Central Intelligence Agency. His strange appearance at this trial led me to conclude that he was still

---

* In New Orleans, the parties and their counsel are allowed to smoke while court is in session, unless the presiding judge specifically forbids it.

working for it. Somebody on Shaw's side had to be representing the interests of the intelligence community.

Although Matthews disappeared immediately after the trial and I was never able to link him directly with the Agency, years later my assumption that the C.I.A. had been aiding Shaw's defense was proved true. At the time of the New Orleans investigation into President Kennedy's assassination, Victor Marchetti had been a high-ranking staff employee at C.I.A. headquarters. In an article published in *True* magazine in 1975, Marchetti referred to the Agency's concern during the Shaw trial:

> I used to attend, among other things, the Director's morning meeting, his morning staff meeting. This was Richard Helms at the time and he held a meeting every morning at 9, which was attended by 12 or 14 of his leading Deputies plus 3 or 4 staffers— the executive assistants to the number one, two and three men in the Agency and also the Press Officer. I often used to take the minutes of this meeting . . . which are a joke because things would be left out or written in a vague fashion so they were meaningless. But during the Clay Shaw trial I remember the Director on several occasions asking questions like, you know, "Are we giving them all the help they need?" I didn't know who *they* or *them* were. I knew they didn't like Garrison because there were a lot of snotty remarks passed about him. They would talk in half sentences like "is everything going all right down there . . . yeah . . . but talk with me about it after the meeting" or "we'll pick this up later in my office." So after several of these over a week or two I began to ask myself what's going on, what's the big concern. I began to ask around . . . and one of the other people who attended the meeting . . . at the time I said, "What's the concern about this trial and this guy Shaw?"
>
> I was then told, "Well . . . Shaw, a long time ago, had been a contact of the Agency. . . . He was in the export-import business . . . he knew people coming and going from certain areas—the Domestic Contact Service—he used to deal with them . . . and it's been cut off a long time ago" . . . and then I was told "well of course the Agency doesn't want this to come out now because Garrison will distort it, the public would misconstrue it."*

---

* In the interview, Marchetti added: "At that time or shortly thereafter this guy Ferrie came up, . . . and I was given a similar kind of explanation, that he's been involved in the Bay of Pigs and been a contract agent or contact at the time. As I say I accepted these explanations on

Of course, at the time we had no proof of Shaw's connections to the Agency nor did we know the extent of the Agency's "help" for him. We proceeded at the trial as if we had a fair chance for a conviction.

In order to show the relationship between Shaw and Oswald, we called Vernon Bundy to the stand. Bundy, it may be recalled, had testified in the preliminary hearing that he had observed Lee Oswald and Clay Shaw meeting together out on the seawall along Lake Pontchartrain. (See Chapter 12.) A round-faced, placid black man in his twenties, he was a part-time presser for Avondale Cleaners. Very much at ease and in control of himself, Bundy repeated in greater detail the story he had told at the hearing: how he had been giving himself a heroin injection when he saw Oswald and Shaw together and overheard their conversation; how Shaw gave money to Oswald; how Oswald placed it in his pocket as one of his yellow circulars supporting Castro fell to the ground; how Bundy used that paper as wrapping for his heroin kit.

This time, however, Bundy added a piece of unexpected drama. Without any warning, he asked the judge to allow him to demonstrate how he knew it was Clay Shaw who was at the lakefront.

"Would you have the gentleman there go to the back of the courtroom?" he asked.

The judge, after a surprised moment of hesitation, nodded his assent. Shaw complied, with bailiffs on each side of him.

Bundy stepped down from the witness chair, then turned Shaw's chair around and sat in it sideways, looking toward the entrance of the court where Shaw was. "Would the gentleman approach me?" asked Bundy. Shaw and the bailiffs moved forward.

"Here I am on top of the seawall with my cooker," said Bundy. Shaw, looking irritated and puzzled, walked down the center aisle of the courtroom.

He watched the way Shaw's foot twisted when he walked. This is how "I identified this man the next time I saw him," he said.

---

face value, never thought more about them until I began to get connected with the Committee to Investigate Assassinations and looked back. One of the reasons I accepted that at face value is usually when you were being put off you were told 'look, it's sensitive and you have no need to know.' Sometimes when it was really sensitive they would give you a phony excuse. . .. His association and contacts could have been extensive and I was just being put off."

Everyone in the courtroom was able to observe that the tall defendant had a slight limp—the result, he later explained, of a back injury received in the Army when lifting a hospital cot.

Afterward, it was plain that courtroom attachés and jurors alike had been impressed with Vernon Bundy's testimony. It certainly was the first time I ever saw a witness take over the courtroom during a trial. I should add that until Bundy told me what he had seen when Shaw met Lee Oswald on the lakefront, I had no idea that Shaw walked with an almost imperceptible limp.

By now we had established the relationship among Shaw, Oswald, and Ferrie. And we had established that Shaw gave money to Oswald in a clandestine setting. We should have known that things were going too well.

The bomb that shattered our case exploded quickly enough. His name was Charles Spiesel. The accountant from New York whom we had belatedly added to our witness list took the stand next. He said that on a trip to New Orleans he met David Ferrie at Lafitte's Blacksmith Shop in the French Quarter. Later they joined Clay Shaw in a building Spiesel recalled as being at "Dauphine and Esplanade," which is approximately where Shaw's residence was located. After everyone relaxed and had a number of drinks, Spiesel said Ferrie and Shaw began discussing the possible assassination of John Kennedy. Although Spiesel was surprised when the subject first arose, everyone had been drinking heavily so the indiscretion of the conversation was understandable to him. He recalled the exchange of comments between Shaw and Ferrie in great detail, each explaining why Kennedy should be eliminated and how it should be done.

On cross-examination, the chief defense counsel uncannily seemed to know just what questions to ask Spiesel. First, Dymond asked if Spiesel had ever publicly complained about "hypnosis and psychological warfare" being used on him. Spiesel replied that he indeed had been hypnotized in New York and New Jersey, and during several visits to New Orleans, in the period between 1948 and 1954.

Asked who hypnotized him, Spiesel said he did not always know. He said he could tell that hypnosis was being tried "when someone tries to get your attention—catch your eye. That's a clue right off."

Dymond then asked him what happened under hypnosis. Spiesel

replied: "They plant certain thoughts in your mind and you are given the illusion that they are true." He added that he had become "rather an expert" at knowing when people were trying to hypnotize him.

Under further cross-examination, Dymond brought out Spiesel's belief that the New York City police had hypnotized him, tortured him mentally, and forced him to give up his practice as an accountant.

"Have you had trouble recently with a communist conspiracy," Dymond asked, "people following you, and tapping your phones?"

"Well," replied Spiesel hesitantly, "not particularly recently."

Then Dymond zeroed in for the kill. Was it not a fact, he asked, that when Spiesel's daughter left New York to go to school at Louisiana State University he customarily fingerprinted her? Spiesel replied in the affirmative.

Dymond then asked if it were not also a fact that he customarily fingerprinted his daughter again when she returned at the end of the semester. Again, the witness acknowledged that this was true.

Dymond then asked him why he fingerprinted her. Spiesel explained that he did this, in effect, to make sure that the daughter who was returning from L.S.U. was the same one he had sent there.

For one very long moment, while I am sure that my face revealed no concern, I was swept by a feeling of nausea. I realized that the clandestine operation of the opposition was so cynical, so sophisticated, and, at the same time, so subtle, that destroying an old-fashioned state jury trial was very much like shooting a fish in a barrel with a shotgun.

Our only hope now was that our subsequent witnesses could drown out the memory of Spiesel. So next we called Perry Russo, perhaps our most important witness. Russo largely repeated the testimony he had given in the preliminary hearing (see Chapter 12), but at the trial he was on the stand much longer—two days, most of which were devoted to cross-examination. To the very end, Russo remained unshaken in his clear-minded insistence that he had seen Clay Shaw and David Ferrie meeting with the young man named "Leon Oswald" and that they had discussed in detail the assassination of the President.

In the course of Dymond's cross-examination, issues raised by journalist James Phelan came up. (See Chapter 13.) Phelan had written and later would testify for the defense that there were inconsistencies between the two memoranda that Andrew Sciambra had written based on interviews with Russo, and Russo's actual testimony at the preliminary hearing. Russo responded that neither of the memoranda contained all the details he thought could have been added, but he had not written the respective notes and it had not been his responsibility to correct them. He went on to say that what he thought was important was what he had just testified to under oath in front of the jury. Then, looking directly at Clay Shaw, he said: "I am absolutely sure the defendant is the man who was there," referring to the meeting about the assassination which had taken place at Ferrie's apartment.

Phelan had built a brief career out of his contention that Russo had mistakenly identified Clay Shaw. Now, with his obviously honest and forceful testimony, the young witness had instantly disposed of Phelan's efforts. So irrelevant had Phelan become, in fact, that later when the defense called him as a witness we did not even send in Andrew Sciambra, who was champing at the bit, to cross-examine him.

To establish that the President had to have been shot by more than one gunman and that there had to have been a conspiracy, we called a number of witnesses from Dallas who saw and heard shooting from in front of the motorcade. William E. Newman, a young design engineer from Dallas, described how he had been only 10 to 15 feet away from the limousine when he saw the first shot hit the President in the front of the head. Kennedy fell backwards violently. The shots, Newman recalled, were coming from the grassy knoll right behind where he was standing. His testimony was corroborated by Frances Newman, his wife. And by James Simmons, an employee of the Union Terminal Railway. And by Mrs. Mary Moorman, a housewife from Dallas, and Mrs. Philip Willis.

Richard Randolph Carr, confined to a wheelchair because of a construction accident, nonetheless traveled from Dallas and testified that he had heard shots from the grassy knoll and had seen a furrow caused by a bullet that missed the President's limousine, cutting a path eastward through the grass in Dealey Plaza. Carr then ran down the outside stairway of the building he was working on and happened to see four men running out of the Book Depository. One walked away, but the other three climbed into a Nash Rambler parked facing north on Houston Street and drove off unimpeded against the traffic. When he told his story to the F.B.I., Carr testified, the agents told him to keep his mouth shut.

Deputy Sheriff Roger Craig corroborated some of Carr's testimony, repeating under oath that he had seen a Nash Rambler driven by a Latin man pull up on Elm Street in front of the Depository and pick up a young man, whom he later took to be Lee Oswald, before speeding away. (See Chapter 7.)

The expert witness we called to demystify the Warren Commission's official explanation of the President's bullet wounds was Dr. John Nichols, an associate professor of pathology at the University of Kansas, who had studied the Zapruder film, slides made from the film, and other photographs of the assassination. The court qualified Dr. Nichols as an expert on pathology and forensic pathology.

To help the jury understand Dr. Nichols's testimony, we had subpoenaed the Zapruder film and twenty-one 8" x 10" color pictures from *Life* magazine. This was the first time in more than five years that the Zapruder film had truly been made public.* To be sure, the F.B.I. had given a copy of it to the Warren Commission, but two critical frames had been mysteriously reversed to create the false impression that a rifle shot to Kennedy's head had been fired from behind.† The National Archives also had a copy for those citizens able to stop their work and make their way to the nation's capital. However, there had been no real public viewing of the Zapruder film. It had been kept in a vault in the Time-Life Building on the Avenue of the Americas in New York City all these years.

Now Al Oser, who was conducting the questioning of Dr. Nichols, asked the court for permission to show the Zapruder film. While the assistant district attorneys were setting up the projector and screen, spectators moved *en masse* from one side of the courtroom to the other so

---

* I persuaded Mark Lane to have 100 copies of the Zapruder film printed and distributed to colleges and universities all over the country and the world.

† Frame 313 showed the instant of the shot striking Kennedy's head. As photographed by Abraham Zapruder, frames 314 and 315 showed the head falling backwards, plainly indicating that the rifle shot had come from the front. Following the F.B.I.'s transposition of these two frames, it was made to appear that the President's head was falling forward, indicating a shot from the rear.

After a routine examination of the subsequent frames, even the Warren Commission was forced to recognize the transposition of frames 314 and 315 and asked the F.B.I. what happened. J. Edgar Hoover explained that an "inadvertent" printing error had occurred.

that they could participate in the viewing of the "first run" of the moving picture of the President's death. The film, clearly illustrating in horrifying detail the fatal shot striking President Kennedy, was shown again and again until every member of the jury understood what had happened. Then Oser asked Dr. Nichols to state as an expert from what direction that shot had come.

"Having viewed these slides and pictures and the Zapruder film," Dr. Nichols said, "I find that it is compatible with the gunshot having been delivered from the front."

Dr. Nichols further testified that the President had been shot not only from the front but also from behind. In lay terms, Dr. Nichols described how the bullets from behind necessarily had entered Kennedy's body from divergent angles, meaning that the riflemen had to be firing from two different positions.

We hoped that Dr. Nichols's testimony would clarify for the jury once and for all the utter impossibility of the Warren Commission's official story that seven entry and exit wounds in President Kennedy and Texas Governor John Connally were caused by one bullet. The government adopted this official posture, which came to be known as "the magic bullet" theory, after the Zapruder film established a maximum time frame for the shooting of 5.6 seconds. In such a short time a lone assassin could have fired only three bullets. Since the government had already concluded that one bullet missed completely (with a fragment striking onlooker James Teague in the cheek) and a second bullet hit the President in the head and shattered his skull, that left a third "magic" bullet, Commission exhibit 399, to account for the remaining seven wounds in Kennedy and Connally.

According to the government's account, the seven wounds were inflicted as follows: The bullet entered the President's back or neck (1) headed downward at an angle of about 17 degrees. It then moved *upward* and departed from Kennedy's body out of the front of his neck (2). It continued into Connally's body at the rear of his right armpit (3). Inasmuch as Governor Connally had been sitting directly in front of President Kennedy, it must be assumed that the bullet somehow moved over to the right far enough to head leftward into Connally. Now the bullet headed downward at an angle of 27 degrees, shattering Connally's fifth rib and departing from the right side of his chest (4).

The bullet continued downward and then entered Connally's right wrist (5), shattering the radius bone. After coming out of the other side of the governor's right wrist (6), it entered his left thigh (7), from which it later fell out.

According to the official story, this bullet was later found in almost perfect condition in a corridor of Parkland Hospital, apparently having fallen from a cot.* The bullet was nearly flawless, deformed slightly only at its base. Curiously, more fragments were found in Governor Connally's wrist than were found to be missing from bullet No. 399.

We did not ask Dr. Nichols to get into a lot of technical jargon in disposing of the magic bullet theory. We just wanted him to point out to the jurors that such an explanation, which was central to the government's lone assassin scenario, defied the laws of both physics and common sense. Once the jury accepted that the magic bullet could not create all seven different wounds in President Kennedy and Governor Connally, our strategy went, it would then have to conclude that there was a second rifleman—and thus a conspiracy.

It was clear to me from the jurors' reactions that our presentation of the evidence of a conspiracy in Dallas had made a deep impression. I did not know if we could ever truly recover from the Spiesel cross-examination, but now it remained for us to link Shaw to the Dallas conspiracy.

The linkage depended largely on the fact that the roly-poly hippie attorney Dean Andrews had admitted receiving a call from "Clay Bertrand" about representing Lee Oswald in Dallas. The pieces of the puzzle would fall into place in the jurors' minds, we hoped, if we could rest our case with persuasive evidence that "Clay Bertrand" was actually Clay Shaw. And so we called as our next witness Mrs. Jesse Parker, a hostess at the V.I.P. room of the New Orleans International Airport. She testified that in December 1966 she saw Clay Shaw sign the room's guest register as "Clay Bertrand." After describing the incident fully, Parker located the signature in the register and then pointed to Shaw as the man who signed it.

We then called Mrs. Elizabeth McCarthy, a handwriting expert

---

* It is of some interest that Jack Ruby had been seen in the halls of Parkland Hospital shortly before the magic bullet was found. Some critics have speculated that Ruby may have delivered it to the hospital.

from Boston, who had studied the V.I.P. room signature of "Clay Bertrand." I asked her if she had reached a conclusion concerning that signature. "It is my opinion," she replied, "that it is highly probable that Clay Shaw signed the signature."

To provide a dramatic finale, we had scheduled as our final witness New Orleans Police Officer Aloysius Habighorst. He was the police desk officer who booked Clay Shaw after we arrested him (see Chapter 11). It will be recalled that Habighorst routinely asked Shaw if he had any alias, and Shaw, apparently greatly shaken by his arrest, replied, "Clay Bertrand." This, of course, was one of the most important pieces of evidence in our case because it came from Shaw himself and directly linked him with the call to Dean Andrews about representing Lee Oswald in Dallas.

We instructed the court attaché to call Officer Habighorst. But before Habighorst could take the stand, Judge Haggerty suddenly ordered the jury removed from the court. Then he informed Jim Alcock, who was questioning at the time, that he was going to rule inadmissible the fingerprint card, signed by Shaw, on which "Clay Bertrand" had been typed in the space designated for "alias." Haggerty went on to say that he would not believe whatever Officer Habighorst said, anyway.

Alcock, angered and flushed, leaped to his feet and protested the judge's ruling and his incredible comment about Habighorst. Haggerty replied that Shaw had been deprived of a constitutional right at the central police lockup when he was asked—without a lawyer being present—whether or not he had an alias.

From time immemorial, this had been standard booking procedure at the central lockup. We knew that there was no constitutional requirement that an attorney be present for routine questions at booking. That was not the law then, and it is not the law even today. But Judge Haggerty was changing the law before our eyes.

Alcock announced in frustration that he would ask for writs from the Louisiana Supreme Court, but I knew that was a futile gesture. In those days appellate courts in Louisiana never granted such writs in an ongoing trial.

On that solemn note the presentation of the state's case against Clay Shaw essentially ended. As we walked out of the courtroom for the break before the defense presented its case, I glanced out through the huge windows, which were open for a change. A feeling of sadness passed over me. I was envisioning our case, like a giant bird with its great wings flapping slowly, sailing through the open windows off into the blue.

Whenever a white-collar defendant goes on trial, the defense attorneys almost invariably begin their presentation with witnesses to show their client's superb reputation in the community. The idea is to establish in the jurors' minds that, whether out of venality or haplessness, the prosecution has made a terrible mistake and is trying the wrong man.

Thus it came as no surprise that Shaw's attorneys led off with a series of witnesses to reaffirm his reputation. They were followed by other witnesses intended to refute various points the prosecution had made, including Dean Andrews, who testified that Shaw was not the "Clay Bertrand" who had called and asked him to represent Lee Oswald in Dallas.*

Rather than go through the entire litany, I shall focus on the testimony of the defense's two most important witnesses. The first was Lieutenant Colonel Pierre Finck, one of the three pathologists who participated in the military autopsy of President Kennedy at Bethesda Naval Hospital in Maryland.

The autopsy had been so tainted in several respects that prior to the trial we wondered whether or not the defense would expose one of the pathologists to the risk of cross-examination in a courtroom. First of all, under Texas law the body should never have been removed from the city until a civilian autopsy had been done by a pathologist at the mortuary in Dallas. Texas officials informed the Secret Service of this

---

* Andrews had previously been found guilty of committing perjury before the Grand Jury when he gave similar testimony under oath, and had been sentenced to five months in the Parish Prison. However, during the Shaw trial his conviction was on appeal to the Louisiana Supreme Court and it could not be referred to. Later, after Andrews lost his appeal, his attorneys approached me, concerned that he would never live through a six-months' sentence with the serious heart condition he had. I knew this was true, and I advised them to file a motion for a new trial. When they responded that the Supreme Court would never grant such a motion, I told them to note on the papers that the motion was approved by the district attorney. It would then be granted *pro forma*, as it was. When the case was sent back to my office, I dismissed the charges. Andrews never served any time, but he did later die from his bad heart.

as the body was being placed in an ambulance, but instead of going to the mortuary, the Secret Service whisked the body to the airport, where it was put on Air Force One and taken to the Bethesda Naval Hospital.

Second, although the civilian doctors at Parkland Hospital had already diagnosed the wound in the front of Kennedy's neck as an entrance wound, the three military pathologists did not probe it, as is standard procedure, to find the bullet or trace its path.

Third, 15 to 20 photographs and x-rays of President Kennedy's body were taken during the autopsy and handed over to Agent Roy H. Kellerman of the Secret Service, yet none of these was ever examined by the Warren Commission. Instead, the chief pathologist, Commander James Humes, arranged for artists to draw pictures of various parts of the autopsy for the Commission. Not even the artists were allowed to see the photos and x-rays. They drew their pictures from the pathologists' verbal recollections. Finally, on Sunday, November 24, 1963, Commander Humes by his own admission burned all his autopsy notes.*

---

* Years later two other important discoveries concerning the autopsy were made. The first was that during the autopsy Commander Humes apparently found an additional bullet that he never acknowledged in his report. On the contrary, he told the Commission he did not find any bullets. The bullet is mentioned in a receipt given to the Bethesda Naval Hospital's commanding officer by the F.B.I. agents to whom it was given. Released under the Freedom of Information Act to Mark Lane, the receipt says:

22 November 1963

From: Francis X. O'Neill, Jr., Agent FBI
     James W. Sibert, Agent, FBI
To: Captain J.H. Stover, Jr., Commanding
    Officer, U.S. Naval Medical School, National
    Naval Medical Center, Bethesda, Maryland
1. We hereby acknowledge receipt of a missle [sic] removed by Commander James J. Humes, MC, USN on this date.

(signed)
Francis X. O'Neill, Jr.
(signed)
James W. Sibert

The discovery of a fourth bullet during the autopsy necessarily meant that more than one shooter hit the President.

The second discovery came in August 1972, when Dr. Cyril Wecht, an eminent pathologist and the coroner of Pittsburgh, Pennsylvania, obtained a court order allowing him to examine President Kennedy's brain at the National Archives. An examination of the brain, which had

We knew, of course, that the defense could not very well bring down Commander Humes as a witness, considering what he had done. That left Dr. J. Thornton Boswell and Lieutenant Colonel Finck. The defense chose Finck, who, oddly enough, also had participated in the autopsy of President Kennedy's younger brother Robert following his assassination on June 4, 1968.

In our trial preparation we had explored extensively all of the available information about the President's wounds and were well prepared to question Dr. Finck. However, we could not be sure in advance which position he would take.

Because of conflicting evidence, there were two completely different official explanations of where Kennedy had been hit from behind. One, based on the testimony of Secret Service agents who were close to the President when he was shot as well as F.B.I. agents at the autopsy scene, placed the rearward wounds slightly more than five inches downward from the collar line and approximately two inches to the right of the spine. This explanation was strongly corroborated by Kennedy's shirt and jacket, each of which had a bullet hole slightly more than five inches below the collarline.

The other official explanation, defended with equal solemnity by the government, was that the rearward bullet struck President Kennedy in the back of his *neck*. This hypothesis not only placed the wound nearly half a foot above the bullet holes in the President's shirt and jacket, which, it was claimed, must have been bunched up high on his back, but also directly contradicted the previous explanation. The second position was more consistent with the idea of an exit wound in the front of the throat, because at least it did not require that bullet to have gone *upward* after coming down at a seventeen-degree angle. But it had other problems. No photograph had ever been released showing an entrance wound at the rear of the neck. Furthermore, the width of the "entrance" wound was measured from the clothing as virtually the same size of the "exit" wound below the Adam's apple. Inasmuch as exit wounds are invariably larger than entrance wounds, this made no sense.

---

been preserved in formalin, might have revealed from what direction, how many times, and where bullets had struck the President's head. Unfortunately, Dr. Wecht could not perform such an examination. The President's brain, it was explained to him, had disappeared.

We listened intently to Dr. Finck's direct testimony, in response to questions by Irvin Dymond, to ascertain which explanation he would support. Dr. Finck sat erect and spoke with great precision. I imagined that his desk probably was kept in perfect order with no unfinished correspondence or unnecessary clutter obscuring the clean walnut top. He was obviously most meticulous, as revealed by his habit of spelling out loud technical medical words after he uttered them—apparently a remnant of his teaching experience.

As it turned out, Dr. Finck arrived from Washington as a spokesman for the "back-of-the-neck" entry. He testified, in effect, that the autopsy strongly supported the likelihood that the President had been killed by one rifleman firing at him from behind, one shot hitting him in the neck and the other striking him in the back of the head and killing him. As his testimony went on, it became apparent that he was using the term "back" in its broadest possible sense to include that part of the back which runs up above the shoulders into the neck.

I glanced at Oser to see if he was ready. He nodded grimly. Oser was a tall, rangy young man with blue eyes and blondish hair. His father had been a judge in this same Criminal District Court for years, and the court had been his destination since the first day he arrived at law school. Foremost among his many trial capabilities, as Dr. Finck was about to find out, was a snapping-turtle tenacity in cross-examination.

As he loped toward the witness chair, Oser greeted Dr. Finck with a warm smile. Within minutes he had the autopsy pathologist back-pedaling at a rapid rate. After Dr. Finck committed himself to the proposition that the entry wound was in the back of the neck, Oser quickly moved to the question of whether the neck wound had been probed at the autopsy. This should have been a standard and routine examination to determine the route of the wound. When Dr. Finck's answer was negative, Oser began pressing him:

> DR. FINCK: I will remind you that I was not in charge of this autopsy, that I was called—

> MR. OSER: You were a co-author of the [autopsy] report though, weren't you, doctor?

> DR. FINCK: Wait. I was called as a consultant to look at these wounds; that doesn't mean I am running the show.

MR. OSER: Was Dr. Humes running the show?

DR. FINCK: Well, I heard Dr. Humes stating that—he said, "Who's in charge here?" and I heard an Army general, I don't remember his name, stating, "I am." You must understand that in those circumstances, there were law enforcement officers, military people with various ranks and you have to coordinate the operation according to directions.

MR. OSER: But you were one of the three qualified pathologists standing at the autopsy table, were you not, doctor?

DR. FINCK: Yes, I was.

MR. OSER: Was this Army general a qualified pathologist?

DR. FINCK: No.

MR. OSER: Was he a doctor?

DR. FINCK: No, not to my knowledge.

MR. OSER: Can you give me his name, colonel?

DR. FINCK: No, I can't. I don't remember.

MR. OSER: Do you happen to have the photographs and x-rays taken of President Kennedy's body at the time of the autopsy and shortly thereafter? Do you?

DR. FINCK: I do not have x-rays or photographs of President Kennedy with me.

Of course he did not have the x-rays or photographs of President Kennedy with him. Our pathologist witness, Dr. Nichols, had asked the government to see the x-rays and photographs of President Kennedy's autopsy, and his requests were denied. Dr. Nichols also had testified that he asked to see the limousine in which President Kennedy had been riding, and the government denied that request also.

Oser now zeroed in on who had been in charge of the autopsy, a question that had long fascinated me.

MR. OSER: How many other military personnel were present at the autopsy room?

DR. FINCK: That autopsy room was quite crowded. It is a small autopsy room, and when you are called in circumstances like that to look at the wound of the President of the United States who is dead, you don't look around too much to ask people for their names and take notes on who they are and how many there are. I did not do so. The room was crowded with military and civilian personnel and federal agents, Secret Service agents, F.B.I. agents, for part of the autopsy, but I cannot give you a precise breakdown as regards the attendance of the people in that autopsy room at Bethesda Naval Hospital.

MR. OSER: Colonel, did you feel that you had to take orders from this Army general that was there directing the autopsy?

DR. FINCK: No, because there were others, there were admirals.

MR. OSER: There were admirals?

DR. FINCK: Oh, yes, there were admirals, and when you are a lieutenant colonel in the Army you just follow orders, and at the end of the autopsy we were specifically told—as I recall it, it was by Admiral Kinney, the surgeon of the Navy—this is subject to verification—we were specifically told not to discuss the case.

MR. OSER: Did you have occasion to dissect the track of that particular bullet in the victim as it lay on the autopsy table?

DR. FINCK: I did not dissect the track in the neck.

MR. OSER: Why?

DR. FINCK: This leads us into the disclosure of medical records.

MR. OSER: Your Honor, I would like an answer from the colonel and I would ask the Court so to direct.

THE COURT: That is correct, you should answer, doctor.

DR. FINCK: We didn't remove the organs of the neck.

MR. OSER: Why not, doctor?

DR. FINCK: For the reason that we were told to examine the head wounds and the—

MR. OSER: Are you saying someone told you not to dissect the track?

THE COURT: Let him finish his answer.

DR. FINCK: I was told that the family wanted an examination of the head, as I recall, the head and chest, but prosectors* in this autopsy didn't remove the organs of the neck, to my recollection.

---

* Prosector is the technical term for a person who makes anatomical dissections. Dr. Finck used the word several times.

MR. OSER: You have said they did not. I want to know why didn't you as an autopsy pathologist attempt to ascertain the track through the body which you had on the autopsy table in trying to ascertain the cause or causes of death? Why?

DR. FINCK: I had the cause of death.

MR. OSER: Why did you not trace the track of the wound?

DR. FINCK: As I recall I didn't remove these organs from the neck.

MR. OSER: I didn't hear you.

DR. FINCK: I examined the wounds but I didn't remove the organs of the neck.

MR. OSER: You said you didn't do this; I am asking you why you didn't do this as a pathologist?

DR. FINCK: From what I recall I looked at the trachea, there was a tracheotomy wound the best I can remember, but I didn't dissect or remove these organs.

MR. OSER: Your Honor, I would ask Your Honor to direct the witness to answer my question. I will ask you the question one more time: Why did you not dissect the track of the bullet wound that you have described today and you saw at the time of the autopsy at the time you examined the body? Why? I ask you to answer the question.

DR. FINCK: As I recall I was told not to, but I don't remember by whom.

It came as no surprise to us that the customary neck probe was not done. However, we were surprised to learn that an Army general who was not a physician had apparently ordered the autopsy pathologists not to do it, and that an admiral had ordered them not to discuss the autopsy.

Even more shocking to me was the next major witness for the defense. I was seated near Jim Alcock at the prosecutors' table and was just lighting up my pipe when I heard Irvin Dymond call "Clay Shaw." The pipe slipped from my mouth. I have never been more astonished. Shaw did not have to testify, because no one can be forced to testify against himself or herself. Yet he must have known by now that we had dug up witness after witness concerning his relationship with David

Ferrie and Lee Oswald and that once he took the witness stand we would cross-examine him at length about this.

Possibly Shaw's attorneys were overconfident following Spiesel's description of his need to fingerprint his daughter and the judge's ruling excluding Shaw's signature admission to the alias of "Clay Bertrand." Or possibly Shaw himself, wanting to gild his already luminous public image, insisted. In any case, he took the stand and testified—under oath—that he had never known Oswald, never used the alias Clay Bertrand, and never called Dean Andrews. And most amazing of all, he testified that he had never even met David Ferrie.

In the normal course of events, that mistake would have put Shaw in a box, gift-wrapped and tied with a bow, for future perjury prosecution. And more immediately, it would have seriously damaged his credibility in the current case because so many witnesses had testified that they had seen Shaw with Ferrie. But this case was hardly normal, and it was clear by now that no jury would find an eminently respectable, prominent, distinguished community leader guilty of conspiring to kill the President, especially following an unforgettable example of genuine lunatic testimony from a prosecution witness.

Early Saturday morning, March 1, 1969, just past midnight, the jury filed into the courtroom and announced that it had acquitted Clay Shaw. I had been prepared for the inevitable verdict and had very little emotional reaction to it. I continued to believe that Shaw had participated in the conspiracy to kill the President, his role having been essentially to set up Lee Oswald as the patsy. But I did not feel vindictive toward Shaw. I did not even dislike him. He simply had done his job as a functionary of the federal intelligence community. And I had done mine as the elected representative of the people of New Orleans.

Following the acquittal, Mark Lane questioned members of the jury, a procedure which is allowed in Louisiana. Their responses indicated that they could not find any motivation for Shaw to have participated in a conspiracy to kill Kennedy, whom he always publicly professed to admire. This did not surprise me. I had known from the outset that we would be unable to make Shaw's motivation clear. That motivation, I believed, stemmed from Shaw's history as a C.I.A. operative and his desire, shared by the hard-core cold warriors in the intelligence community, to stop Kennedy's attempt to turn around U.S. foreign policy. But at the time of the trial the C.I.A. would not acknowledge Shaw's connection with it, and I had no independent evidence either, so I could not even introduce this possible motivation. It was not until later that I discovered the Italian and Canadian press exposés of Shaw's role in Centro Mondiale Commerciale and Permindex. (See Chapter 6.) And it was not until 1975 that Victor Marchetti discussed the Agency's concern for Shaw, and not until 1979 that Richard Helms, the C.I.A.'s deputy director for plans (covert operations) in 1963, first admitted under oath that Shaw had Agency connections.

In a 1979 trial, Helms was asked if he knew Clay Shaw. He responded, under oath:

> The only recollection I have of Clay Shaw and the Agency is that I believe that at one time as a businessman he was one of the part-time contacts of the Domestic Contact Division, the people that talked to businessmen, professors, and so forth, and who traveled in and out of the country.

In a subsequent trial, in 1984, this answer was repeated to Helms, and he was asked, "Do you recall making that statement under oath on May 17, 1979?" He responded, "If it says here I did make it under oath, I guess I did." Helms also conceded then that he had publicly denied this fact when he was the director of the Agency.

Had the jurors been aware of Shaw's Agency connection, the verdict might possibly have been different. Even as it was, every juror Lane questioned agreed that the prosecution had established that President Kennedy had been killed as the result of a conspiracy. To me, this was important. The jurors had acquitted Shaw as an individual, but they had *not* accepted the federal government's great lie about the assassination.

The national press treated the verdict as nothing less than a full vindication of the Warren Commission. Of course, the New Orleans jury had heard evidence concerning only one small corner of what necessarily was a large enterprise. Furthermore, only one individual, whose participation was marginal, had been under consideration. It

251

mattered not. For the moment, the lone assassin myth was resurrected, propped up in a chair by the window and undertaker's rouge applied to its cheeks.

In New Orleans, the reaction of the *Times-Picayune* and the *States-Item* would best be described as dignified jubilation. Unlike their national counterparts, the local media had known all along that we had a first-rate district attorney's office, so they had not become seriously infatuated with the "witness brutality" allegations.

Nevertheless, the local press demanded my resignation. The *States-Item,* in a front-page editorial on March 1, 1969, said:

> District Attorney Jim Garrison should resign. He has shown himself unfit to hold the office of district attorney or any other office.
>
> Mr. Garrison has abused the vast powers of his office. He has perverted the law rather than prosecuted it. His persecution of Clay L. Shaw was a perversion of the legal process such as has not been often seen. . . .
>
> Clay L. Shaw has been vindicated, but the damage to his reputation caused by Mr. Garrison's witch hunt may never be repaired. It is too shameful. This travesty of justice is a reproach to the conscience of all good men and must not go unanswered. Mr. Garrison himself should now be brought to the bar to answer for his conduct.

The next day the *Times-Picayune*'s slightly milder front-page editorial said more or less the same thing. These, it turned out, were merely the first of a number of demands for my resignation by the local press. But I was not about to resign for doing my duty.

To me, the next step was obvious. Although Clay Shaw had won one case, he had created an even better one. On Monday morning, March 3, I filed perjury charges against Shaw. Specifically, I charged him with having testified under oath that he had never met David Ferrie. In fact, Shaw not only knew Ferrie well but frequently had been seen in his company. We had more witnesses to prove this flagrant case of perjury than I had ever encountered as district attorney.

Given my personal choice, I would much rather have let the matter rest once and for all. On the preceding Saturday morning, the jury had relieved me of a great burden. And, truth to tell, I was awfully tired of dancing with the federal government, its mindless intelligence machinery, and the countless battalions of reporters who helped to support the government's deception of the American public about Kennedy's assassination.

However, the choice was not mine. My decision had been made automatically when—contrary to the numerous statements in our files—Shaw had taken the witness stand and, in his grand and courtly manner, made a mockery of the law against lying under oath. There was no more emotion involved in my filing this charge than there is when an airline pilot, informed of bad weather at his destination, changes the course of his airplane to an alternative airport.

Understandably, given the history of this particular case, Shaw promptly sought refuge with the federal government. His attorneys asked the federal court to enjoin me from prosecuting Shaw for perjury. However, there was on the books an explicit statute making it very difficult for any federal court to interfere with a state prosecution.*

Fortunately for Shaw, the federal judicial system shut its eyes to that federal law. The United States District Court *did* enjoin me from prosecuting Shaw for committing perjury, and the federal appellate structure firmly backed up the District Court's ruling all the way. When the assassination of a dead President has been ratified by a live national government, details such as the law very quickly become irrelevant.

In any case, the local newspaper editorials calling for my resignation received from New Orleans citizens the attention they deserved. In the election for district attorney later that year, I received 81,000 votes, the runner-up received 61,000, and the third-place candidate received 7,000.

---

* 28 U.S.C. §2283: Stay of State court proceedings:

"A court of the United States may not grant an injunction to stay proceedings in a State court except as expressly authorized by Act of Congress, or where necessary in aid of its jurisdiction, or to protect or effectuate its judgments."

19

The Majesty
of the Law

MY ARREST BY FEDERAL AGENTS came without warning.

It was early in the morning, June 30, 1971. I had just had breakfast
and read the *Times-Picayune*. I was still wearing my pajamas and
bathrobe and was going up the stairs when the bell rang.

I opened the door, and the men from the federal government poured
in. The man in charge displayed an Internal Revenue Service badge
and held out a piece of paper, while other agents crowded in behind
him. As they fanned out through the rest of the house, he informed me
that I was under arrest and asked if I was armed.

"How can I be armed, when I'm just going upstairs to get dressed?"
I said.

"Well, we're going up with you because we have to take you
downtown to book you."

After I had dressed, with several agents closely watching me, I came
down the stairs. My wife and children were very upset. I told them
there was nothing to worry about.

As I went out the front door flanked by federal agents, I was appalled to see that the sidewalks and driveway in the vicinity of the house were filled with new cars bearing large aerials. Men with walkie-talkies seemed to be all over the place. I noticed some neighbors peering out from their windows, and I could not blame them. Suddenly I was embarrassed.

I was taken downtown to the federal courthouse in a car packed full of agents. There I was mugged, fingerprinted, and put behind bars in a green-walled holding cell. Soon a guard brought me to a courtroom where the magistrate read the formal charges. It seemed that I stood accused of participating in organized crime, specifically of allowing payoffs on pinball gambling.

It is hardly a novelty to hear a man who has been charged by the government say that he was innocent. But for me to say merely that I was innocent would be an understatement of cosmic dimensions.

Put aside that I had never taken a single illegal dollar as district attorney and that it simply was not in my makeup to do so. The plain fact was—as the members of my staff and district attorneys of nearby parishes all realized—that I had enforced the law forbidding payoffs on pinball gambling more rigidly than any previous district attorney ever had. I had done this not because of any soaring sense of virtue or any particular rage about pinball payoffs but because I used my office to enforce every criminal law on the books, whether it was a felony or, as with pinball payoffs, a misdemeanor.

The federal government apparently had not realized this, assuming that like many of the district attorneys in Louisiana I kept one eye closed to pinball gambling payoffs. It had chosen this particular charge, I quickly figured out, because pinball gambling had a federal aspect and this was in its jurisdiction. The federal connection was pretty slender, resting solely on the fact that the pinball machines were manufactured in Illinois. But without such strained legal reasoning the government could come up with no reason to arrest me—unless, of course, it announced the real reason, which I assumed was that I had caused considerable trouble to everyone by investigating the J.F.K. assassination.

After I was released on my own recognizance, Frank Klein picked me up and drove me to the office. Once the initial excitement was over, it was a normal day—except that I made a long-distance call to Boston to talk to F. Lee Bailey, the distinguished trial attorney who was a friend of mine. Lee said he would be delighted and honored to represent me, but there would be one stipulation.

"What?" I asked.

"There will be no fee," he replied.

The 26 months between my arrest and my trial were filled, as always, with trying to keep an understaffed and underfinanced office caught up with the endless overload of work. From time to time, I had to appear as the defendant in the local United States District Court for my own pre-trial proceedings. Bailey's associates were excellent lawyers, and their preparation and court work during this period were splendid, to say the least, leaving me free to concentrate on the details of the district attorney's office. As time went on, however, it became apparent to all of us that the government was in no particular hurry to bring this case to trial.

This simply gave us all the more time to study the material we had obtained from the government. As enunciated by the Supreme Court in the leading case of *Brady v. Maryland,* the federal government is required, during pre-trial discovery proceedings, to supply a criminal defendant with copies of all requested material relating to his case. In my case that material turned out to be prodigious, revealing that the government's investigation of me, involving more than 40 Internal Revenue agents from five southern states, had been under way for several years at the very least. The agents' primary problem had been to make it appear that I was in violation of some law. They had not been able to do this by the usual means of gathering statements from individuals in the pinball business because no one in that business actually knew me.

Accordingly, the federal agents handling my case appeared to have concluded that their only alternative was to create a "make believe" case against me. As most students of covert operations will recognize, the intelligence community is not above constructing such a case against a target individual when circumstances require.

The centerpiece of the government's case turned out to be my old wartime buddy Pershing Gervais. It may be recalled that Gervais was once my chief investigator and had come into conflict with Frank Klein over the Kennedy investigation. (See Chapter 10.) I had dropped Gervais from the office staff after an attorney informed me that Gervais had offered to get a particular case dismissed for him for $750 in cash.

Although Gervais strongly denied the allegation, my position was that the D.A.'s office had to be like Caesar's wife. It was not enough for the office to be virtuous; its virtue had to be unquestioned. Reluctant to accuse my old Army friend of lying and also reluctant to "fire" him, I told him that for some time it had seemed to me that he really was not right for the job of chief investigator. The upshot of a long conversation was that he agreed to resign.

At the same time Gervais told me about the financial problems he was having. I was just beginning a re-election campaign and I had, at least temporarily, more cash from contributions than I needed immediately—although need for money later in the campaign was predictable.

I counted $5,000 out of what I was going to deposit in the campaign bank account within the next few days. I handed it to him, emphasizing that this was a loan and that I expected to be repaid. He accepted it readily and expressed his appreciation.

In early 1970, while federal agents already were constructing a criminal case against me, I became curious about what Gervais was up to since leaving our office. I was aware of his trademark, his large Cadillac, parked out in front of the Fontainbleau Motel at the intersection of Tulane and South Carrollton avenues. He seemed to have a lot of time on his hands, yet plainly was traveling first-class. I asked Lou Ivon to look into it. He began with his contacts on the police force, who knew Gervais, and in a few weeks he had what appeared to be the answer. Gervais, it seemed, had become an entrepreneur in a very unusual enterprise. His office was the lobby or the dining room of the motel, where he was available all day long. The ingenious core of his bizarre operation seemed to be the historical fact that he used to be my chief investigator and also knew half the police force.

Pershing Gervais apparently had become a master of what is known as "playing results." He would select a criminal case which he learned, either from friends on the police force or from court attachés, was not very strong and which the district attorney's office had a low probability of winning. His next stop was to contact the family of the defendant and inform them of his special connection with the district attorney.

After gaining the family's confidence, Gervais would advise them that, despite the serious charges against their son, it was possible for him to arrange for the D.A. to lose the case. Let us say, for the sake of argument, the D.A.'s office lost two out of five such cases in court after a jury trial. Gervais then would call the families of those who were acquitted and announce his success in arranging the outcome of the case. He would collect from them $5,000 or whatever the named fee happened to be—part of which, he would imply, was to go to the district attorney as a payoff.

Evidently Internal Revenue Service agents caught on to what he was up to and developed a case against him. As it turned out, "playing results" was just the beginning of Gervais's suspicious activities. He also collected large amounts of money from various individuals for "authorizing" everything from the operation of a house of prostitution to the opening of a massage parlor to the running of a high-stakes gambling game. By the time the federal agents had completed their investigation against him, they appear to have had him in a very tight vice. And because most of his activities were based on his presumed close relationship to me, they also realized that Gervais was a potential way for them to get at me.

At first, as we learned from the papers we obtained under the *Brady* rule, Gervais informed the I.R.S. agents that there was nothing he could tell them about me because I would not take money and he could not get me to do anything illegal. However, as the vice was tightened, they learned about the money I had loaned Gervais. That was what the federal agents had been looking for. It was all they needed to start building their fictional structure of "bribery."

Sometime in early 1971 Gervais dropped around and explained to me that he had come into some good fortune. Friends in the pinball business had helped him in an enterprise, the particularities of which he never got around to describing. However, his point was that at last he was going to be able to pay back some of the money he had borrowed from me. He would not be able to pay it all at once, but from time to time he would give me $1,000. This seemed agreeable to me, and I let the subject drop from my mind.

After that, Gervais would come by the house to see me occasionally. Only now he was wired for sound—with a transmitter taped under his shirt and a receiver at some outside location, such as in the car of a federal agent near the house.

Inasmuch as I had just undergone painful back surgery, I usually was in bed during his visits. He would ask me how I was feeling, and there would be a brief conversation about nothing in particular. Then he would say something like, "Incidentally, I have another thousand for you. What do you want me to do with it?" My usual reply would be something like, "Just put it on the mantle."

These conversations, of which I recall three or possibly four, presented a problem for the federal agents. In every case they lacked a peg, something that could give Gervais's handing of $1,000 to me a sinister meaning. There was no discussion of my helping the pinball operators violate the law because he knew, perhaps better than anybody, that I would never go along with such a thing.

However, when listening to copies of the taped conversations, which we had obtained under *Brady,* we found that in every tape a lively line or two had been inserted at just the right spot so as to give the rest of the conversation its sinister context.

I happened to remember clearly one of the final conversations that Gervais taped. It had gone along these lines:

GERVAIS: You know, this coming legislature in Baton Rouge could be tough. Some of my friends in the pinball business will really need some help.

GARRISON: What are you telling me for? Why should I help them?

I remembered the conversation because of my longstanding and pronounced lack of interest in dealing with the legislature—except on rare occasions when, for example, I went up to Baton Rouge to obtain a law preventing felons from carrying loaded revolvers. Consequently, I was profoundly astonished when I listened to the copy of the government's tape of this conversation. What I heard, in the presence of attorneys from Lee Bailey's office and my own, was not what actually had been said but, rather, the following:

GERVAIS: You know, this coming legislature in Baton Rouge could be tough. Some of my friends in the pinball business will really need some help.

GARRISON: *I don't see any problem. Forget about it.*

I could not recall from what other tape the new response had been obtained, but it was instantly clear that the reply supposedly coming from me had been inserted. We were appalled that the government would go so far, but I was pleased at the obvious desperation of its agents. If they were this hard up, if they had to be so downright sleazy in their attempt to develop evidence against me, then that meant that their case against me had to be pretty pathetic.

My trial was an elaborate government tableau in the tradition of Franz Kafka. The great issue to be determined was whether or not I had been a corrupt district attorney.

The Justice Department ultimately chose August 20, 1973, to begin the trial, which was expected to last four to six weeks. The election—in which I would be running for a fourth term—was scheduled for November 10. That meant I would be lucky to have five or six weeks afterwards to campaign, although at least four or five months usually is necessary in New Orleans.

Even before the opening of the trial, my major opponent—a former assistant United States attorney—began appearing on television spots. His advertisements provided the public with a colorful contrast. Every morning I was featured on the front page of the *Times-Picayune* as the defendant in a squalid federal bribery case. Meanwhile, every evening there was Mr. Spic and Span on television calling for a return of decency to the district attorney's office.

This was the setting for the case of *The United States of America vs. Jim Garrison, et al.* The "et al." was legalese for my co-conspirators, most of them men I had never set eyes on before my arraignment.*

---

* All of the defendants except myself and two others, Aruns Callery and Robert Nims, were, in fact, pinball owners and/or operators, and by the time the case came to trial, they had pleaded guilty to one charge or another.

Gerald Gallinghouse, the United States Attorney, announced that he personally would be in charge of the prosecution of the trial. All that meant to me was that his judicial district would be totally without the services of a United States Attorney for perhaps six weeks. However, he obviously recognized the paramount importance of this pinball case to the Justice Department, and he made his presence known through the pre-trial activities—a sheaf of legal papers always in his hands, a small American flag ever present in his lapel.

The judge was Herbert Christenberry, at the time the senior judge of the United States District Court for the Eastern District of Louisiana. There were far more complex and significant cases on the docket, but he moved them aside to devote his next six weeks or so to this pinball question.

Judge Christenberry was an austere, stone-faced individual whose stolid expression concealed a volatile temper. Years before, when I was in private practice, I had stood only a few feet away in his court office when he hurled a large law book at a co-counsel of mine who had protested the charge Christenberry had given the jury. He would have thrown one at me as well, but he had none left on his desk.

Christenberry also happened to be the judge who signed the order enjoining me from prosecuting Clay Shaw for perjury in spite of the valid federal statute explicitly forbidding federal interference with a state prosecution.

More than two years after my arrest, trial day finally arrived. My wife and children came to the door as I was about to leave my house that morning. Liz was still in her bathrobe, trying to control the tears welling in her eyes. My children were still very young at the time—young Jim was 14, Virginia 12, Lyon 10½, Elizabeth 9, and Darrow 7. The children sensed that something was happening but were not sure what it was. They would learn later in the day when my wife brought them to court. I kissed them all. "Don't worry," I said, "this is just another day for the D.A.'s office."

At court, as the bits of business which mark a trial's beginning were getting under way, I informed Judge Christenberry I was going to represent myself during the trial. The judge promptly ordered all attorneys to meet him in the conference room. In the smallish chamber, to which the courtroom led directly, I sat down on one side of the table with my attorneys Louis Merhige and Fred Barnett; the United States Attorney and his two assistants sat on the other as we waited for the judge. The prosecutors were looking at me in utter disbelief. All they had ever known me to do as district attorney was to farm out my cases to trial specialists. They had never heard of me during the preceding years when I had earned my keep trying jury cases every day.

My decision to try the case myself had been made after wading, along with Lee Bailey's attorneys, through the mountain of material which represented the government's case against me. It had become increasingly apparent that the whole affair was a fabrication consisting of two separate parts. The first, some sort of financial arrangement which undoubtedly had pre-existed between a number of the pinball operators and at least one member of the police force, was the large one. This pinball arrangement apparently did constitute a conspiracy under the technicalities of federal law, and that made it of value to the federal government if, somehow, it could be connected to my coat tails.

And that is where Pershing Gervais and the government's doctored tapes—the second part of the prosecution's case—came in. This was the small case which they wired to the larger pre-existing case to make the big bomb which they were going to haul into court.

It was plain to me that the government's fraud in connecting me to the pre-existing pinball case had been a criminal activity. However, I also realized that this was almost too much to ask the members of a jury—who had grown up under a government they regarded highly—to believe. An out-of-town lawyer—even one with the great ability of F. Lee Bailey—might not be able to communicate the essentially unbelievable fact of the government's corruption in setting me up.

That was when I decided that *I* had to do it. I knew that most New Orleanians had to be aware of my long fight with the federal government. I knew that most of them sensed, even though they might not know all the details, that my motivation was genuine. Consequently, I concluded, my defense should be nothing less than a continuation of my fight against Washington—with me doing the fighting.

Now Judge Christenberry strode into the chamber and seated himself at the head of the table. He was not enthusiastic about the development, but there really was not much he could do to prevent me from representing myself. He listened as I explained that, while I felt my representation had been excellent, we had a difference of opinion as to how the trial should be handled. Merhige and Barnett confirmed this.

Judge Christenberry turned to me and said that he would go along with my motion to represent myself, so long as I had another attorney at the defense table. He emphasized that he could not have the record show that he let me go to trial unaided.

That was fine with me. When the trial resumed, my longtime friend Lou Merhige was seated at the defense table by my side. The government's first witness was one of the owners of the pinball machines. I had never seen the man before (nor had I ever seen anyone employed by him), and he had never seen me.

Gallinghouse, the United States Attorney, a large, imposing man in a dark blue suit, carefully drew his testimony from him. Yes, the pinball operator said, he had contributed to a fund intended to minimize law enforcement interference with pinball operations in the city. To whom did that money go? To Sergeant Fred Soule of the New Orleans Police Department, the operator replied.

The time came for cross-examination. To whom did Sergeant Soule give the money? He had no idea. Had he ever given any money to me? No, he had not. Had he ever given any money to anyone connected with my office? No. Had anybody in my office ever done any favors of any kind for him or his pinball business? No one had. There were no further questions.

One pinball owner after the other testified, and the pattern continued. Same questions on each direct examination, same answers. Same questions on each of my cross-examinations, same answers.

The next morning I brought a book to court. Lou Merhige picked it up. "What's this?" he asked.

"Something for me to read," I said, "while the United States Attorney continues with his pinball case. Do you really expect me to go along with the pretense that all of this testimony is relevant to anything?"

"You can't do this in Christenberry's court," he said. "He'll stop you."

"No, he won't," I replied. And he did not. I sensed that the judge was restless at first, as I read while the owners testified at length, but

263

apparently he got used to it. Later on, as the seemingly interminable testimony continued, I glanced at the jury. I saw several of its members yawning.

When each machine owner completed his tedious direct testimony, I put my book down and questioned him briefly. I established that we did not know each other, that neither I nor my office ever had done anything for him in connection with his pinball business, and that he had never given any money to me or to anyone representing me. Having established the total irrelevance of the witness insofar as I was concerned, I dismissed him, picked up my book, and resumed reading it.

Finally the government finished with its parade of pinball machine owners. "Call Sergeant Frederick Soule," Gallinghouse announced.

Soule was a smallish, mustachioed man, neatly dressed and wearing a bow tie. He perched carefully on the edge of the witness chair like a parakeet in a bird cage. His testimony for the prosecution added up to a confirmation of his being the receiver of "protection" money from the pinball owners. The high point was his acknowledgment that he had saved up his part and buried it in a large container in his backyard. After his arrest he had dug it up and turned it over to the arresting authorities.

His testimony corroborated that the owners had paid into a protection fund, but it never brought out who had received the money from him and what they did in exchange for it. In short, it did not address the *performance* end which completed the bribery transaction.

I knew from the witness list that the government was not going to call any other officers from the police force. So, I had reasoned, the action on the law enforcement end would have to come from Soule. It never came.

Thus, the cross-examination of Sergeant Soule turned out to be unexpectedly brief. The former police commander of the vice squad testified that I had never asked him to do anything improper. He testified further that my office never had any prior knowledge of pinball raids and that we had a high percentage of convictions in pinball cases.

Now it was time for the star witness for the prosecution. "Call Pershing Gervais," Gallinghouse announced in a stentorian voice.

After some bustle around the entrance doors to the courtroom, Gervais appeared. His hair was gray now, and he was huskier than he had been in our early Army days back at Camp Shelby. He was natty in a cream-colored knit suit, matching shirt, and dark brown tie. He was wearing large, steel-rimmed glasses. Casually strolling down the aisle, he seemed as much at ease as if he were a member of the United States Attorney's staff. He made himself comfortable in the witness chair, then nodded at the members of the jury with a broad smile.

I listened carefully to Gervais's lengthy testimony. Gallinghouse, well aware that the trial had been going for some days without my name coming up once, made the Gervais presentation the crown jewel of his case. The full details of how the hidden recording microphone had been taped to Gervais's body were described. Then the tape recordings were introduced as evidence and played for the jury. Every juror, the judge, the prosecutors, and I all wore earphones while the U.S. Attorney labored at converting overnight a misdemeanor involving the pinball machine owners and a police sergeant named Soule into a major bribery conspiracy involving the district attorney. And with the magic of electronics he made distinct progress in that direction.

My stomach turned each time I heard my voice on the tapes follow Gervais's innuendos with remarks such as "Sure" and "Sounds all right to me." I knew, of course, that each phrase had been selected from another tape and had been taken completely out of context, but the jurors did not. The agents of the intelligence community engineering this particular project had done a good job not only of bottling me up but of tightly screwing on the lid.

There was no doubt in my mind that if a vote had been taken of the jurors at that moment, they would have found me guilty as charged by a vote of 12 to nothing. And I knew full well that, following their verdict, the stone-faced man in the black robe would not have sent me to one of those minimal security "country club" resorts to which some public figures go after a federal conviction. No, it would be the federal penitentiary. Even Lou Merhige, who had made a point of always being upbeat and encouraging, was noticeably unhappy.

There was very little in Gervais's direct testimony that I had not expected. But I was astonished when Gervais said calmly from the witness stand that I had received $150,000 from the pinball operators.

I knew that he would have to go along with the three or four $1,000 payments which matched the secret tapings of his repayments to me, but I had no idea why he had come up with an incredible sum like $150,000.

However, the more I thought about it, the more I realized that Gervais's gigantic figure of $150,000 would be useful to me. The pinball people—or anyone else, for that matter—would have expected gigantic services for that gigantic amount. On the pad in front of me I wrote, "services?" I had the working title for the presentation of my case.

I began my cross-examination of Pershing Gervais in a distinctly laid-back manner. I wanted him to sense that his testimony had not angered me. I understood the jam the Internal Revenue agents had put him in as the result of his highly original short-order brokerage operation at the Fontainbleau Motel. I also understood that he had had no alternative but to answer the United States Attorney's lengthy questioning, which set up the introduction of the government's tapes.

I wanted him to know that none of this had changed me. I was still the same fellow who had served with him when we were both non-commissioned officers back in the Army days.

"Do you remember," I asked, "when we first met?"

"At Jackson Barracks," he said.

"Do you recall when?"

"It would have been prior to World War II."

"Do you remember where we went from Jackson Barracks?"

"I recall we went to Camp Shelby, Mississippi."

"What outfit were we in?" I continued.

"The Washington Artillery of the Louisiana National Guard," he replied.

I could tell from the tone of his voice that he was not on the same frequency with me. It was an evanescent warning that the relationship I thought existed did not exist any more. I brushed it aside and went ahead. This man had been my best friend back in those early Army days.

"What kind of relationship would you say we had in those years?" I asked.

"As related to what?" Gervais asked.

"You recently described our relationship as being acquaintances," I said. "Would you say that when we were in the Army, we were good friends?"

"My good friend was Charlie Weiss," Gervais answered. "You were a friend. We did not socialize."

That reply brought a sudden end to my being laid back. I did not know where the man had gone whom I had known in the Army, but this was not the same person at all. This man, I realized, was as cold as the steel rims on his glasses.

I left the past behind and moved at once to the subject at hand. Directing his attention to the period before he began cooperating with the government, I asked if it was not true that he had told I.R.S. agents I was not concerned with money. He acknowledged this was true. I asked if he had not also told the I.R.S. agents that if I made a mistake on a tax return it would be the result of carelessness, that I was just as likely to overpay my tax as to underpay it. Gervais acknowledged that he had made this statement. Was it not also a fact, I asked, that he had complained that he could not get me to do anything for him at all? He confirmed that this was correct.

Now I took from the table a handful of material and walked back in front of him. I asked him if it was true that the government had obtained a job for him at General Motors of Canada. And that he had to show up only several times a week to collect a salary of $22,000 a year. He answered yes to both questions.

I asked what his title was. He replied that he was a division field manager, the top position at the plant. I then inquired about his qualifications for the job. When he replied that he had none, I walked back to the table.

I busied myself searching through some of the exhibits. I knew what I was after, but I wanted the fact of Gervais's getting $22,000 a year for showing up a couple of times a week to sink into the minds of the jurors.

I picked out copies of two birth certificates and walked back to the witness stand with them in my hand where he could see them. Now I asked him whether, when he joined the Witness Relocation Program, the government had required him to change his name.

Yes, he replied, he had changed his name to Mason, and the Justice

Department had given him new birth certificates for his children, bearing the new last name.

I asked whether these birth certificates had shown the states in which his two children truly had been born, and his reply was that they had not.

I then asked whether this necessarily meant that the two birth certificates, obtained for him by the Justice Department, were forgeries. Gervais looked at the two certificates I had. He agreed that this necessarily was so. Whereupon I handed the two forged birth certificates to the jurors so that they could see what a professional forgery looked like. I remained silent as they examined the art work from the Justice Department. When the jurors had finished, I moved for a recess. I wanted the jurors to have plenty of time to ask themselves why the United States Justice Department would be so interested in convicting someone that they would have birth certificates forged to assure the conviction. I wanted them to reflect upon the majesty of the law.

When Gervais resumed the witness stand, I asked if he remembered any details about the agreement he had made with the Justice Department. He indicated that he did.

Then I showed him a copy of a letter written to him by John Wall, the attorney in charge of the organized crime and racketeering field office of the Justice Department. Gervais recalled receiving the letter.

That meant that I could introduce it into evidence and read it to the jury, which I proceeded to do. The last paragraph concerned the conditions of his keeping the $22,000 position (referred to in the letter as "subsistence") with General Motors of Canada. This paragraph said:

> It was further determined on September 8, 1971, the subsistence is paid *on condition that you not re-enter the United States without the prior approval of the Criminal Division* and that all future payments will be cancelled and the Department of Justice will be relieved of any responsibilities if this condition regarding re-entry is breached.
> [Emphasis supplied.]

The federal Witness Relocation Program had been a measure ostensibly for use in the government's fight against organized crime. The change of name for a witness, for example, was intended to protect the witness from being murdered by the mob or otherwise harmed or intimidated. To go to such lengths when the defendant was a district attorney was absurd. It seemed clear to me that the government had put Gervais into the program solely to make him inaccessible to me for interview or questioning. Although a defendant (or his attorney) has the right to interview all likely witnesses against him prior to his trial, there was no way I could locate this man, whose name had been changed to Mason and who even had been sent off to another country.

Near the end of his Canadian exile, Pershing Gervais finally rebelled against the Justice Department's confinements and gave an interview in May 1972 in Canada to reporter Rosemary James for a New Orleans television station. I had obtained a copy of the transcript and now, in the courtroom, I questioned Gervais about it.

I showed him the transcript, then read it aloud to him, and asked him if he could confirm that he had made the following statements:

ROSEMARY JAMES: You were forced to work for the government?

GERVAIS: But more than that, I was forced to lie for them, that's a better description.

ROSEMARY JAMES: What were you forced to do?

GERVAIS: Well, it became clear in the beginning, it was obscure, it was always hence [sic], you know what we want, you know what we are doing, see. . . . Through the beginning of harassment until that time where I, for the want of a better description, was seduced by the Justice Department, you know, if I could be seduced, as if there was some question somewhere in there, it became clear that they were really interested in but one man, Jim Garrison, and in their minds, they knew that I was the guy who could get him.

ROSEMARY JAMES: Are you saying you got him?

GERVAIS: Oh yeah, no question about that.

He recalled the interview and acknowledged that these had been his statements. Here is another comment which I requested him to confirm:

ROSEMARY JAMES: You are giving me a lot of double-talk here as far as most people are concerned, did they want to investigate people in the pinball industry and Jim Garrison?

GERVAIS: They wanted Jim Garrison.

ROSEMARY JAMES: What do you mean when you say they wanted Jim Garrison?

GERVAIS: They wanted to silence Jim Garrison. That was their primary objective, because if that were not true, I would still be in New Orleans.

ROSEMARY JAMES: Well, now, are you saying that you participated in a deliberate frameup?

GERVAIS: A total, complete political frameup, absolutely.

He agreed that these were his replies, although he suggested he might have been "irresponsible" to have given such an interview. Here is another series of statements which I asked if he recalled having made to the reporter:

ROSEMARY JAMES: What you are saying explicitly is that the government's total case against Jim Garrison is a fraud?

GERVAIS: No question about it. Anything founded and based purely on politics can't be anything but fraud.

ROSEMARY JAMES: It's a whole lie?

GERVAIS: The entire thing.

He admitted that these were the replies he had made when interviewed. At that point, of course, the government's case against me swirled down the drain into the sewer—where it had belonged all along.

But I was not yet through. Now I wanted to reveal the worthlessness of the government's fraudulently altered tape recordings, once and for all. With the help of Lou Merhige I had located an expert, Dr. Louis Gerstman, a professor of speech and hearing science at the City University of New York.

When I called Dr. Gerstman to the stand, the United States Attorney objected vehemently. Nevertheless, the judge recognized Dr. Gerstman as an expert in his field.

Dr. Gerstman's testimony was to the point: He had found the government's prize evidence to be a fabrication of prior tapes that had been spliced together. He cited an example of my voice being out of context with the conversation taking place. He described "technical disparities" occurring between my voice and that of Gervais and the recurrence of inconsistent noise levels. In sum, his testimony was explicit that the government's tapes had been doctored.

I then called as a witness Leon Hubert, a Tulane law professor and former district attorney, whose testimony, essentially, was that my office had done everything possible under Louisiana law to prosecute the pinball operators. In contrast, to show the differing attitudes of other prosecutors in the state, I called the president of the Louisiana District Attorneys' Association. He testified that it had been his policy not to prosecute the owners of pinball machines. I called the district attorney of Jefferson Parish, which represents the other part of metropolitan New Orleans, and he testified that his office never prosecuted pinball cases because there were too many other crimes that required a higher priority.

My closing argument to the jury lasted three hours. I and my two co-defendants were found not guilty.* Unfortunately, there was not sufficient time to get a re-election campaign off the ground, and my opponent won by 2,000 votes.

My last day in the office where I had been district attorney for 12 years was a Saturday. The place was practically deserted. The floors were scattered with crumpled paper. The wastebaskets overflowed with artifacts collected by a group of people who had worked together for years.

I was cleaning off the top of my desk when I became aware that Andrew Sciambra was standing in front of me. He had tears in the corners of his eyes.

---

* This was not the last time the federal government tried to frame me. Along with the main case, I had been charged with income tax evasion for failing to pay taxes on the money I never received from the pinball people. This second trial was held in early 1974, after I had completed my term as district attorney. I defended myself again and was again found not guilty. The government's case this time collapsed even more ignominiously than the first one had. It simply became obvious to the jurors that I had not received any illegal income from the pinball business or any other racket and the government was unable to produce a scintilla of evidence that I had engaged in income tax evasion.

20

The Secret Sponsors

> Whenever you have eliminated the impossible, whatever remains, *however* improbable, must be the truth.
>
> *The Sign of Four,*
> Sir Arthur Conan Doyle

MUCH HAS HAPPENED since Clay Shaw's trial and my trial. Leading public figures like Lyndon Johnson, Earl Warren, Allen Dulles, Charles Cabell, and Earle Cabell have all died. And important characters in my New Orleans investigation like the virulent anticommunist Guy Banister and his private detective associate Jack Martin have gone unnoticed to their graves.

Others have died in undeniably mysterious circumstances. Lee Oswald's Dallas friend and baby sitter George de Mohrenschildt was found shot to death, a shotgun nearby, hours after arranging to be interviewed by an investigator from the House Select Committee on Assassinations. The coroner's verdict was suicide.

David Ferrie, as described in Chapter 11, was discovered dead in his New Orleans apartment with two unsigned suicide notes by his side. The coroner decided that death was due to natural causes.

Deputy Sheriff Roger Craig left Dallas and moved to New Orleans as the result of an attempt on his life. He grew homesick for Dallas, however, and moved back. His car was blown up while he was in it, but he survived. Then he was found shot to death at his home. The coroner's verdict was suicide.

Jack Ruby, having been treated at the Dallas Sheriff's office for a cold, was sent to the hospital when it got worse. Shortly thereafter it was announced that he had cancer, and shortly after that it was announced that he had died from the cancer.

Lee Harvey Oswald, of course, was shot by Ruby in front of a television audience of millions and a virtual wall of Dallas police officers. Though there is no mystery about the precise cause of death, Ruby's stated reason for killing Oswald—to save Mrs. Kennedy the burden of having to attend Oswald's trial—remains as questionable as ever, particularly in view of Ruby's ties to organized crime on the one hand, and to the F.B.I. and the C.I.A. on the other.

Clay Shaw died on August 14, 1974, and the circumstances were also odd. One day, a neighbor of Shaw's saw some men carrying a body on a stretcher in the front door of Shaw's carriage house. The entire body, including the head, was covered with a sheet. The neighbor, finding this unusual, called the coroner's office, which promptly sent its investigators to Shaw's residence. By the time they arrived, the place was empty. After a day of inquiry, the Orleans Parish coroner's investigators learned that Shaw had just been buried in Kentwood, in Tangipahoa Parish where he was born.

A death certificate signed by Dr. Hugh Betson attested that Shaw's death was due to natural causes—lung cancer. The New Orleans coroner, Dr. Frank Minyard, concerned about the circumstances and the speed of the burial, decided to obtain a court order for the exhumation of Shaw's body in Kentwood so that he could assure himself that Shaw had not died as a result of foul play. But before he could get the order, word of what he had in mind reached the media. Immediately, the newspapers published heated editorials protesting the callous desecration of Shaw's remains, proclaiming his right to be left in peace, and hinting that this was an attempt to revive my past charges of Shaw's involvement in President Kennedy's assassination. The coroner reconsidered, there was no exhumation, and Shaw's body has been left in repose.

I have no idea what happened to some of those who figured prominently in this saga: Kerry Thornley, Oswald's look-alike acquaintance from his Marine days; former F.B.I. Agent James Hosty; Oswald's friend Ruth Paine; and our witness Vernon Bundy.

Some have prospered. Richard McGarrah Helms, the C.I.A.'s deputy director for plans (covert operations) when the assassination occurred, was promoted to Agency director in 1966. In 1973, he retired to become ambassador to Iran, until 1977, when he became a private business consultant. Johnny Carson has turned into a late-night TV icon. N.B.C., C.B.S., *Newsweek*, *Time*, *Life*, and the *New York Times* have all gone on just as before.

So have some important witnesses. For example, Perry Russo operates a property rental business of his own in New Orleans and drives a taxicab on the side. Julia Ann Mercer, married to a successful businessman, is a housewife in the Midwest. And Pershing Gervais is a bailbondsman in Baton Rouge.

With one exception, the members of the special group in the New Orleans D.A.'s office who carried out the J.F.K. investigation are still involved with the law in one way or another. Andrew Sciambra is now a magistrate in the Criminal District Court in New Orleans. Lou Ivon is a member of the state legislature. Al Oser became a judge of the Criminal District Court until his retirement and is now a senior partner in a New Orleans law firm. Jim Alcock also became a Criminal District Court judge in New Orleans and now practices law in Houma, Louisiana. Charles Ward sits as a judge on Louisiana's Fourth Circuit Court of Appeal. D'Alton Williams practices real estate law in New Orleans. And Numa Bertel is chief of the Indigent Defender Service at the Criminal District Court. Frank Klein returned to our office, and later moved on to become the chief assistant district attorney in Placquemine Parish, south of New Orleans, but, I am sad to say, died of cancer in 1986.

As for myself, following my defeat for a fourth term as district attorney and my acquittal in the government's phony tax evasion case against me, I spent four years in private law practice, wrote a novel, and then was elected to my present office as a judge on the Louisiana Fourth Circuit Court of Appeal.

However, my interest in the assassination of President Kennedy and its implications never ended. The assassination critics have continued to turn up new information—which has continued to be disregarded by the United States government. To me, among the most significant revelations were the belated discovery that an additional bullet had been found in President Kennedy's body at the autopsy scene, the disappearance of President Kennedy's brain, and of course the confirmation by both Victor Marchetti and Richard Helms that Clay Shaw had been an agent of the Central Intelligence Agency. (See Chapter 18.)

In 1978 and 1979 the House Select Committee on Assassinations conducted its hearings, and while well on its apparent course of attempting to breathe new life into the moribund Warren Commission report, stumbled reluctantly to the conclusion that Kennedy "was probably assassinated as a result of a conspiracy."* Before disbanding, it called upon the Justice Department to consider reopening the investigation and delivered a secret report detailing the fresh leads its work had developed. The result of that request was nearly a decade of silence.†

More than anything, what has changed in the years since President Kennedy's assassination is our national consciousness. We have been through so much. There were, for example, the assassinations of Martin Luther King, Jr., Robert Kennedy, Medgar Evers, and Malcolm X. There were the assassination attempts on presidential candidate George Wallace and on Presidents Gerald Ford and Ronald Reagan. We have lived through nine horrifying years of the Vietnam War, the trauma of Watergate, the revelations during the 1970s about the C.I.A., and more recently, the Iran/*contra* affair. This extraordinary succession of events has ended our innocence.

Looking back today with new information and new insights, it is possible to put together an informed historical speculation of what

---

* The House Committee was left with no other alternative after its acoustics experts discovered that, in addition to the shooting from behind President Kennedy, a rifle had been fired from the grassy knoll in front of him. Nevertheless, the committee concluded that the frontal shot had missed completely, so Lee Oswald remained the killer of President Kennedy. This was a roundabout way of saying that the Warren Commission really was almost right, except for the detail of the extra rifleman up ahead. The committee added that it was theoretically possible for the grassy knoll rifleman and Lee Oswald to have acted independently, in which case there might not have been a conspiracy after all.

† It was broken, rather anticlimactically, in September 1988 by the news that six months earlier the Justice Department had advised the chairman of the House Judiciary Committee it had found "no persuasive evidence" of a conspiracy.

happened to President Kennedy and why. I believe that what happened at Dealey Plaza in Dallas on November 22, 1963, was a coup d'etat. I believe that it was instigated and planned long in advance by fanatical anticommunists in the United States intelligence community; that it was carried out, most likely without official approval, by individuals in the C.I.A.'s covert operations apparatus and other extra-governmental collaborators, and covered up by like-minded individuals in the F.B.I., the Secret Service, the Dallas police department, and the military; and that its purpose was to stop Kennedy from seeking détente with the Soviet Union and Cuba and ending the Cold War.

A coup d'etat has been described as "a sudden action by which an individual or group, usually employing limited violence, captures positions of governmental authority without conforming to the formal requirements for changing officeholders, as prescribed by the laws or constitution." A successful coup requires a number of elements: extensive planning and preparation by the sponsors (those responsible for the coup); the collaboration of the Praetorian Guard* (officials whose job is to protect the government, including the President); a diversionary cover-up afterwards; the ratification of the assassination by the new government inheriting power; and the dissemination of disinformation by major elements of the news media. If this concurrence of events has a familiar sound, it is because this is exactly what happened when John Kennedy was murdered.

I do not know precisely when the planning and preparation for the coup began. In a sense, it may have been as early as late 1960 when the C.I.A. prepared a dossier analysis on the President-elect. Such a psychological profile surely would not have contemplated assassination of the President, but its purpose was to help the C.I.A., or some elements within it, further its goal of manipulating foreign policy. It probably was not until later, when Kennedy had veered toward détente and conventional means of controlling policy had failed, that assassination became an option in the minds of some of the C.I.A.'s Cold War establishment.

---

* During the Roman empire, the Praetorian Guard constituted the imperial bodyguard. These carefully selected special soldiers, led by high-ranking officers of the empire, were the only troops in Rome. Some of them were always with the emperor no matter where he was. As a consequence, in a crisis they could make or break the emperor.

Just who did the plotting is not clear either. But certainly Guy Banister was involved in questionable assassination-related activities very early. Representatives of his organization, Friends of Democratic Cuba, were the first ones to impersonate Lee Oswald when they tried to buy 10 pickup trucks for the Bay of Pigs invasion from the Bolton Ford dealership in New Orleans in January 1961. (See Chapter 4.) By the summer of 1963 Banister was deeply involved in anti-Castro activity, ranging from training guerrillas north of Lake Pontchartrain to collecting ammunition for raids on Cuba. That Banister was working with the C.I.A. at this time is no longer open to serious dispute.

Another one of Banister's tasks that summer of 1963 was the sheepdipping of Lee Oswald to make him appear to be a dedicated communist. Although no one has ever succeeded in locating a genuine New Orleans chapter of Fair Play for Cuba, Banister had Oswald out on the streets handing out leaflets in its name. He provided Oswald with a room up on the third floor of the Newman Building and met with him from time to time in his own office. This sheepdipping, courtesy of Banister, succeeded exactly as planned. Following the assassination, Oswald was immediately branded a communist, with his leafleting activity in New Orleans cited as the prime evidence.

The sponsors of the assassination also arranged numerous scenes where Lee Oswald was impersonated in hopes of laying a trail of incriminating evidence at his feet. (See Chapter 5.) The most significant of these impersonations occurred in Mexico City in October 1963, when Oswald reportedly contacted the Soviet Embassy and the Cuban consulate, ostensibly to arrange a trip to the Soviet Union. The reason this particular impersonation stands out is that all the "documentation" for it was provided by the C.I.A. This evidence—which included C.I.A. memos, photographs of a man who obviously was not Oswald, and tapes of phone calls to the Soviet Embassy that were not of Oswald's voice—was insultingly flimsy. To me, this meant that while some elements within the C.I.A. participated in the Oswald impersonation charades and thus were doing the necessary preparatory work of setting up the scapegoat for the assassination, other elements within the Agency remained uninformed about the plot, or indeed might have been trying to discover the truth.

Oswald appears to have been extensively manipulated by the C.I.A.

for a long period prior to the assassination and may well have believed that he was working for the government. Oswald was also an F.B.I. confidential informant, a job that provided additional control over him and may have given him a reason to believe he was actually penetrating the plot to assassinate the President. His association with the F.B.I. raises a question. To what extent did the F.B.I. and the Secret Service cooperate in the pre-assassination planning? It appears to me that neither agency took any discernible positive action prior to the assassination—although there clearly was distinct inactivity when activity was called for.

This brings us to the second necessary element for a successful coup: the cooperation of the Praetorian Guard. A coup d'etat needs the support neither of a large number of government officials nor of a broad base of the population. The managers of the coup may well represent the views of only a tiny minority of the populace, but if they have key elements of the Praetorian Guard on their side, the majority becomes irrelevant.

In the United States, the modern counterparts to the Praetorian Guard are the secret police of the intelligence community, beginning with the smallish, close-at-hand Secret Service and extending on through the F.B.I., the intelligence divisions of various federal departments, the Defense Intelligence Agency, and the Central Intelligence Agency. Without key elements of this modern-day Praetorian Guard, a coup d'etat in the United States would be impossible. With them, however, a coup can be unstoppable.

The Praetorian Guard is vital to a successful coup because it has the capability of allowing the defensive protection of the leader to vanish at a crucial moment. The removal of the Emperor Caligula in seconds, leaving as the new emperor the stuttering Claudius, was almost casual following the quiet withdrawal of the protection of the guard. And almost equally casual was the removal of President Kennedy in less than six seconds, leaving Lyndon Johnson as the new President.

A telexed warning of an attempt to assassinate the President in Dallas on November 22 or 23 had apparently been sent to every F.B.I. special agent in charge across the country and had been quietly ignored. (See Chapter 17.) The protective bubble for the President's limousine had been left off by the Secret Service. The windows and roofs of buildings along the parade route had not been secured. (See Chapter 2.) And the parade route had been changed at the last minute so that the motorcade would have to make a sharp turn, thus slowing it to less than ten miles per hour. (See Chapter 7.) All of this added up, essentially, to the withdrawal of the President's protection by the modern-day Praetorian Guard, leaving him vulnerable to the rifle fire coming at him from the grassy knoll in front of him and from at least two locations in buildings behind him.

Precisely how many shots were fired, from precisely where, and by whom are questions that remain unanswered. But one thing I am quite sure of is that Lee Harvey Oswald did not fire at anyone on November 22, 1963. His negative nitrate test, his abysmal marksmanship record in the Marines, his generally unaggressive personality, the poor quality of the Mannlicher-Carcano rifle he allegedly bought through the mail and used, and the lack of any evidence of his involvement in the Tippit murder all confirm that he killed no one, that he was merely, as he claimed, "a patsy."

The President's blood hardly had cooled before the well-organized cover-up began. The hijacking of his body in an ambulance to Air Force One, over the vociferous objection of Texas officials at Parkland Hospital, allowed the body's quick removal before the required local autopsy could reveal that he had been hit from both front and back. Lyndon Johnson was promptly sworn in as the new President to head off the alarming possibility of a national security emergency. Then the plane made its getaway from Love Field and headed for the military autopsy waiting at the U.S. Naval hospital in Bethesda, Maryland. There the Hippocratic oath and any serious search for truth would suddenly be swept aside in the face of the first rule of the military—to obey orders without question. (See Chapter 18.)

Once Air Force One took off and Kennedy's body was airborne, it finally could be announced officially that the President had been shot only from behind. It could be announced that a lone assassin, a disoriented young Marxist drifter with no motive and no supporters, had done it all and that the Dallas police already had him under arrest in the office of Captain Will Fritz, the chief of homicide. The feared emergency was over. The United States government was in good hands.

The coup d'etat had accomplished its objective with clock-work precision. The life had been ripped from the chief executive of the United States government, and major changes in American foreign policy would be arriving not in months or weeks but in the next several days.

Meanwhile, the cover-up was progressing. The Secret Service sent Governor John Connally's clothing, along with all the evidence it contained, to be laundered and then proceeded to scrub down the presidential limousine, again washing away crucial traces of blood, bone, and bullets. (See Chapter 17.) Later its agents would "investigate" Lee Oswald's office in Guy Banister's operation and fail to find anything remotely suspicious. (See Chapter 3.)

The F.B.I. hushed up the fact that it had been informed of a plot to kill the President five days before the actual assassination and began bullying witnesses like Fenella Farrington (see Chapter 5) and trying to silence others like Richard Randolph Carr (see Chapter 18). It went so far as to alter the statements of witness Julia Ann Mercer, who identified Jack Ruby as the man she had seen dropping off a rifleman on the grassy knoll an hour before the assassination. (See Chapter 17.)

The Dallas homicide unit managed to lose two rifles found in the Texas School Book Depository, one of them a highly accurate 7.65 Mauser (see Chapter 7); it never bothered to check out Deputy Sheriff Roger Craig's report that he had seen a Nash Rambler station wagon carrying four men, including Oswald, leave from in front of the Depository and even denied hearing of such a thing (see Chapter 16); it concealed for ten months Oswald's negative nitrate test (see Chapter 7); it concealed, altered, and fabricated crucial ballistics evidence in the Tippit murder (see Chapter 15); and most important, it allowed Jack Ruby to kill Oswald in the basement of police headquarters surrounded by dozens of officers. Ruby had at least helped set up the assassination and because of this may have been put in a position by the assassination's engineers where he had no alternative but to eliminate Oswald. Ruby's act of violence, silencing the one man who might have identified the assassination's sponsors, was the capstone of the cover-up.

With the cover-up such a stunning success, the stage was now set for the ratification of the assassination. The surviving elements of the new government—from Lyndon Johnson, J. Edgar Hoover, and Earl Warren on down—were quick to see the advantages of supporting the scenario that no coup d'etat had occurred and that our democracy was safely intact, that a lone malcontent had murdered the President in a meaningless, random act of violence. And they were quick to understand the message of those who had engineered the assassination—that there was a forceful consensus that wanted the Cold War resumed at its pre-Kennedy intensity. There is no evidence that Johnson, Hoover, Warren, or Allen Dulles had any prior knowledge of or involvement in the assassination, but I would not hesitate to classify all of these men as accessories after the fact.

As soon as the non-participating elements in the intelligence community saw that a coup d'etat had occurred, they moved quickly to support the official story. Motivated in some instances by self-preservation and in others by a belief that Kennedy had brought the assassination on himself by compromising too often with the Soviets, the remainder of the government—from high elected officials to heads of departments and agencies—lined up to add their solemn voices to the growing chorus chanting the great lie.

This is the way of all successful coups d'etat. In the early 17th century, Sir John Harington, the English poet, described it in a few lines:

> Treason doth never prosper: What's the reason?
> For if it prosper, none dare call it treason.

The beginning of the formal ratification process came when Congress allowed President Johnson, the heir to power, to appoint the Warren Commission, including ex-C.I.A. Director Dulles, to investigate the murder. The Commission's report, carrying the prestige and credibility of its highly respected chair, put the official government stamp of approval on the lone assassin fairy tale. For the government, reluctant to face the pre-assassination involvement of the C.I.A. and the participation of its other intelligence agencies in the cover-up, such a ratification must have seemed the easy way out. For many years afterwards, federal officials did their best to prop up this crumbling edifice as critics tore it apart, leaving almost no one still believing in the lone assassin scenario.

With the murder plainly unsolved, a succession of Presidents and attorneys general, each with the resources of the F.B.I. and the entire federal government at their command, made no effort to get to the truth.

On the contrary, when I attempted a real investigation of the assassination, federal officials sought to suppress the truth. I received no cooperation when I sought to subpoena key witnesses like Allen Dulles. I found crucial federal records destroyed, altered, classified as secret, or sealed by the federal government for 75 years. I found myself denounced by the President, the attorney general, and the Chief Justice. I found my investigation infiltrated and subverted by federal agents. And ultimately I found myself on trial in a trumped-up federal case. That is what happens to you when you do not go along with the new government's ratification of the coup.

The government's cover-up and ratification of the assassination have been aided by a flood of disinformation appearing in the major media. Dissemination of disinformation is the last element necessary for a successful coup d'etat, and it also happens to be one of the specialties of the C.I.A. For many years the Agency secretly had on its payroll journalists ostensibly working for the major media but in fact disseminating propaganda for consumption by the American people. It has also subsidized the publication of more than 1,000 books. As Richard Barnet, the co-director of the Institute for Policy Studies, put it:

> The stock in trade of the intelligence underworld is deceit. Its purpose is to create contrived realities, to make things appear other than they are for the purpose of manipulation and subver-

sion. More than two hundred agents . . . pose as businessmen abroad. The C.I.A. has admitted that it has had more than thirty journalists on its payroll since World War II. "Proprietary" corporations—Air America and other agency fronts, fake foundations, student organizations, church organizations, and so forth—are all part of the false-bottom world that has ended up confusing the American people as much as it has confounded foreign governments.

For 25 years the American people have been bombarded by propaganda pointing insistently to a variety of irrelevant "false sponsors" as the supposed instigators of the Kennedy assassination. (False sponsor is a term used in covert intelligence actions which describes the individual or organization to be publicly blamed after the action, thus diverting attention away from the intelligence community.) Americans have been so thoroughly brainwashed by such disinformation, paid for by their own taxes, that many of them today are only able to sigh mournfully to one another that they "probably never will know the truth."

Meanwhile, an unending stream of news service releases, newspaper articles, television "documentaries," magazine features, and books repetitively reinforce this bewilderment and continue to point the public's attention in the wrong direction. The incredible accumulation of false sponsors laid upon the American people includes Lee Harvey Oswald, the K.G.B., Howard Hughes, Texas oil barons, organized crime, and Fidel Castro.

The original false sponsor was the scapegoat himself, Lee Harvey Oswald. Nominated for the role by the intelligence community, he was formally endorsed by the Warren Commission and others at the highest levels of the United States government. However, over time it became increasingly apparent that the lone assassin fairy tale had fallen apart, and most of its supporters simply fell silent.

Consequently, I was surprised to find recently that *Time* magazine, long an ardent supporter of the lone assassin explanation, continues to be loyal to the original false sponsor, Lee Oswald. One must acknowledge a certain magnificence in the total dedication here, the sustained lack of thought through 25 years. In its August 1, 1988, review of the novel *Libra* by Don DeLillo, which although fictional is an interesting and provocative treatment of both Kennedy's assassination and his alleged assassin, *Time* finds fault with the book's argument that "the plot to kill the President was even wider and more sinister than previously imagined." There is a simpler possibility, the magazine authoritatively concludes: "A frustrated, angry man looked out a window, watched the President ride by, and shot him dead."

When I read that brief, neat disposition of one of history's most complicated and significant events, I realized that there is not much one can say to a publication which obviously has all the answers.

One of the most intriguing false sponsors is Fidel Castro. Frequently over the years—particularly when I was making speeches at universities—I would encounter people who enthusiastically agreed with me that it was not possible for Oswald to have killed Kennedy unaided. However, they then would add that they believed that Fidel Castro had engineered the assassination. I would answer by examining the logic of this proposition.

First I would point out that at a critical time during the C.I.A.'s attempted invasion of Cuba in 1961, the acting chief of the Agency beseeched the President to provide jet fighter plane support from nearby U.S. Navy aircraft carriers. Kennedy refused, and the invasion failed catastrophically. Next I would explain that during the Cuban missile crisis in 1962, Kennedy refused to bomb or invade Cuba, as a number of his military and intelligence advisers urged him to do. Finally, I would remind the audience that one of the factors helping to resolve the missile crisis was Kennedy's personal assurance to the Soviet Union that the U.S. would make no further attempts to invade Cuba, a decision which deeply disturbed the operational elements of the C.I.A., which had been training anti-Castro Cubans at guerrilla camps in Florida and Louisiana for precisely that objective. At this point it usually was sufficient for me to ask but one question: "Do you truly believe that Fidel Castro would have liked to see Kennedy removed as President, that he would have preferred to have Lyndon Johnson in power?"

One could pose many more questions to those who advocate the idea of Castro as an engineer of Kennedy's murder. Could Cuban commmunists really have established the necessary operational base and penetration of key police elements in Dallas, one of the most conservative cities in the United States? Would these communists have received the extensive cooperation from Dallas officials, the F.B.I., and the C.I.A. that the actual assassins evidently received? And are we really to believe that Fidel Castro had Lee Oswald hand out his inflammatory leaflets in New Orleans and later ordered the same fellow to go to Dallas and kill President Kennedy? Are we to suppose that Castro would have had only one man working for him? Fortunately, perhaps because of the very insanity of such a proposition, the false sponsorship of Castro has faded.

I was aware, of course, of the brief vogue of the "Southwest oil billionaires" as backers of the assassination. However, this was never in vogue with me, not even briefly, because it simply did not fit my initial—and unchanging—belief that the critical connections were to the intelligence community. True, George de Mohrenschildt was in the oil business and was a member of the Petroleum Club in Dallas. But in my talks with de Mohrenschildt it became clear to me that he was used—not by the Southwest oil billionaires but by the intelligence community. His duties were limited to escort supervision of Oswald, at the conclusion of which he was dispatched to his "government-oriented" business in Haiti while the final arrangements were made establishing Oswald as the scapegoat for the assassination. (See Chapter 4.)

The visit of "Jim Braden" (Eugene Hale Brading) to the offices of the Hunt family, of Texas petroleum fame, a few days before the assassination appears to have been a one-shot deception gambit. (See Chapter 16.) The same kind of one-time visit to the Hunt offices was made, also just before the assassination, by Jack Ruby—who was no more in the oil business than "Braden" was. The intention of these decoy moves was to fuel speculation that the Texas oil business might have sponsored the assassination.

Such brief decoy visits reminded me of the "mis-direction" move with which every major professional football team commences a number of its running plays. Upon receiving the ball, the runner takes a half step to his left and, while the opposing defense is off and running in the wrong direction, then heads off to his right at full speed. The professional football players, however, are only amateurs when it comes to mis-direction. The real pros work in the operations directorate of the Central Intelligence Agency.

Of course, the primary and most lasting false sponsor has been organized crime, the Mafia, the mob. Many of the books ostensibly criticizing the government's official explanation of the assassination seem designed simply to leave readers with the firm conviction that the mob murdered John Kennedy. As with any powerful myth, there are some elements of truth to it. The C.I.A. has worked with the Mafia over the years, and there is certainly evidence that many mob figures hated President Kennedy—and his brother, Attorney General Robert Kennedy. And mob-related individuals do figure in the scenario.

For some elements of organized crime, pre-Castro Cuba had been rich pickings with its wide-open gambling for American tourists. Later, in furtherance of its private war against Castro, the C.I.A. made arrangements with some of these mobsters—most notably Santos Trafficante and John Rosselli—to help it accomplish the assassination of Fidel Castro. Other mob-oriented individuals, like Jack Ruby, were still adept at collecting arms and ammunition for anti-Castro adventures. It was hardly surprising then, after President Kennedy's murder, that the Agency continued to use its helpful new friend, the mob, for the fragrance its very name provided as a false sponsor. The unarguable criminality of its varied enterprises added greatly to the continued confusion being manufactured by the Agency's disinformation machinery and caused many eyes to turn away from the Company as a possible sponsor. For these mobsters, in turn, the Agency had become a new and generous godfather.

The Agency used its new friends not only for murder and gunrunning, but for other purposes as well. Imagine my surprise, for example, upon thumbing through a volume of the House Select Committee on Assassinations when I read a report provided by the C.I.A. It stated that "Jim Garrison, while still district attorney of New Orleans, had participated in a secret meeting in a Las Vegas hotel with John Rosselli." Of course, this was absolutely false, but I considered it no small honor to have the disinformation machinery of the government's main clandestine operation smear me with its most powerful potion— association with the mob.*

Far more significant than this minor slander has been the Agency's success in persuading many otherwise thoughtful Americans to believe that organized crime itself somehow accomplished the sophisticated social engineering that resulted in the elimination of President Kennedy. I suggest that we examine this contention with a little old-fashioned reasoning.

It will be recalled that the original route scheduled for the motorcade did not go right past the Texas School Book Depository, where Oswald had been working since October when Ruth Paine obtained a job interview for him there. (See Chapter 5.) In fact, as late as the morning of the assassination the motorcade route was still diagramed on the front page of the *Dallas Morning News* as continuing on Main Street to the center of Dealey Plaza. (See Chapter 7.) Is it really believable that the mob could have changed the route of the motorcade on the morning of the assassination?

Never mind the succession of books which purportedly reveal organized crime as the engineer of Kennedy's murder. (See Afterword.) If it can simply be shown how the mob changed the route of the motorcade on the morning of the assassination—just that one single, simple, item—I could accept at least the possibility that the mob killed President Kennedy. Without that explanation, I must be suspicious of the people who say they believe the Mafia carried out the assassination.

It appears to me that someone with considerable force and influence wanted to have Lee Oswald close to the motorcade. Whoever this was

---

* The periodic allegations that I am on friendly terms with organized crime figures are amusing, in light of my record. As district attorney of New Orleans I ended the lottery racket for the first time in a century, I cleaned up the Bourbon Street clip joints for the first time in anyone's memory, and I closed down the last houses of prostitution in the city. In a town where no district attorney had ever before been reelected, the citizens of New Orleans kept me in office for 12 years, three full terms. In 1987, after ten years on the appellate bench, I was reelected to another ten years without opposition. The citizens of New Orleans obviously are as amused by the absurdity of these mob charges as I am.

It has been my policy not to respond to each of the many canards which have been part of the campaign to discredit my investigation, nor to waste time trying to prove negatives. For what it is worth, however, I do not even know Carlos Marcello, the man with whom I am most frequently linked by my detractors. Nor, for that matter, did I ever in my years as district attorney come upon any evidence that he was the Mafia kingpin the Justice Department says he is.

decided, in effect, "If we can't put Lee Oswald along the parade route, then we'll put the parade route next to Oswald." Who could more likely accomplish that change—the capos who work for Anthony (Fat Tony) Salerno, or clandestine operations elements of the intelligence community? The employees of Tony (Big Tuna) Accardo, or elements of the Praetorian Guard which, having the duty to protect the President, also have the power to decide where, when, and how he travels?

Placing Lee Oswald somewhere along the parade route would have been of value only to whoever had sheepdipped him to appear to be a communist and supporter of Fidel Castro. Was it organized crime that sheepdipped Oswald, or was it Guy Banister, veteran of the O.N.I., the F.B.I., and the C.I.A.? Was Oswald working out of some Mafia restaurant, or was he working out of Guy Banister's offices along with David Ferrie, a small army of anti-Castro Cuban guerrillas, and a host of intelligence community operatives?

Could organized crime have insured that the version of the front page of the *Dallas Morning News* offered to the Warren Commission as evidence no longer showed the originally scheduled route of the motorcade? (See Chapter 7.) Could the mob have obtained Governor Connally's clothes, sending them out to be drycleaned after the arrival of the President's limousine at Parkland Hospital, thus removing all evidentiary marks? Could the Mafia have whisked Kennedy's body past the Texas authorities, who wanted it kept for the local autopsy as Texas law required, and got it aboard Air Force One? Could the Mafia have placed in charge of the President's autopsy an Army general who was not a physician? Could the Mafia, in the course of the autopsy, have ordered the pathologists not to probe the neck wound lest a bullet from the front be found lodged in the spine? Could the Mafia, afterwards, have ordered the chief pathologist, Commander Humes, to burn his original autopsy notes? Could the Mafia have arranged for President Kennedy's brain to disappear from the National Archives?

Upon close examination, then, the false sponsors all fall of their own weight. What remains as the only likely sponsor with both the motive and the capability of murdering the President is the covert action arm of the Central Intelligence Agency.

Invisible as it is dangerous, the covert operations apparatus of the C.I.A. has become far and away the most powerful element in the intelligence community. It is the closest to the top levels of the government and, at least since the 1950s, has assumed a steadily increasing role in the determination of foreign policy.

As distinguished from intelligence collection, covert operations include the development and distribution of propaganda (the euphemism is disinformation), the raising of secret armies, the staging of coups d'etat, and even murder—everywhere and anywhere, internationally and domestically, but always hidden. Such concealed operations represent more than two-thirds of the C.I.A.'s total activity, as a result of which the covert operations directorate constitutes, as former C.I.A. officer Philip Agee once put it, "a secret political police . . . the Gestapo and S.S. of our time."

It is improbable that an elaborate plan to assassinate the President received official approval from John McCone, the C.I.A. director in 1963, or Richard Helms, deputy director for plans (covert operations). But it may well have been conceived at lower echelons of the Agency and been carried out in collaboration with extra-governmental individuals or organizations* precisely to avoid leaving any paper trail to top C.I.A. officials, who may have conveniently looked the other way. We have recently seen such a quasi-governmental creature, composed of a mixture of government officials and private citizens, in the Iran/*contra* affair which Congress investigated in 1987. That particular mixture of official power and civilian assistance, also seen in the Watergate affair, was described by one of the high-ranking officers participating in it as the "Enterprise."

I believe that the Iran/*contra* enterprise may well be the historical descendant of a considerably more powerful enterprise that killed President Kennedy. Both were brainchildren of the C.I.A. covert action directorate; both utilized a combination of Agency veterans and mysterious civilians to carry out their sinister, illegal operations; both were steeped in far rightwing ideology; and both were totally unaccountable. The continuity here is frightening indeed. To me, it

---

* The most obvious of these were the anti-Castro adventurers, both Cuban and American, whom the Agency had trained at its guerrilla camp north of Lake Pontchartrain, and mob-connected individuals like Jack Ruby.

appears that the dream of the late C.I.A. director William Casey of an ongoing "off-the-shelf" operation to handle extremely delicate and controversial covert actions as an untraceable instrument of the Agency has been a living reality for a quarter century, going back at least to the assassination of President Kennedy.

Unlike the false sponsors, the C.I.A. clearly had the capability to accomplish the assassination. In 1975 a Senate committee headed by Frank Church found that the Agency had planned a number of assassination operations, using everything from poison to machine guns and sometimes mob hit men. The committee was not mandated to inquire into domestic assassinations, but it did find that the Agency had repeatedly conspired to remove foreign leaders who were implementing policies it did not like.

In 1953, with Allen Dulles directing the operation by radio out of Geneva, Switzerland, the Agency launched a well-organized coup against the government of Iran. As a result, Premier Mohammed Mossadegh was overthrown, the imperial throne was restored, and the Shah was reinstalled on it.

In 1954 in Guatemala, Jacobo Arbenz, although not a communist, was governing with distinctly liberal policies. When some military leaders began a plot against the democratically elected leader, the Agency moved in to support them with armed fighter planes. Arbenz ended up fleeing the country.

In 1960, Patrice Lumumba, a strong national leader and the first premier of the Congo (Zaire today), became an Agency target. Like Mossadegh of Iran and Arbenz of Guatemala, Lumumba was not a communist. Nevertheless, C.I.A. Director Dulles authorized the expenditure of up to $100,000 to "remove" Lumumba. Shortly thereafter, the Agency's deputy director for plans, Richard Bissell, asked C.I.A. scientist Joseph Scheider to make preparations to assassinate an unnamed "African leader." Scheider made a list of toxic biological materials which would cause fatal diseases indigenous to Africa. In his testimony before the Church Committee, Scheider admitted delivering a lethal bouquet to the Agency's station chief in the Congo and instructing him that he was to assassinate Lumumba.

However, the poison never had to be used. In January 1961, Lumumba—now temporarily out of office and a political prisoner—

was placed on a plane allegedly bound for Bakwanga in Katanga Province. In mid-flight it was redirected to Elizabethville in the same province, an area where the inhabitants were known to be hostile to Lumumba. Some weeks afterwards it was reported that Patrice Lumumba had escaped but then had been murdered by hostile villagers. The C.I.A.'s direct involvement in the murder of Lumumba is unclear, but in 1978 former C.I.A. Africa specialist John Stockwell said a high Agency official had described to him how he drove around with Lumumba's body in his car, "trying to decide what to do with it."

The Church Committee found that, in addition to plotting the murder of Patrice Lumumba, the C.I.A. on a number of occasions plotted the murder of Fidel Castro, using such novel devices as poisoned diving suits and toxic cigars. Furthermore, the committee found that the Agency had actively encouraged the assassinations of other foreign leaders, including Rafael Trujillo of the Dominican Republic in 1961, President Ngo Dinh Diem of South Vietnam in 1963, and General René Schneider of Chile in 1970. The committee's sobering conclusion was that the C.I.A. repeatedly had planned or helped plan the assassination of a number of national leaders.*

This was confirmed by former Agency officials. According to one of them, William Harvey, the C.I.A.'s program of removing foreign leaders included the "capability to perform assassination." Richard Bissell, former deputy director for plans, also acknowledged that assassination was included in the "wide spectrum of actions" available to eliminate chiefs of state who were a problem. It seems fair to state, then, that the C.I.A., from long experience, had the necessary capability to assassinate President Kennedy.

Equally important, it had the motivation. Contrary to what most Americans assume, the C.I.A. was not created solely to gather intelligence.† From its beginnings in 1947 the primary reason for its existence, as exemplified by the dominant role of its operations directorate, was the defeat of what it perceived as a monolithic commu-

---

* This did not include the systematic assassination of tens of thousands of village leaders and suspected Viet Cong carried out in Vietnam under the C.I.A.'s Operation Phoenix.

† Not even primarily, according to Agency critics such as Philip Agee, Ralph McGehee, John Stockwell, and others.

nism. The hard-line Cold War obsession of the C.I.A. during the Truman and Eisenhower administrations—that the Soviet Union was committed to the destruction of the United States and the conquest of the entire world—was shared by its brother agency, the F.B.I., under J. Edgar Hoover and by many others in the government.

President Kennedy had campaigned and taken office on a note which suggested that his administration would continue the policy of no compromise with the Soviets. However, it gradually became clear that his philosophy did not truly lend itself to the long-established hard line. From his refusal to let General Cabell have the requested jet fighter support for the Agency's faltering Bay of Pigs invasion, to his rejection of the recommendations to bomb and invade Cuba during the missile crisis, to his insistence over the initial opposition of his military advisers that the U.S. sign the nuclear test ban treaty in Moscow, to his decisions in 1963 to withdraw from Vietnam and consider restoration of diplomatic relations with Cuba, Kennedy was following a different drum beat.*

To the hard-line, war-oriented elements of the American power structure, for whom the C.I.A. operations directorate had been created and for whom it functioned, this was nothing less than "selling out to the communists."

In retrospect, the reason for the assassination is hardly a mystery. It is now abundantly clear from the course that U.S. foreign policy took immediately following November 22, 1963, why the C.I.A.'s covert operations element wanted John Kennedy out of the Oval Office and Lyndon Johnson in it.

The new President elevated by rifle fire to control of our foreign policy had been one of the most enthusiastic American cold warriors— although as vice-president he had become of necessity a closet cold warrior. Lyndon Johnson has been described by the writer Fred Cook, a highly regarded observer of the Washington scene, as "a man with

---

* Actually, Kennedy seems to have had very little real support in Washington for the policy of military restraint to which he had come by 1963. His own secretary of defense, Robert McNamara, acknowledged in 1984 that as late as 1965 he was convinced that the United States would win in Vietnam. Dean Rusk, President Kennedy's secretary of state, made a similar acknowledgment. One has to wonder just who in the U.S. government in 1963 did support Kennedy's lonely decision against our continued military involvement in Southeast Asia.

limited knowledge of foreign affairs" who by experience and tempera-
ment was "oriented to think in military terms."

Johnson had originally risen to power on the crest of the fulminating
anti-communist crusade which marked American politics after World
War II. Shortly after the end of that war, he declaimed that atomic
power had become "ours to use, either to Christianize the world or
pulverize it"—a Christian benediction if ever there was one. Johnson's
demonstrated enthusiasm for American military intervention abroad,
which earned him the sobriquet "the senator from the Pentagon,"
contrasted starkly with President Kennedy's intention of total withdrawal from Vietnam.

It was no surprise, then, that following President Kennedy's death
and Lyndon Johnson's swearing in as President, some dramatic changes
in American foreign and military policy took place. Kennedy's order to
have the first thousand Americans returned home from Vietnam by
December was promptly rescinded.

Of even greater consequence, on the Sunday afternoon following the
assassination, after solemnly making an appearance at the eulogy for
Kennedy at the Capitol Rotunda, Johnson met with Henry Cabot
Lodge, the U.S. ambassador to South Vietnam, in the Executive Office
Building. He informed Lodge that he was not going to lose Vietnam,
that he was not going to see Southeast Asia go the way of China, that
"Saigon can count on us."

In August of 1964 the Gulf of Tonkin incident occurred—or, at
least, so the American public was told. The entire affair carried the
musky fragrance of the intelligence community. "While on routine
patrol in international waters," it was announced from Washington,
"the U.S. destroyer Maddox underwent an unprovoked attack." An
invisible enemy vessel, it seemed, had fired an invisible torpedo which
fortunately missed the Maddox cruising off the coast of North Vietnam. Shortly afterwards a similar incident took place involving
another U.S. naval vessel. Once again the enemy, deceptive as ever, left
no evidence of the attack.

Johnson soundly denounced this "open aggression." He appeared on
national television to inform the American citizenry that "renewed
hostile actions against United States ships on the high seas in the Gulf
of Tonkin have today required me to order the military forces of the

United States to take action in reply." Congressional leaders of both parties, he said, had assured him of passage of a resolution making it clear "that our government is united in its determination to take all necessary measures in support of freedom and in defense of peace in Southeast Asia."

The Gulf of Tonkin resolution, passed on August 7, 1964, with only two Senators dissenting, gave Johnson the power to take whatever military action he felt necessary in Southeast Asia. This declaration of war against North Vietnam, however unofficial, had been accomplished just over a year after John Kennedy's American University speech in which he had eloquently expressed his hope for peace.

Promptly following the congressional resolution, American planes began their first bombardment of North Vietnam. The U.S. Pacific Command was ordered to prepare for combat. In 1965, more than 200,000 American troops poured into South Vietnam. In 1966 and 1967, upwards of 300,000 more followed. By the time the U.S. signed the Paris Agreement in January 1973, more than 55,000 Americans and millions of Vietnamese were dead.

Thus was President Kennedy's foreign policy reversed "without conforming to the formal requirements for changing office holders, as prescribed by the laws or constitution"—the very definition of a coup d'etat. This was the major consequence of the assassination of John Kennedy, and the real reason for it.

Is all this plausible? It might not have seemed so 25 years ago. However, now that we know some of the true history of the C.I.A. and its covert operations, the answer is a distinct yes. Assassination is precisely what the Agency knows how to do and what it has done all over the world for policy ends.

With the passage of time, we can see the enduring results of President Kennedy's assassination. The nation is still recovering from its tragic nine-year adventure in Vietnam. The C.I.A. continues to run our foreign policy without any real control by either Congress or the President—only now the Agency stands far back in the shadows, appearing to distance itself from the enterprise at hand, using private citizens and intermediaries to guarantee its insulation. The Justice

Department, knowing all that we know now, still refuses to conduct an honest investigation into the most important political assassination of our time. Twenty-five years after President Kennedy's murder, it may be too late.

However, it is not too late for us to learn the lessons of history, to understand where we are now and who runs this country. If my book can help illuminate this for a younger generation who never knew John Kennedy, then it will have served its purpose.

Afterword

Is the Mafia Theory a Valid Alternative?

By Carl Oglesby*

FOR CLOSE TO TWO DECADES NOW, the vast majority of American people have believed, contrary to the Warren Commission, that President Kennedy was killed by a conspiracy.

Within the broad popular rejection of the lone-gunman theory of the crime, however, there is enormous difference of opinion as to what the nature of this conspiracy might be.

Jim Garrison has laid out in *On the Trail of the Assassins* the theory that I believe most of the serious students of this mystery will recognize and accept as the most complete, most natural, and most straightforward way to read the totality of the current evidence. Speaking for myself as a writer and activist on the J.F.K. case for many years, I see compelling documentary support for Garrison's leading ideas, which I would paraphrase as follows:

> (a) Rabidly anticommunist elements of the C.I.A.'s operations division, often moving through extra-governmental chan-

* Carl Oglesby is a founder/director of the Assassination Information Bureau, widely credited with helping to build the popular demand in the 1970s for a congressional investigation of the J.F.K. murder. He is the author of several books, including *The Yankee and Cowboy War* (1976), an attempt to explain the underlying political context of the J.F.K. conspiracy and the toppling of Nixon at Watergate ten years later.

nels, were deeply involved at the top of the assassination planning and management process and appear to have been the makers of the decision to kill the President.

(b) The conspiracy was politically motivated. Its purpose was to stop J.F.K.'s movement toward détente in the Cold War, and it succeeded in doing that. It must therefore be regarded as a palace coup d'etat.

(c) Oswald was an innocent man craftily set up to take the blame. As he put it, "I'm a patsy."

For all its structural logic and its virtually audible resonance with contemporary American experience, Garrison's theory of the crime is perhaps too challenging, too frightening, and too deeply contradictory of very basic American myths (*e.g.,* that we are a law-abiding republic) to stand a chance of official recognition or even civil consideration by the intelligentsia and the media.

Garrison's line of reasoning raises basic questions about the legitimacy of the American state. Never mind that Garrison is a staunch patriot with Grant Wood roots and a long, happy career in the U.S. Army and J. Edgar Hoover's F.B.I. before joining the district attorney's office in New Orleans; his vision of this crime is, I believe, nonetheless the most radical and cogent statement we can find of the predicament of American constitutionalism. One cannot follow Garrison's reasoning in serenity. Though Garrison is the furthest thing from a Marxist, an American cannot face his analysis without risking a crisis of political faith. He threatens to make Hamlets of all who listen to him—children of a slain father-leader whose killers, for all we know, still in secret possess the throne. He confronts us with the secret murder at the heart of the contemporary American dilemma. His whole terrifying narrative forces down upon us the appalling questions: Of what is our Constitution made? What is our vaunted citizenship worth? What is the future of democracy in a country where a President can be assassinated under conspicuously suspicious circumstances while the machinery of legal action scarcely trembles?

That is a brutal subtext. Garrison's reconstruction of the murder of the President tells us, in so many words, that what we call our Constitution has become, to some of us, secretly and shamefully, a laughing-stock. Key components of government, critical to the integrity of policy intelligence systems, appear to have been occupied and manipulated by a secret force that we can barely identify and hardly conceive of opposing.

Maybe Garrison's political and historical realism will prove too intensely challenging for general consumption. We Americans like to regard ourselves as pragmatic about politics, but this seems to mean that we tend to believe what makes us happy and not to believe what confuses and depresses us. Garrison's analysis of the J.F.K. murder challenges us to be unhappy about our political environment and to adopt a perspective that could easily put us at odds with it. This is not the way to be popular.

So Garrison's theory of the crime, despite being the most reasonable, the most realistic, and the most securely grounded in the totality of the evidence, is therefore not the official theory. The official theory used to be the Warren Commission's idea that Oswald was like a heart attack, something out of the blue, without significance beyond himself. But the Warren Commission's theory fell away bit by bit to the digging of patient volunteer researchers, and in 1976 the House of Representatives voted to create the Select Committee on Assassinations in order to reinvestigate the case. This was in effect a vote of no-confidence in the Warren Commission.

The House Assassinations Committee then proceeded to spend more than a year and $3 million in reinvestigating the J.F.K. case and reconstructing the official theory.

This new official theory—semi-official, perhaps we should say, since the F.B.I. will still have none of it—was framed and adopted by the House Select Committee on Assassinations in 1979 in its final report and then amplified and extended in 1981 in *The Plot to Kill the President,* by the committee's chief counsel, G. Robert Blakey, and its senior staff writer, Richard Billings (himself an important minor character in Garrison's narrative; see Chapters 8 and 13).

For comparison with Garrison's theory, the leading ideas of Blakey's theory can be summarized as follows:

(a) Oswald alone did shoot and kill J.F.K., as the Warren Commission deduced.

(b) An unknown confederate of Oswald's, however, also shot at the President, firing from the celebrated "grassy knoll." This shot missed.

(c) Apart from the question of the number of assailants in the attack, Oswald acted as the tool of a much larger conspiracy.

(d) The conspiracy behind Oswald was rooted in organized crime and was specifically provoked by J.F.K.'s anti-crime program. Singly or in some combination, prime suspects are Carlos Marcello and Santos Trafficante, godfathers respectively of the New Orleans and Tampa Mafias, and Teamster racketeer James Hoffa. Each one had the motive, means, and opportunity to kill J.F.K.

Blakey is an accomplished academic and a Washington lawyer of considerable experience and connection. He is close to the Kennedys. He was on Robert Kennedy's organized-crime strike force. He wrote the latest revision of the federal criminal code. He wrote the R.I.C.O. statute, which makes it possible for citizens to bring conspiracy charges against racketeers. He taught at Cornell Law School before coming to the committee; now he teaches at Notre Dame Law School. He is not conventionally pompous and yet presents himself as an embodiment of scholarly values and tends to judge condescendingly those who do not share his views.

In his book, Blakey cannot simply ignore Garrison, since Garrison's investigation turned up key individuals (Ferrie and Banister) whom Blakey finds crucial to his own theory. Instead, Blakey viciously attacks the former New Orleans district attorney.

Garrison, Blakey writes, was motivated by "a thirst for publicity. National headlines were what he was after when he agreed to brief representatives of *Life* and CBS." Yet Blakey knows that "national headlines" were in the nature of the subject, that the strong involvement of the media and the public were required in order to move the stone of the federal cover-up, and that in any case it was *Life* and the rest that came to Garrison first, not the other way around. Blakey's co-author, Billings, was in fact the *Life* editor dispatched by upper management in 1967 to sound Garrison out on his willingness to collaborate against the conspiracy.

But Blakey cannot stand to credit Garrison's work even when he must admit its importance to his own. Garrison "stigmatized . . . by his conduct" whatever "bona fide evidence" existed in his "array of charges," Blakey writes, continuing:

> It would require the surprising disclosure of the findings of a Senate committee on intelligence in 1976 to prevent Garrison's probe from effectively ending any hope that the federal government would take a second look at the work of the Warren Commission. In short, Garrison's case was a fraud.

It is preposterous to blame Garrison, of all people, for the federal government's refusal to take this case by the horns. Blakey tries to pretend that there was something about Garrison's "conduct" that "stigmatized the evidence." It had nothing to do with Garrison's "conduct" as a district attorney, however, when federal officials in Washington, D.C., refused to serve his subpoenas. It was not because Garrison's charges were unfounded that the governor of Ohio refused to extradite an extremely critical witness (Gordon Novel) to Louisiana. It was because the government does not want the people to know the truth about the J.F.K. assassination.

Moreover, it was not the Church committee as such or any of its "surprising disclosures" that persuaded the House to reopen the J.F.K. case; it was the growing insistence of popular concern and, in the aftermath of Watergate, the murders of John Rosselli and Sam Giancana while they were sworn witnesses under federal protection.

Blakey's basic accusation against Garrison—insinuation is the better word, since Blakey is too much the lawyer to slander Garrison outright—is that Garrison approached the J.F.K. case as the stooge of Carlos Marcello. Here is how Blakey and Billings phrase it in their book:

> As for the organized-crime aspect of Oswald's associations in New Orleans, where it had been overlooked by the F.B.I. and the Warren Commission, it had been studiously avoided by the District Attorney for reasons we believed had become apparent.

What were these reasons, "apparent" as Blakey believes they had become? Without ever actually saying it explicitly, Blakey conveys the impression that Garrison must have been secretly under Marcello's control. Blakey even unearths charges of which Garrison was acquitted long ago and writes as though the charges were borne out:

> Garrison was tried but acquitted in 1971 of federal charges of taking payoffs from underworld pinball operators, despite evidence that included incriminating tape recordings of Garrison and the seizure of $1,000 in marked money from Garrison's home.

Blakey sees fit not to explain why these "incriminating tapes" and this "marked money" failed to convince a jury that Garrison was guilty. Blakey chooses not to tell his readers that Garrison's chief accuser in the pinball trial, Pershing Gervais, publicly admitted that he had been pressured and rewarded to perjure himself against Garrison. Why does Blakey pass silently over the abundant indications that Garrison was framed in the pinball case by enemies at the federal level who wanted him out of the district attorney's office?

But what of Blakey's theory that Oswald was the agent and J.F.K. the victim of Marcello?

On first look, there is much to recommend it. The attitude of certain mobsters toward the one administration in American history that actually did try to destroy them is a fascinating and perhaps pivotal aspect of this case (and one which Blakey was hardly the first to see); but Blakey knows very well that his Mafia hypothesis has never been rigorously probed and contested.*

Clearly, the Mafia is present in the drama of John Kennedy's 1,000 days. It appears in J.F.K.'s life before his presidency, is embroiled and entangled with his administration, and survives his attempt to throttle it. The now-familiar instances of this presence are basic:

· The Mafia stole the Illinois vote for the J.F.K. ticket in 1960, thus delivering the White House.
· The Mafia supplied Kennedy with mistresses such as Judith Campbell Exner during the first year of his White House tenure.

---

* The new book by David E. Scheim, *Contract on America,* essentially restates Blakey's theory without adding to the evidence.

· Mafia assassins answered the call of the C.I.A. to try to kill Castro in 1961 and 1962 and became formal agents of the U.S. government.

And yet throughout Kennedy's tenure, paradoxically, the same Mafia was locked with the Justice Department in an unprecedented struggle that for a while seemed to threaten the Mafia's continued existence.

Furthermore, Jack Ruby was certainly a Mafia errand man. He may have been on a Mafia-directed errand when he shot Oswald. If it was really the Mafia that killed Oswald, then that might be because the Mafia wanted to keep the case out of court. What might have motivated such an interest? Why should the Mafia have cared enough about Oswald to liquidate him? Unless the Mafia had something to do with the assassination of Kennedy, why should it have cared about Oswald at all? It is only natural to suppose that the Mafia had something to hide; it is easy to jump to the conclusion that the Mafia must be the principal culprit.

However, a longer historical perspective makes it equally clear that the presence of the Mafia in illicit affairs of state does not necessarily mean that the Mafia stands there alone and unsupported. Besides the aforementioned C.I.A. sponsorship of Mafia hit men against Fidel Castro, the best-established historical examples of positive association between the Mafia and elements of the U.S. government are ones in which the Mafia served as the junior partner:

· The Navy's Operation Underworld of the World War II years in which the U.S. government bought Mafia protection against Nazi sabotage on the East Coast docks in exchange for favors involving Lucky Luciano.
· The Army's alliance with the Mafia in General George Patton's Sicilian campaign in World War II.
· The C.I.A.'s use of Mafia force to destroy communist-dominated unions in Marseilles during the early Cold War.

In none of these cases was the Mafia dominant over the government; in none did the Mafia provide the motivation for the relationship or the leadership within it. The Mafia, for example, did not invite itself into the C.I.A.'s secret war against the Cuban revolution. The Mafia was recruited into that campaign by Richard Bissell and Colonel Sheffield Edwards, top-level C.I.A. operations officers. Similarly, if the Mafia was present in the Dealey Plaza assassination, it remains to be seen whether it was present as a principal or as an agent, whether as a prime mover or as a secondary technical service responsible to a larger combination secretly licensed by disaffected elements of the national intelligence services.

The Mafia theory of the J.F.K. assassination is most helpful and interesting when viewed as a step in the evolution of the official perception of the case. It is an improvement over the lone-assassin theory, but its basis in fact still seems tenuous.

For example, if Marcello knew Oswald at all, never mind well enough to see what kind of an assassin he would make, and if Marcello or his lieutenants therefore reached out to Oswald, either to recruit him directly or to find means of controlling him indirectly—all of which is implied by Blakey and is necessary to his theory—then there must have been a bridge of some kind, a link, a connection, between Marcello and Oswald. How did Marcello know, or know about, Oswald?

The House investigation discovered a total of four people who were known both to Oswald and to individuals at the middle and lower levels of the Marcello organization. The first was Oswald's mother, Marguerite, who once had dated men connected with the Marcello organization. The second was Oswald's uncle and surrogate father, Charles Murret, an alleged bookie in the Marcello gambling apparatus. The third was not even an acquaintance of Oswald's but a man named Emile Bruneau who filled in for the absent Murret in helping Oswald get released from jail in August 1963 following the leafleting incident. (See Chapter 2.)

The only Oswald-to-Marcello contact of any substance was the fourth, David Ferrie, who is indeed extremely interesting. Ferrie is said to have piloted Marcello back from Guatemala after he was deported there by Attorney General Robert F. Kennedy. He occasionally freelanced as an investigator with an attorney, G. Wray Gill, who sometimes represented Marcello.

But investigation also determined that Ferrie had piloted for the

C.I.A. as well (on a contract basis at the time of the Bay of Pigs) and that he was close to intriguing individuals who were *not* Mafiosi, *not* distinguished by any special connection to Marcello. One of these was a leader of the anti-Castro Cuban Revolutionary Council (C.R.C.), Sergio Arcacha Smith. Another was W. Guy Banister, an ex-F.B.I. officer and professional anticommunist engaged in the training and equipping of commando units for paramilitary actions inside Cuba. Oswald himself knew Banister directly and associated with C.R.C. exiles.

Thus, the one individual who might conceivably link Oswald to Marcello in any serious way, Ferrie, can much more readily be seen linking Oswald, through Arcacha Smith and Banister, to the C.I.A., with which both Banister and Arcacha Smith were associated.

Further, the Mafia theory fails to explain the evident complicity of the government in the cover-up. One of the major aspects of this case is the fact that members of the national intelligence community—the F.B.I., the C.I.A., possibly the Office of Naval Intelligence—have continually tried to suppress information bearing on some of its core issues, such as other C.I.A. assassination projects, Oswald's military counter-intelligence background and Ruby's ties to the mob. If it was just a few dons and thugs who condemned the President, why did the government's entire investigative apparatus stand paralyzed?

The most questionable step that Blakey took in the projection of his Mafia theory, however, was to classify as secret (or silently allow to be classified as secret) a 285-page report prepared for the Assassinations Committee by one of his own principal researchers, a young attorney named Edwin Juan López, on the question of Oswald's purported trip to Mexico City in late September and early October 1963.

This trip is important in Blakey's case against Oswald because it was in Mexico City at that time that Oswald was said to have phoned and visited the Soviet embassy and the Cuban consulate, loudly announcing his name and, by one disputed account, his belief that J.F.K. should be killed. It is suggested by some in fact that Oswald, during his stay in Mexico City, specifically met with the Soviet K.G.B.'s master of assassinations.

The Assassinations Committee's investigation, however, turned up compelling suggestions that the Oswald seen in Mexico City was a completely different person from the Oswald known to all. (1) A C.I.A. photo said to be of Oswald leaving the Soviet embassy is not Oswald's image. (2) A tape recording of Oswald talking on the phone with a Soviet diplomat is not Oswald's voice. (3) A Cuban diplomat who had three angry confrontations with Oswald said repeatedly and in detail that the Oswald of Mexico City was not the Oswald of Dallas. (4) The one eyewitness who said she saw Oswald in the Cuban consulate could not describe him correctly to House investigators.

The capstone of this is that López himself, the author of the suppressed report, has risked violating his oath of secrecy to say publicly and under oath that he believes Oswald to have been impersonated in Mexico City by people who were trying to set him up. Surely if Oswald was being impersonated and belied by people who wanted him remembered as a dangerous person, then this fact in itself, apart from all the other evidence exculpatory of Oswald, would lend great credibility to his basic protest that he was framed.

And would this not be important news? That someone or some group had framed Oswald to take the blame for the assassination? Would this not oblige us to put back into suspense our official condemnation of Oswald? If he were in prison now and these facts were found, would he not deserve a new hearing and a new presumption of innocence? Not to Blakey.

Blakey pretended to be dispassionate and objective and to serve only the cause of truth when he came to the Assassinations Committee in 1977. He began his tenure with a promise "to let the sun shine in" on whatever he found. Blakey nonetheless suppressed the López report, paid no attention to the doubts it apparently raises, declined even to mention the López investigation or report in the more than 400 pages of his book, and plunged straight on with the inherited myth that Oswald was not only madman enough to shoot the President but madman enough to spread advance warning of his intentions directly and profusely in the beam of U.S. intelligence systems.

*   *   *

As a Washington co-director of the Assassination Information Bureau, which was created early in the 1970s to build a movement for a new J.F.K. investigation, I watched Blakey from a short distance and sometimes close up over a period of about a year and a half as he prepared and presented his theory of the assassination for the committee's review and approval. At first I supported his Mafia theory for basically strategic reasons. It was at least a conspiracy theory that was not rightwing, it could command an official consensus, and it thus appeared strong enough to get the case properly reopened and activated by the Justice Department. Blakey believed the committee's then-fresh leads pointed to the Mafia. Many of us who were watching thought he was mistaken, and that the leads would punch right through the Mafia cover and track straight back to several departments of official U.S. intelligence. That was the gamble and the deal: Let the government start pulling the Mafia string, we thought, and we will see what else it brings with it.

Then came the Reagan era and the total freeze-out from government sympathy of any project in the least memorializing of the Kennedys. Blakey did not take the offensive when the F.B.I. rudely closed the Justice Department's door in his face, basically telling him and the committee, "We don't buy it, so you're out of luck."

Why did Blakey choose not to fight harder and more publicly about it? Why did he seem to retire from the fray?

But then: Why did he try to crucify Garrison? Why did he not credit Garrison for the contribution Garrison has made to the development of this case, though working with a fraction of Blakey's resources and under the intense pressure of an active covert opposition?

Why did Blakey ignore the evidence turned up by his own investigators that the Cuban exile community was equally well positioned to kill a President as was the Mafia? Why did he ignore the fact that this Cuban exile community was the creature of the C.I.A.'s operations directorate?

Perhaps there is, after all, a simple explanation for these curious lapses. At the very end of the Blakey-Billings book, sandwiched between the list of principal sources and the bibliography, there is the following paragraph, the book's final utterance:

> Pursuant to agreement with the Select Committee on Assassinations, the Central Intelligence Agency and the Federal Bureau of Investigation reviewed this book in manuscript form to determine that the classified information it contained had been properly released for publication and that no informant was identified. Neither the C.I.A. nor the F.B.I. warrants the factual material or endorses the views expressed.

This may be one of the most significant paragraphs in the book. It should be printed in the front instead of the back, where everyone would be sure to read it and have it in mind as they encounter the steps of Blakey's argument.

There is, in any case, no such addendum to be tied to the work of Jim Garrison. *On the Trail of the Assassins,* you can be sure, was not reviewed, censored, and approved for publication by the C.I.A. and the F.B.I. Garrison's voice indeed emerges here as one of the great uncensored voices of our day.

Endnotes

I HAVE ATTEMPTED in these endnotes to provide a source or sources for every reference in the text, and have purposely avoided cluttering the text with citations. A great number of the notes are to the full Warren Commission report of 1964 or to the 1979 report of the House Select Committee on Assassinations. Certain abbreviations are used to save space with respect to these items.

The Warren Commission report (*Report of the President's Commission on the Assassination of President John F. Kennedy,* [Washington: U.S. Government Printing Office, 1964]) is cited as WCR. The 26 volumes of Warren Commission hearings and exhibits (Volume I, Volume II, etc.) are cited as 1WCH, 2WCH, etc. Commission Exhibits are also noted, as CE, and deposition exhibits are also noted, with the name of the deponent and Ex. Commission documents, housed at the National Archives in Washington, and occasionally cited separately, are noted as CD.

The House Select Committee report (*Report of the House Select Committee on Assassinations* [Washington: Government Printing Office, 1979]) is cited as HSCR. The 14 volumes of hearings and exhibits are cited as HSCH1, HSCH2, etc.

Some caveats are in order. Many of the conversations I had with colleagues, prospective witnesses, and other sources of information were neither recorded nor summarized in contemporaneous memoranda. Other conversations and interviews were memorialized in one form or another, but the records have subsequently been lost or stolen. Indeed, an entire filing cabinet of documents which I stored after leaving the district attorney's office was stolen while I was working on the first draft of this book. Most of my references to that material were in the form of notes written on cards and pieces of paper with which I worked. While I still have my own notes, I no longer have many of the original documents, passages from which I quote.

Nevertheless, both to aid in the flow of the narrative and to give readers the feel of how events actually unfolded, I have occasionally set forth what is essentially dialogue reconstructed from my memory, and I have frequently quoted from my notes, when the original is no longer available. Where there is an existing source for dialogue, it is given in these endnotes; if a conversation is from memory, it is not sourced. When there is an existing documentary source, it is also given here; when something comes from my notes of material later stolen, that fact is noted here.

Four books, cited frequently, are listed in these notes by the authors' last names only. They are: Warren Hinckle and William Turner, *The Fish Is Red: The Story of the Secret War Against Castro* (New York: Harper & Row, 1981); Henry Hurt, *Reasonable Doubt* (New York: Henry Holt and Co., 1985); Mark Lane, *Rush to Judgment* (New York: Holt, Rinehart & Winston, 1966); and Anthony Summers, *Conspiracy* (New York: McGraw-Hill, 1981). My book, *A Heritage of Stone* (New York: G.P. Putnam, 1970), is cited as *Heritage*. Some matters are covered in virtually all the books on the President's assassination; in such cases I have given a few representative citations.

Introduction

xii: the jury accepted: See Chapter 18.

xii: Dallas police closed the case: See Chapter 2.

xii: The F.B.I. agreed: See Chapter 2.

xii: the concealment of . . . evidence: See Hurt, pp. 432-434; Lane, p. 229; *New York Herald Tribune,* December 18, 1964. Hurt says in 1985 that "of the 375 cubic feet of sealed evidence, all but 12 feet have been released to the public." Hurt, p. 434.

xiii: two-thirds of the public: A Harris poll reported that 66 percent of the American people believed the assassination was the result of a conspiracy. *New York Times,* May 30, 1967. By 1981, another Harris survey indicated that 80 percent of the people believed this. Hurt, p. 34.

xiii: received a telexed warning: See Chapter 17.

xiii: rifle fire coming from the grassy knoll: See Chapter 2.

xiii: a nitrate test: See Chapter 7.

xiii: Jack Ruby. . .was observed: See Chapter 17.

xiv: his brain disappeared: See Chapter 18.

xiv: burned in the fireplace: See Chapter 18.

xiv: the House Select Committee on Assassinations: HSCR, *Findings and Recommendations,* p. 1.

xv: I was vilified in the press: See Chapter 13.

xv: brought false charges of corruption: See Chapter 19.

xv: Assassination by our C.I.A. is. . .established historical fact: See Chapter 20.

xvi: at American University: Commencement address, June 10, 1963, *Public Papers of the Presidents of the United States, John F. Kennedy, 1963* (Washington: Government Printing Office, 1964), p. 462; *New York Times,* June 11, 1963, p. 16.

CHAPTER 1: **The Serenity of Ignorance**

7: other witnesses who had seen Ferrie: My notes of this extensive series of interviews were among the stolen files.

7: brought to my office for questioning: *Ibid.*

8: at the skating rink: *Ibid.*

8: continued on from Houston to Galveston: *Ibid.*

11: a gratuitous statement: *Ibid.*

11n: the Committee . . . concluded: See Chapter 20.

11n: one of the possible indications: HSCR, *Findings and Recommendations,* p. 145: "The committee was puzzled by Oswald's apparent association with Ferrie. . . ."

CHAPTER 2: **The Awakening**

13: shooting from the grassy knoll: See later in this Chapter.

13: protective bubble had been removed: WCR, p. 43. The Warren Commission was told that the bubble top was not bullet proof and that the skies had cleared.

13: had inquired extensively: The Warren Commission was inaugurated on November 29, 1963. Its final report was issued September 24, 1964. WCR, p. viii.

15: produced by Sylvia Meagher: Sylvia Meagher and Gary Owens, *Master Index to the J.F.K. Assassination Investigations* (Metuchen, N.J.: Scarecrow Press, 1980).

15: Julia Ann Mercer. . .saw: 19 WCH, Decker Ex. 5323, pp. 483-484.

16: she reported this unsettling incident: Hurt, pp. 114-116.

16: According to [Lee Bowers's] testimony: 6WCH, pp. 286-287.

16: an affidavit given [by J.C. Price] to the Sheriff's office: 24 WCH, CE2003, p. 222; 19WCH, Decker Ex. 5323, p. 492.

16: Joseph Smith . . . ran: 7 WCH, p. 353.

16: S.M. Holland . . . described the shooting: 6WCH, pp. 243-244.

16: O.V. Campbell . . . said the shooting: 3WCH, p. 274.

17: from a point . . . near the railroad tracks: 22WCH, CE1381, p. 638.

17: James Tague . . . said: 7WCH, p. 557.

17: Billy Lovelady . . . recollected: 6WCH, p. 338.

17: Abraham Zapruder . . . described the police officers: 7WCH, p. 572.

17: Forrest Sorrels . . . testified: 7WCH, p. 345.

17: William Newman . . . said: 24WCH, CE 2003, p. 219.

18: L.C. Smith . . . ran "as fast as I could": 19WCH, Decker Ex. 5323, p. 516.

18: Malcolm Summers . . . recalled the moment: *Ibid.,* p. 500.

18: Jean Hill . . . admitted: 6WCH, p. 211.

18: the testimony of Lee Bowers: *Ibid.,* p. 288.

19: Sergeant D.V. Harkness . . . testified: *Ibid.,* p. 312.

20: Joe M. Smith . . . who was told: 7WCH, p. 535.

20: [Joe M. Smith] responding to questions: *Ibid.*

21: all of the Secret Service agents assigned: WCR, pp. 52, 446.

21: Sergeant Harkness's testimony revealed: 6WCH, p. 312.

21: Jean Hill . . . was halted in the parking lot: Hurt, p. 119.

22: had been questioned for a total of 12 hours: WCR, p. 180.

22: could not be mere sloppiness: Chief Curry "recognized" that "we were violating every principle of good interrogation." WCR, p. 200; 4WCH, p. 152.

22: the testimony of Lieutenant Colonel Allison G. Folsom, Jr.: 8 WCH, p. 307; 19WCH, Folsom Ex., p. 622.

23: 544 Camp Street: 23WCH, CE1414, p. 3.

25: We interviewed young Steele: My notes are gone. The Warren Commission also had interviewed Steele; see 10WCH, pp. 62, 64.

25: when Oswald was arrested on August 9 on Canal Street: 4WCH, pp. 432-433.

25: contrary to standard Bureau procedures: Quigley, it should be noted, told the Warren Commission it was "the usual practice" to destroy notes after a report had been completed. *Ibid.,* p. 433.

26: a radio debate on station WDSU: WCR, p. 408; Summers, pp. 307-308.

26n: temporarily transferred . . . Quigley: 4WCH, p. 440.

27: two other addresses on the 600 block of Magazine Street: WCR, p. 403.

27: Reily . . . actively supported the anti-Castro movement: Summers, p. 313.

27: Alba described Oswald's interest: 10WCH, p. 220.

27n: Alba . . . testified in 1978: HSCR, *Findings and Recommendations,* p. 146.

CHAPTER 3: **War Games**

36: Guy Banister's widow: The notes of this interview were stolen.

37: the few remaining index cards: These notes were also stolen, but not until after the publication of *Heritage;* the list appears on page 113.

39: a copy of the report: This was also in my files which were stolen some years ago.

39n: Hinckle, pp. 198-203.

40: As we later learned from . . . Gordon Novel: See Chapter 14.

40: The Schlumberger Corporation: According to the *New Orleans States-Item* of April 25, 1967, "50 to 100 crates" of ammunition, rifles, grenades, landmines, and the like were found in Guy Banister's storeroom, "labeled 'Schlumberger.' " See Paris Flammonde, *The Kennedy Conspiracy* (New York: Meredith Press, 1969), p. 119.

42: the Secret Service . . . synopsis: 23 WCH, CE1414, p. 828.

43n: what [Delphine Roberts] later admitted to others: Summers, pp. 324-325.

CHAPTER 4: **The Social Triumphs of Lee Harvey Oswald**

44: a "commitment to Marxism": WCR, pp. 23, 390, 423.

45: [Nelson Delgado's] testimony: 8WCH, p. 133.

45: colloquy between Delgado and . . . Wesley J. Liebeler: *Ibid.,* pp. 237, 246.

46: [Daniel Powers's] dialogue with . . . Albert E. Jenner, Jr.: 8WCH, pp. 285-286.

46: the testimony of John E. Donovan: 8WCH, p. 293.

46n: Donald Peter Camarata: *Ibid.,* pp. 316-317.

46n: Peter Francis Connor: *Ibid.,* p. 317.

46n: Allen D. Graf: *Ibid.,* pp. 317-318.

46n: John Rene Heindel: *Ibid.,* p. 318.

46n: Mack Osborne: *Ibid.,* p. 322.

46n: Richard Dennis Call: *Ibid.,* p. 323.

47: Thornley's testimony: 11WCH, pp. 82-115.

47: Atsugi, I discovered: See Michael R. Beschloss, *Mayday* (New York: Harper & Row, 1986), p. 46.

47: a list of those files concerning Oswald: See *Heritage,* p. 37.

48: Oswald applied for a premature discharge: WCR, pp. 688-689.

48: His steamship ticket: 26WCH, CE2665, p. 21; CE2673, p. 29; WCR, p. 690.

48: stated that Oswald flew straight on: WCR, p. 690; 18WCH, CE946, p. 162.

49: checked into his Helsinki hotel: 26WCH, CE2676, p. 32.

49: James A. Wilcott . . . told the House Select Committee: *New York Times,* March 27, 1978, p. A14; HSCR, pp. 198-199; Hurt, p. 203; Summers, pp. 159-160.

49: had denied . . . that Oswald was ever employed by the Agency: WCR, p. 327.

49: a series of contacts with Soviet officials: WCR, p. 691; Hurt, p. 214.

49: dramatic appearance at the American Embassy: WCR, p. 747; 18WCH, CE908, pp. 97-98.

49n: an executive session: Hurt, pp. 193–194.

49n: was convicted of lying: See Thomas Powers, *The Man Who Kept the Secrets: Richard Helms and the CIA* (New York: Alfred A. Knopf, 1979), pp. 298-305.

50: announced that he had told Soviet officials: WCR, p. 748.

50: the . . . F.B.I. . . . stated: WCR, p. 748; 26WCH, CE2718, p. 92.

50: had given Oswald a "clean bill": WCR, p. 748.

50: Oswald was sent to Minsk: 16WCH, CE24, pp. 98-99.

50: applied at the American Embassy in Moscow to return: 18WCH, CE931, pp. 133-134, 102.

50: met Marina: 16WCH, CE24, p. 102.

50: were married: 22WCH, CE1111, pp. 72-73.

50: neither government objected: WCR, p. 709.

50: Oswald "had not expatriated himself": WCR, pp. 752-760.

51: the loan of $436 was granted: WCR, pp. 709-712, 770-773.

51: no reason why Oswald's passport should not be renewed: WCR, p. 757; 18WCH, CE979, p. 382.

51: the Passport Office gave . . . a clean bill of health: WCR, p. 751.

51: There was only Spas T. Raikin:`Summers, p. 217; 26WCH, CE2655, pp. 2-10, WCR, p. 713.

51: moved to Fort Worth: WCR, p. 713.

51: worked at the Leslie Welding Company: WCR, p. 715-716.

51: when George de Mohrenschildt and his wife came over: Hurt, p. 220.

51n: when Oswald applied for his passport again: WCR, pp. 773-774.

52: moved to Dallas: WCR, p. 718.

52: seeking a new job: *Ibid.;* 19WCH, Cunningham Ex., pp. 397-405.

52: writer Henry Hurt has observed: Hurt, p. 219.

52: was given the job [and] had access: *Ibid.*

52: setting the type: *Ibid.,* p. 220.

53: welcomed . . . by the White Russian community: WCR, pp. 719-721.

53: these were the people who helped Lee and Marina: *Ibid.*

53: Oswald's most frequent associate: WCR, p. 282; see 9WCH, pp. 166-284, for the de Mohrenschildt deposition.

54: Max Clark [and] his wife Katya: 9WCH, p. 219.

54: had seen . . . *Das Kapital:* 8WCH, p. 382.

54n: researcher Harold Weisberg: Harold Weisberg, *Whitewash II* (New York: Dell, 1966), pp. 45-50.

55: de Mohrenschildt had been operating under deep cover: Summers, pp. 499-500; HSCH12, p. 61.

55n: de Mohrenschildt committed suicide: Summers, p. 499.

55n: his deposition was taken: 9WCH, pp. 166-284.

56: dozens of photostats of job applications: 21WCH, Rachal Ex., p. 282; 22WCH, CE1398, p. 736; 23WCH, CE1943, p. 741; 23WCH, CE1945, p. 745; 23WCH, CE1949, p. 747; 23WCH, CE1950, p. 752; 23WCH, CE1951, p. 753.

57n: his local draft board card: 24WCH, CE1990, p. 21.

57n: his Department of Defense ID: *Ibid.*

57n: His . . . passport application: 22WCH, CE1114, p. 77.

57n: his discharge form: 23WCH, CE1944, p. 744.

57n: this man with the scar was always present: These witness statements were also stolen.

60: a fascinating book: William R. Corson, *The Armies of Ignorance* (New York: Dial Press, 1977), pp. 30-31.

CHAPTER 5: **Setting Up the Scapegoat**

62: regarded by many as a source of cover for the C.I.A.: "At one time, many A.I.D. field offices were infiltrated from top to bottom with C.I.A. people." John Gilligan, director of A.I.D. during the Carter administration, quoted in George Cotter, "Spies, Strings, and Missionaries," *The Christian Century* (Chicago), March 25, 1981.

62: When Marina and her daughter reached Dallas: WCR, pp. 729-730.

62: Lee returned to Dallas: WCR, p. 736.

63: got the job: WCR, p. 738.

63: a series of small rooms: WCR, pp. 737-738.

63: that they had been classified as secret: I was told this by our English archivist, and never pursued it. Appendix 1 of James Hepburn, *Farewell America* (Vaduz, Liechtenstein: Frontiers Press, 1968), is entitled "National Archives Classified Documents Pertaining to the Kennedy Assassination." It includes CD 848, "Michael & Ruth Paine tax returns '56-'58." An inordinately large number of documents relating to the Paines were also classified. See *Heritage,* pp. 134-135.

63: Lee Oswald himself, according to the government, was in Mexico City: See WCR, pp. 730-736.

63: A C.I.A. memo: Hurt, pp. 231-235; HSCH4, p. 219.

64: a murky snapshot: Hurt, opposite p. 263.

64: the C.I.A. ordered Mexican authorities: HSCH3, pp. 82, 157, 232-233; HSCH11, pp. 203-204.

64: Duran told author Anthony Summers: Summers, p. 377.

64: Azcue was shown photographs: *Ibid.,* p. 374.

65: obtained under the Freedom of Information Act: Summers, p. 386.

65: the Agency claimed: Hurt, pp. 233-234.

65: Edwin Juan López: "On Trial: Lee Harvey Oswald," LWT Productions, London, 1986. Aired on Showtime cable TV in the United States, in November 1986 and January 1987. López's 285-page report was not released.

65: One of these tableaux: From my notes of the Farrington investigation, in my possession.

67: A "Leon Oswald" appeared at the home of Sylvia Odio: Michael L. Kurtz, *Crime of the Century* (Knoxville, Tenn.: University of Tennessee Press, 1982), p. 219.

67: Mrs. Lovell Penn found three men: *Ibid.,* p. 220.

67: a young man using the name of "Lee Oswald": *Ibid.*

67: arrived at the Downtown Lincoln Mercury dealership: 10WCH, p. 353.

68: drove like a madman: 26WCH, CE 3078, p. 685.

68: go back to Russia: *Ibid.*

68: "He won't want to buy a car": 10WHC, pp. 353-354.

68: already forgotten: *Ibid.*

68: Frank Pizzo . . . was much more positive: *Ibid.,* p. 349.

69: Eugene Wilson's testimony: 26WCH, CE3078, p. 685.

69: loftily stated: WCR, p. 320.

70: Oswald was called at the Paine household: 11WCH, p. 481.

70: Thornley's testimony: *Ibid.,* pp. 82-115.

70: I had my staff begin inquiring: My original notes of this aspect of the investigation are also gone.

71: a routine check of police records: *Ibid.*

73: Jenner had asked how tall: 11WCH, p. 89.

74: had just moved from the Neely Street apartment: On April 24, Oswald helped his wife move to Mrs. Paine's; he then took the bus to New Orleans. Marina joined him there May 11. WCR, pp. 726-730.

75: As [Spencer] described it: The Spencer notes were also among the stolen files.

75n: concluded that these were genuine: WCR, p. 127; HSCR, *Findings and Recommendations,* p. 55.

75n: Groden . . . wrote a dissent: HSCR, p. 295.

76: a lengthy . . . 50-page affidavit: This document was also in my stolen files.

76n: Rosselli was enlisted by the C.I.A.: Summers, pp. 268, 494. Rosselli's name is spelled "Rosselli" in the Warren Commission volumes and "Roselli" in the House Select Committee volumes, and variously in other books. I have used "Rosselli" throughout, for consistency.

77: Rosselli's assignment: *Ibid.,* p. 263.

77: appeared before a Senate committee: *Ibid.,* p. 503.

77: the remains of Mr. Rosselli: *Ibid.,* pp. 502-503.

77n: Sam Giancana: *Ibid.,* p. 502.

78: we later discovered a letter: This letter is also part of my missing Thornley files.

CHAPTER 6: **Deep Cover**

79: [Andrews] admitted to the Warren Commission: 11WCH, pp. 331-333.

80: Andrews's testimony: *Ibid.,* pp. 325-339.

80: had described Clay Bertrand: *Ibid.,* p. 335.

80: citizenship problems: 26WCH, CE3094, pp. 704-705.

80: Bertrand's height had shrunk: 11WCH, p. 334.

80: Andrews told them, "Write what you want": *Ibid.*

87: articles in the Italian Press: *Paesa Sera* (Rome), March 4, 11, 12, 14, 16, and 18, 1967; see Roberto Faenza and Edward Becker, *Il Malafare: Dall'America di Kennedy all'Italia, a Cuba, al Vietnam* (Milan: Mondadoro, 1978) (cited below as Faenza and Becker), pp. 128, 326, 330, 389; Roberto Faenza and Marco Fini, *Gli Americani in Italia* (Milan: Feltrinelli, 1976); and Robert D. Morrow, *Betrayal: A Reconstruction of Certain Clandestine Events from the Bay of Pigs to the Assassination of John F. Kennedy* (Chicago: Henry Regnery, 1976), p. 92.

88: described . . . by writer Paris Flammonde: Paris Flammonde, *The Kennedy Conspiracy* (New York: Meredith Press, 1969), pp. 214-224.

88: it had expelled the Centro: *Le Devoir* (Montreal), March 16, 1967; Faenza and Becker, p. 320.

89: *Le Devoir* . . . wrote in early 1967: *Le Devoir*, March 16, 1967.

89: *Paesa Sera* stated: March 4, 1967.

89: As for Permindex: *Ibid.;* Faenza and Becker, p. 321.

CHAPTER 7: **The Front Page**

91: The "admission note": 17WCH, CE392, pp. 11-12.

92: Arnold Rowland: 2WCH, pp. 165-190.

92: Barbara Rowland: 6WCH, pp. 177-191.

92: a statement [Carolyn Walther] gave to the F.B.I.: 24WCH, CE2086, p. 522.

92n: Mrs. Rowland recalled: *Ibid.,* p. 181.

93: Toney Henderson . . . was waiting: 24WCH, CE2089, p. 524.

93: the testimony of . . . Amos Euins: 2WCH, pp. 201-210.

93: when interviewed by Sergeant D.V. Harkness: 6WCH, p. 313.

94: as if it were white: 2WCH, p. 207.

94: as being black: Lane, p. 281.

94: not be certain: 2WCH, p. 207.

94: "bald spot": *Ibid.*

94: looked like it was white: *Ibid.,* p. 208.

94n: Stanley Kaufman . . . described a client: 15WCH, p. 526.

94n: John Powell surfaced later: Summers, pp. 74-75.

95: As Craig recalled it: 6WCH, pp. 260-273; and in numerous interviews with me.

95: a Nash Rambler: 6WCH, p. 267.

95: a young white man: *Ibid.,* p. 270.

95: "a Negro": *Ibid.,* p. 267.

95: Richard Randolph Carr had observed: Hurt, p. 119. Carr also testified at the Shaw trial; see Chapter 18.

95n: Craig came to see me: I had numerous interviews with Craig, all of which confirmed, and expanded upon, his Warren Commission testimony.

95n: He told Captain Will Fritz . . . about the Nash Rambler: 6WCH, p. 270.

95n: Deputy Sheriff Buddy Walthers drove out: *Ibid.,* p. 271.

95n: Fritz later denied: Hurt, p. 125.

95n: a news photo that turned up six years after: Hurt, ninth page following p. 138.

96: was described as a Latin man: In letters to my office from Dallas witnesses.

97n: found no fingerprints: 4 WCH, p. 23.

97n: police excitedly announced: WCR, p. 566.

97n: an internal F.B.I. memo: Hurt, p. 108; cf. HSCR, p. 53.

97n: Drain was questioned about the supposed palm print: Hurt, p. 109.

98: described the discovery of the rifle: 7WCH, pp. 105-109; 24WCH, CE2003, p. 228.

98: an engineering degree and also operated a sporting goods store: Hurt, p. 102.

98: Weitzman identified it: 7WCH, p. 108.

98: Craig was also there: Hurt, p. 102; and numerous interviews with me.

98: Boone executed a sworn affidavit: 19WCH, Decker Ex. 5323, p. 507.

98: Wade told the media: 24WCH, CE2169, p. 831.

98: three empty cartridges . . . were found: WCR, p. 79.

98: no ammunition clip was ever found: Hurt, pp. 103-104.

99: was found to have a badly misaligned sight: 26WCH, CE2724, p. 104.

99: A film taken by Dallas Cinema Associates: This film was shown to me by Richard E. Sprague. It, along with a massive amount of photographic evidence compiled by Sprague, is now in the archives of Western New England College, Springfield, Massachusetts.

100: Oswald had been seen in the lunchroom: WCR, pp. 151-152.

100: a pop bottle that did not have Oswald's fingerprints on it: 4WCH, p. 266.

100: The nitrate test results: WCR, pp. 560-561. The Commission reported that "Oswald's hands reacted positively to the test. The cast of the right cheek showed no reaction." WCR, p. 560. Faced with the complications posed by the latter finding, the Commission simply stated, "the test is completely unreliable . . . ." WCR, p. 561.

101: "How did he get way down here on Elm?": Why the route was changed, and when it was changed, are both matters of controversy. The Warren Commission was told that the change was necessary to avoid a difficult turn beyond the railroad overpass, to depart on Stemmons Freeway toward the Trade Mart. 4 WCH, pp. 168-170; 7WCH, pp. 336-338; 24WCH, CE2116, p. 546. However, the reasoning is quite flawed. Remaining on Main Street would have called for a 100-degree turn, after the underpass, in a completely clear area, with all traffic diverted, and the crowds nowhere around. Instead, a 120-degree turn was chosen, in a crowded and extremely accessible area. There are also people who say that a map of the amended route was published some time before November 22, but no such document has surfaced. Most significant to me is the map of the Main Street route on the front page of the November 22 *Dallas Morning News,* and the fact that this map was *not* shown to the Warren Commission.

102: introduced as a Commission exhibit: 22WCH, CE1365, p. 617.

103: the Agency's disastrous Bay of Pigs invasion: Hinckle, pp. 82-95.

104: asked for Cabell's resignation: *Ibid.,* p. 112.

104: Dulles (also fired by President Kennedy): *Ibid.*

CHAPTER 8: **Covert Operations**

107: The car . . . was registered to the International Trade Mart: See Chapter 18.

107: McGehee . . . would recall: *New Orleans Times-Picayune,* February 7, 1969, p. 15.

108: Morgan recalled: *Ibid.,* and see *New Orleans Times-Picayune,* March 1, 1969, p. 20.

109: David Ferrie had worked . . . for Gill: Summers, pp. 337-338.

110: the day before Oswald left New Orleans: WCR, pp. 726-730.

110: the number Ferrie called: From Bell Telephone Company records in New Orleans: "Chicago, Ill. - WH-4-4970 - Amount $3.85 - Your number 524-0147."

111: an F.B.I. interview with Lawrence Meyers: 25WCH, CE2267, pp. 191-192; 25WCH, CE2266; and see HSCH9, pp. 805-941.

114: Lou Ivon had located . . . Jimmy Johnson: These notes, part of our extensive investigation of David Ferrie, were all stolen. Ivon and Alcock have confirmed the content of these passages for me.

115: Alcock found that Ferrie had deposited: *Ibid.*

115: a private detective agency . . . report: *Ibid.*

115: I glanced down at the list: *Ibid.*

CHAPTER 9: **The Bonds of Friendship**

117: Jules Ricco Kimble: Signed statement of Kimble, October 10, 1967.

117: a member of far-right groups: HSCR, p. 392.

117n: a friend of James Earl Ray: *Ibid.*

119: a young friend of his, David Logan: These notes were also stolen.

119: Nicholas Tadin . . . went out to New Orleans Airport; *Ibid.*

120: Raymond Broshears: *Ibid.*

122: an extensive statement [from] Edward Whalen: Memorandum from James L. Alcock to Jim Garrison, September 18, 1967.

CHAPTER 10: **The Ides of February**

132: John Miller . . . came down from Denver: There is, of course, no record of this meeting, although Andrew Sciambra recalls it as I do.

CHAPTER 11: **Checkmate**

141: priestly garments: Ferrie was a "bishop" in "an obscure sect called the Orthodox Old Catholic Church of North America." Hurt, pp. 263-264.

141: Two suicide notes were found: Only one was quoted in the press. See *New Orleans States-Item,* February 23, 1967, and *New Orleans Times-Picayune,* February 23, 1967.

141: To leave this life: *Ibid.*

142: the coroner announced: *New Orleans States-Item,* February 24, 1967.

144: We had already questioned Shaw once at the office: All the notes of Shaw's interrogations were in the stolen files.

145: we questioned him once at great length: *Ibid.*

146: his address book: *Ibid.*

146: our written opposition: *Ibid.*

146: Shaw's attorneys produced a man: *Ibid.*

147: on one of the pages of Oswald's address book: 16WCH, CE58, p. 58.

147: Dallas had not yet acquired: We were so informed by the Dallas Post Office in 1966.

CHAPTER 12: **Confrontation**

149: One newsman asked Clark: *New York Times,* March 3, 1967.

150: a Justice Department spokesman announced: Statement (undated) prepared by Justice Department spokesman in response to a request for public clarification made by one of Shaw's attorneys, Edward F. Wegmann.

150n: the indictment: *New Orleans Times-Picayune,* March 23, 1967.

151: Shaw's . . . preliminary hearing: *New Orleans States-Item,* March 14, 1967, p. 1.

152: use hypnosis and Sodium Pentothal: *Ibid.,* March 17, 1967, pp. 1, 12.

152: Russo responded: For complete coverage of Russo's testimony, see *New Orleans States-Item,* March 14, 1967, pp. 1, 14; and March 15, 1967, pp. 1, 4, 6.

156: both testified strongly and clearly: *New Orleans States-Item,* March 15, 1967, pp. 1, 4, 6; March 17, 1967, p. 12.

156: More than two decades later, Russo's candor: One of several interviews I had with Russo, summer 1988.

157: Bundy testified: *New Orleans States-Item,* March 18, 1967, p. 12.

CHAPTER 13: **The Assault**

160: Earl Warren announced from Tokyo: United Press International, dispatch from Tokyo, September 4, 1967.

162: Alvin Beaubeouf . . . admitted: Beaubeouf called Lynn Loisel, the person in our office who had allegedly threatened him, and said he was fed up with being pressured into saying things against me. He then came to our office with his attorney, Hugh Exnicios. I told Exnicios that neither I nor Loisel should be present, and sent them to meet with Lou Ivon and Charles Ward. They ultimately took a sworn statement from Beaubeouf in which he stated he had never been threatened by our office and that the statements to that effect were untrue. He also stated that there were, of course, no secret tapes because the alleged conversations had never taken place. Mr. Exnicios and Lou Ivon both recently recalled the incident clearly.

162: "The Vice Man Cometh": *Saturday Evening Post,* June 8, 1963, pp. 67-71.

162: "Rush to Judgment in New Orleans": *Ibid.,* May 6, 1967, pp. 21-25.

164: *Life* articles about organized crime: *Life,* September 1, 1967, p. 15; September 8, 1967, p. 91.

164: I was described: *Life,* September 8, 1967, pp. 94-95.

164: *Time . . .* ran a series of articles: March 3, 1967; March 10, 1967; and see June 30, 1967, on the NBC show.

165: The *New York Times Magazine . . .* article: September 11, 1966, pp. 52, 154.

166: Marlene Mancuso . . . wrote in a memo to us: After I had copied this extract from the memo, the original was returned to the files which were subsequently stolen.

167: Sciambra wrote a memorandum: *Ibid.*

168: "The Case of Jim Garrison": N.B.C., June 19, 1967.

170: Dean Andrews . . . was indicted: See Chapter 18.

170: found guilty of perjury: *Ibid.*

171: I made my reply: N.B.C., July 15, 1967.

171: I learned that R.C.A. had become: See Kenneth Bilby, *The General: David Sarnoff and the Rise of the Communications Industry* (New York: Harper & Row, 1986), pp. 156, 167.

171: aired on four successive evenings in June: June 25-28, 1967.

CHAPTER 14: **The Company**

176: President Kennedy had adopted a highly distrustful stance: See generally, Hinckle, pp. 96-102.

177: a landmark speech at American University: See Introduction.

177: to withdraw all American military personnel: Kenneth O'Donnell and David F. Powers, *Johnny, We Hardly Knew Ye* (Boston: Little, Brown, 1970), p. 382.

177: a secret National Security Council memo: Howard Zinn, *A People's History of the United States* (New York: Harper & Row, 1980), p. 462.

178: observed . . . Kenneth O'Donnell: O'Donnell and Powers, p. 383.

178: instructed . . . Robert McNamara: *Ibid.,* p. 382.

178: threatened to strip the C.I.A.: After the Bay of Pigs fiasco, President Kennedy said he wanted to "splinter the C.I.A. into a thousand pieces and scatter it to the winds." *New York Times,* April 25, 1966.

179: through interviews and press conferences: The *New Orleans States-Item* of April 25, 1977, referred to Novel as "one of history's most loquacious fugitives."

179: he announced that the Schlumberger bunker business: *Ibid.*

180: the *New Orleans States-Item* . . . article: *Ibid.*

180: Novel's . . . draft of a letter: See Michael Canfield and Alan J. Weberman, *Coup d'État in America* (New York: Third Press, 1975), pp. 37-38. And see E. Howard Hunt, *Give Us This Day* (New Rochelle, N.Y.: Arlington House, 1973), p. 46; and Rosemary James and Jack Wardlaw, *Plot or Politics* (New Orleans: Pelican, 1967), p. 11.

180n: five Irish-Americans were acquitted: See Shana Alexander, "The Patriot Game," *New York Magazine,* November 22, 1982, p. 58.

182: DeBrueys pleaded executive privilege: See HSCR, pp. 192-193.

183: I finally stumbled across . . . the F.B.I. report: CD197. For an account of Nagell's story, see Hinckle, pp. 226-229. My own notes of my meetings with Nagell are gone. Hinckle and Turner had access to some of his written statements when they were working on their book.

185n: conviction was reversed: Hinckle, p. 228.

186: an account of Nagell's arrest by East German police: This clipping was in my stolen files.

CHAPTER 15: **Shell Game**

193: investigations of the murder of J.D. Tippit: See WCR, pp. 156-176.

194: rhetorically posed the question: See Hurt, p. 139.

194: Tippit was shot: 6WCH, p. 448; 24WCH, CE2003, pp. 202, 215; Lane, p. 188.

194: had returned to his rooming house: WCR, pp. 163-164.

194: virtually impossible: WCR, p. 165, concedes it is at least a 15-minute walk.

194: Domingo Benavides: 6WCH, p. 452.

195: Warren Reynolds: 11WCH, pp. 435-436.

195: Reynolds had been shot: *Ibid.,* p. 437.

195: Markham's testimony: 3WCH, pp. 304-321, 340-342; 7WCH, pp. 488-506.

195: trying to talk: 20WCH, Markham Ex. No. 1, pp. 583, 590.

195: she informed Mark Lane: Lane, p. 180.

195: under oath she denied: 7WCH, pp. 503-504.

195: black hair: WCR, p. 167.

195: how that identification went: 3WCH, p. 310.

196: the ambulance driver and his helper: Lane, p. 194.

196: Mr. and Mrs. Donald Higgins: *Ibid.*

196: T.F. Bowley: 24WCH, CE2003, p. 254.

197: interviewed . . . Acquilla Clemons: Lane, pp. 193-194; Lane interviewed, filmed, and taped Mrs. Clemons in Dallas in March 1968.

197: Frank Wright: Lane, p. 194; *New York Times,* October 12, 1964; *New Leader,* October 12, 1964.

197n: Lane's . . . work: See Lane, pp. 171-208.

198: a book by Michael Kurtz: Michael L. Kurtz, *Crime of the Century* (Knoxville, Tenn.: University of Tennessee Press, 1982), p. 138.

198: transcripts of the messages: See 25WCH, CE1974, pp. 832-940; *Heritage*, pp. 71-72.

198: the gun allegedly taken from Lee Oswald: 3WCH, p. 301; 7WCH, p. 54.

199: had conducted an autopsy: 3WCH, pp. 473, 475.

199: sent only *one* bullet: See Lane, pp. 195-200.

199: Courtlandt Cunningham . . . testified: 3WCH, p. 475.

200: finally added four cartridges: 3WCH, pp. 474-476.

200: Bureau lab promptly reported back: 3WCH, p. 511.

201: *two* of the cartridge cases had been manufactured by: WCR, p. 172.

201: it became embarrassingly apparent: 6WCH, pp. 450-451; 7WCH, p. 47.

201: Poe informed the Warren Commission: 7WCH, pp. 68-69.

201: Barnes . . . too was unable: 7WCH, pp. 275-276.

CHAPTER 16: **Escape of the Assassins**

204: From . . . Craig . . . I already knew: See Chapter 7.

205: arrested at the Dal-Tex Building: See Hurt, pp. 122-124.

205: Jim Braden: See 24WCH, CE2003, p. 202.

206: Tom Tilson . . . had heard: "On Trial: Lee Harvey Oswald," LWT Productions, London, 1986.

209n: Walthers subsequently was murdered: *Dallas Morning News,* January 11, 1969. According to the Sheriff's office, the previous day Walthers and his partner had responded to a tip that "an escaped convict and his woman companion" were located at a particular hotel room. They reportedly went to the hotel without phoning in to headquarters, and as they accosted the suspect, Walthers was shot, and his partner was knocked unconscious. When the partner recovered, the suspects were gone and Walthers was dead.

210nn: the House Select Committee did: HSCH4, pp. 367-386.

CHAPTER 17: **The Reluctant Investigators**

216: Julia Ann Mercer's statements: 19WCH, Decker Ex. 5323, pp. 483-485.

219n: Jack Ruby had a special relationship: Jurt, p. 177; Summers, pp. 456-465; HSCR, pp. 369-370.

219nn: I sent the committee copies of Mercer's statements: 12HSCH, pp. 16-17.

220: Walter . . . made out a statement: My copy of this statement was among my stolen papers.

222: made public years before by C.A. Hamblen: WCR, pp. 332-333; Hurt, p. 402.

222n: The Secret Service's performance: See Hurt, p. 84; WCR, p. 58; 5WCH, pp. 64-65.

222nn: Oswald had written the Navy secretary: 19WCH, Folsom Ex., pp. 713, 695.

223: Oswald's address book contained the name of . . . Hosty: 16WCH, CE18, p. 64.

223: a list of the contents . . . omitted: The Hosty entry was missing from CD205, purporting to be a transcription of Oswald's address book. Later, CD385 was submitted to the Warren Commission, with the entry. See discussion in HSCH11, pp. 424-425.

223: "lead information": *Ibid.,* p. 424. The House Select Committee on Assassinations considered the incident "trivial." HSCR, p. 190.

223: an item appeared in the press: *Washington Post,* October 22, 1975; see Hurt, pp. 252-254.

224: Shanklin ordered him to destroy it: HSCR, p. 195; HSCH11, pp. 424-425.

225: I heard a story . . . from . . . Jim Gochnour: Richard Sprague first heard the Gochnour story and told me about it. I tracked Gochnour down and confirmed it.

226: According to . . . Jack Revill: 19WCH, CE831, pp. 780-784.

CHAPTER 18: **The Trial of Clay Shaw**

232: Reeves Morgan testified: *New Orleans Times-Picayune,* March 1, 1969.

232: John Manchester . . . "checked out" all strange cars: *Ibid.,* February 7, 1969.

234: Marchetti referred to the Agency's concern: *True* magazine, April 1975. Marchetti evidently first indicated an Agency interest in the Clay Shaw trial in a December 21, 1973, interview with Zodiac News Service, but it was little noticed. After the *True* article, Mark Lane's Citizens Committee of Inquiry interviewed Marchetti and issued a press release on April 22, 1975. See also Hinckle, p. 269.

235: we called Vernon Bundy to the stand: *New Orleans Times-Picayune,* February 8, 1969.

236: On cross-examination . . . Dymond asked Spiesel: *Ibid.*

237: fingerprinted his daughter: Hurt, pp. 274-275.

237: we called Perry Russo: *New Orleans Times-Picayune,* March 1, 1969, pp. 2, 24.

238: William E. Newman . . . described: *Ibid.,* p. 20.

238: Richard Randolph Carr . . . testified: *New Orleans Times-Picayune,* February 20, 1969, p. 24.

239: Deputy Sheriff Roger Craig corroborated: *New York Times,* February 15, 1969, p. 13.

239: Dr. John Nichols's testimony: *New Orleans Times-Picayune,* February 28, 1969, pp. 1, 6, 7.

239nn: J. Edgar Hoover explained: HSCH1, p. 100.

240: maximum time frame: WCR, p. 115.

240: one bullet missed: WCR, p. 117.

240: the government's account [of] the wounds: WCR, pp. 86-96; Lane, pp. 74, 76.

241: the bullet was later found: WCR, p. 95; 6WCH, pp. 128-134; 17WCH, CE399, p. 49.

241: more fragments were found: Lane, pp. 76-77.

241: we called . . . Mrs. Jesse Parker: *New Orleans Times-Picayune,* February 20, 1969, p. 28.

241: Mrs. Elizabeth McCarthy: *Ibid.,* March 1, 1969, p. 24.

241n: Jack Ruby had been seen: Lane, p. 73.

242: to rule inadmissible the fingerprint card: *Ibid.,* February 20, 1969, p. 1; Shaw's attorneys suggested that their client had signed a card with a blank space for aliases and that someone, presumably Habighorst, had later filled in "Clay Bertrand." The judge did not allow the jury to decide whom to believe.

242: That was not the law: It is a close question and seems to depend upon (1) whether the questioning is a routine part of the booking process, and (2) whether the booking officer had reason to believe that he might be eliciting an incriminating response. Habighorst had no idea at that time that the question was important to us. See *Miranda v. Arizona,* 384 U.S. 436 (1966); *Rhode Island v. Innis,* 100 S.Ct. 1682 (1980).

242: ask for writs: *New Orleans Times-Picayune,* February 20, 1969, p. 1.

243: under Texas law the body should never have been moved: WCR, p. 58.

244: had already diagnosed the wound: 16WCH, CE387, p. 981; Lane, p. 46.

244: 15 to 20 photographs and x-rays: 16WCH, CE387, p. 982-983.

244: drew their pictures: 2WCH, p. 349.

244: Commander Humes by his own admission: 17WCH, p. 48; 12WCH, p. 373; HSCH1, p. 330; HSCH7, p. 257. See generally, Hurt, Chapter 3: "The Autopsy of the Century."

244n: told the Commission he did not find: 2WCH, p. 364. Humes was very positive in his testimony. He noted that x-rays had been taken of the President's entire body and that they showed "no evidence of a missile in the President's body at any point."

244n: Released . . . to Mark Lane, the receipt says: *L.A. Free Press,* "Special Report Number One," 1978, p. 17.

244n: The President's brain . . . had disappeared: HSCH1, pp. 332-373; 17WCH, CE394, p. 26.

245: Finck . . . also had participated: Thomas T. Noguchi, *Coroner* (New York: Simon & Schuster, 1983), p. 95.

245: two completely different official explanations: WCR, pp. 88-92; Lane, p. 65; 17WCH, CE394, p. 26.

246: Dr. Finck's . . . testimony: After the trial, I had a transcript of Dr. Finck's testimony prepared.

247: Dr. Nichols's . . . requests were denied: *New Orleans Times-Picayune,* March 1, 1969, p. 24.

247: asked to see the limousine: *Ibid.*

249: I was told not to: Dr. Finck said that he "was told that the family wanted no examination of the neck organs." *New York Times,* February 25, 1969, p. 18.

250: Shaw . . . took the stand: *Ibid.,* February 28, 1969, p. 19.

250: Lane questioned members of the jury: Lane informed me of his interviews immediately afterwards.

251: Helms . . . responded under oath: *Hunt v. Weberman,* S.D. Fla. 1979.

251: In a subsequent trial: *Hunt v. Liberty Lobby,* S.D. Fla., No. 80-1121-Civ.-JWK, deposition of Richard McGarrah Helms, June 1, 1984, p. 37.

CHAPTER 19: **The Majesty of the Law**

256: that material turned out to be prodigious: There were many, many cartons full of material, all of which I left in the D.A.'s office, without a backward glance, when I departed.

258: their investigation against [Gervais]: *Ibid.*

258: nothing he could tell them about me: See below.

260: *United States vs. Jim Garrison:* S.D. La., No. 71-542-Cr.

260n: Aruns Callery and Robert Nims: Callery was a prominent executive with the Sugar Bowl, whom I believed I had seen around town once or twice. I had never met Nims, and I have not seen either of them since.

268: a letter written to him by John Wall: After having been introduced as an exhibit, the letter was read into the record. I reread it in my closing argument. I have the transcript.   .

269: interview [with] Rosemary James: I subpoenaed the transcript of the James-Gervais interview as broadcast on WWL-TV. I read from the TV transcript during my final argument.

CHAPTER 20: **The Secret Sponsors**

273: undeniably mysterious circumstances: Sylvia Meagher lists 25 "mysterious deaths" of key individuals; *Master Index,* p. 323.

273: The coroner's verdict [on de Mohrenschildt] was suicide: Summers, p. 499.

274: The coroner's verdict [on Craig] was suicide: *Dallas Morning News,* May 16, 1975, p. 5D. Craig's father found him beside a rifle. A note nearby said that Craig could not stand the pain any more. The pain, his father explained, was from an auto accident two years before and from a gunshot wound six months before. Both incidents seemed a bit unusual.

274: attested that Shaw's death was due to natural causes: card on file at the office of the New Orleans coroner.

274: The coroner reconsidered: confirmed by Dr. Minyard in a recent interview with the author.

275: Richard McGarrah Helms: John Patrick Quirk, ed., *The Central Intelligence Agency* (Guilford, Ct.: Foreign Intelligence Press, 1986), p. 233.

275: wrote a novel: *The Star-Spangled Contract* (New York: McGraw-Hill, 1976).

276: "was probably assassinated as a result of a conspiracy": HSCA, Report, p. 1.

276: to consider reopening the investigation: HSCR, p. 481.

276n: concluded that the frontal shot had missed: HSCR, p. 43.

276n: theoretically possible: HSCR, p. 97.

276n: "no persuasive evidence": *New Orleans Times-Picayune,* September 4, 1988; Associated Press dispatch, September 3, 1988.

277: coup d'etat has been described: *Encyclopedia Britannica.*

282: none dare call it treason: Sir John Harington, *Epigrams,* Bk. iv, No. 5, "Of Treason" (1613).

283: sealed by the federal government: See Introduction.

283: had on its payroll journalists: See Congressional Quarterly Almanac, 1967, pp. 360-361; *New York Times,* February 26, 1967, February 20, 1976, December 25-27, 1977; *Washington Post,* February 18, 1967; *Los Angeles Times,* February 26, 1967; Carl Bernstein, "The C.I.A. and the Media," *Rolling Stone,* October 20, 1977.

283: more than 1,000 books: Report of the Senate Select Committee to Study Government Operations with Respect to Intelligence Activities (the Church Committee), Book I, pp. 192-193.

283: As Richard Barnet . . . put it: Richard J. Barnet, "The 'Dirty Tricks' Gap," in Robert L. Borosage and John Marks, eds., *The C.I.A. File* (New York: Grossman, 1976), p. 225.

285: during the C.I.A.'s attempted invasion of Cuba: See Hinckle and Turner, *The Fish Is Red,* pp. 82-95.

285: the acting chief of the Agency: General Cabell was in charge of the C.I.A.; Director Dulles was on a speaking engagement in Puerto Rico "in order not to arouse suspicion that something big was up." *Ibid.,* p. 87.

285: during the Cuban missile crisis: Hinckle, pp. 133-135, 141, 155-156.

285: no further attempts to invade Cuba: *Ibid.* Indeed, Ambassador William Atwood was meeting with the Cuban ambassador at the United Nations and actually called Fidel Castro on behalf of President Kennedy shortly before the assassination to discuss a possible restoration of diplomatic relations. Atwood also arranged for a French journalist, Jean Daniel, to meet with President Kennedy before taking a trip to Cuba, to discuss U.S.-Cuban relations. Daniel was in a meeting with Castro when they received the news that Kennedy had been shot.

House Select Committee investigators interviewed Castro at length. He noted the profound effect that Kennedy's American University speech in June 1963 had had on him. See HSCH3, pp. 221-226; HSCH10, p. 165; and see Summers, pp. 419-427, 430-432, 453.

286: The visit of "Jim Braden": Hurt, pp. 123-124.

286: one-time visit . . . by Jack Ruby: *Ibid.*

287: the C.I.A. made arrangements: For a detailed account of the C.I.A.'s several attempts to assassinate Fidel Castro, see generally, Hinckle. See also the Church Committee, Final Report, Volume IV, *Alleged Assassination Plots Involving Foreign Leaders,* Senate Report No. 94-465, November 20, 1975; also published by W.W. Norton, New York, 1976.

287: Jack Ruby . . . collecting arms and ammunition: Lane, pp. 294-297; Summers, pp. 464-465.

287: thumbing through the final summary: HSCH4, p. 146..

290: as former C.I.A. officer Philip Agee once put it: Philip Agee, "Introduction: Where Myths Lead to Murder," in Philip Agee and Louis Wolf, eds., *Dirty Work: The C.I.A. in Western Europe* (Secausus, N.J.: Lyle Stuart, 1978), pp. 18, 23. See also Ralph McGehee, *Deadly Deceits: My 25 Years in the C.I.A.* (New York: Sheridan Square Publications, 1983), p. xi.

291: had planned a number of assassination operations: Church Committee, *Alleged Assassination Plots Involving Foreign Leaders.* And see John Ranelagh, *The Agency: The Rise and Decline of the C.I.A.* (New York: Simon & Schuster, 1986), pp. 336-345.

291: coup against the government of Iran: William Blum, *The C.I.A.: A Forgotten History* (London: Zed Books, 1986), pp. 67-76. Many sources for this and the incidents which follow in the text can be found in Blum's book. See also Darrell Garwood, *Under Cover: Thirty-Five Years of C.I.A. Deception* (New York: Grove Press, 1985), which includes as an appendix a Chronology by Tom Gervasi listing more than 80 major C.I.A. covert operations, 1946-1983.

291: a plot against [Arbenz]: Blum, pp. 77-89.

291: Lumumba . . . became an Agency target: *Ibid.,* pp. 174-176.

292: drove around with Lumumba's body: John Stockwell, *In Search of Enemies* (New York: W.W. Norton, 1978), p. 105.

292: plotted the murder of Fidel Castro: Church Committee, *Alleged Assassination Plots Against Foreign Leaders;* and Hinckle, *passim.*

292: Rafael Trujillo . . . President Diem . . . and General René Schneider: *Ibid.*

292: according to . . . William Harvey: Church Committee, Interim Report, *Instituting Assassinations: The "Executive Action" Capability,* testimony of June 25, 1975, p. 34.

292: Richard Bissell . . . also acknowledged: *Ibid.,* testimony of July 22, 1975, pp. 30-32. Bissell said there was "a wide spectrum of actions" available "to eliminate the effectiveness of foreign leaders," including "the most extreme."

292n: Operation Phoenix: See Ernest Volkman, *Warriors of the Night* (New York: William Morrow and Co., 1985), pp. 255-256; Zinn, p. 468; and Victor Marchetti and John Marks, *The C.I.A. and the Cult of Intelligence* (New York: Alfred A. Knopf, 1974), pp. 245-246.

292nn: Agency critics: See Philip Agee, *Inside the Company* (New York: Stonehill, 1975); John Stockwell, *In Search of Enemies* (New York: W.W. Norton, 1978); Ralph McGehee, *Deadly Deceits: My 25 Years in the C.I.A.* (New York: Sheridan Square Publications, 1983).

293: described by the writer Fred Cook: Fred Cook, *What So Proudly We Hail* (Englewood Cliffs, N.J.: Prentice-Hall, 1968), p. 73.

294: to Christianize the world: Ronnie Dugger, *The Politician: The Life and Times of Lyndon Johnson* (New York: W.W. Norton, 1982), p. 392.

294: met with Henry Cabot Lodge: Tom Wicker, *L.B.J. and J.F.K.* (New York: William Morrow, 1968), p. 205.

294: left no evidence of the attack: See Zinn, p. 467.

294: Johnson soundly denounced: *Ibid.* Zinn characterizes the Gulf of Tonkin incident as "a fake," and says "no torpedo was ever fired on the Maddox."

295: Promptly following the congressional resolution: See generally, Joseph C. Goulden, *Truth is the First Casualty: The Gulf of Tonkin Affair—Illusion and Reality* (New York: Rand McNally, 1969). And see Zinn, supra; and Carl Oglesby, "Presidential Assassinations and the Closing of the Frontier," in Sid Blumenthal and Harvey Yazijian, eds., *Government by Gunplay* (New York: New American Library, 1976), pp. 200-201.

295: more than 55,000 Americans and millions of Vietnamese had died: Zinn, p. 436.

Afterword: Is the Mafia Theory a Valid Alternative?

299: its final report: *Report of the Select Committee on Assassinations*, U.S. House of Representatives, Ninety-Fifth Congress, second session, March 29, 1979. See especially, "Findings and Recommendations" volume.

300: "a thirst for publicity. . .": G. Robert Blakey, *The Plot to Kill the President* (New York: Times Books, 1981), p. 47.

301: It would require. . . : *Ibid.*, pp. 45-46.

301: As for the organized crime aspect. . . : *Ibid.*, p. 178.

302: Garrison was tried . . . : *The Plot to Kill the President*, p. 50.

302n: The new book by David E. Scheim: David E. Scheim, *Contract on America* (New York: Shapolsky Books, 1988).

306: to say publicly and under oath . . . : "On Trial: Lee Harvey Oswald," LWT Productions, London, 1986. Aired on Showtime cable TV in the United States, in November 1986 and January 1987.

307: At first I supported: Carl Oglesby and Jeff Goldberg, "Did the Mob Kill Kennedy," *Washington Post*, February 25, 1979.

308: Pursuant to agreement . . .: *The Plot to Kill the President*, p. 401.

Index